Death, Dying
&Bereavement

Also published by
SAGE Publications
in association with
The Open University

Health, Welfare and Practice: Reflecting on Roles and Relationships
edited by Jan Walmsley, Jill Reynolds, Pam Shakespeare and Ray Woolfe

Disabling Barriers – Enabling Environments
edited by John Swain, Vic Finkelstein, Sally French and Mike Oliver

All three books are Course Readers for the Open University Diploma in Health and Social Welfare.

Details of the Diploma and the related courses are available from The Information Officer, Department of Health and Social Welfare, The Open University, Walton Hall, Milton Keynes MK7 6AA, UK.

Death, Dying &Bereavement

edited by

Donna Dickenson

and

Malcolm Johnson

The Open
University

in association with
The Open University

SAGE Publications
London • Thousand Oaks • New Delhi

SAGE Publications Ltd
6 Bonhill Street
London EC2A 4PU

SAGE Publications Inc
2455 Teller Road
Thousand Oaks, California 91320

SAGE Publications India Pvt Ltd
32, M-Block Market
Greater Kailash – I
New Delhi 110 048

British Library Cataloguing in Publication data

A catalogue record for this book is available from the British Library.
ISBN 0-8039 8796-X
ISBN 0-8039 8797-8 (pbk)

Library of Congress catalog card number 92–050904

Typeset by Mayhew Typesetting, Rhayader, Powys
Printed in Great Britain by The Cromwell Press Ltd,
Broughton Gifford, Melksham, Wiltshire

Contents

Acknowledgements

The authors and publishers wish to thank the following for permission to use copyright material.

Ellen Jaffe Bitz for 'For Rose Albert' and 'How to Live with Ghosts'.

British Medical Association for material from Sheila Awooner-Renner (1990) 'I desperately needed to see my son', *British Medical Journal*, Vol. 302, 9 February; and Tom Heller (1989) 'Personal and medical memories from Hillsborough', *British Medical Journal*, Vol. 299, 23–29 December; Robert Buckman (1984) 'Breaking bad news: why is it still so difficult?', *British Medical Journal*, Vol. 288, 26 May; Peter Maguire and Ann Faulkner (1988) 'Communicate with cancer patients: 1. Handling bad news and difficult questions' and 'Communicate with cancer patients: 2. Handling uncertainty, collusion, and denial', *British Medical Journal*, Vol. 297, 8 October; and D.W. Yates, G. Ellison, S. McGuiness (1990), 'Care of the suddenly bereaved', *British Medical Journal*, Vol. 301, 7 July;

British Sociological Association and the author for material from Tony Walters (1989) 'Modern death: taboo or not taboo?', *Sociology*, 25(2): 293–301;

Cambridge University Press for material from David Clark (1982) 'Death in Staithes in the early twentieth century' from *Between Pulpit and Pew*;

Churchill Livingstone for material from Gavin Fairbairn (1986) 'When a baby dies – a father's view', *Nursing Practice*, 1: 167–8;

Andre Deutsch Ltd for material from Rosemary and Victor Zorza (1980) *A Way to Die*;

Faber and Faber Ltd for Douglas Dunn (1985) 'December' in *Elegies*; material from R.S. Downie and K.C. Calman (1987) 'Paternalism and moral deficiency' in *Healthy Respect* and Elizabeth Forsythe (1990) *Alzheimer's Disease: The Long Bereavement*; and with Farrar Straus and Giroux, Inc for Philip Larkin (1977) 'Aubade' in *Collected Poems*. Copyright © 1988, 1989 by the Estate of Philip Larkin;

Guardian News Service Ltd for Jane Martin (1989) 'Doctor's mask on pain', © *The Guardian*, 5.4.89; and Clare Williams (1991) 'First Person', © *The Guardian*, 29.5.91;

David Higham Associates Ltd on behalf of the author and New Directions Publishing Corporation for Dylan Thomas (1952) 'Do not go gentle into that good night' from *Poems of Dylan Thomas*. Copyright © 1952 by Dylan Thomas;

The Lancet for material from (1990) 'Assisted death', Institute of Medical Ethics Working Party on the Ethics of Prolonging Life and Assisting Death, *The Lancet*, 8 September;

Macmillan Publishers Ltd and St Martin's Press, Inc. for material from Lindsay Prior (1989) 'Social distribution of sentiments' in *The Social Organisation of Death*;

Lesley Moreland for 'Ruth: death by murder', compiled from articles written on the death of her daughter;

Nursing Times for George Castledine (1984) 'When life moves on', *Nursing Mirror*, 25 April 1984, Vol. 158;

Penguin Books Ltd. and Alfred A. Knopf, Inc. for material from Philippe Ariès (1981) *The Hour of Our Death*, trans. Helen Weaver, Allen Lane. Translation copyright © 1980 Alfred A. Knopf, Inc.;

Plenum Press for material from Dennis F. Thomson (1980) 'Paternalism in Medicine, Law and Public Policy' in *Ethics Teaching in Higher Education*, eds. Daniel Callahan and Sisela Bok, Hastings Center Publication;

Research Press for material from Evelyn Gillis (1986) 'A single parent confronting the loss of an only child' in *Parental Loss of a Child* by T.E. Rando, pp. 315–19. Copyright © 1986 by T.E. Rando;

Joseph Rowntree Foundation for material from Maureen Oswin (1990) 'The grief that does not speak', *Search*, Winter, 4: 5–7 (also included in *Am I Allowed to Cry* by Maureen Owsin, Souvenir Press, 1991);

Scutari Projects Ltd for material fron Anon. (1990) 'A student's story' in 'Ethics and the loss of innocence' by G. Fairbairn and D. Mead, *Paediatric Nursing*, June 1990;

Sinclair-Stevenson Ltd for material from David Widgery (1991) 'Not going gently' in *Some Lives!*;

Society for Applied Philosophy for material from Henk ten Have (1992) 'Euthanasia in the Netherlands', *Philosophy Today*, No. 11, September;

The Society for the Psychological Study of Social Issues for material from Colin Murray Parkes (1988) 'Bereavement as a psychosocial transition: processes of adaption to change', *Journal of Social Issues*, 44(3): 53–65;

Abner Stein on behalf of the author and Delacorte Press/Seymour Lawrence, a division of Bantam Doubleday Dell Publishing Group, Inc. for material from 'Tell me a Riddle' from *Tell Me a Riddle*, by Tillie Olsen. Copyright © 1956, 1960, 1961 by Tillie Olsen;

Anselm Strauss and Barney Glaser for material from (1970) 'Dying trajectories: the organization of work and expectations of dying' in *Anguish: the Case History of a Dying Trajectory* by Anselm Strauss, Sociology Press;

The Tablet Publishing Co Ltd for Elizabeth Dean (1991) 'Sitting it out', *The Tablet*, 28.5.91;

Robert G. Twycross for material from (1990) 'Assisted death: a reply', *The Lancet*, 29 September;

Every effort has been made to trace all the copyright holders, but if any have been inadvertently overlooked the publishers will be pleased to make the necessary arrangement at the first opportunity.

Introduction

A death-denying society is what the influential French historian Phillipe Ariès claimed ours to be, in his important book *The Hour of Our Death*. Like much else in his writing this was not an uncontested opinion, but it is one which has been widely taken up. The ensuing debate can be observed within the covers of this book and it could be summarized by saying that there is great awareness at a social level, even if public rituals have diminished, but that in our personal lives we are less willing than our forebears to talk openly about life, death and beyond. Despite the trend, renewed interest is abundantly evident and this resource book is both a product of it and a response.

There can be no doubt that contemporary Western societies have handed over the business of dying and its aftermath to a variety of professionals who have largely taken over traditional family and neighbourhood roles. In Britain (in common with most developed countries) almost 70 per cent of deaths now occur in hospitals or other institutional settings, where doctors, nurses, physiotherapists, pharmacists and others manage what Anselm Strauss calls the dying trajectory. Once life has left the body the funeral industry provides a comprehensive range of services which remove death from the home and disconnect it from those who mourn. Such a distancing approach, however, has been challenged since the early 1960s by the rise of the modern hospice movement which has emerged as a new and powerful force progressively sponsoring new methods and attitudes.

It is common practice for academic authors to introduce their writings with complaints about the paucity of serious study of their topic. Thanatologists can make no such observation. On the contrary the literature of the ages contains vast quantities of speculation and analysis, through fiction and academic endeavour, about human mortality. Theologians and philosophers in all cultures and historical periods have treated death as a serious subject, whilst novelists and poets find it an irresistible theme. And yet, there are inevitable shortcomings. The medical literature on palliative care is largely unavailable to readers outside the profession. At the same time published work in nursing, psychology, sociology, ethics and history is widely distributed and rarely brought together, reflecting the reality that as a field of study for carers of all sorts, we are in a new era.

So this is a book which has been designed for the growing numbers who, either as paid carers or as family members, friends or volunteers, are involved with the support of dying or bereaved people. For them the theologian's concern with eschatology (the study of 'last things') is of less pressing importance than knowing about new treatments to relieve pain, the tested guidelines for breaking bad news or how to decide what their views are on euthanasia. Yet a wholly practical approach does not seem justified, for whoever engages in the caring role must themselves reflect on the great mystery of death and confront their own fears.

As a response to this essential mix of knowledge, information, reflection and experience the collection of over sixty contributions which makes up *Death, Dying & Bereavement* ranges broadly, juxtaposing academic research with practitioner and personal accounts. Each section also contains portions of literature or poetry which illuminate the dominant themes.

Of all subjects, death cannot be owned by any one discipline or area of study. It cannot belong only to science, only to art, only to poetry, only to philosophy, theology or religion. It is part of all of these and many others. Nor can it be the exclusive province of any particular profession – not only medicine, not only nursing, not only the clergy. By the same token proper understanding of the conclusion of life must embrace the vast range of human experience as well as systematic study. If we are to relate to dying people and those who are bereft by the loss of loved ones, our attention must be directed to the whole fabric of the complex tapestry.

No attempt has been made in the structure of the book to create an integration of the diverse literature contained within it. Simply by laying one set of insights or data next to others from different intellectual and practice traditions, we hope to stimulate in readers a willingness to fashion their own connections. None the less there is an organizing framework created by the four parts, each of which has its own introduction in which we draw attention to the key contributions of each item. Part 1 provides a general consideration of a wide range of issues to do with loss and dying, while the remaining three parts are arranged more or less chronologically, from dying through death till mourning.

Part 1, starting with a careful and evocative anthropological description of death rituals in an Edwardian English seaside town, sets a familiar and comforting tone. In Staithes dying is dignified and profoundly social. This provides a starting point for successive articles which encompass great sweeps of history and contrast the lonely, modern tragedy of terminal illness in the poverty-stricken inner city. Before we reach the noble lines of Donne and the indignation of Dylan Thomas, we recognize the contemporary reality of multi-cultural living where new religions clank against an increasingly secular society.

New themes are even more prominent in Part 2, where high-technology medicine has complicated deathwork, bringing an uneasy partnership of law and ethics into the picture. Organ transplantation represents one set of moral dilemmas whilst assisted death and advance directives present others which are equally testing. The harrowing but deeply moving extract from Tillie Olsen's *Tell Me a Riddle* provides a literary counter-balance, and first-person accounts add a personal note here, as in other parts.

The humane aspects of dying are linked in Part 3 with the new scientific procedures at the centre of palliative medicine. Even when the focus is on treatments and therapies, the constant theme is good communication, openness and honesty. The final part concerns itself with bereavement and grief and what can be done to diminish their pain. Psychological studies and evaluations of practice sit side by side with Wordsworth's observations on epitaphs and Douglas Dunn's contemporary poem which concludes the book with the unsolved mysteries of living and dying.

Whilst we see the book as principally serving the needs of many different kinds of students pursuing courses in palliative care and counselling, it is also for the established practitioner wishing to be updated and the more general reader (perhaps even some who know they are dying) who wants a rich source of material about the end of life. To meet the needs of such a diverse readership it was necessary to have a much larger number of articles and pieces than is common in academic readers. To achieve this arrangement, it was agreed that there would be an upper limit on the length of any one contribution and where necessary longer articles would be edited to an appropriate size. It is our view that this process has been wholly positive. However, we also hope that in cases where the selections from longer works are presented, readers will feel sufficient interest to trace and read the original publications.

A formative influence on the structure and content was the book's place as a set text within the Open University course K260 *Death and Dying*. The studentship for the course is most likely to have the same range as for this book as an independent volume; but it will probably contain large numbers of nurses, doctors and those from the professions allied to medicine, along with other sorts of care workers, clergy, police and funeral directors, volunteers and unpaid carers. For them the Reader links with interactive study texts, audio, video, television and tutorial support. The course, like this book, is both multidisciplinary in an academic sense and multi-occupational, bringing together the understanding and skills of a variety of contributors to enable better experiences of dying and mourning.

Reference has been made to the hospice movement as a stimulus to better care and more research. Its influence has had a direct bearing on the preparation of this book. Dr Gillian Ford, one of the founders with Dame Cicely Saunders of St Christopher's Hospice in Sydenham, south London, took time out in the late 1980s from her post as Deputy

Chief Medical Officer at the Department of Health to become Director of Education at St Christopher's. There she found the demand for courses on palliative care so overwhelming that she looked for alternative ways of meeting the burgeoning need. Prompted by Professor Norman McKenzie, she turned to the Department of Health and Social Welfare at the Open University. The course and this associated publication are direct outcomes of Dr Ford's energy and initiative. We thank her for assisting us at every stage and for chairing the course Advisory Group. Particular thanks must also go to our colleagues on the Course Team, Dr Jeanne Katz, Alyson Peberdy, Dr Moyra Sidell and the Course Manager Margaret Allott. All of them have made major contributions to this Reader. Rae Smyth as Course Team secretary has typed and interpreted huge quantities of text with great efficiency. We acknowledge their part warmly and with genuine thanks.

More than half of the academic and practice-related articles are original pieces commissioned for this book. We are grateful to colleagues all over the UK and beyond who have responded to our invitations and for ensuring that this collection is now the most wide-ranging Reader on the subject yet published.

Donna Dickenson
Malcolm Johnson

PART 1   LIFE AND DEATH

Introduction

Addressing the eternal questions of life and death presents a daunting prospect. World literature, philosophy, religion and history present us with an endless source of material which is necessarily inconclusive. Fortunately our task is not to present our readers with a digest of this vast body of work. It is more focused and instrumental. So this first part offers a selection of contributions which contextualize the *contemporary* experience of dying and death. It provides powerful sketches of the awesome struggle humankind has with the reality of mortality, whilst concentrating on the ways in which the past and the present influence the attitudes, rituals and practices which operate in modern societies at the end of life.

David Clark's beautifully observed anthropological account of death in Staithes at the turn of the century provides an evocation of much of the current debate about 'the world we have lost'. Its precise descriptions of the complex of religious, metaphysical and folk beliefs about death and the associated rituals, public and private, are not confined to a seaside town in the staunchly traditional north-east of England. On the one hand it offers a universal picture of the interweaving of fear, hope, respect, celebration, mourning, ceremonial and petty concerns which have surrounded death everywhere and in every age. As an opening piece it stimulates many of the questions and debates which follow in the rest of the book.

From the local and the particular we move to the great canvas of history addressed by Phillipe Ariès in his monumental survey of death. Here we can only offer a taster of a huge scholarly work which has excited much controversy and debate since it was first published in French in 1977. In a characteristically Gallic review Ariès does not hesitate to interpret history or to make judgements. The passage reproduced propounds the view that modern societies are death-denying societies which are unwilling to face the inescapable facts of death. He argues that this attitude explains the professionalizing of death and its sanitization by the funeral industry.

David Widgery a general medical practitioner in the East End of London, illustrates Ariès's theme from his own experience of working largely with poor people. He sees the loneliness and desolation which impoverished city life can inflict on the terminally ill. His stark images of modern urban human neglect contrast with the persistence of an earthier, more communal experience which has survived in present-day Ireland. Rosemary Power's descriptions, so reminiscent of Staithes almost a century earlier, depict a society more at ease with death. Again we see an elaborate pattern of symbolic and functional behaviour which firmly locates the dead person where he or she was in life – within the family, the locality, the church, and the timeless essence of Ireland.

One significant change not alluded to in the first four articles is the increasing ethnic and religious diversity to be found all over the world. Shirley Firth addresses an important dimension of this newly acknowledged mix, as she examines the religious, cultural and family patterns of Sikh and Hindu communities in Britain. Attention is drawn to the distinctive attitudes to health, illness and dying which require reactions from health professionals quite different from those predominant in the host culture. The need of Hindus to die lying on the floor, in the midst of their family, to the accompaniment of ritual chanting is juxtaposed with the clinical atmosphere of typical hospital wards.

Tony Walter's lively review of the debate about the existence of a death taboo in present-day society picks up themes from Ariès. In subjecting the question to critical scrutiny, he embraces a great deal of the post-war writing about death, drawn from many disciplines. His systematic and critical survey suggests that the social restrictions on discussion about death are diminishing, but that individuals still feel constrained about exploring their own feelings about mortality.

The next four articles are of a much more practical nature, exploring the demographic reasons for the dramatic changes in the experience of death in the twentieth century and ways in which society provides services for the dying. Clive Seale explains how the control of premature death, which has produced a greater expectation of life, has made death largely the preserve of old age. Using data from two major studies of people living at home with terminal illnesses, he maps the current patterns of family and professional care. These findings are corroborated and developed by Christina Victor, who takes a macro-view of mortality rates and the causes of death, placing them in the broad context of social policy and provision. She identifies a range of challenges to health and social care systems, if they are to provide an adequate response to the needs of dying people.

Taking the particular case of sudden death, by suicide, Stella Ridley continues the practical approach by mapping the incidence of self-inflicted death and the limited services which relate to it. But she also raises more philosophical questions about the meaning and the taking of life which are treated more fully in Part 2. In a similar vein, Mary Bradbury's questioning of what constitutes a good or a bad death combines anthropological and theological considerations with observations about the medical management of terminal illness. These two short pieces act as valuable linkages between the global subjects at the start of this part and much of the rest of the book.

The selection of poetry and prose which follows reflects the ideas, concerns, practices and beliefs uncovered by the preceding articles. The extracts from the mid-Victorian *Child's Own Magazine* portray a middle-class Christian version of death designed to comfort children and likely to incur the wrath of Ariès. John Donne, Philip Larkin and Dylan Thomas, however, have no illusions about death, although they respond to it in characteristically different ways: Donne with a comforting romanticism, Larkin with clinical realism and Thomas with exuberant defiance – such a contrast with Kahlil Gibran's calm spirituality.

At the close of the part are two brief but arresting personal stories of the experience of someone else's death. Jane Martin and Mary Benjamin both remind us of the emotional strength that professional carers need if they are to work well in the midst of dying and grief. These contemporary statements reflect the same, universal, concerns which captured the great Russian writer Leo Tolstoy; but the mixture of philosophical reflection and literary anguish he displays is a marked contrast in style and analysis.

1

Death in Staithes

David Clark

Death in Staithes in the early twentieth century

With the exception of accidental fatalities, death in Staithes in the early part of the century almost invariably took place in the home, where the sick and the dying were the immediate responsibility of the family, to whom also befell the task of laying the dead to rest in an adequate and befitting manner. In the midst of their bereavement, therefore, the kinsfolk were kept busy by funeral preparations and various related tasks. The first duty was that of laying-out the body, known in Staithes as 'the lying-out'. As one old man put it, 'When a person passed away the first thing they did was go for the board – the lying-out board.' This board, upon which the corpse was stretched out was kept in the workshop of the village joiner, who also performed the duties of undertaker. 'Lying-out', however, was the charge of a handful of women who were recognized in the village as qualified to carry out the work and who, from their painstaking attention to detail, appear to have taken considerable pride in their task.

The process began with the washing of the body and the tying-up of the jaw; the corpse was then wrapped in a white sheet and laid on the board in the centre of a double bed. White woollen stockings were used to cover the feet, a pillow was placed on each side of the head and another sheet, meticulously folded in a series of horizontal pleats which ran down its entire length, was laid over the body. Finally, a large white handkerchief covered the face. The linen used in the laying-out was of the finest quality and that edged with Maltese lace was particularly popular. In common with the practice in many other areas and classes of society, the material was usually purchased well in advance. [. . .]

Thus laid out, the corpse became the object of formalized visits on the part of kin and friends, who upon calling at the house would be invited to go upstairs to see the dead person for the last time. 'Would you like to have a look at him?', was the usual question asked of

Extract from *Between Pulpit and Pew*, Cambridge: Cambridge University Press, 1982, pp. 128–38 (abridged).

visitors, who would then be escorted upstairs. The person watching over the corpse would then lift the face cloth for a few moments to allow a final view of the deceased, at which point the visitor was expected to touch the body as an expression of sympathy or, as one man put it, 'to show that they always held out goodwill while the person was alive'. Following a few moments of silence the visitor would return below to the other members of the family.

After the initial separation of the dead person, the stage leading up to the burial had all the aspects of liminality associated with the middle phase of the rite of passage; we see therefore the suspension, not only of normal conventions and patterns of behaviour, but also, one feels, of time itself. The progression of day and night became meaningless as clocks were stopped and members of the family sat up throughout the night, dozing in chairs and taking it in turns to go to sit by the body. Mirrors and pictures were carefully covered over with white napkins and curtains remained drawn.

Meanwhile, funeral preparations continued to occupy various individuals – the joiner, in the construction of the coffin, and the women, in the baking of the special funerary foods. One woman, known as the 'bidder', was specially employed at this time to announce the day and time of the funeral throughout the village. Her task took her to every house in Staithes, at each of which she would knock at the door and 'bid', or invite, the household to attend. Sunday was the preferred day for funerals, despite the charging of double burial fees. Since sabbatarian observance prohibited working on the Sabbath, all who wished to attend were free to do so. [. . .] Coffin bearers were usually recruited from close kin; as one old lady put it, the rule was that 'you always went as near as you could'. The bearers were always of the same sex as the deceased. The servers at the funeral tea, known locally as 'waitresses', were usually neighbours.

On the day of the funeral itself, and at the appointed hour, a group of villagers would congregate outside the house of the deceased. Inside, when all members of the immediate family were present they would gather around the open coffin (or 'box' as Staithes people habitually refer to it), whereupon the minister or priest placed one hand upon it, and delivered a short extempore prayer of thanks for the life of the dead person and the comfort of the mourners. [. . .] At the conclusion of the prayer the coffin lid was fixed in position and at this point special sweet 'funeral biscuits', along with glasses of port, or occasionally spirits, were taken to the people outside. Clay pipes and tobacco were passed around among the men on a special black patterned funeral plate which each family kept for such occasions. The bearers also received food and drink for, as one man put it, 'they used to like a glass before the lifting'. [. . .] As members of the family left the house, care was taken to leave the door open in the belief that this facilitated the departure of the dead person's soul. Then, with the coffin resting on the chairs, all present would sing the first verse of a funeral hymn. Still singing, the bearers took the coffin and began moving away in the direction of the chapel. [. . .]

Behind the bearers in the funeral procession came the women who would later serve at the tea. Six or eight in number, they wore black hats with white crocheted shawls and black silk sashes. With characteristic meticulousness, the women walked in pairs, one wearing her sash diagonally from the left shoulder and the other wearing hers from the right in order to form an inverted V pattern. The minister followed, then came a separate group made up of the bereaved family and finally the rest of the company. [. . .] After the service had taken place in the chapel it was necessary to carry the coffin some one and a half miles to the graveyard of the parish church at Hinderwell. Even today Staithes has no cemetery of its own. In the days before motor transport this meant a steep climb out of the village followed by a tiring walk along the cliffs. [. . .]

At the foot of the hill, and before returning to prepare the funeral tea, the serving women stepped to one side and watched as the others left the village. The processions were evidently a spectacular sight. Male coffin bearers wore small white bows or rosettes in their lapels – three men with them on the right side and three on the left side. The bows had to be worn on the side nearest to the coffin. Women bearers wore black skirts, white shawls and white hats. Behind the bearers came the men, wearing seal-skin caps or bowler hats, dark blue jerseys and serge trousers. Then came the women, all in black. [. . .]

At the committal it was the duty of the grave-digger to throw soil down onto the coffin during the final obsequies and when the prayers were completed a hymn would be sung at the graveside; 'Gather at the River' was a popular choice. The company then set off back to the village where they were met at the top of the bank by the serving women who divided them into small groups for the funeral tea. [. . .] Large attendances at funerals, coupled with the smallness of the fishermen's cottages, made a collective meal impossible and gave rise to the practice of holding the meal in several different households. Very often a neighbour having a slightly larger house would offer assistance by putting it at the disposal of the waitresses. In later the years the problem was overcome by holding the funeral tea in the relevant chapel Sunday Schoolroom. Smoked ham, fruit cake (known as 'funeral bread') and Madeira cake were the traditional foods for the tea, which was manifestly an expensive affair. During one funeral I attended, I was told by a man in his early seventies that in the past, 'the poorer class o' person often had to spend his last penny paying for everything', whilst in an interview another man remarked, 'nearly everyone had a small insurance out to cover the cost of the fees and the funeral tea'. There were also funeral clubs into which weekly subscriptions were paid. [. . .]

The funeral tea may be seen as the first in a series of rites of incorporation, bringing the group together in a final acknowledgement of the death, whilst at the same time preparing the bereaved for their return from the fraught liminal phase and their subsequent re-entry into the regulated pattern of group life. Consequently, when the family returned to their home after the funeral, the white napkins would be removed from the mirrors and pictures and the curtains partially opened. While it was true that the bereaved family had to follow a host of mourning rules and injunctions for many weeks, there was a steady divestment and relaxation of sanctions, which progressively admitted the re-entry of the mourner into a normal role in the community. The emphasis throughout this re-admission, however, was on a *gradual* progression. [. . .] For women in particular, mourning represented a protracted period wherein onerous restrictions on movement and dress were only gradually removed during subsequent months. For example, women frequently ceased to attend chapel for as much as a whole year; indeed, one old lady told me that 'some never went for five or six years – they used to think it wasn't reverent'. Not only attendance at chapel, but any appearance outdoors in the early weeks and months after the death was considered improper and gave rise to unfavourable comment. [. . .]

More permanent reminders of the death were kept in the house for years to come. Throughout the Victorian period and on into the early twentieth century it was common to have special mourning cards printed to commemorate the death of a member of the family. The cards were solemnly funereal in design and style and contained various biographical details of the dead person.[1] [. . .] Large cards such as this (some seven inches by nine) were framed and hung on the walls, whilst smaller ones were often tucked behind picture frames or mirrors. Grim reminders they must have been to a community where death was such a frequent and untimely visitor.

Death in Staithes today

Whilst listening to old people talking of the beliefs and ritual surrounding death in the early part of the century I was continually impressed by their detailed and highly specific accounts. These displayed a remarkable internal consistency and few differences appear to have existed between funerals taking place at the different religious institutions in the village. Even funerals at the parish church differed from those in the chapels only in so far as the company had to walk to the church at Hinderwell beforehand. When we turn to the subject of death in the contemporary situation, however, a number of important changes are immediately apparent and various traditional practices appear to have been abandoned or modified. I could find no evidence, for example, for the continuance of the custom of covering up mirrors and pictures in the death house. Similarly, bearers are no longer of the same sex as the dead person; in fact, to have bearers at all is now rather exceptional, since the duty frequently falls to the undertaker's staff. Curtains are still drawn in the house of the dead, but now only on the day that death occurs and then again immediately before the funeral. The practice of printing special death cards ended in the 1940s. Perhaps the most significant innovation is the emergence of a number of specialist organizations which increasingly concern themselves with the processes of death and dying. It is a transformation which has stripped the family of one of its traditional functions, so that some of the familial and communal rituals previously associated with the death of a villager have disappeared beneath a general trend towards standardization. [. . .]

The professionalization of death

In Staithes today, and in contrast to the situation in the early part of the century, the immediacy of death as a communal event has been considerably attenuated. For most villagers contact with death takes place at a distance or through intermediaries, in the form of bureaucratically organized agencies which perform the duties and tasks once held to be the responsibility of the family or community. We may call this process the professionalization of death since it perpetrates the notion that competence to deal with the practical matters associated with death is vested solely in specially trained professionals, who in conducting their work seek to emphasize the ascendancy of their skills in this matter over any related ones held by the family. Professionalization has thereby resulted in a vastly different set of responses to the problem of death.

First of all, it is important we recognize that the home is no longer the only setting in which death is likely to take place. Other alternatives exist, such as hospitals, residential homes and geriatric units, which in assuming responsibility for care of the dying have taken death not only out of the home, but also out of the village. At the same time the duties of the undertaker, transferred from village joiner to local Co-operative Society and then aggrandized in the role of 'funeral director', have been made to include many of the responsibilities formerly borne by relatives and neighbours. Thus, when death occurs in one of these institutions it is common for the body to be removed to the funeral director's memorial house rather than to the individual's home, and for the preparation of the corpse and laying-out to be done by the funeral director rather than by the traditional female specialists in the village. [. . .] Formal announcement of the death and notification of the date and time of the funeral have ceased to be jobs for the 'bidder' and whilst news of the death still travels quickly, it is usual for the funeral director to arrange for publication of details in the death and obituary column of the local evening newspaper. [. . .] Similarly, making the coffin, once a task for the local joiner, is now arranged by the funeral director, who in addition to ordering flowers and wreaths also makes provision for the preparation of the funeral tea by outside caterers. One woman summed the changes up thus, 'Now the Co-op has it all – tea, flowers, box – he'll put it in t' paper and everything.' Even the laying-out board itself has become the property of the North Eastern Co-operative Society, and hangs on a gate next to the village store.

Burial and cremation

Perhaps the greatest innovation coming from those professional agencies who now concern themselves with death has been the introduction of cremation as an alternative form of disposal of the dead. Its implications for any analysis of death in the village are considerable. During the period of fieldwork in Staithes there were thirty-five funerals. Three of these took place entirely at the crematorium and two were at the Roman Catholic Church. Of the remaining thirty, twenty-two were held in one or other of the three chapels and eight took place in the parish church. Six out of ten funerals were burials, whilst the remainder were cremations. These figures almost reverse those for the country as a whole, which show that in 1974 approximately 60 per cent of all deaths in Britain were followed by cremation.[2] What interpretation can we give to this local phenomenon? Two possibilities exist. The first is that, in common with the situation in many other areas, a considerable distance must be travelled to the nearest crematorium, thereby creating undue expense and making the funeral itself a lengthy and tiring affair. Practical considerations may therefore militate against the choice of cremation among villagers. Alternatively we might consider whether or not there are to be found in the village any indication of values and attitudes *vis-à-vis* cremation which might prevent it from being regarded as an acceptable means of disposal of the dead. [. . .]

In fact a far more satisfactory explanation can be found. As should become increasingly apparent, the people of Staithes have never allowed considerations of time or cost to interfere with what they consider to be the right and proper way of bidding farewell to the dead. Popular though the notion of the parsimonious Yorkshireman may be, it is not confirmed here; indeed cremation, which requires no grave-plot or headstone, is cheaper than interment. The high figures for burial are rather, we suggest, the product of a particular aversion to cremation, combined with a deep-seated preference for the traditional ritual.

Notes

1. Similar cards were used by Roman Catholics, especially on the Continent.
2. From *Resurgam* – the Journal of the Federation of British Cremation Authorities, 1975: 19–22.

2

Death denied

Phillipe Ariès

In the early twentieth century, before World War I, throughout the Western world of Latin culture, be it Catholic or Protestant, the death of a man still solemnly altered the space and time of a social group that could be extended to include the entire community. The shutters were closed in the bedroom of the dying man, candles were lit, holy water was sprinkled; the house filled with grave and whispering neighbours, relatives and friends. At the church, the passing bell tolled and the little procession left carrying the *Corpus Christi*.

After death, a notice of bereavement was posted on the door (in lieu of the old abandoned custom of exhibiting the body or the coffin by the door of the house). All the doors and windows of the house were closed except the front door, which was left ajar to admit everyone who was obliged by friendship or good manners to make a final visit. The service at the church brought the whole community together, including latecomers who waited for the end of the funeral to come forward; and after the long line of people had expressed their sympathy to the family, a slow procession, saluted by passersby, accompanied the coffin to the cemetery. And that was not all. The period of mourning was filled with visits: visits of the family to the cemetery and visits of relatives and friends to the family.

Then, little by little, life returned to normal, and there remained only the periodic visits to the cemetery. The social group had been stricken by death, and it had reacted collectively, starting with the immediate family and extending to a wider circle of relatives and acquaintances. Not only did everyone die in public like Louis XIV, but the death of each person was a public event that moved, literally and figuratively, society as a whole. It was not only an individual who was disappearing, but society itself that had been wounded and that had to be healed.

From *The Hour of Our Death*, London: Allen Lane, 1981, London: Peregrine Books, 1983, pp. 559–63. This brief extract from Ariès's large and important volume contains one of his principal theses, but all too little of the elaborate argument contained in the book. It is included here as a sampler of an impressive if controversial contribution to the historical and cultural analysis of death.

All the changes that have modified attitudes toward death in the past thousand years have not altered this fundamental image, this permanent relationship between death and society. Death has always been a social and public fact. It remains so today in vast areas of the Latin West, and it is by no means clear that this traditional model is destined to disappear. But it no longer has the quality of absolute generality that it once had, no matter what the religion and the culture. In the course of the twentieth century an absolutely new type of dying has made an appearance in some of the most industrialized, urbanized and technologically advanced areas of the Western world – and this is probably only the first stage.

Two characteristics are obvious to the most casual observer. First is its novelty, of course, its contrariness to everything that preceded it, of which it is the reverse image, the negative. Except for the death of statesmen, society has banished death. In the towns, there is no way of knowing that something has happened: the old black and silver hearse has become an ordinary grey limousine, indistinguishable from the flow of traffic. Society no longer observes a pause; the disappearance of an individual no longer affects its continuity. Everything in town goes on as if nobody died anymore.

The second characteristic is no less surprising. Of course, death has changed in a thousand years, but how slowly! The changes were so gradual and so infinitesimal, spread out over generations, that they were imperceptible to contemporaries. Today, a complete reversal of customs seems to have occurred in one generation. In my youth, women in mourning were invisible under their crepe and voluminous black veils. Middle-class children whose grandmothers had died were dressed in violet. After 1945, my mother wore mourning for a son killed in the war for the twenty-odd years that remained to her.

The very rapidity and suddenness of the change have made us take stock of it. Phenomena that had been forgotten have suddenly become known and discussed, the subjects of sociological investigations, television programmes, medical and legal debates. Shown the door by society, death is coming back in through the window, and it is returning just as quickly as it disappeared.

The change is rapid and sudden, there is no doubt of that; but is it really as recent as it appears to the journalist, the sociologist, and to ourselves, dazed as we are by the acceleration of pace?

The beginning of the lie

After the second half of the nineteenth century, an essential change occurred in the relationship between the dying man and his entourage.

Obviously, the discovery that one's end was near has always been an unpleasant moment. But people learned to overcome it. The Church saw to it that the doctor carried out the role of herald of death. The role was not a coveted one, and it required the zeal of the 'spiritual friend' to succeed where the 'earthly friend' hesitated. When the warning did not happen spontaneously, it was part of the customary ritual. But in the later nineteenth century it became more and more problematical, as we see from a story in Tolstoy's 'Three Deaths', which appeared in 1859.

The wife of a rich businessman had contracted tuberculosis, as happened so often at that time. The doctors have pronounced her condition hopeless. The moment has come when she has to be told. There is no question of avoiding it, if only to allow her to make her 'final arrangements'. But here is a new element: the distaste of the entourage for this duty has increased. The husband refuses 'to tell her about her condition', because, he says, 'It would kill her. ... No matter what happens, it is not I who will tell her.' The mother of the dying woman is also reluctant. As for the dying woman, she talks about nothing but new treatments; she seems to be clinging to life, and everyone is afraid of her reaction. However, something has to be done. Finally the family enlists an old cousin, a poor relation, a mercenary person who throws herself into the task. 'Sitting beside the sick woman, she attempted by a skilfully manoeuvred conversation to prepare her for the idea of death.' But the sick woman suddenly interrupts her, saying, 'Ah, my dear! ... Don't try to prepare me. Don't treat me like a child. I know everything. I know that I haven't much longer to live.' Now they can begin the classic scenario of the good death in public, which has been momentarily disturbed by the new reluctance regarding the warning.

Behind this reluctance, even when it grates under the satirical pen of Tolstoy, there is the love of the other, the fear of hurting him and depriving him of hope, the temptation to protect him by leaving him in ignorance of his imminent end. No one questions the idea that he ought to know, yet no one wants to do the dirty work himself; let someone else take care of it. In France the priest was all ready, for the warning had become part of his spiritual preparation at the last hour. Indeed, the priest's arrival will be interpreted as the sign of the end, without it being necessary to say anything else.

As for the patient, and Tolstoy describes this very well, he does not really need to be warned. He already knows. But his public acceptance would destroy an illusion that he hopes to prolong a little longer, and without which he would be treated as a dying person and obliged to behave like one. So he says nothing.

And everyone becomes an accomplice to a lie born of this moment which later grows to such proportions that death is driven into secrecy. The dying person and those around him continue to play a comedy in which 'nothing has changed', 'life goes on as usual' and 'anything is still possible'. This is the second phase in a process of domination of the dying by the family that began among the upper classes in the late eighteenth century, when the dying man chose not to impose his last wishes in a legal document but entrusted them directly to his heirs.

A new relationship had been established that brought the dying man and his entourage closer on an emotional level; but the initiative, if not the power, still belonged to the dying. Here the relationship persists, but it has been reversed, and the dying man has become dependent upon the entourage. It is useless for Tolstoy's heroine to protest that she is being treated like a child, for it is she who has placed herself in that position. The day will come when the dying will accept this subordinate position, whether he simply submits to it or actually desires it. When this happens – and this is the situation today – it will be assumed that it is the duty of the entourage to keep the dying man in ignorance of his condition. How many times have we heard it said of a husband, child or relative, 'At least I have the satisfaction of knowing that he never felt a thing.' 'Never felt a thing' has replaced 'feeling his death to be imminent'.

Dissimulation has become the rule. These feats of imagination inspired Mark Twain to write a story about the tissue of lies maintained by two nice old maids in order to conceal from each of the two invalids they are taking care of, a mother and her 16-year-old child, the fact that the other is dying.

This dissimulation has the practical effect of removing or delaying all the signs that warned the sick person, especially the staging of the public act that once was death, beginning with the presence of the priest. Even in the most religious and churchgoing families, it became customary in the early twentieth century not to call the priest until his appearance at the bedside of the patient could no longer come as a surprise, either because the patient had lost consciousness or because he was unmistakably dead. Extreme Unction was no longer the sacrament of the dying but the sacrament of the dead. This situation already existed in France by the 1920s and 1930s, and became even more widespread in the 1950s.

Gone are the days of the solemn procession of the *Corpus Christi*, preceded by the choirboy ringing his bell. Gone, long gone, the days when this procession was welcomed sadly by the dying man and his entourage. It is clear that the clergy finally had had enough of administering to cadavers, that they finally refused to lend themselves to this farce, even if it was inspired by love. Their rebellion partly explains why, after Vatican II, the Church changed the traditional name of Extreme Unction to the 'anointing of the sick', and not always the terminally sick. Today it is sometimes distributed in church to old people who are not sick at all. The sacrament has been detached from death, for which it is no longer the immediate preparation. In this the Church is not merely recalling the obligation to be fully conscious when one receives the unction. It is implicitly admitting its own absence at the moment of death, the lack of necessity for 'calling the priest'; but we shall see that death has ceased to be a moment.

In the nineteenth century the disappearance of pious clauses from the will had increased the importance of the final dialogue: the last farewells, the last words of counsel, whether in private or in public. This intimate and solemn exchange has been abolished by the obligation to keep the dying man in ignorance. Eventually he left without saying anything. This was almost always the way the very old, even the conscious and the pious, died during the 1950s and 1960s in France, before the influx of new modes of behaviour from America and northwestern Europe. 'She didn't even say good-by to us,' murmured a son at the bedside of his mother. He was not yet accustomed to this stubborn silence, or perhaps to this new modesty.

3

Not going gently

David Widgery

Social change in the twentieth century, within which medical science played only a minor part, has extended the expectancy of life for all classes. At the turn of the century, it was unusual to live to three score years and ten. The poignant epitaphs in the older East End graveyards at Abney Park and Mile End show why. Death in childhood was commonplace and many adults perished in their thirties and forties. Infectious illness was the principal cause of mortality and, before the antibiotic era, GPs had a largely ceremonial and comforting role since they were unable to materially alter the course of illness. But by the end of the century, the proportion of old and very old (75 years or more) in the population had increased, in East London, to about one in six. And this is low compared with the coastal retirement areas and depopulated rural Britain: the East End's high levels of immigration keep its population artificially young. Not only do people live longer but, in general, the birth rate has fallen. [. . .]

Rather than old age being some universal state of being, it reflects quite precisely the class circumstances of the life that preceded it. We are born physiologically broadly equal, but by our sixties our bodies bear the evidence of occupation and social conditions. Our duration of life and cause of death will be the end products of the inequalities in the use made of our bodies. And for surprising numbers of male manual workers, retirement after a hard working life, which was as physically demanding in their fifties as in their twenties, is followed by premature death from preventable causes, from a stroke, lung cancer, or a heart attack. Perhaps more tragically still, an East End working life will often be followed, not by well-earned retirement but a non-fatal stroke or early dementia (Alzheimer's disease) which will render a once independent and active person chronically dependent. There can be few more devastating changes than the transformation which occurs when a stroke renders a previously articulate and agile partner speechless and chair-bound. Or when a wife of forty years deteriorates mentally so as to require constant supervision, incapable of anything but repetitive, uncomprehending gibberish.

Extract from *Some Lives!*, London: Sinclair-Stevenson, 1991, pp. 124–38 (abridged).

But to talk about the old as 'geriatric' is to see them immediately as ill and therefore dependent. Whereas many are, within the biological limits of the ageing process, active, alert and fiercely independent. It is to see them simply as an age category rather than individual people who deserve respect as mothers and lovers and storytellers and historians. For every person over 65 who has a home help, there are nine who don't. For everyone living in a local authority old people's home, there are fifty who don't.

Rather than 'suffering' from old age, East End pensioners are done down by something very much simpler – lack of finances. And the principal cause of that poverty is a paltry state pension which rewards the generation who fought through both the Great Depression and the Blitz with a mean stipend which bears no relation to real wage levels. The retired workers who have lived thrifty lives but who have neither property nor investments are likely in their old age to be very poor by general standards. Poor means often cold and at risk of death during extreme winter weather. It means eating a very basic diet with little variety and often low in vitamins, on foil trays from the Meals on Wheels during the day and out of tins at night and weekends. It means shabby, well-worn clothing, purchased secondhand and infrequently cleaned. It means rarely a car and seldom a washing machine. It means a life spent indoors watching the TV to the end and hoping the knock on the door is not an intruder. One doesn't need any statistical equipment more complicated than a pair of eyes to observe this. Look, for example, at the foray at the knitted clothes stall at East End jumble sales and observe the broken boots and laddered stockings in any geriatric outpatients. Watch pensioner couples, perplexed by prices, putting too costly items back on to supermarket shelves. See the queue for sweet tea and free biscuits at the pensioners' clubs or the old gentlemen in the back of the public bar nursing their half pints hour by hour. Look into the eyes of a pensioner living alone (one in six of British households) and, by and large, you will not see serenity and comfort but fear, impatience and the desire to be somewhere, anywhere, else. [. . .]

Death is the great truth of all our lives; however sharp-witted, fit or rich, we can't avoid it, and yet, in the modern world, we are unlikely to have experienced it at home. When people want their dying to be put in hospitals, it is only partly because they hope for treatment which will save them. In reality it is because we can't face death. It's everywhere in fiction: it is said a Californian child will have seen 2,000 deaths on TV by the time it's five. But we know nothing of it firsthand, how unappeasable and cruel it is, what it's like when it happens. Instead we tidy it away with 'floral tributes', funeral directors and the witless rhetoric of the crematorium dirge. For death, for most working-class patients, isn't usually kind or 'a release' or all the other slippery phrases which lie about it. It's the final confirmation that many of life's possibilities have been confiscated. To take the pain and the injustice out of death is the meanest sentimentality. It is something starker: I have seen too often the gasping and fading in a room which has accumulated only the most meagre of possessions, the last struggle of a body that has known little luxury and much settling for less.

As a doctor, your next encounter is with a corpse which you are, for the purposes of cremation, required to examine in the rear of the undertaker's. The front lounges of these places are well upholstered, full of cigarette smoke and euphemisms, but the bodies are usually stored out of sight in a clanking garage-like morgue whose slightly putrid smell is not completely masked by detergent. The body is now cold, stiff and often toothless, in a galvanized container. Death makes people ugly. Ugly because inert; the sweat and lung-suck and heartbeat gone. Hard to believe this person has ever worked, thought, journeyed, fantasized or procreated. Now a passenger at the rites, while taped organs intone and priest pontificates.

GPs are still required to 'certify' death, another ritual which is legal rather than medical. And this is a moment, and an important one, to meet relatives who are grieving. A family who have been nursing a terminally ill patient at home sometimes need a formal statement of death, a piece of paper to make it real. What you say at this moment is important; even the banal words of sympathy can mean a lot. At least East Enders know how to mourn: they have to. Like the old Irish and Jewish families, all ages sit with each other and the body. Rooms fill with relatives you don't know, sobbing, clutching and supporting each other, streaming sons and tearful grandchildren assembled instantaneously even at 4 a.m. You feel for the absent pulse, shine a light into unresponsive pupils, shake endless hands and refuse sweet tea, swallowing instead a bitter mixture of relief and sadness. A moment which is very strong.

It is more painful to be called to a person who has died unattended and alone. These are the bodies keeled over in the toilet or stiff in a stale bedroom, blue and contorted in the time they have lain undiscovered. Once I was called to a flat where a man had become depressed, drunk himself to death and sat for six days rotting on top of a vast mound of empties, like a Guy Fawkes consumed by drink instead of flames. The smell was rich and sickly and he was almost impossible to reach and examine on his pyre of debris. Unexpected death is also frightening, although mostly the ambulance service is called before the GP and takes the body to the hospital, often attempting revival even if it is clear the person is dead. I remember trying to haul a stocky butcher, who had died of a heart attack at 2 a.m. in front of the TV, on to his bed, which seemed a better resting place. But he doubled up as we lifted him and the raised intra-abdominal pressure made it look as if he took a breath. His widow insisted on mouth to mouth again, and even though it was quite hopeless I complied for a decent interval. 'Why did you take so long?' is the question either spoken or unspoken when one arrives at a deathbed. But it is rare that speed much alters the course of events, although it is important for those who are to live on to feel everything has been done that could have been. As Epicurus says, death is no misfortune for him who died but for those who survived.

But how death is observed, the respect or otherwise human bodies are afforded, surely marks a measure of our degree of civilization. In one week the local paper reported four East End deaths which were last exits of horror and neglect. A hospital porter in his fifties lay in a filthy local pond because 'the locals thought it was a bag of rubbish'. A Stepney pensioner was found dead only after a neighbour complained of a smell coming from his door. A Poplar widower hanged himself with a tie and a Hoxton man died alone of hypothermia after falling in his bedroom. Earlier in 1990, a 91-year-old demented man lay dead in the grounds of Hackney Hospital for three weeks before discovery. A 67-year-old Clapton man drowned in a pool of roadside water that had developed when sewers had become blocked with mud and litter. During the 1989 flu epidemic, some of the Borough of Hackney's old people's homes were reported as being damp and draughty with a shortage of towels and sheets, intermittent hot water, dirty toilets and uncarpeted floors.

What is then bewildering is that such time, money and emotion are spent on the outward show of grief when it is all too late. But so little is done about the care of the old when they are living. What do we all want but a gentle death, near to those we have loved, with some sense that we have done some of what was possible and changed things for the better? To die peacefully *is* our greatest desire; to have 'come to terms' with death and no longer be petrified by the advance of 'the cure of all diseases'. To die fighting death is to cause yourself intractable pain. And I can remember people who have willed themselves to stay alive and the agony their demise has therefore become. A policeman with lung cancer who silently quaked with fury at the injustice of his illness. His family kept denying his death was a possibility and in futile solidarity pretended business as usual while he became skin and bones before their eyes. Yet other people can derive an almost exhilarating sense of purpose from the same situation and, instead of desperate anguish, derive great focus and intensity. [. . .]

It would be nice to think we were just departing to a congenial reunion of all those others we have loved who have died, waiting to welcome us to Hotel Eternity. Nice but implausible. What does linger is something almost more powerful, which is memory. It is the world which is given to us, as Cicero states, 'as an inn in which to stay, but not to dwell'. It is what we have done in life that lives on, not the trumped-up version of eternity which is worshipped in dank cemeteries and gravestone jingles. What we deserve to remember is real courage, not bogus virtue lauded at the funerals. How few deaths are 'acceptable': I was angry and hurt even when a 96-year-old friend died. Indeed you can get lost in a pit of grief, determining you will never laugh or dance or joke again. But humans are enormously adaptable, have ways of healing their mental as well as physical pain. It's not the passage of time that matters, however, but what you do with it. Only with effort do we extract from the irreplaceable something that falls into place. [. . .]

What is odd is that in our apparently highly sophisticated society, we are still cowardly about facing death. More incompetent and less civilized than the Greeks or even the Victorians. And that, even at the grave, there is such injustice. A great man's funeral is rich in decorum, music, honour and dignity. The pauper dies alone, floating like waste paper in a pond and puddle or rotting in the council flat.

4

Death in Ireland: deaths, wakes and funerals in contemporary Irish society

Rosemary Power

While many of the rituals that once surrounded the processes of death and burial have been lost in contemporary Irish society, more survive than is the norm in Western Europe. Death is still a major event for which people prepare, by keeping up life insurance payments in order to pay for their funeral, by writing wills, by acquiring a burial plot, and sometimes, particularly in the country areas, by buying a shroud in which to be buried. A good death requires both spiritual and practical preparation.

Throughout Ireland religious practice is common. About 90 per cent of the population of the Republic of Ireland and over 40 per cent of the population of the six counties of Northern Ireland would regard itself as Catholic. A high proportion of Catholics would practice their religion regularly, and, although there is evidence that the numbers who do so are declining, in particular in poorer urban areas, nearly all would observe the rituals appropriate to major events in their life. While there are a relatively small number of Protestants in the Republic, a slight majority of the population of Northern Ireland regards itself as Protestant. The largest denomination is the Presbyterian Church, followed closely by the (Anglican) Church of Ireland. There are also Methodists and Baptists, and a significant number of subscribers to small, mainly fundamentalist, denominations. While regular practice among Protestants is less widespread than among Catholics, most would observe Church rituals at the major rites of passage. The attitudes to death referred to in this article are especially relevant to the mixed Protestant/Catholic society of the North of Ireland, in particular to that of the city of Belfast. While certain practices, such as those associated with praying for the dead or invoking the Virgin Mary, are almost entirely confined to Catholics, most forms of practice and ritual surrounding death will be found on both sides of the community.

While dying in hospital has become common, and the hospice movement provides an institutional alternative to hospital, many people, given the choice, elect to die at home.

It is usually the intention of the close family to ensure that they do not die alone. Prayers are often said as a person dies, and at some stage a priest or minister may be present. If he is not present at the death itself, he is likely to be called in soon afterwards, in the case of a Catholic priest, to anoint the body and say prayers for the dead. Folk rituals concerning the moment of death may take several forms. After death it is usually the prerogative of a close relation to close the eyes and mouth of the deceased. In many houses all the clocks are stopped and mirrors are covered. The curtains of the death-room and of the house will be drawn and will not be opened again until the family returns to the house after the funeral. (On the day of the funeral, it is still common for the curtains of the other houses in the street to be closed while the remains are being taken out.) While it was a custom until recently for local women to wash the body – a custom usually deputed to a couple of women in every street, such duties are now usually, but not always, performed by the undertaker, the exceptions being when close women relatives decide to perform this service themselves. Until fairly recently the undertaker came to the house after a bereavement, to take measurements for a coffin, and, if embalming was necessary, to perform it in the house. The body was then laid out on the bed of death until shortly before the funeral. Nowadays, undertakers usually remove the body and place it in a coffin. While sometimes, in particular among the middle classes, the remains are taken to a funeral parlour, it is customary to have the coffin brought home and left open in the best room.

The coffin is placed on trestles in the living room, with the lid laid aside. People who have known the deceased then come to view the body and to pay their respects. People of all ages, including young children, may be present during the wake. In Catholic households the visitors will customarily say a prayer, and perhaps a part of the rosary. A small altar with candles and a religious picture or some such item will have been set up. One South Armagh informant said that a piece of yew is provided which mourners use to sprinkle holy water over the body in the form of a cross. A mass card, notification that a mass is to be said on behalf of the deceased, is laid in the coffin. In both Protestant and Catholic households a family member deputed to be present is then shaken by the hand and offered condolences. Tea, or in some cases alcohol, is offered in another room and it is regarded as discourteous not to accept. It is considered bad form to leave the corpse unattended in Catholic households and people will stay up at night in order to prevent this and take turns at praying. In Protestant households the corpse is also viewed but prayers are not offered for the deceased. There is less emphasis on watching with the corpse, and it may be laid out alone, for example in an upstairs bedroom. Catholics and Protestants go to the wakes of people of the opposite persuasion.

Protestants are inclined to be buried in secular clothes, which commonly comprise of a suit for a man, and either a dress or night-clothes for a woman. Catholics, especially in rural areas, may be buried in a shroud. It is normal to bury Catholics with a rosary in their hands, usually one that belonged to the deceased.

It is traditional to have alcohol at 'wakes', the period during which the corpse is at home, and to offer a drink to all comers, unless the designation 'house private' has appeared in the newspaper death notice. Drinking alcohol does not always occur these days, though a Belfast Protestant informant spoke of recent wakes in which an extra glass of Guinness was still poured for the deceased; and of others at which heavy drinking occurred. The wake games of the past, decried down the centuries, would on the whole be frowned upon today. However, 'weddings should be sad and wakes should be happy' still largely applies, at least where the deceased has lived a normal span of years. It is essential to speak well of the dead.

Although the custom of kissing or otherwise touching the dead is no longer considered necessary, viewing the deceased is still regarded as normal. If the corpse is for some reason badly disfigured, for example as the result of a car accident, the undertakers may suggest the coffin is brought home closed. However, the close family are then deemed, by themselves and others, to suffer additional grief.

It is normal for the funeral to occur shortly after the death, in some cases on the following day. By means of a death notice in one of the local papers, and by word of mouth, people will have been informed of the time of the service.

Shortly before the body is removed, the coffin is closed in the presence of the family and usually with a clergyman in attendance. At the appointed time the coffin is lifted out of the house, followed by the close family and the bearers. It may be carried a short way at this stage. In parts of the Mournes, a religiously mixed mountainous area, the front door of the house is hardly ever opened except when a coffin is taken out. Sometimes something reminiscent of the deceased will be placed on the coffin, though it will be removed while the coffin is inside the church. A football jersey may be put there in the case of a young person, or, in certain circumstances, a flag.

In the case of many, but not all, practising Catholics the coffin is brought to the church the night before the funeral. The reception is marked by a brief service conducted by a priest. The coffin is left in front of, or near to, the altar overnight. The Protestant custom is to bring it to church directly before the funeral service.

The funeral service is almost always conducted in church by a member of the clergy. In the case of Catholics it will always include prayers for the dead and nearly always a homily. Sometimes, in particular among Protestants, there will be, instead of a church service, a private service in the home or in a funeral parlour. It is nearly always conducted by a member of the clergy. It is not uncommon for Protestants to be cremated, especially in Belfast, but among Catholics burial is normal.

It is a matter of form for people to come to funerals if they knew the deceased or if they know the family and wish to support them at the time of loss. This means that funerals can be very large and that people unlikely to meet under other circumstances may walk together and even help bear the coffin together. The coffin may be taken most of the way to the cemetery in a hearse, especially if the commercial areas of the city have to be crossed, but it is customary to start off on foot, with male members of the family and their associates carrying the coffin. The carrying is done in shifts and other selected mourners may be invited to take a turn. The custom of women helping to carry the coffin is new and is still only occasionally seen. The main body of the mourners walk behind, and in some instances, even though the coffin is placed in a hearse, it moves slowly in order to enable the mourners to follow on foot, a practice that often causes traffic delays. Catholic funerals customarily take place in the late mornings, and Protestant funerals in the early afternoons.

Until about fifteen years ago, women attended the church service but rarely if ever followed the coffin to the cemetery or watched it being placed in the grave. One informant, speaking of the funeral of her father who died in the Troubles in the early 1970s, said, 'In those days only republican women went to funerals.' She had not seen her father buried and felt that her own grieving had been incomplete in consequence. Customs changed and when her mother died and was buried beside him, she was able to attend all parts of that ceremony. However, while a funeral's chief mourners may now be women, it is not unknown to see only men following the cortege on foot (even if the deceased is a woman), though nowadays women mourners may follow behind in a car.

Lowering the coffin into the grave is usually accompanied by ritual, and it may be followed at Catholic funerals by the recitation of part or all of the rosary, which will be led by the presiding priest. Until fairly recently, at both Protestant and Catholic funerals, the grave was closed while the mourners were present: now they may throw a token handful of earth into the grave, but the actual filling will be done later by grave-diggers. One member of the family is deputed to have his hand shaken by the departing mourners.

At one time it was common for the mourners to return to the death-house for refreshments, but this practice is declining, perhaps because funerals have become larger, and the house may be said to be 'private' – for members of the immediate family only. Other alternatives are that the chief mourners will stand a round of drinks for the other mourners in a nearby bar, or, more formally, a selected group will be invited to a meal at a local hotel. In rural areas, heavy drinking in a local bar may take place after the funeral, especially if the deceased was elderly and celebration is deemed appropriate.

While the funeral marks the end of the initial rituals, there are rites still to be observed, particularly by Catholics. A month to the day after the death will be the 'month's mind', a mass said for the repose of the dead person. Other masses will be said on the anniversary of the death. In addition, every Catholic diocese has a 'Cemetery Sunday', a day on which people visit the graves of their dead and tidy them, and a brief service takes place. A secular custom common on both sides of the religious divide is placing an In Memoriam notice in the local newspapers, in particular for the early anniversaries of the death. These notices are often accompanied by a brief and intensely personal verse, usually of homemade construction.

Many people claim that they have had forewarning of a death. Sometimes too, the presence of the person is said to be sensed at the moment of their death or shortly afterwards, and may be interpreted as the dying person saying farewell to someone. These private experiences are common on both sides of the community, even where formally-held theological beliefs deny that such events can occur.

Where people have lived their full span, death need not be regarded as unwelcome. In the Irish language one of the formulae traditionally used when taking farewell of a person is to wish them 'Bás í nÉirinn', Death in Ireland. In a society bled by emigration, it was a loving wish. While in Ireland today, traditions are being lost in favour of a more sanitized version of funerals, death rituals are still sufficiently rich to provide a degree of comfort, both for a person planning their own funeral, and for their family. One informant advised, speaking of a clergyman: 'Ask Jimmy to bury you. You'll get a great send-off.'

Note

This is a shortened version of the original article.

The author wishes it to be known that this version of her article is a more authentic representation of her research than the version originally published in the first printing.

Thanks are due to all my informants, and to those who read and commented on this paper in draft.

Bibliography

Maurna Crozier, 'Powerful Wakes: Perfect Hospitality', in Chris Curtin and Tom Wilson (eds), *Ireland from Below* (Galway University Press, n.d./c. 1991), pp. 70–91.

Kevin Danaher, *In Ireland Long Ago* (Dublin, The Mercier Press, 1962). 'The Wake', pp. 169–76 contains traditional oral accounts of the wakes of the recent past.

Seán Ó Súilleabháin, *Irish Wake Amusements* (Dublin, The Mercier Press, 1967). This contains a historical perspective and folklore accounts of wakes and attendant practices.

5

Approaches to death in Hindu and Sikh communities in Britain

Shirley Firth

Hindus and Sikhs live in many parts of Britain and most try to maintain their own religion and culture as far as possible. However, living in a country with a different culture, belief systems and family patterns can create problems for Asians because they may not be able to follow their traditional practices at a time when they would most wish to. Those who have come from rural areas may have little experience of Western medical techniques and intensive care units. Ignorance and lack of sensitivity on the part of medical or social work personnel about the religious beliefs and cultural outlook of patients can make an already frightening situation worse, particularly in hospital, where language may be an additional barrier. There are rituals which need to be done at the moment of death, which make it essential for at least family members to be present; failing to do this can have long-term consequences.

Hindu beliefs

Hindus have emigrated from India, East Africa, the West Indies, Fiji or Malaysia, and speak Hindi, Gujarati, Panjabi and other regional languages. Hindus belong to different classes and castes, reflecting ancient social and occupational divisions. Priests, who come from the highest class, the Brahmins, are required for funeral and post-mortem rituals (Burghart, 1987; Sulivan, 1989).

There is an immense diversity of religious and cultural beliefs and practices, but most Hindus follow 'Sanatan Dharma', the eternal religion, code or law. They may worship God in one form, such as Shiva, Krishna or Mataji (the Mother), or in many forms, believing that underlying these is one Ultimate Reality.

My gratitude to all those who advised me on the current paper: Dr Tanaji Acharya, Prof. S.N. Bharadwaj, Dr Amrit Bening, Dr Desai, Ram Krishan and Eleanor Nesbitt, Dr Kanwaljit Kaur Singh, Dr Yashvir Sunak, Dr Harcharan Sanir, Darshan Singh, Piara Singh Sambhi and many members of the Hindu and Sikh communities.

Material for this article has appeared in Firth, 1988, 1989, 1991, and Berger, 1989.

Certain commonly held beliefs are important in understanding Hindu approaches to death. Hindus believe that we are reborn many times as part of a cosmic cycle involving all living things. During this life-time our good and bad thoughts and actions generate good or bad *karma*, which determines what happens to us after death. A truly holy soul will be with God in heaven or, according to other beliefs, merges with Ultimate Reality. Less perfect souls are reborn as humans if they have been good, or else as animals or even insects. Unexplained suffering and handicaps may be understood as a person's previous *karma*. It is important to prepare for death by scripture reading, meditation, prayer and fasting so that when the time comes there is no attachment to family or possessions and one is ready to go. Such a death in old age is a good death and may be anticipated to the exact day and time. It should take place on the floor, with God's name or the scriptures being chanted and holy Ganges water and *tulsi* (basil) leaf in the mouth (Firth, 1989, 1991).

Sikh beliefs

Sikh men are recognizable because of their turbans and beards, although some wear neither; women usually wear a trouser suit, *salvar kameze*. Initiated Sikhs wear the five Ks, symbols of the faith, at all times. These are uncut hair, *kesh* (spirituality); the comb, *kangha* (discipline, neatness and cleanliness); the sword, *kirpan* (readiness to defend the faith, the poor and the oppressed); the steel circle, *kara*, on the right wrist as a reminder to use the hands only for good and as a symbol of divine unity and infinity (Cole and Sambhi, 1978: 128); and shorts, *kachh* (restraint, modesty and purity). They are usually worn in Britain as an undergarment. The turban is a mark of identity. Women cover their heads in the *gurdwara*, the place of worship, and may do so in the presence of men.

Sikhism arose out of Hinduism in the sixteenth century, reflecting the caste system. As a symbol of the equality of all people there is a shared meal (*langar*) in the *gurdwara* available to everyone. There is no hereditary or ordained priesthood, although in *gurdwaras* there is a knowledgeable man, *granthi*, who is paid to read the scriptures contained in the *Guru Granth Sahib* and lead services. However, anyone may do this, including women, who have equal status (Cole and Sambhi, 1978: 64).

Sikhs also believe in *karma* and reincarnation. After death those who are rid of their self-centredness and spiritual blindness come into God's presence, but those who are not spiritually ready are reborn according to their *karma*. A truly spiritual person who meditates is said to know of his approaching death and prepare for a good death. Life should be lived in such as way that death does not take one unawares.

Talking about death

Although Hindus and Sikhs believe in principle that it is important to know about death in advance in order to be prepared, death in Britain is a less familiar part of life than it would be in India where life expectancy is much lower and where more deaths would occur at home in the extended family situation. In Britain there are greater expectations that doctors and modern medicine will be able to do something.

> Asians like the idea of symptom clearance. If you can stop a cough or fever the person is cured. It is difficult to say the effects are of an underlying disorder. There is a feeling that you should be able to keep people alive. Indians find it harder to accept that illness is terminal, they may feel that one says so out of malice. I have a relative of 50 with motor neurone disease who can't accept that nothing can be done medically. More and more people want to blame someone. (Sikh doctor)

According to the doctor quoted above, the death of the elderly in the Asian community in Britain occurs in a very different context to India, because there

> the elderly in villages have more of a sense of preparation for death. Here there is a feeling that one can keep the old alive, without any preparation for death. Many people feel, 'Now we are wealthy, let's bring the old folks here.' It is making a mistake because the elderly are sad and lonely, uprooted from the familiar environment where they had a role to play and a sense of continuity. There they were useful and accepted, with a full day. Here they are lost and lonely, and the [younger] women work, whereas there they did not. In India the older generation would keep old folks at home because they would have had the experience of supporting the dying at home, but here people expect health care professionals to do it.

Telling a person she or he has a terminal illness or telling the relatives is felt to be necessary yet it should be done in a way which does not lead to the patient's loss of hope, particularly in the case of a premature death, where the belief that this is due to bad *karma* may make it difficult to come to terms with (Neuberger, 1987: 25). Hindu and Sikh doctors may also be in a dilemma because sometimes the patient or relative collapses emotionally on being told that an illness is terminal, yet they are also aware of the longer-term emotional and spiritual needs of the family: 'The majority of patients don't want to know – the relatives may have an inner idea, but they don't want to know. They may cry or become hysterical.' One Hindu doctor told a son, on the basis of reports from the hospital, that his father was not likely to live more than six months. Having been reassured by the hospital that the father would be alright, the son did not believe the doctor and was not prepared for or present at his father's death, which was emotionally shattering for him.

Lack of communication between Asians and medical staff may cause great frustration, especially in hospital, if they are kept in the dark about the prognosis and miss actually being present at the point of death. Sometimes it is felt that lack of sensitivity on the part of doctors and nurses borders on racism, particularly when assumptions are made about the patient's or relative's capacity to understand what is going on because of real or perceived language difficulties. This is well illustrated in the case of a graduate Panjabi woman who had a heavy accent. She did not understand the implications of her husband's treatment and was not told, so kept demanding more help and care and came to be thought of as a nuisance. Her 15-year-old daughter ended up as an interpreter. It was also assumed incorrectly that the father could not understand English, although his problems of communication were due to partial paralysis of his throat and the daughter was expected to pass messages on to him.

Caring for the dying

In spite of the difficulties involved in informing relatives, they want to know when death is imminent so that they can make the right preparations.

> In hospitals, when someone is near death he must have his next of kin with him because there are a few religious rituals to be performed. When we know he is near death we start reciting the *Bhagavad Gita* or religious books. The only people who can perform this service for the dying patient are their own. The nurses and doctors won't do it, so obviously we must be told [death is imminent] rather than keeping this news away, and only being told after the death has happened. I know it's not easy to say, 'Look, he is going to die.' It's easier to say, 'He's alright, nothing to worry about', and then you are given a telephone call, 'Sorry we couldn't save him.' But there are rituals to be done before the person dies, and chanting the Gayatri Mantra is evergreen and gives you power, strength, satisfaction and peace. (Panjabi Brahmin)

Sikhs have similar views about being present, but for Hindus it is especially important because there is a belief that unless the rituals at the time of death are performed properly the dying person will not pass on to the next life but will remain a ghost. This spells disaster not just for the patient but also for the family subsequently. In one Gujarati family the death of an aunt was complicated by the fact that the family were not permitted to place Ganges water on the patient's lips. This is so holy it washes away the sin of the dying.

> An aunt was dying of cancer, everybody knew she was dying, the doctors told the family, and the whole family was present at the death. But when the doctors switched off the life-support machine they wouldn't let the family give Ganges water or perform any last rites to this lady, and even today after ten years it still affects the family that they weren't able to do this. If they want to have a social occasion like a wedding in the family or something, they must do some penance first, because they say she died without water, therefore her soul is still not free, and her family is not free,

and they've got to keep performing all these rites that they weren't able to
during her death, until the soul is free . . . for at least seven generations.
(Gujarati woman)

Even without such an extreme situation, the failure of the family to be
present can have long-term consequences for the family.

Nurses should let the family be present when the soul leaves, because if the
person dies without the family there, then that person will not be thinking
of God but of his family who weren't there. Not only would the family be
affected, but the dying person, who would have to take rebirth. The family
couldn't take part in any social occasions or anything because it would
always be hanging over them that they hadn't been present at the death, so
no good omen will occur for them to perform for a very long period. The
person's whole extended family would be affected, uncles, aunts, distant
cousins. (Gujarati woman)

The moment of death

The idea of death at home and on the floor is recognized by most
Indians to be impractical in Britain, although elderly Hindus have been
known to get out of bed and lie on the floor.

The belief is that you should die on the floor. Here a lot of people die in
hospitals and a lot of us families are very shy to [ask for what we want]. We
feel out of place, like a Muslim praying on the factory floor. (Panjabi Brahmin)

Clearly, the needs of Indian patients may conflict with the needs of the
ward as a whole and the chanting or singing could be very disruptive
unless a separate room were to be made available. A Sikh doctor,
having observed disturbances by Sikh families around dying patients,
made sure in the case of his own dying niece that visitors were
restricted to the immediate family and then the *granthi* was called: 'He
sang hymns and we asked him to leave when the machine was switched off. The nursing staff left us for a good hour.'

Ending or prolonging life

Hindus and Sikhs believe life should never be artificially ended,
although the boundaries between active 'killing' or euthanasia and
'allowing to die' are acknowledged to be hard to draw at times. A
Panjabi doctor said that on principle he would always treat
aggressively (to prolong life):

I can't dream of a Hindu considering euthanasia; one would want to know
that everything had been done, because of one's attachment, and because of
guilt that one hadn't done one's duty. There would be enormous pressure
from others that not enough is being done, so that doesn't allow you to do
anything but treat aggressively. . . . I can't imagine a Hindu signing
something like a living will. That is far too intellectual.

However, switching off a life-support machine when it is clear that death is imminent or the person is brain-dead is acceptable in principle, if difficult to accept in practice.

After death

Because there are fewer taboos against women weeping or against men showing emotion than in Anglo-Saxon society, a great deal of distress may be shown on the death of a Hindu or Sikh relative and this may disturb staff and other patients. A Sikh nurse described another woman who had a stillbirth in the maternity unit and the English nurse thought she was being very extreme because she was expressing her grief very loudly. A couple of her relatives and her mother-in-law were also wailing and 'making a scene' in a way which would be regarded as quite normal and the 'done thing' in a village setting at home but was regarded as abnormal here. The nurses, not surprisingly perhaps, kept telling them to 'keep your voices down' but the Sikh nurse said they needed to get it out of their system and work it out.

The family may wish to wash and dress the body in the hospital, although it will have to be done again immediately before the funeral, so many families prefer to leave this until later when they can obtain help from more experienced members of the community. Most Hindus and Sikhs will allow the nurses to help lay out the body and remove tubes, etc., but there are taboos against women touching men and vice versa, so men may prefer to deal with the body of a male member of the family. Post-mortems may be disturbing to some but often they will be accepted if the reasons are adequately explained and they help to explain the death. Sikhs wish to wear the five Ks at all times, even in hospital, and so these should not be removed at death.

If for any reason the family are not present at the moment of death this will be particularly traumatic, as has been seen, and they may want to know what the last words of the patient were. These last words are treasured and give an indication of the mental state of the dying person, which, if positive, gives a great deal of hope and comfort to the bereaved.

Conclusion

From the point of view of the patients and their families what is wanted is sensitivity: 'Carers don't have an idea about cultural diversity – but they only need to listen for a few minutes to be sensitive' (Sikh doctor). This sensitivity needs to be manifested from the outset – over the details of nursing care, such as ensuring there is plenty of water for washing after bedpans and before prayers; allowing Sikhs to keep the five Ks on or within reach and understanding their intense feelings about these; respecting strict dietary rules and the intense modesty of Asians, particularly of women patients, regarding male doctors and nurses; and finally showing openness and willingness to communicate with patients and relatives so that mutual compromises can be made and no one dies alone.

Indians, particularly those from the subcontinent, are members of a family first and individuals second: this fact needs to be recognized in helping people deal with death and bereavement. It is this which also provides mechanisms for coping with the loss in a social context, providing an ongoing support system.

References

Berger, A. (ed.) (1989) *Perspectives on Death and Dying*. Philadelphia, PA: Charles Press.

Burghart, R. (ed.) (1987) *Hinduism in Great Britain: the Perpetuation of Religion in an Alien Cultural Milieu*. London: Tavistock.

Cole, W.O. and Sambhi, P.S. (1978) *The Sikhs, their Religious Beliefs and Practices*. London: Rou.

Firth, S. (1988) 'Hindu and Sikh approaches to death and bereavement'. Unpublished paper, Panjab Research Group, Coventry.

Firth, S. (1989) 'The good death: approaches to death, dying and bereavement among British Hindus', in A. Berger (ed.), *Perspectives on Death and Dying*. Philadelphia, PA: Charles Press.

Firth, S. (1991) 'Changing patterns of Hindu death rituals in Britain', in D. Killingley, W. Menski and S. Firth, *Hindu Ritual and Society*. SY, Killingley.

Neuberger, J. (1987) *Caring for Dying People of Different Faiths*. London: Lisa Sainsbury Foundation, Auston Cornish Publishers.

Sulivan, L.E. (1989) *Healing and Restoring: Health and Medicine in the World's Religions*. New York: Macmillan.

6

Modern death: taboo or not taboo?

Tony Walter

'Death - and talk about it - is the one great taboo of our age'

(Radio Times, 24 February 1990).

The above is typical of dozens more quotes from the quality press, from reports and leaflets for the bereaved. It is a strange taboo that is proclaimed by every pundit in the land, and when virtually no Sunday is without at least one newspaper discussing death, bereavement, hospices, or funerals. Nor is this frequent discussion of a taboo subject unique to the UK. Simpson's 1979 English language bibliography lists over 650 books on the subject, while his 1987 update adds another 1,700 books produced between 1979 and 1986. So what is going on?

In this article, I ask: (a) Is death taboo? if so, in what sense, and for whom. Any adequate answer must also be able to explain: (b) Why, if death is not taboo, the constant proclamation of it as such? And if it is in some sense taboo, how is that every year since at least 1955 (when Gorer published his article 'The pornography of death') has seen dramatic announcements that the taboo has only just been discovered?

With the exception of the now dated Gorer (1955, 1965), there is surprisingly little sociological research in the UK on the subject. What research on death there has been has largely come under the rubric of medical sociology (e.g. Williams, 1981, 1989, 1990), and particularly within the hospital setting (e.g. Field, 1989; McIntosh, 1977), though Jupp (1990), Miller (1974), Naylor (1989), Prior (1989), Smale (1985) and Walter (1989b, 1990a) are exceptions. True, Elias wrote *The Loneliness of Dying* (1985), but this book reflects a continental European tradition. There is nothing in the UK like the thanatological textbooks of American sociologists (Charmaz, 1980; Kamerman, 1988; and Kearl, 1989). No British sociological theory includes human awareness of mortality as a central feature of the human condition (as does Peter Berger, 1967), while even the sociology of religion leaves

From *Sociology*, May 1992, 25(2): 293–310 (abridged).

the subject well alone (though see Pickering's brief 1974 article on rites of passage). While journalists, counsellors and historians in the UK write on the subject frequently, British sociologists have kept death at arm's length.

Outside of British sociology, the flood of academic deathwork continues unabated. In the USA, sociologists and psychologists have published many thousands of articles on death since the seminal works of Feifel (1959) and Fulton (1963). Historians in North America, Britain and Europe – though not in Latin Europe (Vovelle, 1980) – picked up the baton in the 1970s. Why this flood of publications at this particular time? [. . .]

The taboo thesis

Now to define my two major terms: taboo, and death. In everyday usage, the word 'taboo' refers to something prohibited, forbidden, by custom rather than by law. It may be something too terrible even to think of, its reality denied. Or, more weakly, it may simply not be mentioned in conversation.

But what is it that may not be mentioned or even thought of – the process of dying, or the state of being dead? my own demise, or the demise of one I love? the idea of not existing, or the physical corpse? In this article I concentrate on the weak taboo – talking about death, both mine and yours. At places I touch on the stronger version – denial – though, as Kellehear (1984) argues, this Freudian concept is more the domain of the psychoanalyst.

Popular assertions that death is taboo in the modern world have their academic counterparts. By far the most quoted – in the UK, Europe and N. America – are Geoffrey Gorer's *Death, Grief and Mourning in Contemporary Britain* (1965) and Phillipe Ariès's *The Hour of Our Death* (1981). Both writers maintain that death is uniquely badly handled by modern society.

Gorer argues that though we have retained some minimal funeral ritual, World War I marked the beginning of the end of mourning rituals. He claims that if problematic experiences such as bereavement are not handled ritually, psychological problems will emerge for the individual, while death will resurface socially in what he had earlier (1955) termed 'the pornography of death': a society that refuses to talk of death personally becomes obsessed with horror comics, war movies and disasters.

Gorer's argument explains much. It explains how the media can be obsessed with death even at a time when individuals find it impossible to talk about their own personal grief. It explains both how death can be a taboo topic, and how Gorer's bereaved interviewees could have been so eager to talk: he had given them 'permission', and all the feelings that no one else wanted to hear came pouring out. His theory could even explain the flood of academic material on death that has developed, especially in the USA, since the 1950s and that shows no signs of abating – like the 'pornographic' media coverage, it is death at a remove, death abstracted, intellectualized, professionalized and depersonalized.

Gorer has been widely criticized, however. He romanticizes Victorian mourning rituals, which Morley (1971) argues were in fact largely generated for the profit of crepe and other manufacturers. [. . .] Historian Jennifer Leaney (1989) suggests that the modern denial of death began in the early nineteenth, not the twentieth century (see, for example, Jacobs, 1899), while Jupp (1990) sees World War II as the key to popular modern attitudes to death. Rosenblatt et al. (1976: Ch. 4) argue that 'denying' death by removing stimuli that remind the bereaved of the deceased is far from uniquely modern and – from the perspective of learning theory – may be psychologically healthy. [. . .]

Ariès, like Gorer, argues that death is inevitably problematic; along with sex, it is one of the major ways in which 'nature' threatens 'culture'. Death must therefore be 'tamed', which societies traditionally do through religion and through ritual. But over the past few centuries, individualism, romanticism and secularism have undermined the rituals, and the modern individual is left naked before death's obscenity. Today we are the heirs both of a Victorian romanticism which made the loss of the loved one ('thy death') unbearable, and of a twentieth-century denial that forbids (Ariès, 1974), or at least hides (Ariès, 1981), death.

Ariès, like Gorer, explains much. The combination of the Victorian *thy* death and the modern *forbidden* death explains, for example, what appear in the USA to be two opposing trends: the denial of death implicit in American hospitals and in the lack of mourning, and the continuing tradition of Americans viewing the body (Ariès, 1981: 596–601). [. . .]

Ariès too has many critics. His historical epochs, apparently sweeping across Europe regardless of culture and religion, offend more careful historians, and in particular his depiction of modern America as the final chapter of a unilinear European history wears very thin. Mount's (1982) demolition of Ariès's earlier claim (1962) that it is only in the last century or two that people could afford to get too fond of their children also holds good for his claim that they did not invest enough emotionally in spouse or children to feel their loss. Ariès rarely mentions the deaths of women (Smale, 1985), and he relies heavily on documentation about the rich. The poor have always been buried without much ritual, and are probably dispatched with more respect in modern welfare states than in any other epoch.

Criticism of Gorer and Ariès, however, must always be tempered by humility. Misleading, partial or downright wrong they may be, but they have put the subject on the academic - if not the British sociological - map. [. . .]

Undoubtedly, evidence exists that death is impolite in some circles, but the taboo thesis as commonly stated is grossly overdrawn and lacking in subtlety. In the rest of this article, I will outline seven alternative theses - modifying or critiquing the taboo thesis - and which I suggest offer ways towards comprehending the complexity of changing attitudes and practices toward death.

1 Taboo plus coda

One possible modification is to accept much of the Gorer/Ariès thesis that death has become something of a taboo since the end of World War I, at least among the middle classes, but to add that it is now ceasing to be - not least because of the work of scholars such as Gorer and Ariès. In other words, the taboo thesis needs bringing up to date and refining along class and gender lines.

Elias (1985: 27) argues that modern people distrust ritual and formality, so these are not available as a means of expressing grief. Unfortunately, modernity - or the Anglo-Saxon male form of modernity - also fosters a certain reserve, so many of us are unwilling to express ourselves personally either. So both forms of self-expression - ritual and personal - are out of bounds, creating embarrassment when talking with dying friends.

I would argue, however, that in some sections of society this is changing. Not that ritual is coming back, but that personal expression is. The counter culture of the 1960s reacted against rationality, asserting that feelings (of all kinds) should be expressed, not repressed; and it reacted against hypocrisy, requiring me to be authentic, to 'be myself'. Though bereavement was doubtless far from the minds of the early hippies, the implications for the dying and bereaved are clear. They should talk about their feelings. The old norm that it was courageous for the dying and their carers not to talk about what was happening gave way, and it became courageous *to* talk about it (Wouters, 1990). The 1960s saw Cicely Saunders (du Boulay, 1984) founding the British hospice movement, and Kübler-Ross (1970) promoting in North American hospitals the right and the necessity of the dying to talk openly about their feelings. Saunders is the very opposite of the hippy in terms of personality, but the whole philosophy of the movement she founded is very much in tune with those expressive elements of the counter culture that have since become institutionalized as part of postmodern culture. Associated with this personal expressiveness are two other cultural currents, the green and women's movements, which also did not set out to consider dying and bereavement but have profoundly affected both. [. . .]

This argument explains the otherwise absurd spectacle of intelligent

men and women repeatedly rediscovering that death is taboo. It identifies them as people whose childhoods pre-dated the 1960s and who
were therefore socialized to deny or at least ignore death, but who
were influenced by 1960s expressionism and began to want to express
hitherto repressed feelings. Media and academic obsession with death
represents, in this view, a genuine attempt to break out of taboo, rather
than mere pornography as Gorer would have it. [. . .]

2 Not forbidden, but hidden

The taboo thesis, and the taboo plus coda modification, are theories
about culture. A directly opposing explanation is in terms of demographic structure, and was classically put forward by Blauner (1966).

Blauner points out that before modern medicine and public health
drastically reduced death rates, the vast majority of adults who died
did so in the prime of life. They left behind a massive gap – social,
economic and psychological – especially for families who depended on
them. In this context, belief in an afterlife could bring considerable
comfort, while comprehensive deathbed, funeral and mourning rituals
helped survivors come to terms with their loss and restructure their
roles and relationships. In the modern world, by contrast, most deaths
are of the elderly. Their children have grown up, become financially
viable and derive emotional satisfaction from themselves having
become parents. When gran dies, it may be sad, it may be the end of
an era, but the gap she leaves has long been filled. Directly contrary
to Ariès, who believes we still retain much of the pain of 'romantic
death', Blauner argues that we miss the deceased today *less* than in
previous centuries. We therefore do not need elaborate rites of passage,
nor even beliefs in an afterlife. [. . .]

But in so far as this fulfilled death in old age does become typical,
the more unprepared are those who lose someone before that age.
Blauner's thesis certainly helps account for the acute grief and isolation
of such people, which could well be mistaken as evidence of a general
taboo by the therapists or counsellors to whom they turn for help. [. . .]

Blauner's thesis also pinpoints a very real isolation of the majority of
the bereaved. Because death is relatively rare nowadays, and because
the elderly person who has died may well not have been widely known
by the friends of those left behind, the grief of the bereaved is not
shared. [. . .]

So the bereaved today often *are* isolated, and may well report being
treated as lepers. Lacking others who share the loss of *this particular*
individual, they may seek support from others who have experienced
this particular *category* of loss (of a remaining parent, of a child, or of
a spouse). Bereavement organizations provide contact with precisely
such people.

Blauner's thesis argues that death in modern society is not taboo; rather, it is simply no great deal. It is not forbidden, but hidden. His thesis explains the perception by experts of death as a taboo subject in terms of the untypical bereavements that they work with. The next two explanations – concerning professions, and frameworks of meaning – go further in pinpointing exactly where the unease with talking about death is located.

3 Limited taboo

The limited taboo thesis argues that it is not modern society per se, but particular key occupational groups within it, that find death peculiarly difficult to handle.

In the mid-nineteenth century, priests were supplanted by doctors and public health officials as the experts on death (Ariès, 1981; Illich, 1976; though see Porter, 1989), and today most of the routine procedures that take place in the days before and after a death are determined by medical and public health, rather than spiritual, considerations. Doctors and public health officials, however, are dedicated to keeping people alive and healthy, so death represents failure for them. In the Chicago hospital where in the 1960s Kübler-Ross first attempted to gain permission to interview dying patients, she was blocked by doctors claiming that the patients could not cope with such conversations. In the event, she found all but one of eventually three hundred patients were relieved and delighted to be able to talk. The nurses on the wards relented first, while the doctors took longest to accept they had been wrong (Kübler-Ross, 1970).

In the book in which she records this, however, Kübler-Ross insists that it is our society, rather than the hospital, that has imposed the taboo. [. . .] To a certain extent, Kübler-Ross, a hospital psychiatrist, may have mistaken her world of the hospital for society as a whole.

Kellehear (1984: 715–17) points out that patients who collude with their doctors in avoiding talk of death need not be denying death in a psychoanalytic sense, but may simply be avoiding conversational embarrassment since they know doctors don't like the subject. And although most people now die in hospital, most of the course of a terminal illness is typically spent at home and in contact with nurses rather than doctors (German, 1980), so the death-denying practices of hospital medicine may not be as salient for the dying and for their families as medical psychologists and sociologists have sometimes implied (Kellehear, 1984: 718). Actually in the USA, doctors now usually inform dying patients of their prognosis (Veatch and Tai, 1980), though this is by no means yet the norm in the UK (Williams, 1989).

The other occupational group that has taken over from clergy in interpreting death for us are mass media personnel: the movie directors and news reporters who produce Gorer's death 'pornography'. Every time there is a disaster, it is not only reported, it is repeatedly reconstructed in the media. I have argued elsewhere that these reconstructions are attempts to make sense of the limits of technology and of power, and so provide images that mediate between the otherwise disparate experiences of death as uniquely personal and death as global (Walter, 1989a). Whatever they are, the media have extraordinary power to interpret death for us. And yet, surely, for those who work in the media world of youth and glamour, death is also an embarrassment. [. . .]

It seems then that the two professions to which our society has entrusted the interpretation and ritualization of death – medicine and the media – are, or have been, almost uniquely embarrassed by the subject. It is therefore not so much society as a whole, but these two key institutions, for whom death is, or was, taboo. [. . .]

4 Disparate frames

Following Goffman (1974), Perakyla (1988) argues that there are four separate frames within which death is perceived in hospital – the practical, the biomedical, the lay and the semi-psychiatric. There is no necessary consistency between these frames, which can help account for some otherwise puzzling phenomena. For example, medics and nurses frequently say (lay frame) they would not want for themselves the intensive chemo- and radiotherapy that they routinely (biomedical frame) give to their patients.

I have observed similarly disparate frames governing the funeral process. There is little if any coherence between the public health frame that governs much of the procedure, the theological frame that governs the liturgy of the funeral service itself, and the psychological frame within which grief is increasingly understood nowadays. No wonder bereaved people look to funeral directors to see them through these bizarre few days. In sum, experience of death is typically postmodern, in that meaning has become fragmented. [. . .]

Frame analysis helps account for two things. First, it explains why people have difficulty finding a language about death, and why conversations between two or more people who are using different frames can be fraught. Second, it explains the flood of thanatological literature (academic in the USA, largely journalistic in the UK) as a desperate search for a new frame within which death may be understood.

There is one frame which is emerging as front runner, which Perakyla calls the semi-psychiatric. The seminal work here is Kübler-Ross (1970) with her concept of dying as a series of psychological stages, and the associated concept of bereavement as a similar series of stages, each ending with some kind of acceptance. The extent to which this framework is taking over others, such as the biomedical and the practical, has been satirized by Douglas (1983) and criticized from a symbolic interactionist perspective by Charmaz (1980: 148–55) among others.

5 Ritual enemy

Lofland (1978: 88–92) observes that social movements typically need real or symbolic enemies if they are to mobilize support, they need giants to slay – the green movement, for example, requires pollution, the feminist movement requires patriarchy. What Lofland terms the 'Happy Death Movement' – the movement to humanize the experience so that the dying are treated as whole persons, rather than medical failures or social embarrassments – typically invokes an idealized happy death of the past, and then contrasts this with today's reality, riven with denial, secrecy and taboo. The constant assertion that death is taboo plays this function of evoking an enemy, which is why the assertion persists even as more people talk about the subject. (Lofland's elegant analysis helps explain the continuing popularity of Ariès and Gorer, despite the substantial criticisms levelled at them.)

6 The universal taboo

Another approach may be derived from Becker (1973) and Dumont and Foss (1972). Becker, in a re-interpretation of Freud and Kierkegaard, argues that the denial of death is not the modern condition, but the human condition. The fear of the *id*, for Becker, is not the fear of sex but the fear of death, and the human personality is a process of repressing this knowledge. For Becker, then, all societies are premised on the denial of death. This then would account for both the death-denying aspects of modern culture, and the possibility that death is not uniquely problematic for modernity.

Dumont and Foss's extended literature review, *The American View of Death: Acceptance or Denial?*, is not so well known. They argue that any society must both deny and accept death. Society must deny death if it is to get on with its everyday business, yet it must accept it if its members are to retain contact with reality.

Their argument is rather unusual in facing up to the ambiguity and paradox so markedly missing in simple assertions that modern society 'denies' death or that death is 'the taboo of the late twentieth century'. No society's handling of death is that simple, because human mortality is not that simple. Their argument also explains how people can debate endlessly and inconclusively whether death is or is not taboo. You can choose your answer depending on where you look and in order to fit your own particular experience of bereavement. It is noticeable that pundits, and the bereaved themselves, typically 'prove' the existence of

the death taboo simply by presenting examples (Kellehear, 1984: 718).
[. . .]

But this phenomenon of differential perception of what is 'typical' does not explain why many of the more educated members of our society – people who are used to weighing evidence carefully – are convinced, unequivocally, that death is taboo. To this end, we turn to our final explanation.

7 Individual and society

Edmund Leach (1961) observes that the English word *time* covers two different experiences: repetitive, cyclical time (springtime and harvest, bedtime), and irreversible, linear time (the day Kennedy was assassinated, the Thatcher years). The unrepeatable events of linear time threaten traditional cultures which assert a changeless social order in which all of life re-enacts some primal order (Eliade, 1954). Unfortunately for such societies, time does move on, there is history, people and things die. So funeral rituals in traditional societies re-assert the other – cyclical – time, in order to counter the irreversible change that has actually occurred. Biologically, death follows birth; ritually, birth – expressed in rebirth or resurrection – follows death. Death must lead to the regeneration of life if the cyclical nature of time, and therefore the culture itself, is to be affirmed. At the same time, in a traditional society where identity is rooted in the group more than in the individual, death does not threaten the individual to the extent it does in the modern world. In traditional societies, death threatens not individuals, but groups and their culture – hence the need for communal death rituals (Bloch and Parry, 1982: 1–15; Malinowski, 1949).

In modern societies, the reverse holds. Our culture is premised on change, on history. We value the young, rather than the elderly, who may depart without disturbing the onward march of progress (cf. Blauner, 1966). But modern society invests identity largely within the individual, whom death does indeed threaten (Slater, 1974). [. . .] Today, communal and religious death rituals that once functioned to affirm culture fall into disuse, and personal therapy and one-to-one bereavement counselling arise to support bewildered individuals.

In sum, Becker has failed to see a crucial distinction. Ideal typically, death is denied by traditional *cultures* and by modern *individuals*. It is a mistake therefore to say that 'modern society cannot cope with death'; it deals with it very nicely thank-you, with its elevation of youth, education, and progress. But along with this societal acceptance goes the most intense personal pain, so intense that others are unwilling to share it. [. . .]

We now can understand why the terms taboo and denial are so easily misused. Kellehear (1984) is surely right to warn us not to think psychological denial by individuals adds up to a death-denying *society*. But he is only half right to say that societies do not deny death; some traditional cultures surely do just that.

Conclusion

Social scientists, the original formulators of the thesis that death is the taboo of the twentieth century, are now having second thoughts. Meanwhile however, popular pundits are identifying death as a 'new' taboo, and it seems that many dying and bereaved people agree with them. So what is actually happening to how death, and in particular how the dying and bereaved, is treated in our society? This article has examined the taboo thesis to see whether it can be modified to account for the complexity of current attitudes and practices.

References

Ariès, P. (1962) *Centuries of Childhood*. London: Cape.

Ariès, P. (1974) *Western Attitudes Toward Death: From the Middle Ages to the Present*. Baltimore, MD: Johns Hopkins University Press.

Ariès, P. (1981) *The Hour of Our Death*. London: Allen Lane.

Becker, E. (1973) *The Denial of Death*. New York: Free Press.

Berger, P.L. (1967) *The Social Reality of Religion*. London: Faber.

Blauner, R. (1966) 'Death and social structure', *Psychiatry* 29: 378–94.

Bloch, M. and Parry, J. (eds) (1982) *Death and the Regeneration of Life*. Cambridge: Cambridge University Press.

Charmaz, K. (1980) *The Social Reality of Death*. Reading, MA: Addison-Wesley.

Douglas, C. (1983) *A Cure for Living*. London: Hutchinson.

Du Boulay, S. (1984) *Cicely Saunders*. London: Hodder.

Dumont, R.G. and Foss, D.C. (1972) *The American View of Death: Acceptance or Denial?* Cambridge, MA: Schenkman.

Eliade, M. (1954) *The Myth of the Eternal Return*. Princeton, NJ: Princeton University Press.

Elias, N. (1985) *The Loneliness of Dying*. Oxford: Blackwell.

Feifel, H. (ed.) (1959) *The Meaning of Death*. New York: McGraw Hill.

Field, D. (1989) *Nursing the Dying*. London: Tavistock/Routledge.

Fulton, R. (1963) *The Sacred and the Secular: Attitudes of the American Public toward Death*. Milwaukee, MN: Bulfin Printers.

German, C. (1980) 'Nursing the dying', in R. Fox (ed.), The Social Meaning of Death. *Annals of the American Academy of Political and Social Science*, 447.

Gilmore, A. and Gilmore, S. (eds) (1988) *A Safer Death*. London: Plenum.

Goffman, E. (1974) *Frame Analysis*. Cambridge, MA: Harvard University Press.

Gorer, G. (1955) 'The pornography of death', *Encounter*, October.

Gorer, G. (1965) *Death, Grief and Mourning in Contemporary Britain*. London: Cresset.

Houlbrooke, R. (ed.) (1989) *Death, Ritual, and Bereavement*. London: Routledge.

Illich, I. (1976) *Limits to Medicine*. London: Marion Boyars.

Jacobs, J. (1899) 'The dying of death', *Fortnightly Review*, new series, LXXII (392), 1 Aug: 264-9.

Jupp, P. (1990) *From Dust to Ashes: the Replacement of Burial by Cremation in England 1840-1967*. London: The Congregational Memorial Hall Trust.

Kamerman, J.B. (1988) *Death in the Midst of Life*. Englewood Cliffs, NJ: Prentice Hall.

Kearl, M.C. (1989) *Endings: a Sociology of Death and Dying*. Oxford: Oxford University Press.

Kellehear, A. (1984) 'Are we a "death-denying" society? A sociological review'. *Social Science and Medicine*, 18 (9).

Kübler-Ross, E. (1970) *On Death and Dying*. London: Tavistock.

Leach, E. (1961) 'Two essays concerning the symbolic representation of time', in *Rethinking Anthropology*. London: Athlone.

Leaney, J. (1989) 'Ashes to ashes: cremation and the celebration of death in nineteenth-century Britain', in R. Houlbrooke (ed.), *Death, Ritual and Bereavement*. London: Routledge.

Lofland, L. (1978) *The Craft of Dying*. London: Sage.

McIntosh, J. (1977) *Communication and Awareness in a Cancer Ward*. London: Croom Helm.

Malinowski, B. (1949) 'Death and the reintegration of the group', in *Magic, Science and Religion*. New York: Doubleday.

Miller, J. (1974) *Aberfan: a Disaster and its Aftermath*. London: Constable.

Morley, J. (1971) *Death, Heaven and the Victorians*. London: Studio Vista.

Mount, F. (1982) *The Subversive Family*. London: Cape.

Naylor (née Page), M. (1989) 'The funeral: death rituals in a northern city'. Unpublished PhD, Leeds University.

Perakyla, A. (1988) 'Four frames of death in modern hospital', in A. Gilmore and S. Gilmore (eds), *A Safer Death*. London: Plenum.

Pickering, W.S.F. (1974) 'The persistence of rites of passage', *British Journal of Sociology*, 25: 63-78.

Porter, R. (1989) 'Death and the doctors in Georgian England', in R. Houlbrooke (ed.), *Death, Ritual, and Bereavement*. London: Routledge.

Prior, L. (1989) *The Social Organisation of Death*. London: Macmillan.

Rosenblatt, P.C. et al. (1976) *Grief and Mourning in Cross-Cultural Perspective*. Washington, DC: Human Relations Area Files Press.

Simpson, M. (1987) *Dying, Death and Grief: a Critical Bibliography*. Philadelphia, PA: University of Philadelphia Press. (1979 edition, New York: Plenum.)

Slater, P. (1974) *Earthwalk*. Garden City, NY: Doubleday.

Smale, B. (1985) 'Deathwork: a sociological analysis of funeral directing'. Unpublished PhD, University of Surrey.

Veatch, R. and Tai, E. (1980) 'Talking about death: patterns of lay and professional change', in R. Fox (ed.), The Social Meaning of Death. *Annals of the American Academy of Political and Social Science*, 447.

Vovelle, M. (1980) 'Rediscovery of death since 1960', in R. Fox (ed.), The Social Meaning of Death. *Annals of the American Academy of Political and Social Science*, 447.

Walter, T. (1989a) 'Deathwatch', *Third Way*, 12 (5): 6.

Walter, T. (1989b) 'Secular funerals', *Theology*, 92 (Sept.): 394-402.

Walter, T. (1990a) *Funerals*. London: Hodder.

Williams, R. (1981) 'Mourning rituals: their application in Western culture', in P. Pegg and E. Metz (eds), *Death and Dying*. London: Pitman.

Williams, R. (1989) 'Awareness and control of dying: some paradoxical trends in public opinion', *Sociology of Health and Illness*, 11 (3): 201–12.

Williams, R. (1990) *A Protestant Legacy: Attitudes to Death and Illness among Older Aberdonians*. Oxford: Oxford University Press.

Wouters, C. (1990) Paper given to the BSA Sociology of Emotion Group, Birmingham.

7

Demographic change and the care of the dying, 1969–1987

Clive Seale

The expectation of life at birth varies widely between countries and in most has increased dramatically during the twentieth century. In the UK, average life expectancy in 1980 was 73.7 years, compared to a figure for all African countries of 49.7 (United Nations, 1991). At the beginning of the century, expectancy in the UK had been nearer African levels. In 1910–12 it stood at 51.5 for males and 55.4 for females (Devis, 1990). Underlying this spectacular shift is a reduction in infant mortality and a general decline in mortality from infectious diseases. Better sanitation, nutrition and other material conditions as well as improvements in medical care have contributed, but still have much more to contribute in many Third World countries.

Largely due to increases in life expectancy, there have been changes in the household composition of elderly people in Britain since the beginning of the century. Dale et al. (1987), covering the period since 1945, show that there has been a trend towards living alone, or with a spouse only. With increasing age, there are increasing levels of illness and dependency, and because women tend to live longer than men these problems are concentrated amongst elderly women.

However, household composition is not solely determined by the facts of longevity. Historical studies (e.g. Laslett, 1983) suggest that long-standing cultural preferences determine people's willingness to live in multi-generational households, often (and wrongly) assumed to have been a universal norm in pre-industrial Britain. Laslett found that people in countries of the Mediterranean and Eastern Europe were, in pre-industrial times, more likely to live in multi-generational house- holds than Europeans further west, such as the British. Waerness (1989) presents data that suggest that such patterns have been main- tained, with the nuclear family – albeit with elderly relatives living in the neighbourhood – being the preferred cultural norm in Western Europe.

This study from which this paper derives was funded by the Medical Research Council and conducted in collaboration with Ann Cartwright while Clive Seale was a Research Officer at the Institute for Social Studies in Medical Care, London.

Changes in longevity and cultural preferences about household structure have consequences for the sources of informal support that the elderly can expect to draw upon. This in turn has implications for formal services. As most people who die in Britain are elderly – 79 per cent in 1986 were 65 and over and 55 per cent 75 and over (OPCS, 1989) – so the problems of the older population have much in common with the problems of the dying. This is not always recognized by those writing about the care of dying people, as the influence of the hospice movement has tended to focus attention on terminal care, which largely concerns cancer (Seale, 1991a). Those who die of cancer are, on average, significantly younger than those dying of other conditions (Seale, 1989). A larger proportion of the 'young elderly' rather than those over 75 are affected.

Reported here are the results of two surveys, one describing the needs of a nationally represented sample of 785 adults dying in 1969, and the other carried out eighteen years later on 639 people; which aimed to repeat and update the earlier study. Because the samples were drawn in the same way, comparisons can be made to identify trends in need, household composition and sources of support.

Methods

The methods of the studies are fully described in two books (Cartwright et al., 1973; Cartwright and Seale, 1990). Both were based on random national samples of death certificates of people aged 15 and over, taken from randomly selected areas of the country. Interviewers visited the home of the person who had died, or whoever had registered the death, to identify and interview the individual who knew most about the last twelve months of the deceased person's life. Response rates were high: 82 per cent for the earlier study, 80 per cent for the later one.

Respondents were taken through a structured questionnaire that enquired into many aspects of the life and care received by the person who died. This included the symptoms and restrictions they suffered from, the care received from family and friends, general practitioners, community nurses, in hospitals, hospices and other institutions, the level of awareness about their illnesses and a number of questions about the respondents' involvement and experiences since the death. In both 1969 and 1987 the largest group of respondents consisted of spouses of the deceased (39 per cent in 1969, 36 per cent in 1987), with other close family members (daughters and sons, for example, being 30 per cent and 26 per cent of respondents) also commonly found. However, in the 1987 study there was a higher proportion of respondents who were officials of one sort or another, usually staff in residential homes. In the earlier study these constituted only 3 per cent of respondents. In 1987 this had risen to 11 per cent. This change in itself reflects changes that had occurred in the population during the years since 1969.

Table 7.1   *Age and sex of deceased, 1969 and 1987*

	1969			1987		
	Male %	Female %	All %	Male %	Female %	All %
<65	36	22	29	29	16	22
65–74	34	28	31	30	17	23
75+	30	51	40	41	67	55
All (100%)	504	454	958[1]	383	412	800

[1] Data was missing on two death certificates.

Source: Cartwright and Seale, 1990

Age and gender

In line with the continuing increases in life expectancy throughout the twentieth century, the people who died in 1987 tended to be older than those in 1969. Taking the initial samples of death certificates, in 1969 40 per cent of the people were aged 75 or more, compared to 55 per cent in 1987. Table 7.1 shows this separately for men and women, indicating that for women the proportion dying at age 75 or more had risen from a half of all women, to two-thirds.

Symptoms and dependency

Respondents were asked on both occasions to report whether certain symptoms were experienced at all during the last twelve months of life and, for symptoms reported at this stage, how long they had been experienced by the person who died. The major changes since 1969 concerned the duration of some of the symptoms: mental confusion, depression and incontinence were all experienced over a longer time period by people in the later study. Controlling for age showed that these increases were all related to the greater proportion of people aged 75 or more in the 1987 study.

Comparison of the restrictions experienced by people who lived at home during the last twelve months of life was made difficult by the fact that slightly different wording was used on the two occasions. However, on both occasions respondents were asked to say which of a number of areas of restrictions had been experienced by the people who died. These included such activities as getting in and out of the bath, dressing and undressing and washing. Again, the major changes concerned the length of time that such restrictions were experienced. In 1969 30 per cent had needed help with at least one of these for a year or more. By 1987 this had risen to 52 per cent.

Once again, the rise in dependency levels are a reflection of a general population which contains a higher proportion of very old people than two decades previously. In 1972, in the first General Household Survey (GHS), 21 per cent of respondents reported a long-standing illness, with 16 per cent of all respondents saying that this limited their activities (OPCS, 1975). By 1988, these figures had risen to 33 per cent and 19 per cent respectively (OPCS, 1990). Both in the GHS and the two surveys reported here, restrictions were experienced more frequently for women than men, reflecting women's greater life-span. A survey by OPCS examining the prevalence of disability amongst adults in Great Britain (OPCS, 1988) reached similar conclusions, with 63 per cent of women aged 75 and over being judged disabled, but only 53 per cent of men in the same age category.

The surveys suggest, then, that the need for care in the last year of life had risen since 1969, and that this was in line with more general changes in the older population. But it is important to remember that these represent trends only, and that a proportion of the people in both samples were able to look after themselves until very close to death. Thirty-five per cent of those living at home in 1987 suffered no restriction while at home, and this is true of 32 per cent of those aged 65 and over and 27 per cent of those aged 75 and over. Similarly, the high proportions of elderly disabled reported by OPCS (1988) reflect a generous definition of disability. As Nicholas Scott, Minister for the Disabled in 1988, when the OPCS survey reported, pointed out:

> Many of those included would not regard themselves as either disabled or in need of special help. . . . [Older people] would consider the relatively minor limitations of hearing, vision or movement recorded by the survey as in fact normal for their age. (*The Guardian*, 29 September 1988)

Household composition and care from family and friends

Table 7.2 shows that the proportion living alone had doubled by 1987. While those living with their spouse only had increased slightly, there were reductions in those living with people other than their spouse.

Once again, this reflects trends in the population as a whole. General Household Survey data (OPCS, 1990) show a change in the proportion of households consisting of one person only, from 17 per cent in 1971 to 26 per cent of households in 1988. The proportion of the population living in a household without children had also risen: from 42 per cent to 54 per cent. This is associated, too, with a rise in the numbers of the widowed, from 7 per cent of the adult population in 1972 to 10 per cent in 1988 (OPCS, 1975, 1990).

The trend towards living alone in the two studies of people who had died was largely due to the greater numbers of women living alone. In

Table 7.2 *Household composition, 1969 and 1987[1]*

| | 1969 | 1987 |
	%	%
Alone	15	32
With spouse only	32	38
With spouse and others	20	14
With others only	33	16
Number of deaths (100%)	670	580

[1] Excludes those in hospital or institution all year, and sudden deaths of those under 65.

Source: Cartwright and Seale, 1990

the 1969 study only 19 per cent of women in the sample lived alone and 10 per cent of men. In 1987, 44 per cent of women lived alone and 20 per cent of men. People living alone in the 1987 sample were in a particularly unfortunate situation for potential sources of help. They were the least likely to have any children or siblings alive and were most likely to be widowed or divorced and old. They were also the group most likely to progress to institutional care.

Those living with others, but without a spouse, were the next oldest group, although this type of household was about half as common as those living alone. They were also quite likely to be elderly widows and to be single people, but, perhaps because they were somewhat more likely than those living alone to have children or siblings alive, they could live with them when they started becoming restricted. In fact this group reported the highest proportion of long-term restriction, a condition which, if they had been living alone, would have meant a larger proportion entering institutional care.

Those living with their spouse only were the next most elderly group, as well as this being the most common type of household. With an average level of restriction, and being more likely than average to have children alive, their prospects, both in terms of need for help and for sources on which they could draw, were better than the previous two groups. Such people were more likely to be men, and this was even more likely to be true with the youngest group: those living with their spouse and others. This last group was the smallest, but all had children alive and less than a fifth experienced long-term restriction. Both of these last two household groups contained high proportions of people dying from cancer, suggesting that cancer patients were more likely to have access to sources of informal care than sufferers from other terminal conditions.

Clearly, this pattern of household composition and gender is produced largely because women outlive their husbands more frequently than the reverse. Overall, demographic change since 1969 has meant that fewer family resources are available to cope with the increasing needs. Elderly widows are particularly disadvantaged in this respect, and the results illustrate the progression of events that so many of these widows will have experienced; from caring for a dependent husband, to bereavement and the difficulties of adjustment to living alone with grief and, perhaps, increasing dependency in themselves.

Where restrictions were reported, respondents in the 1987 study were asked who had helped, and who had borne the brunt of care. Analysis of the replies showed the average number of relatives and friends helping in 1987 (2.0) was significantly lower than for 1969, when the figure was 3. However, this varied a great deal across the different types of households, with people living alone having an average of 1.7 such helpers, and people living with their spouses and others having 3.1. Women were most likely to bear the brunt of caring: 43 per cent were wives or daughters of the deceased, only 21 per cent husbands or sons.

Formal care

Since 1969 there has been a growth in specialist care for the terminally ill, led by the hospice movement (Seale, 1989). Some aspects of the quality of care given by hospices was judged by respondents to be better than that provided by hospitals, yet by 1987 hospice care – either in-patient or domiciliary – was received by only 6.9 per cent of the sample, and these were almost exclusively people dying from cancer (Seale, 1991b). When considering the care of people who die from other illnesses, the expertise developed by the hospice movement – if not the broad philosophy of the approach – may be less relevant (Seale, 1991a). It remains the case that most of the medical and nursing care provided to those who die is given by hospitals, general practitioners and community nurses.

Between the two time points there was a 50 per cent increase in the number of hospital admissions during the last year of life. Length of stay, however, had reduced considerably, in line with general trends in hospital admission practice over the years. Cartwright et al. (1973) report that the estimated average length of stay in NHS hospitals for the 1969 sample was 61 days; by 1987 this had reduced to 38 (Cartwright, 1991). In part this is due to the increased numbers in residential homes, thereby reducing the numbers in long-stay geriatric wards. By 1987 the proportion living in old people's homes for the whole of the year before death had risen from 9 per cent in 1969 to 15 per cent. National statistics reveal that between 1969 and 1987 there was an overall increase in the provision of institutional care for the elderly in England, with an overall increase in places in residential and nursing homes taken by those aged 65 and over from just over 130,000 to almost 210,000. By far the largest increase was in the private provision of this type of care, from 17,369 places in 1969 to 84,946 in 1987 (Government Statistical Service, 1982, 1990).

Concurrently, there was also an increase in the need for care at home and this was coupled with a reduction in the availability of care from family and friends. One area where help had increased to meet the need was that provided by the home help service. The proportion receiving such help had risen from 10 per cent in 1969 to 24 per cent of the people who lived at home in the last year of life. Again, national statistics record that provision of home helps increased during the period concerned (Government Statistical Service, 1982, 1990). Nevertheless, respondents' perceptions of the need for home help had not changed significantly, suggesting that this increase had left the same level of demand.

At the same time, home visiting by general practitioners had declined, with 23 per cent of those living at home receiving no home visits in 1987, compared to 12 per cent in 1969. Frequent consultations at either home or surgery (defined as twenty or more in the year before death) had also become less common, declining from 29 per cent to 19 per cent. Criticisms by respondents in 1987 of the general practitioner centred on the perceived unwillingness to visit (Cartwright, 1990). However, there was some indication that general practitioners had become better at communicating: more respondents in 1987 thought the deceased's doctor was easy to talk to – 87 per cent compared to 75 per cent. Further, 82 per cent in 1987 compared to 69 per cent in 1969 thought the doctor had time to discuss things. Perhaps extra time was gained by not going on home visits!

The pattern of home visiting by community nurses had also changed, with people in 1987 receiving less frequent visiting in 1987, spread over a longer period of time. Twenty-eight per cent of those receiving such help had it for a year or more in 1987, compared to 15 per cent in 1969. Daily visiting, however, was less common (41 per cent compared to 56 per cent). Nevertheless, in spite of the increase in self-care needs since 1969, respondents were no more likely in 1987 to judge the level of provision of domiciliary nursing inadequate. It may be that changes in the way nurses cared for patients and their families had reduced the need for frequent visiting. Nationally, there were more district nurses employed in 1987/88 than fifteen years previously, by a factor of 1.6, and the treatment rate for patients aged 65 and over, measured in terms of numbers seen for first treatments, had risen by a factor of 1.7 (Government Statistical Service, 1982, 1990). However, national statistics are not available for those in their last year of life; the studies of people who had died suggest a district nursing service that had become more thinly stretched for this client group.

Alternatively, other services may have been filling the gaps: for example, in 1987 chiropodists were almost twice as likely to have visited those who needed help with cutting their toenails (40 per cent of those needing help as opposed to 23 per cent in 1969). This is in line with national statistics, which show a rise in those treated by the chiropody service between 1969 and 1987 by a factor of 2.18 (Government Statistical Service, 1982, 1990).

In general, then, the pattern of service provision for people in their last year of life has undergone some changes since 1969, in part being a straightforward increase in volume (as in the case of home helps, residential care and chiropody) to meet the increased needs. The pattern of hospital, general practitioner and domiciliary nursing care, however, did not conform to this, with services superficially at least looking more thinly stretched. Clearly in the case of home visiting by general practitioners this had led to an increase in perceptions of inadequacy amongst respondents. To explain why this did not happen in other areas, further analysis of what has happened over the years to the process of care would be needed.

Conclusion

Increasing life expectancy means that people dying in 1987 had a rather different set of problems from those dying in 1969. Physically, they were in greater need, and having fewer family members around them to support them there was more dependence on formal services for help. The particular problems of elderly women (who live longer than men and who also tend to have married men older than them) are highlighted by the studies. These are often women who have themselves looked after people who have died, most commonly their husbands, and who now live alone.

Arber and Ginn (1991), in a paper that analyses the position of elderly women revealed by General Household Survey data for 1985 to 1987, suggest that the elderly possess three sets of resources: material and health resources, and access to sources of care in their communities. These authors found that in all three respects elderly women were at a disadvantage. The ideologies of the New Right, influential in policy-making in the 1980s, stressing self-provisioning by the individual elderly person and their immediate family, and the market-led provision of state welfare services, are likely to disadvantage elderly women still further. As Arber and Ginn state:

> Publicly-funded provision of health care or domiciliary services can mitigate the effects of low income, poor health, or lack of informal carers, and prolong independence . . . [thus preventing] the most visible and distressing loss of independence – unwilling admission to an institution.

The findings from the two studies of those who had died suggest that public provision of domiciliary support had just about kept up with the needs of people living in private households, although there is no room for complacency, as is revealed by the problems over home visiting by general practitioners. The higher proportion of those who die who spend time in residential care does not reflect so well on the adequacy of public provision, if its aim is to support independent living in the year before death.

Naturally, the data from the two studies of those who died, and the picture revealed by official statistics and surveys of the elderly, are all reported in terms of statistical facts and trends, and do not necessarily reflect the realities of every individual situation. However, when thinking overall about service provision they are important. Much thinking about the care of those who die has focused on terminally ill cancer patients who, by virtue of their age, tend to have access to informal family care. Statistically, this group is *not* particularly disadvantaged in terms of access at least to the resource of informal care, as those who die from cancer are more likely to live in families (Seale, 1991a). Statistical study of demographic trends reminds us that in considering the needs of those who die, the elderly widow living on her own may be as important an image to bear in our minds as the terminally ill cancer patient. A focus on pain control and bereavement support may be less relevant when the key needs are for long-term home help with self-care, and where the person dies leaving no one to grieve for them.

Perhaps at the root of this is the fact that people's status as 'dying' is often only recognized when terminal illness is present. If it is not present, people are seen as 'living', even if seriously ill. If we are to raise the status of the care of the elderly in the same way as the hospice movement has raised the status of cancer care, we may need to recognize that we are all at different stages on the road to death, with some nearer than others. The care of the elderly *is* the care of the dying, just as it is also the care of the living.

The practical implications of this are that people who currently consider themselves to be working with 'the elderly' are also working with 'the dying'. This can no longer be solely the province of those working with people medically predicted as having but a short time to live.

References

Arber, S. and Ginn, J. (1991) 'Gender and later life: a sociological analysis of resources and constraints'. Paper presented to the 1991 British Sociological Association Annual Conference, University of Manchester.

Cartwright, A. (1990) *The Role of the General Practitioner in Caring for People in the Last Year of their Lives* (pamphlet). London: King's Fund.

Cartwright, A. (1991) 'The role of hospitals in caring for people in the last year of their lives', *Age and Ageing*, 20.

Cartwright, A., Hockey, L. and Anderson, J.L. (1973) *Life before Death*. London and Boston, MA: Routledge & Kegan Paul.

Cartwright, A. and Seale, C.F. (1990) *The Natural History of a Survey: an Account of the*

Methodological Issues Encountered in a Study of Life before Death. London: King's Fund.

Dale, A., Evandrou, M. and Arber, S. (1987) 'The household structure of the elderly population in Britain', *Ageing and Society*, 7: 37–56.

Devis, T. (1990) 'The expectation of life in England and Wales', in Office of Population Censuses and Surveys, *Population Trends 60*. London: HMSO.

Government Statistical Service (1982) *Health and Personal Social Services Statistics for England*. London: HMSO.

Government Statistical Service (1990) *Health and Personal Social Services Statistics for England*. London: HMSO.

The Guardian (1988) 'Minister spurns disability action', 29 September.

Laslett, P. (1983) 'Family and household as work group and kin group: areas of traditional Europe compared', in R. Wall, J. Robin and P. Laslett (eds), *Family Forms in Historic Europe*. Cambridge: Cambridge University Press.

Office of Population Censuses and Surveys (OPCS) (1975) *General Household Survey 1972*. London: HMSO.

Office of Population Censuses and Surveys (OPCS) (1988) *The Prevalence of Disability among Adults*. London: HMSO.

Office of Population Censuses and Surveys (OPCS) (1989) *Mortality Statistics 1986*. London: HMSO.

Office of Population Censuses and Surveys (OPCS) (1990) *General Household Survey 1988*. London: HMSO.

Seale, C.F. (1989) 'What happens in hospices: a review of research evidence', *Social Science and Medicine*, 28: 551–9.

Seale, C.F. (1991a) 'Death from cancer and death from other causes: the relevance of the hospice approach', *Palliative Medicine*, 5: 12–19.

Seale, C.F. (1991b) 'A comparison of hospice and conventional care', *Social Science and Medicine*, 32 (2): 147–52.

United Nations (1991) *Demographic Yearbook*. New York: United Nations.

Waerness, K. (1989) 'Caring', in K. Boh, M. Bak, C. Clason, M. Pakratova, J. Ovortrup, G.B. Sgritta and K. Waerness (eds), *Changing Patterns of European Family Life: a Comparative Analysis of 14 European Countries*. London and New York: Routledge.

8

Health policy and services for dying people and their carers

Christina R. Victor

In this article the current pattern of mortality in England and Wales is outlined and the configuration of service provision for dying people and their carers is described. Following this the patterns of service organization and the broad social and policy contexts which determine the provision of care to this group are set out.

Patterns of mortality

In order to understand the service needs of dying people and their carers it is important to be aware of the patterns of mortality within society, the main demographic characteristics of those who die and the principal causes of death.

Death in Britain is a highly medicalized event. Under the 1836 Births and Deaths Registration Act a doctor is required to certify both death and the immediate and underlying cause of death. Collation of information from these death certificates provides information about the pattern of deaths or mortality in Britain. Such data form a useful background to identifying the service needs of dying people and their carers.

In 1987 there were 566,994 certified deaths in England and Wales, the majority of which, 450,630 (79 per cent), were of people aged 65 and over (see Table 8.1). Despite all the attention focused upon them, premature deaths (those before the age of 65 years) represent only a minority of all deaths. For example, in the 45 to 54 age range there were 22,452 deaths in England and Wales. However, in order better to understand the patterns of mortality within the area it is necessary to relate this to the population size within each age group. One useful indicator expresses the total number of deaths per 1,000 total population in that age group. Table 8.2 demonstrates that the pattern of deaths within England and Wales shows a J-shaped curve. Mortality is relatively high in the first year of life and then decreases during childhood. From the age of 15 years mortality then steadily increases with age, although at all ages women illustrate lower mortality rates than men.

Table 8.1 *Deaths by age and sex: England and Wales, 1987 - crude deaths*

	Male	Female	Total
<1	3,637	2,635	6,272
1–4	578	489	1,067
5–14	713	483	1,196
15–24	3,200	1,164	4,364
25–34	3,218	1,708	4,926
35–44	5,823	3,897	9,720
45–54	13,678	8,774	22,452
55–64	41,367	25,000	66,367
65–74	82,021	56,858	138,879
75–84	94,060	103,354	197,414
85 +	31,882	82,455	114,337
Total	280,177	286,817	566,994

Source: OPCS (1989) Table B.

Table 8.2 *Death rates by age and sex: England and Wales, 1987*

| | Rate per 1,000,000 ||
	Male	Female
<1	5,238	4,009
1–4	440	392
5–14	225	161
15–24	781	296
25–34	884	476
35–44	1,671	1,125
45–54	5,007	3,225
55–64	15,973	9,135
65–74	41,225	22,753
75–84	96,301	60,065
85 +	191,548	158,560
Total rate for all ages	10,654	10,304

Source: OPCS (1989) Table B and Table 1.

As well as the general pattern of mortality the cause of death is also an important issue when considering the service needs of dying people. The main causes of death in England and Wales in 1987 are shown in Table 8.3. Overall the most important are diseases of the circulatory system, such as heart attacks and strokes, which account for 47 per cent of male deaths and 49 per cent of female deaths. Deaths from cancer, which has been the focus of most of the literature concerned

Table 8.3 Deaths by underlying cause: England and Wales, 1987*

	0–14*		15–24		25–44		45–64		65+		All	
	M	F	M	F	M	F	M	F	M	F	M	F
Infectious diseases	135	93	43	37	107	54	266	208	653	779	1,204	1,171
Neoplasms	196	182	288	169	1,859	2,638	18,103	16,650	53,879	48,487	74,325	68,126
Endocrine	73	66	66	45	283	79	800	598	2,991	4,809	4,213	5,597
Blood diseases	19	23	13	7	23	29	116	100	729	1,264	900	1,423
Mental disorders	15	12	94	25	178	52	191	161	3,662	8,047	4,140	8,297
Nervous system	231	164	191	86	339	262	764	733	3,726	4,457	5,251	5,702
Circulatory	68	64	129	85	2,256	801	27,117	10,322	103,029	127,190	132,599	138,462
Respiratory	251	191	91	69	295	208	3,016	1,889	26,059	25,006	29,712	27,363
Digestive	42	26	27	27	349	240	1,580	1,242	5,416	8,720	7,414	10,255
Genitourinary	12	6	6	12	41	42	247	236	3,157	3,937	3,463	4,233
Pregnancy and childbirth	–	–	–	13	–	33	–	–	–	–	–	46
Skin	–	1	–	–	5	4	20	25	151	528	176	558
Musculoskeletal	4	5	5	9	15	47	143	267	1,055	3,642	1,222	3,970
Congenital	431	405	80	65	121	92	154	124	150	172	936	858
Perinatal	119	72	–	2	–	1	3	1	–	–	122	76
Ill-defined	829	568	11	7	59	18	84	34	521	1,778	1,504	2,405
Injury or poisoning	498	286	2,156	506	3,111	1,005	2,441	1,184	2,785	3,851	10,991	6,832
All	2,923	2,164	3,200	1,164	9,041	5,605	55,045	33,774	207,963	242,667	278,172	285,374

* excludes deaths under 28 days.

Source: OPCS (1989) Table C

with death and dying, account for 26 per cent of all deaths and 37 per cent of deaths of those aged under 65 years.

The pattern of mortality is not, however, constant across the different age and sex groups. At different ages there are variations in the importance of the different causes of death. Accidents and violence are most common amongst causes of death in the younger age groups. These groups will, therefore, present quite a different set of service requirements from the older age groups where circulatory diseases, cancers and respiratory diseases are important sources of death.

The analysis of the current patterns of mortality in England and Wales illustrates several important points which have to be taken into account when considering the issue of services for dying people and their carers. First, death is most common amongst the older age groups. Consequently many of the issues surrounding the provision of care to dying people are those which apply to the general area of the care of older people. Secondly, death from cancers, which have been the focus of much of the literature in this subject area, represent only a minority of deaths at any age. Thirdly, and following on from this, many deaths are, therefore, 'unexpected', particularly amongst younger age groups, where a large percentage of deaths are the result of accidents. The issue of providing appropriate care and services for dying people therefore ranges across the entire spectrum of health care provision from paediatrics to geriatrics.

Care of the dying: patterns of care

Data about patterns of mortality within England and Wales provide a crude indication of the needs of dying people and their carers. The focus upon the event of death does not provide us with any information about the circumstances of the individual before their death and the actual experience of death. Such data are not collected routinely upon a national basis. However, Cartwright et al. have undertaken two surveys in 1969 and 1987 (1973: 1990) which attempted to look at the care received and circumstances of a random sample of adults who had died, by collecting information about the last year of life from relatives, friends and others who knew the deceased.

The vast majority of deaths in Britain, about 60 per cent, now take place in hospital. In urban areas it is probable that this percentage is very much higher. However, this overall percentage of deaths at home, about 25 per cent, is a higher percentage than in some Scandinavian countries where the majority of deaths are not at home. This trend for deaths to take place in hospitals represents a marked change with the situation before 1945 when most deaths took place at home.

However, although deaths may take place in hospital, Cartwright and Seale (1990) have indicated that most of the care of the dying patient takes place at home or in other social settings such as nursing homes. In their 1987 sample of adult deaths in England, 12 per cent of those who died had spent some time in an old people's home or nursing home. The variety of agencies involved in the care of the dying are, therefore, highly diverse and include public and voluntary agencies.

The pattern of household circumstances of dying people affects their needs for care. Given that the majority of those who die are elderly, their household circumstances reflect those of the population of older people. Cartwright and Seale's survey reported that 32 per cent of those who died lived alone, and 38 per cent lived with only their spouse. Women were more likely to live alone than men – this reflects a general pattern in the elderly population. Compared with the survey conducted in 1969, the number of those people dying who lived alone had more than doubled from 15 per cent to 32 per cent whilst the percentage living with others (not their spouse) decreased from 53 per cent to 30 per cent. The percentage living and dying in institutional care increased from 3 per cent to 10 per cent. These changes in the household circumstances of dying people represent two important social changes: the trend for the establishment and maintenance of independenti households by both young adults and those in the post-retirement age groups.

The needs of dying people and their carers are very diverse given the variety of different causes of death which were described earlier. Seale (1990) has described the types of problems reported by people in their last year of life. Common symptoms included mental confusion, pain and incontinence as well as problems with 'activities of daily living' such as self-care like bathing, shaving and cutting toenails. Overall 59 per cent reported health restrictions in the year prior to death and 65 per cent needed help with the activities of daily living; 52 per cent had required help with these activities for one year or longer. It is probably important from a policy perspective to distinguish between deaths preceded by a period of disability and those where the mortal event has no such antecedent.

Who provides care to those people who die following a period of disability or restricted activity? Overall 16 per cent of care to dying people was provided from official sources such as district nursing or general practitioner services. The pattern of care provision varies with the age and household circumstances of the dying person. The most vulnerable group are those who live alone and who are supported by a network of relatives. We might expect that such people would be well supported with help from official sources. However, Seale (1990) reports that even for those living alone only a minority 38 per cent received care from official sources. The bulk of care to dying people is therefore provided from non-formal sources and reflects the general pattern of care provision to older people, with spouses and daughters being the prime source of such care (Green, 1988).

Almost one-half of main carers reported that they could have done with more help in caring for the dying person whilst 45 per cent reported that their own health problems made caring difficult (Seale, 1990). These data indicate that there is a vast well of unmet need amongst those who are caring for dying people which also mirrors the general pattern of care provision in the community for older people.

Resources and service provision

Perhaps the key assumption upon which the National Health Service (NHS) had been planned was the notion that there was a 'fixed' amount of illness in the community which the NHS would gradually diminish. Consequently, it was assumed that expenditure on the NHS would eventually decline and level off, once existing diseases had been eliminated. It soon became evident that this was a false premise and expenditure on the NHS has increased steadily. Ham (1985) indicates that, at 1949 prices, expenditure per capita on health care increased from £437 in 1949 to £1,490 in 1984. In 1949 total expenditure on the NHS was £437 million; by 1984 this had risen to £16,695 (Ham, 1985). The cost of the services has increased threefold in real terms and it now represents 6.2 per cent of Gross National Product as compared with 3.9 per cent in 1948. These expenditure increases prompted the following comment from the Royal Commission on the NHS: 'the demand for health care is always likely to outstrip supply . . . the capacity of health services to absorb resources is almost unlimited' (HMSO, 1979: 51).

A key factor in determining the current pattern of services to dying people is the way that the health care budget is distributed. We may consider the distribution of the health care budget in four main ways: between geographical regions; between different sectors of the service (e.g. hospital versus community); between varying client groups; and between differing age groups. Acute hospital in-patient care accounts for one-third of all NHS expenditure. Despite numerous attempts to redress the balance, hospital medicine, because of its greater 'prestige', has managed to maintain a stranglehold on the allocation of NHS resources. The result of this dominance of acute hospital medicine is that community forms of provision are constantly under-funded. For dying people this may be manifest in the insufficient provision of community nursing, hospices and nursing home provision.

Within the local authority sector there is also a competition for finite resources both between social services and other departments and within social services between client groups. How decisions are made between competing services within social service departments remains difficult to articulate empirically. However, statutory duties of the local authority towards children mean that these services often take priority over the needs of other client groups. Typically the local authority provides domestic and meals services. However, it is questionable as to how appropriate some of the typical social services are in meeting the needs of dying people and their carers. The implementation of the community care reforms which stress the provision of services which meet the needs of clients rather than fitting clients to services may improve the situation.

Coordination of care

To meet the diverse needs of dying people appropriately a variety of different agencies are required. However, in meeting these needs a number of problems arise, including differences in the geographical areas served by the varying agencies and lack of clarity about the boundaries of responsibility between agencies and professions.

The geographical areas served by these different agencies are not necessarily coterminous. For example, Parkside DHA in Inner London relates to three different local authorities (Brent, the Royal Borough of Kensington and Chelsea, and the City of Westminster) and two Family Health Service Authorities (FHSAs) (Kensington, Chelsea and Westminster, and Brent and Harrow). Such problems of overlapping boundaries are most acute in inner-city districts and may well result in a less than optimal service being provided to those who are dying, especially if they require help at home before the mortal event.

In organizing the care of dying people and their carers there are a variety of agencies involved. As well as overlapping administrative boundaries in many circumstances, there are no clear professional boundaries between the responsibilities of those organizing and providing care to older people in both hospital and community settings. The system of providing care is characterized by fragmentation of responsibility and a multiplicity of agencies and professionals involved. For example, home nursing is the province of the District Health Authority, whilst home caring is provided by the local authority social services department. Co-ordinating care under such circumstances is, therefore, problematic and largely the result of historical events which have vested responsibilities for social and health care provision between varying agencies which have not developed in a coordinated and coherent fashion.

There is another layer of provision, that of the voluntary sector. Voluntary agencies are involved in the provision of a wide range of services to dying people and their carers. Indeed many of the innovations in service provision such as hospice care and bereavement counselling originated in this sector. Within a local area voluntary agencies may be specific to that locality or be branches of national organizations such as the Crossroads Care Attendant Schemes. The hallmark of the voluntary sector is that it is very dependent upon local activists and enthusiasm. We may distinguish between agencies providing care to people who die, such as the Crossroads Care Scheme for the very disabled, and those specifically aimed at those with a terminal illness, such as the hospice movement. A particularly fertile and innovative part of the voluntary sector has been the development of services for people with AIDS. Agencies such as the Terrence Higgins Trust, London Lighthouse and the Mildmay Mission have developed a plethora of services for those in the terminal phases of AIDS.

We may speculate as to why the voluntary sector has been the source of much innovation. The enterprise and enthusiasm of the voluntary sector have much to commend them. However, from a wider perspective there are problems with the development of services by this sector. First, the patchy availability of such schemes adds to the current pattern of geographical inequality in care provision observed within the formal sector. Secondly, such services may be adopted by the formal sector without proper evaluation and study, which means that services may be adopted by the statutory sector for emotive reasons without proper evaluation.

Community care

An important policy context is that of the trend towards community care. Across the range of Western industrial societies there is a trend towards decreased institutional provision and a greater emphasis upon the care and maintenance of those with long-term care needs in their own homes for as long as possible. To achieve this, priority is being given to the development of domiciliary provision and the encouragement of measures designed to prevent or postpone the need for long-term care in hospital or residential homes. Thus, it is argued, care of the dying is a responsibility which should be shared by all, and not one which solely involves statutory services. In this manifestation community care is seen as the responsibility of the family with state services only playing a rather residual role. The receipt of services by only a minority of the dying is the manifestation of this policy. Despite current policy taking too little account of changes in family and household formation, policy is not stressing the need to mobilize the resources of the informal sector, notwithstanding evidence that care is supplied mainly by family and friends rather than the wider community.

Conclusion

The provision of care to dying people and their carers illustrates most of the key issues confronting the health and social welfare system in Britain. First it is important to take into account the epidemiology of death and dying. Most people who die are elderly and they die from a variety of diseases, not just cancers which have dominated the debate about services for the dying. Such a broad perspective makes it difficult to generalize about this group. The dying are not a homogeneous social category and, in developing services and policy, the diversity of the group must be recognized. The pattern of service provision to this group reflects the fragmentation of responsibility between agencies resulting from a variety of historical circumstances which have proved difficult to change. The power of the medical profession and the dominance of the hospital sector result in the concentration of death in hospital, where the ethos of acute care may be inappropriate for those who are in the 'terminal' phases of their illness. The separation of primary, secondary and home care services and the lack of coterminosity of the areas served results in problems in the co-ordination of services. Overcoming these difficulties requires a fundamental overhaul of the way that services are provided.

References

Cartwright, A., Hockey, L. and Anderson, J.L. (1973) *Life Before Death*. London and Boston, MA: Routledge & Kegan Paul.

Cartwright, A. and Seale, C.F. (1990) *The Natural History of a Survey: an Account of the Methodological Issues Encountered in a Study of Life before Death*. London: King's Fund.

Green, H. (1988) 'General Household Survey (GHS)', *Informal Carers*. London: OPCS, HMSO.

HMSO (1979) *Royal Commission on the National Health Service*. London: HMSO.

Ham, C. (1985) *Health Policy in Britain* (2nd edn). London: Macmillan. p. 38.

OPCS (1989) *Mortality Statistics: England and Wales 1987: Cause*. London: HMSO.

Seale, C. (1990) 'Caring for people who die', *Ageing and Society*, 10: 413-28.

9

Sudden death from suicide

Stella Ridley

The concept of illness in our society carries with it the possibility of treatment, and the hope of the relief of suffering. Death following illness is one possible outcome of a progression of events which fall into a sequence and become meaningful in retrospect, according to the kind of illness and the settings in which it occurs.

It is far harder to find or create meaning in sudden death from suicide or self-inflicted injury. For the individual who chooses to commit suicide it would seem that life has become a struggle with no meaning, or a terror from which death is the only escape. The one factor common to suicide or self-inflicted injury is the intention to harm the self; the question common to those left behind is 'Why?' About a third of those who take their own lives give little or no warning and leave no clue as to the reasons behind their feelings of despair; often their family and friends are no wiser. Others talk of suicide and death for a period beforehand, and then take their lives; this is reflected in the tripled rate of suicide for hospital inpatients compared with the general population (Ritter, 1989: 99). A further group attempt suicide and survive, but with perhaps a higher risk of completing the act on a subsequent attempt.

In 1989 the deaths of 4,361 people in the United Kingdom were officially attributed to suicide or self-inflicted injury; to put this in perspective it is roughly equivalent to the number who died of leukaemia (Central Statistical Office, 1991). Suicide statistics are of doubtful accuracy and this can be taken to be the minimum. Coroners are often reluctant to deliver a suicide verdict and this tends to be determined by the means of death; for example, hanging or death from fumes from a motor vehicle exhaust pipe leading into a car are normally seen as valid indicators, while road traffic accidents are rarely interpreted as showing suicidal intent. It is thought that in excess of 20,000 people attempt suicide each year.

If one-third of those who take their lives give no warning of their intention, there are many others among those who are contemplating suicide who do offer signs. In 1953 Chad Varah formed the Samaritans organization, in response to the suicide of a young girl, with the aim of being there for those who were suicidal or in despair, to listen to what they had to say, and to offer emotional support or befriending in times of crisis. The organization is now divided into 185 local branches throughout the UK (with others world-wide), staffed by 22,500 trained and selected volunteers from a wide cross-section of society, who answered 2.5 million calls in 1990. The callers range in age from children to the elderly, through all socio-economic groups. A fundamental tenet is that every caller has a need to be listened to, in confidence, and to have his or her feelings acknowledged and respected. This includes a respect for the caller's right to choose to end his or her own life.

The question of choice is of paramount importance. Alvarez (1971) describes suicide as an act of choice, when life is not worth living. Listening to individuals who are profoundly suicidal, often it would seem to them that there is no choice open, and that suicide is the only way out. This constitutes not so much a choice as a forced choice, where there is no alternative but to die.

In 'A Letter from Jill' (from Foster and Smith, 1987: 53–4) reproduced as the Appendix to this article, Jill says at the end of her suicide note, 'I can't not kill myself after writing this.' This lack of choice is echoed by descriptions given by others:

> It was as if I'd already gone over, somehow – the problem was not how to die but would have been how to stay alive. (After an incompleted suicide)

Tolstoy, in 'Death and the meaning of life', says:

> The truth was that life was meaningless. It was as though I had just been living and walking along, and had come to an abyss, where I saw clearly that there was nothing ahead but perdition. And it was impossible to stop and go back, and impossible to shut my eyes, in order that I might not see that there was nothing ahead but suffering and imminent death, – complete annihilation. (Tolstoy, 1899; see pp. 89–92 in this Reader)

How can someone be empowered to make an open choice between life and death instead of this forced choice? The Samaritans say they are concerned with 'the affirmation of life and its quality'. On a practical level this entails recognizing suicidal feelings, and encouraging the caller to talk of his or her fears and expectations, to acknowledge plans he or she may have for ending life, and to talk of the feelings that have led up to the present day. Acceptance rather than denial of distress, a belief in what the caller says rather than 'Oh you can't really mean that', are ways in which the caller may learn that he or she is really being heard. There is no formula, each Samaritan volunteer finds his or her own way to facilitate the kind of real human contact that can open a route back into life for someone who has become isolated and without hope. However, it can be a precarious path; depression often inhibits action. As it begins to lift there can sometimes be a critical period when suicidal ideation still exists and increasing energy at last allows for an active suicide attempt.

Do the activities of the Samaritans help to prevent suicide? Brian

Barraclough (1987) finds little consistent relationship between local suicide rates in towns where there were Samaritan branches and those without, but concluded that suicidal people were certainly attracted to the organization.

Are certain groups of people more vulnerable to suicide? Sadly, yes. Suicide is a major cause of death, second only to road accidents, in the 16–24 age group. A high number of older people also take their lives, but suicide accounts for a much smaller proportion of deaths in this age range. Certain occupational groups run a higher risk too, health care professionals and farmers among them. A high proportion of those attempting suicide have suffered major changes or life events in the preceding year. Twice as many males as females take their lives, and the method varies. Male deaths are more likely to be of a violent nature, such as hanging, while the single commonest method for women is by overdose. Violent methods carry a greater risk of completion (Ritter, 1989); the higher rate of non-fatal deliberate self-harm among girls and women may be related to this. The chosen method does have considerable significance, and varies widely across different cultures.

Many who read this will know from first-hand experience what it feels like to be suicidal, or will have known someone who has died in this way. Feelings of loneliness and despair are difficult to share, and friends and family may seem to turn a blind eye to distress because it touches too deeply on hidden fear and pain of their own. Finding the words to describe these feelings, and someone who will listen to and accept them, may be one step towards discovering meaning where, for a time, there threatened to be none.

References

Alvarez, A. (1971) *The Savage God*. London: Weidenfeld & Nicolson.

Barraclough, B. (1987) *Suicide: Clinical and Epidemiological Studies*. Beckenham: Croom Helm.

Central Statistical Office (1991) *Annual Abstract of Statistics*, London: HMSO.

Foster, S. and Smith, P. (1987) *Brief Lives*. London: Arlington Books.

Ritter, S. (1989) *Bethlem Royal and Maudsley Hospital Manual of Clinical Psychiatric Nursing Principles and Procedures*. London: Harper Collins Nursing.

Tolstoy, Leo (1899) 'Death and the meaning of life', in *A Confession*, trans. Leo Wiener. New York: Thomas Y. Crowell & Co. (Abridged version reproduced on pp. 89–82 of this Reader.)

Appendix: A letter from Jill

On 28 December 1984, Jill died, aged 15 years, on the Liverpool to Manchester railway line. She told her parents she was taking the dog for a walk, tied him in a safe place and threw herself under a train. She left a letter.

Dear Mummy,

Please don't waste too much effort on a large funeral after all the heartache I have caused you, it is hardly worth it. I am sorry it happened at Christmas. I killed myself because I had made a mess of so many things.

I know you feel that that isn't true, but it was. It was never your fault, mind. I love you and Daddy very dearly, always remember that. I could just not get the act together, that's all. My future didn't seem very attractive. I think I was just one hell of a cracked-up person. I have always felt inferior. I could never talk to anyone and know they had respected what I have said. Maybe I didn't let it show before because then I was younger and adulthood seemed a long way away and I thought as I got older my thoughts would change. Sadly they didn't.

Always remember me as you thought I was, not as a stupid person, which is how I feel about myself.

I can't not kill myself after writing this. (Sorry)

Love, Jill xxxx

Your disobedient daughter

10

Contemporary representations of 'good' and 'bad' death

Mary Bradbury

'Good' and 'bad' deaths in different societies

An important question we can ask is 'For whom is a death "good"?' As we can only guess whether the death was 'good' or 'bad' for the deceased, this concept would appear to be the concern of the survivors; indeed, the issue as to whether a death is 'good' or 'bad' is essentially social.

People in many different societies enter into discussions as to whether a death was 'good' or 'bad' and it is useful to look to non-industrial groups before turning to contemporary British society. In non-industrial societies 'good' deaths are those that demonstrate some kind of control over events and can be seen to represent a victory over nature. In the Ugandan 'good' death, given below, one can see how important it is that people predict that death is imminent and prepare for it. No women are present in this example as the Lugbara traditionally segregate the sexes at the deathbed.

> A man should die in his hut, lying on his bed, with his brothers and sons around him to hear his last words; he should die with his mind still alert and should be able to speak clearly even if only softly; he should die peacefully and with dignity, without bodily discomfort or disturbance; . . . he should die loved and respected by his family. (Middleton, 1982: 142)

'Good' deaths are those where people can exert control over events. This sense of control is given expression in mortuary rituals that deny the finality of death by claiming that death represents rebirth. Bloch and Parry (1982) show how 'good' deaths serve to reassert the power of the group and reassure the survivors that the deceased has indeed gone on to a new life. They suggest that 'good' deaths may actually increase the 'productiveness' of the group, in terms of crops, successful hunting or human fertility.

'Bad' deaths are uncontrolled; they happen at the wrong place at the wrong time. 'Bad' deaths preclude the chance of regeneration, both for the individual and the group.

Suicide is often viewed as the supremely 'bad' death. While suicide may be seen by an individual as the only way to assert control over destiny, society is helpless. Unlike suicide, self-sacrifice is often positively sanctioned by society. While suicide is presented as a selfish act of personal frustration or despair, self-sacrifice claims to be selfless (Durkheim, 1952). In reality, however, there is a great deal of ambiguity surrounding these archetypal 'bad' and 'good' deaths and, as Bloch and Parry point out, there can be disagreement as to whether a death was a suicide or an example of self-sacrifice.

Contemporary representations of death: recent findings

A recent study aimed to discover current representations of death among medical staff, deathwork professionals (such as the funeral director, the coroner and the registrar) and widows who were nominally Church of England. The findings suggest that our representations of death are still very strong, although they have undergone certain changes. There are several contrasting representations of what constitutes a 'good' death: the traditional sacred 'good' death, the medicalized 'good' death and the 'natural' 'good' death. As one would expect in a complex society, these different representations complement and conflict with each other in an ever-changing kaleidoscope of attitude and behaviour.

Sacred 'good' deaths: a Christian example

The afterlife is a reality for people with religious faith and their concepts of 'good' death appear to follow the non-industrial beliefs that a 'good' death signals an entry into heaven and that whatever sorrow the mourners may feel should be tempered with a sense of celebration and joy.

However, in modern society, this traditional sacred representation of a 'good' death has undergone certain changes. Few deaths occur without some kind of medical intervention and descriptions of what made a death 'good' or 'bad' are interwoven with medical ideas of a 'good' death.

Medicalized 'good' deaths

The majority of deaths take place in a medical context of some kind, whether in a hospital ward, under the supervision of a GP or in an accident and emergency unit. In this context, it is not surprising that we have embraced those medical techniques which allow us to control death to some extent, either by prolonging life or easing pain.

Ariès (1981) bemoans this 'medicalization' of death and gives the impression that this is something which is always imposed on the dying. This is not necessarily the case. One must also remember that medical intervention saves lives; for example, surgery after an accident or the use of insulin for a diabetic.

The 'natural' deaths and 'good' deaths

There are also 'good' deaths which do not take place in a medical or sacred context. These 'natural' deaths are usually unexpected and appear to be desirable because of the absence of fear or pain. While the concept of 'natural' death is not new, the idea of a 'natural' death which is also 'good' is a modern, secular, development. Beier (1989), in an analysis of 'natural' and 'good' deaths in the seventeenth century, found that 'natural' deaths, such as death in childbirth and in old age, were not necessarily regarded as 'good', because they lacked the essential element of human control.

An alternative representation of 'natural' 'good' deaths is held by some people who have actively rejected the idea of medical intervention used to prolong the life of the terminally ill. For them, a 'good' death is one where the only medical intervention that takes place is that of pain relief. In many ways these 'natural' deaths really represent 'less-medicalized' deaths.

In both instances, the essential ingredient of control of the death has been reinterpreted. In the first example one gains control through accepting nature, in the second one does so by fighting the medical system.

Thus, among the bereaved, one can identify three broad categories of 'good' death – sacred, medical and natural. These representations are a function of people's beliefs and the conditions of a death. For example, if someone without religious belief dies then few people will feel comfortable discussing the death in terms of the afterlife. Instead, they are more likely to talk about painlessness, dignity and such like.

Medical practitioners and deathwork professionals

Of course, medical practitioners and deathwork professionals also have representations of 'good' and 'bad' death which affect the way they treat the dying, the body and the next of kin. Sometimes there are conflicts between the representations of a 'good' death held by the bereaved and those of the professional. This is illustrated by the following quote from an experienced casualty doctor:

> If you bring them in and they are obviously dead, you will wait ten minutes so the relatives think you have done something. (Doctor, 1991)

The representation of the medical 'good' death was so strong among this medical team that they agreed to stand around a long-dead corpse for ten minutes for the 'benefit' of the next of kin who was anxiously waiting outside. Yet they had no way of knowing that such behaviour would be a comfort to that person, who may have strongly objected to any kind of intervention.

A funeral director's concern appears to be to present a positive image of the deceased and the manner of the death – in short, to make all deaths appear 'good'. Efforts are made to make the body as life-like and reposeful as possible through embalming and the use of make-up. These activities are overtly targeted at the bereaved and have nothing to do with the spiritual well-being of the deceased.

> I once spent eight hours embalming a person, I had to suture an arm back on – the relatives didn't know. (Funeral director, 1990)

Trying to make the body look life-like is not so much a symptom of our denial of death, as Becker (1973) argued, but the embalmer's denial of 'bad' death by the attempt to make all deaths appear peaceful.

> I am against personal visual identification, unless [the body appears to] lie there serenely asleep. But if the body is disfigured, then its probably unwise to let somebody [view] who is not, as it were, used to it. (Coroner, 1991)

While the rationale for such behaviour is one of kindness and care, a more cynical interpretation is that it makes the customer easier to handle. Similar management of the dying and the bereaved was observed by Glaser and Strauss (1965) and Sudnow (1967) in their studies of hospital deaths.

Summary

To summarize, we currently have multiple representations of what makes a death 'good' or 'bad'; representations formed by our cultural heritage, our medical model of health and illness and our psychological states. It seems particularly important that medical practitioners and deathwork professionals realize that the bereaved may not share their representations of what makes a death 'good'.

References

Ariès, P. (1981) *The Hour of Our Death*. Harmondsworth: Penguin.

Becker, H. (1973) *The Denial of Death*. New York: Free Press.

Beier, L. (1989) 'The good death in seventeenth-century Britain', in R. Houlbrooke (ed.), *Death, Ritual, and Bereavement*. London: Routledge.

Bloch, M. and Parry, J. (eds) (1982) *Death and the Regeneration of Life*. Cambridge: Cambridge University Press.

Durkheim, É. (1952) *Suicide: A Study in Sociology*. London: Routledge & Kegan Paul.

Glaser, B. and Strauss, A. (1965) *Awareness of Dying*. Chicago, IL: Aldine.

Middleton, J. (1982) 'Lugbara death', in M. Bloch and J. Parry (eds), *Death and the Regeneration of Life*. Cambridge: Cambridge University Press.

Sudnow, D. (1967) *Passing On*. Englewood Cliffs, NJ: Prentice Hall.

11

Little Henry; or, God will take care of me

H.M. Benson

DID you ever, dear children, think of a time coming when your dear father or mother might be taken from you? Oh, no, you are ready to say, I never thought of such a dreadful thing. I am sure I should break my heart if my own dear mother or father were to die. Well, so little Henry once thought, and so he said, but alas! he did lose his kind father, and although he was only seven years of age, he knew what sorrow was then. It was a mournful day for Henry, when he walked by the side of his poor weeping mother, and with her followed the remains of his father to the grave. 'I shall never see him any more' he thought within himself. 'He will never again call me his own little Henry', and then his tears flowed fast, and he held his mother's hand tighter, as if he were fearful of losing her also.

Poor child! when he returned home the house seemed so desolate, and he went sorrowfully up to his little bedroom, and kneeling down quite alone, he sobbed as if his heart would break; shortly, however, he brushed off the tears and began to pray. 'Lord, look upon me now,' he said, 'and be my Father. Help me to love my mother and do every thing I can for her.'

He then rose, more comforted, and on going down stairs was met by his mother, and in a moment was in her arms. She did not speak, but Henry felt the big tears on her cheek, and knew *why* she wept; so he looked up into her face and said, 'Mother dear, you have *me* still. Father is gone to heaven. He is happy there. God is *my* father now. He will take care of me. I am your own little Harry, and I will *try* to be good.

From *The Child's Own Magazine for 1856*, London: The Sunday School Union, pp. 156-9.

I shall soon grow up to be a man, and then, mother dear, nobody shall hurt you.'

'You are indeed my own good little boy,' replied his mother, 'and I bless God that you are left to me; so we will try to dry up our tears, knowing that God *will* take care of us.'

And now, dear children, you will wish to know how poor little Henry got on. On the Sunday following his father's funeral, he went as usual to the Sabbath school, but he could hardly hold up his head, his heart was so sad. His kind teacher was deeply grieved, and, drawing him towards her, while she gently took his hand, said, 'My poor child, look up. Your heavenly father will never leave nor forsake you. You must now try to comfort your mother all in your power. Remember, dear, God is a "father to the fatherless".'

Many other tender and encouraging words his teacher added, so that little Henry was cheered; and when school was over, he hastened home to tell all the things his teacher had been saying. It was a lovely Sabbath morning. The air was so fresh, the little birds were singing, and the sun shone so sweetly, making every thing in nature look gay. Henry, however, did not observe the general gladness of creation, he hurried down the lane leading to his home, and, running in, exclaimed, 'Oh, mother dear, I am sure now that God will make us happy again. Teacher says God will never leave nor forsake us, and I am sure God would not say so if He did not mean it. Mother, God is a father to the fatherless, so do not weep any more, for I am sure I believe God, and I want *you* to believe just as I do.'

The mother raised her little boy on her knees, and while she kissed him, silently praised God who had given her such a comforter in her child, at the same time resolving that however poor and desolate she might be, her hope and trust should ever be in God.

Well, time went on, and Henry grew fast. When he was fourteen years of age, he had to go far away from his mother, but still God was with him, taking care of him, and preserving him from evil. When he became a man, God prospered him in the world, and then, like a dutiful son, he did not forget his mother, who had during his early days been obliged to work hard in order to maintain him. Every year he sent her home a sum of money which enabled her to have many comforts in her declining days; and what was better, there always came with it a sweet pious letter, making the widow's heart to sing for joy.

Now, dear children, this is a true story, and I want you to remember it, because the same God that took care of little Henry can and will take care of you. But remember, that Henry asked God in prayer to do so, and God heard and answered him, because he asked in faith, that is, he *believed* God was able to do it. And then he asked in the name of Jesus Christ, through whom alone little children must expect to be heard. Henry too was in *earnest* when he prayed. Children are often thinking of other things when they kneel down to pray. Now this is nothing else than mocking God, because He *looks* into children's hearts, and knows whether they really mean what they are saying or not. You must, dear children, be in earnest about every thing, *especially* in prayer; and then, if it should please God to remove from you by death, your dear parents or friends, you will be able, like little Henry, to go and ask *earnestly* that you may be taken care of by your Father who is in heaven, who has promised never to leave, never to forsake you. And now, in bidding you farewell, I will leave with you a sweet text, which you can learn for the next Sabbath school lesson. You will find it in St. John's Gospel, 16th chapter, 23rd verse: 'Whatsoever ye shall ask the Father in my name, he will give it you.'

12

The dream

T.R.S.

LITTLE BOYS AND GIRLS, THIS IS FOR YOU

'OH, what a sweet dream! – oh, what a lovely dream! Oh, mamma, you don't know what a charming sight these eyes saw but a short time ago!' These simple words were from the lips of a dying child to her mother. The child was ill in a little cot in the bedroom of her mother, who was anxiously watching her child with all the love of a parent's heart; and delighted once more to hear the voice of her dear little one, she replied, 'What, my dear child – what sight has my Lucy seen?' 'Oh, mamma – mamma!' said the charmed girl, 'Such a sight! I thought I was in heaven, and on my head was such a lovely crown of sweet flowers; a golden harp was in my hand, and when I just touched one of its chords, such sweet sounds came, like most delightful music; and I sang to it with all my power. There was dear little Reuben – yes, darling brother Reuben, that used to be so kind and make me little boats to sail on the water; and he looked so happy: he didn't cry, mamma, like he did before he died and was buried in the cemetery. There was dear little baby, too – poor Mary, that was so pretty, with white hair, and such beautiful blue eyes. But, oh, mother, I can't tell you about it, it was so wonderful! Don't cry, mamma; for doesn't the Bible say, if you're good, both you, papa, and brother William, shall go? I shall soon go to help them to sing; and you'll stop to comfort them, mamma, when they cry because I'm gone, won't you, mamma? Dry your tears; for then all of us will be together, so happily, in heaven.'

The beautiful simplicity of her innocent child

From *The Child's Own Magazine for 1856*, London: The Sunday School Union.

deeply impressed the parent. Alas! soon Lucy died; but her mamma had a great comfort. She knew Lucy was with baby and Reuben, in heaven!

13

Death be not proud

John Donne

Death be not proud, though some have called thee
Mighty and dreadfull, for, thou art not soe,
For, those, whom thou think'st, thou dost overthrow,
Die not, poore death, nor yet canst thou kill mee;
From rest and sleepe, which but thy pictures bee,
Much pleasure, then from thee, much more must flow,
And soonest our best men with thee doe goe,
Rest of their bones, and soules deliverie.
Thou art slave to Fate, chance, kings, and desperate
    men,
And dost with poyson, warre, and sicknesse dwell,
And poppie, or charmes can make us sleepe as well,
And better than thy stroake; why swell'st thou then?
One short sleepe past, wee wake eternally,
And death shall be no more, Death thou shalt die.

From *Complete Poetry and Selected Prose of John Donne*, ed. J. Hayward. London:
Nonesuch Press, 1978.

14

Aubade

Philip Larkin

I work all day, and get half-drunk at night.
Waking at four to soundless dark, I stare.
In time the curtain-edges will grow light.
Till then I see what's really always there:
Unresting death, a whole day nearer now,
Making all thought impossible but how
And where and when I shall myself die.
Arid interrogation: yet the dread
Of dying, and being dead,
Flashes afresh to hold and horrify.

The mind blanks at the glare. Not in remorse
– The good not done, the love not given, time
Torn off unused – nor wretchedly because
An only life can take so long to climb
Clear of its wrong beginnings, and may never;
But at the total emptiness for ever,
The sure extinction that we travel to
And shall be lost in always. Not to be here,
Not to be anywhere,
And soon; nothing more terrible, nothing more true.

This is a special way of being afraid
No trick dispels. Religion used to try,
That vast moth-eaten musical brocade
Created to pretend we never die,
And specious stuff that says *No rational being
Can fear a thing it will not feel*, not seeing
That this is what we fear – no sight, no sound,
No touch or taste or smell, nothing to think with,
Nothing to love or link with,
The anaesthetic from which none come round.

From *Times Literary Supplement*, 29 November 1977.

And so it stays just on the edge of vision,
A small unfocused blur, a standing chill
That slows each impulse down to indecision.
Most things may never happen: this one will,
And realization of it rages out
In furnace-fear when we are caught without
People or drink. Courage is no good:
It means not scaring others. Being brave
Lets no one off the grave.
Death is no different whined at than withstood.

Slowly light strengthens, and the room takes shape.
It stands plain as a wardrobe, what we know,
Have always known, know that we can't escape,
Yet can't accept. One side will have to go.
Meanwhile telephones crouch, getting ready to ring
In locked-up offices, and all the uncaring
Intricate rented world begins to rouse.
The sky is white as clay, with no sun.
Work has to be done.
Postmen like doctors go from house to house.

15

Do not go gentle into that good night

Dylan Thomas

Do not go gentle into that good night,
Old age should burn and rave at close of day;
Rage, rage against the dying of the light.

Though wise men at their end know dark is right,
Because their words had forked no lightning they
Do not go gentle into that good night.

Good men, the last wave by, crying how bright
Their frail deeds might have danced in a green bay,
Rage, rage against the dying of the light.

Wild men who caught and sang the sun in flight,
And learn, too late, they grieved it on its way,
Do not go gentle into that good night.

Grave men, near death, who see with blinding sight
Blind eyes could blaze like meteors and be gay,
Rage, rage against the dying of the light.

And you, my father, there on the sad height,
Curse, bless, me now with your fierce tears, I pray.
Do not go gentle into that good night.
Rage, rage against the dying of the light.

From *The Collected Poems*, New York: New Directions Publishing Corporation, 1952.

16

The Prophet

Kahlil Gibran

Then Almitra spoke, saying, We would ask now of Death.

And he said:

You would know the secret of death.

But how shall you find it unless you seek it in the heart of life?

The owl whose night-bound eyes are blind unto the day cannot unveil the mystery of light.

If you would indeed behold the spirit of death, open your heart wide unto the body of life.

For life and death are one, even as the river and the sea are one.

In the depth of your hopes and desires lies your silent knowledge of the beyond;

And like seeds dreaming beneath the snow your heart dreams of spring.

Trust the dreams, for in them is hidden the gate to eternity.

Your fear of death is but the trembling of the shepherd when he stands before the king whose hand is to be laid upon him in honour.

Extract from *The Prophet*, London: Heinemann, 1979, pp. 93-4.

Is the shepherd not joyful beneath his trembling, that he shall wear the mark of the king?

Yet is he not more mindful of his trembling?

For what is it to die but to stand naked in the wind and to melt in the sun?

And what is it to cease breathing but to free the breath from its restless tides, that it may rise and expand and seek God unencumbered?

Only when you drink from the river of silence shall you indeed sing.

And when you have reached the mountain top, then you shall begin to climb.

And when the earth shall claim your limbs, then shall you truly dance.

17

Doctor's mask on pain

Jane Martin

On 1 August 1988, with eagerness and some trepidation, I began my first 'house job' as a junior doctor, at a district general hospital in the north of England. On 12 September, in a similar hospital some 250 miles to the south, my father died.

I was on call the day I heard he had been admitted with extensive secondary cancer and was not expected to live much longer. It was a busy night: at one point four patients with acute myocardial infarction (heart attack) arrived almost simultaneously on the geriatric ward where I was working. We were all up all night. At around 4 a.m. I grabbed a cup of coffee in the ward kitchen with the husband of one of my patients. He mentioned that his daughter had begun travelling through the night from her home on the south coast: she had set aside her own life and its commitments to be with her parents in their time of crisis. I nodded reassuringly through the haze of exhaustion, and wondered why the world had gone suddenly mad.

I left the following day, after twenty-four hours' continuous duty and some hastily snatched sleep and arrived in time to be with my mother and father during the last three days of his life. He was a gaunt skeleton: my mother had hidden from me the true extent of his illness, in order not to impose further stress on me during my first few weeks as a doctor, in order to allow me to care for others while others cared for my dad.

We kept vigil day and night. My mother was alone with him at the moment of his death, which was right and good. I have seen how easy it is to die but for her it was the first encounter, and she was startled and relieved; how much harder was all the suffering than the leaving of it.

Afterwards I stayed with my mother for nearly two weeks, arranging my father's affairs, the funeral, trying to help her through those first bewildering days. She is 72 and has known no other husband or lover.

When I returned to work, I was informed that part of my 'compassionate leave' would be deducted from my annual holiday entitlement. It was difficult to comprehend the mentality that could conceive of the nightmare through which I had just lived as being interchangeable with

From *The Guardian*, 'First Person', 5 April 1989.

a *holiday*. With this dawned the realization that nobody at work was going to acknowledge my desperate need for time to reflect, to grieve for my father in a way which had not been possible when my role had, of necessity, been that of supporting my mother.

In re-donning the white coat, it seemed, I had covered up my claim to be a human being with the capacity to be hurt and the right to crawl away and lick my wounds. I felt confused by all the role-swapping and began to re-evaluate my behaviour as a doctor.

The care my father was given by nursing staff had been superb, and their attitude to the grieving relatives almost as unblemished, except for the unbelievable crassness of one or two individuals. My identity was challenged one night by a new nurse. Suddenly realizing, she laughed: 'Oh, you're with the man dying in room seven. That's all right then.' When the strain was really beginning to tell, I had turned in anguish to a student nurse and whispered: 'It's all the waiting that's so terrible.' 'Yes,' she said, 'it must get really boring.'

Could *I* ever be as unthinkingly cruel to a patient or their relatives? Surely not. Really? Not after a weekend on call, fifty-six hours of continuous duty when I'm so tired I can scarcely remember my own name?

The stereotype of the doctor must be called into question if we are not to be dehumanized by the job. Doctors cannot pretend to stand back in scientific detachment from human suffering. Most of us work with people, not test-tubes, and under our white coats we suffer too. I may grieve for my father, but only in my own time, what precious little there is of that. For my patients, I must not grieve, although, were I a nurse, a few tears would be permissible.

It would benefit both our own emotional health and that of our patients if doctors could refashion this outmoded macho image of invulnerability. I need the space to work through my grief and put it behind me. How wonderful it would be to be able to speak of death with colleagues in terms other than those of 'turning up the toes' or any of the other euphemisms medics use to shield themselves from the reality. Instead I work my horrendous hours, storing up the pain until it erupts in a flood of exhausted irritability when I come off duty.

Last week I was called to see a patient who had begun to deteriorate rapidly. It had already been decided that nothing more could be done to save him. I confirmed that he was, indeed, dying and the staff nurse hurried away to telephone his wife, adding: 'It's all right. We'll stay with him.' My role as the doctor was now superfluous.

Instead of going off to fill in forms and order investigations, I chose to sit with the man for the half-hour it took him to die. His wife arrived an hour later and I broke the sad news. Her first words were: 'Oh! He couldn't even wait for me!' But I was then able to describe to her exactly how he had died: peacefully, in no pain, holding my hand. It seemed to bring her comfort and some solace.

But it wasn't really doing my job.

18

The first day

Mary Benjamin

'This is Sally,' the sister said. 'She was knocked down by a car on her way to school two days ago. Head injury. Over the first twenty-four hours she developed severe cerebral oedema which we couldn't control. We did the first set of brainstem function tests in the evening and they were negative. They will be repeated some time this morning so we can tell her parents when they come in. As far as we are concerned, there is basic care of a ventilated patient to carry out and we will assist with the tests later on.

'Most of the active treatment was stopped yesterday. We are waiting for the results of the second set of tests before we discontinue ventilation: they have to be done twice for legal purposes. I'm going to show you how we look after a ventilated patient, the routine observations and so on: I'll do most of the work this morning, obviously, I want you to watch me and ask questions when you see something you don't understand and I'll explain everything.'

I understood all that the sister had said. This patient was brain-dead. Her condition had been caused by uncontrollable swelling of the brain due to the blow she had suffered in the accident. This patient, my first intensive care patient, was a 13-year-old girl. She did not look dead. A Cape ventilator stood chugging faintly at her bedside and there was an endotracheal tube in her mouth connected via a couple of lengths of rubber tubing to the ventilator, but otherwise she looked, quite literally, as though she were asleep. Until that moment I had thought that this notion must be exactly what it sounds to be, an easy cliché: but it was true. Sally's heart beat on: the monitor beside her bed showed normal sinus rhythm. Intravenous infusions kept her blood pressure up to normal despite the death of her brain's regulating centres. Thus she was pink, warm, apparently comfortable in her white sheets.

We looked after Sally. There was a lot to do: more than I would have thought possible for a single patient. At the time I wondered what this implied for the future, Sally was, I had been told, no longer on 'active

---

Editors' note: The author of this account, a nursing sister on an intensive care unit, chose the pseudonym 'Mary Benjamin' - a name which has personal significance for her - in order to protect patient confidentiality.

treatment'; yet her care kept an experienced sister busy. Later I realized that one major reason for this was that with my near-total ignorance and complete inexperience I had more than doubled Caroline's workload that day, although it was true that there was a core of essential work to be done. In addition to the basic care of mouth and eyes and pressure areas there were drugs to be given, to preserve the kidneys in case the girl's parents should change their minds (for they had refused to consider the prospect the day before) and allow their use for transplant: IV fluids to regulate; vital signs to record and urine to measure. Nothing, I noticed, was done that could prejudice the girl's condition. Until the diagnosis of brain death was confirmed there seemed to remain, behind the continuation of basic life support, ventilation, hydration, even the range of passive movements through which Caroline taught me to take Sally's limbs, the unspoken thought that we must always, even in such a case, assume until the last that she could recover; and beyond even that, that we must always and in every case preserve the person's dignity.

Caroline talked to Sally as she worked. Although the sister knew her patient was almost certainly beyond hearing or seeing or sensing anything which was done to or around her, she spoke: warning her of any disturbance, of a turn or a movement of arms or legs or that one of us was going to clean her teeth. All intensive care nurses, I found, do this. It was a habit I quickly developed myself. Many intensive care unit patients receive drugs to paralyse and sedate them to allow ventilation and to keep them at rest; from talking to those suffering this kind of forced unresponsiveness, who may yet hear and be reassured by the communication, it is a very short step to speaking to those who will never respond again. I have caught myself more than once, when treatments have failed, talking to the corpse I am laying out for the mortuary; some nurses, I know, were once upon a time even taught to do this, in order to preserve patients nearby from realizing what had happened. Fortunately this kind of paternalistic reasoning is less prevalent nowadays.

The girl's pupils were fixed in size and dilated, not reacting to light. She did not blink when a wisp of cotton wool was applied to her eyeball. She did not breathe when disconnected from the ventilator. Also, it could be demonstrated that she was not prevented from reacting by paralysing or sedating drugs. In the general hospital at the time an EEG (electroencephalogram, a measurement of the brain's electrical activity) was always recorded, although it is not necessary for the legal performance of the tests and the recording can in some cases be misleading, since it can pick up electrical activity only in the most superficial structures of the brain. I discovered later on that the EEGs were done for research purposes. Sally's recording consisted of uninterrupted flat lines: there was no activity at all in those parts of the brain which can be investigated in this way.

The second set of brainstem function tests were carried out, as the law requires, by two doctors, one at least being a consultant, who were not connected with any transplant team. Their inevitable conclusion was that the child was indeed brain-dead. When her family arrived they would be told, although the previous day's results had to some extent prepared them for bad news. Then, some time in the afternoon, assuming that the family had not changed their minds about transplantation, Sally would be taken off the ventilator and her body as well allowed to die in peace.

The nurse from the afternoon shift heard our report and nodded. She had heard it all before, had been in this situation before. She too was a sister; chosen to care for Sally not so much for the girl's own sake as for the support her experience would enable her to give to the family. Our morning's work finished, Caroline and I left for the staff room and lunch.

The family had arrived when we returned. They had heard the bad news and had come to say goodbye, still refusing, as was their absolute right, to grant permission for organ donation. I admit that I tried to look both knowledgeable and inconspicuous. I did not think the family's emotional state would be improved if they knew that Sally's nurse – even a nurse who would only be with her for half an hour – had qualified precisely two days before. Also I had no wish to be asked questions. I did not know what I could say. It was a scene which would be repeated many times over the coming years: the parents were waiting, knew they were waiting, for the return of the consultant who would take their daughter off her 'life-support machine'. Making it worse, if this were possible, was the fact that Sally's parents were divorced. The three people around the bed were her father, her mother and her mother's new boyfriend.

The two men did not seem like enemies. The arrangement may have been very civilized and friendly from the start or they may have been drawn together by shock and grief; I had no way of knowing; it was not my business. I did not know, from what I had been told, that Sally's father now lived alone. I did not know whether he would have to go home alone that night. Together with his ex-wife he held his daughter's hand. Beyond all reason and, from things they said among themselves, knowing quite well that it was beyond all reason, they talked to her; although they as well as I knew the diagnosis and had looked into Sally's uninhabited eyes.

'She can't hear us, can she, Nurse?' The mother's question, expecting the answer 'No'.

'No, she can't.' This at least I could answer with some conviction. The mother nodded; it was as though she needed just one more confirmation. They asked no more. The sister came back. I left the bedside again and a short time later the consultant arrived. Not long after, the shift ended. With the other nurses I walked towards the plastic doors.

We had to pass by Sally's bed. The screens were an imperfect barrier, but I could neither stop nor stare. I caught only a brief glimpse of the family, of the still body, as I walked past. Half an hour later I was drinking a cup of tea at home.

19

Death and the meaning of life

Leo Tolstoy

In my writings I advocated, what to me was the only truth, that it was necessary to live in such a way as to derive the greatest comfort for oneself and one's family.

Thus I proceeded to live, but five years ago something very strange began to happen to me: I was overcome by minutes at first of perplexity and then of an arrest of life, as though I did not know how to live or what to do, and I lost myself and was dejected. But that passed, and I continued to live as before. Then those minutes of perplexity were repeated oftener and oftener, and always in one and the same form. These arrests of life found their expression in ever the same questions: 'Why? Well, and then?' [. . .]

The questions seemed to be so foolish, simple, and childish. But the moment I touched them and tried to solve them, I became convinced, in the first place, that they were not childish and foolish, but very important and profound questions in life, and, in the second, that, no matter how much I might try, I should not be able to answer them. Before attending to my Samára estate, to my son's education, or to the writing of a book, I ought to know why I should do that. So long as I did not know why, I could not do anything, I could not live. Amidst my thoughts of farming, which interested me very much during that time, there would suddenly pass through my head a question like this: 'All right, you are going to have six thousand desyatínas of land in the Government of Samára, and three hundred horses, – and then?' And I completely lost my senses and did not know what to think farther. Or, when I thought of the education of my children, I said to myself: 'Why?' Or, reflecting on the manner in which the masses might obtain their welfare, I suddenly said to myself: 'What is that to me?' Or, thinking of the fame which my works would get me, I said to myself: 'All right, you will be more famous than Gógol, Púshkin, Shakespeare, Molière, and all the writers in the world, – what of it?' And I was absolutely unable to make any reply. The questions were not waiting, and I had to answer them at once; if I did not answer them, I could not live.

From *A Confession*, trans. Leo Wiener, New York: Thomas Y. Crowell & Co., 1899 (abridged).

I felt that what I was standing on had given way, that I had no foundation to stand on, that that which I lived by no longer existed, and that I had nothing to live by.

My life came to a standstill. I could breathe, eat, drink and sleep, and could not help breathing, eating, drinking and sleeping; but there was no life, because there were no desires the gratification of which I might find reasonable. If I wished for anything, I knew in advance that, whether I gratified my desire or not, nothing would come of it. If a fairy had come and had offered to carry out my wish, I should not have known what to say. If in moments of intoxication I had, not wishes, but habits of former desires, I knew in sober moments that that was a deception, that there was nothing to wish for. I could not even wish to find out the truth, because I guessed what it consisted in. The truth was that life was meaningless. It was as though I had just been living and walking along, and had come to an abyss, where I saw clearly that there was nothing ahead but perdition. And it was impossible to stop and go back, and impossible to shut my eyes, in order that I might not see that there was nothing ahead but suffering and imminent death, – complete annihilation.

What happened to me was that I, a healthy, happy man, felt that I could not go on living, – an insurmountable force drew me on to find release from life. I cannot say that I *wanted* to kill myself.

The force which drew me away from life was stronger, fuller, more general than wishing. It was a force like the former striving after life, only in an inverse sense. I tended with all my strength away from life. The thought of suicide came as naturally to me as had come before the ideas of improving life. That thought was so seductive that I had to use cunning against myself, lest I should rashly execute it. I did not want to be in a hurry, because I wanted to use every effort to disentangle myself: if I should not succeed in disentangling myself, there would always be time for that. And at such times I, a happy man, hid a rope from myself so that I should not hang myself on a cross-beam between two safes in my room, where I was by myself in the evening, while taking off my clothes, and did not go out hunting with a gun, in order not to be tempted by any easy way of doing away with myself. I did not know myself what it was I wanted: I was afraid of life, strove to get away from it, and, at the same time, expected something from it.

All that happened with me when I was on every side surrounded by what is considered to be complete happiness. I had a good, loving and beloved wife, good children and a large estate, which grew and increased without any labour on my part. I was respected by my neighbours and friends, more than ever before, was praised by strangers, and, without any self-deception, could consider my name famous. With all that, I was not deranged or mentally unsound, – on the contrary, I was in full command of my mental and physical powers, such as I had rarely met with in people of my age: physically

I could work in a field, mowing, without falling behind a peasant; mentally I could work from eight to ten hours in succession, without experiencing any consequences from the strain. And while in such condition I arrived at the conclusion that I could not live, and, fearing death, I had to use cunning against myself, in order that I might not take my life. [. . .]

The former deception of the pleasures of life, [. . .] no longer deceives me. No matter how much one should say to me, 'You cannot understand the meaning of life, do not think, live!' I am unable to do so, because I have been doing it too long before. Now I cannot help seeing day and night, which run and lead me up to death. I see that alone, because that alone is the truth. Everything else is a lie. [. . .]

'My family – ' I said to myself, 'but my family, my wife and children, they are also human beings. They are in precisely the same condition that I am in: they must either live in the lie or see the terrible truth. Why should they live? Why should I love them, why guard, raise and watch them? Is it for the same despair which is in me, or for dullness of perception? Since I love them, I cannot conceal the truth from them, – every step of cognition leads them up to this truth. And the truth is death.'

'Art, poetry?' For a long time, under the influence of the success of human praise, I tried to persuade myself that that was a thing which could be done, even though death should come and destroy everything, my deeds, as well as my memory of them; but soon I came to see that that, too, was a deception. It was clear to me that art was an adornment of life, a decoy of life. But life lost all its attractiveness for me. How, then, could I entrap others? So long as I did not live my own life, and a strange life bore me on its waves; so long as I believed that life had some sense, although I was not able to express it, – the reflections of life of every description in poetry and in the arts afforded me pleasure, and I was delighted to look at life through this little mirror of art; but when I began to look for the meaning of life, when I experienced the necessity of living myself, that little mirror became either useless, superfluous and ridiculous, or painful to me. [. . .]

'Well, I know', I said to myself, 'all which science wants so persistently to know, but there is no answer to the question about the meaning of my life.' But in the speculative sphere I saw that, in spite of the fact that the aim of the knowledge was directed straight to the answer of my question, or because of that fact, there could be no other answer than what I was giving to myself: 'What is the meaning of my life?' – 'None.' Or, 'What will come of my life?' – 'Nothing.' Or, 'Why does everything which exists exist, and why do I exist?' – 'Because it exists.' [. . .]

Rational knowledge in the person of the learned and the wise denied the meaning of life, but the enormous masses of men, all humanity, recognized this meaning in an irrational knowledge. This irrational knowledge was faith, the same that I could not help but reject. That was God as one and three, the creation in six days, devils and angels, and all that which I could not accept so long as I had not lost my senses.

My situation was a terrible one. I knew that I should not find anything on the path of rational knowledge but the negation of life, and there, in faith, nothing but the negation of reason, which was still more impossible than the negation of life. From the rational knowledge it followed that life was an evil and men knew it, – it depended on men whether they should cease living, and yet they lived and continued to live, and I myself lived, though I had known long ago that life was meaningless and an evil. From faith it followed that, in order to understand life, I must renounce reason, for which alone a meaning was needed.

PART 2   PREPARING FOR DEATH

Introduction

The remaining three parts of this Reader follow a chronological pattern: preparing for death in Part 2, caring for dying people in Part 3, and bereavement in Part 4.

'Preparing for Death' is perhaps a slightly ambiguous title for Part 2. To avoid confusion, we should make it plain that this is no 'how-to' manual. The readings in Part 2 are concerned with some of the great uncertainties which people confront in facing death. This part deals primarily with the period when serious illness is perhaps suspected but not definitively diagnosed, or when the diagnosis is known to be terminal but the prognosis is not certain.

In facing death, people confront not only what are sometimes called the 'existential uncertainties' – those about the very meaning of existence – but also other doubts: about whether they *are* seriously ill, about what to do in relation to family or work responsibilities, about the likely course of their illness, about whether to consent to particular kinds of treatment, about whether to contemplate organ donation. Those caring for them must also consider other ethical, legal and professional questions: whether it is ever right to impose treatments paternalistically, how to deal with disagreement in the care team, whether it is ever permitted to assist death.

These kinds of uncertainties are illustrated with great immediacy by the example of Alzheimer's disease in 'My husband the stranger', a first-person account by Elizabeth Forsythe. Forsythe is frank about her own uncertainties and ignorance in trying to decide whether her husband's increasingly strange behaviour was or was not dementia. She speaks honestly about her negative feelings, including bewilderment, anger and her own temporary breakdown, as well as her conviction that caring for a person dying with Alzheimer's disease can heal as well as hurt. 'His dying brought us back together again after many years of difficulty and much distress. [. . .] Watching the disintegration of somebody close and experiencing it within yourself is painful, but in the end all the anguish need not be a waste,' she concludes.

Much literature on caring for dying people tends to assume that the terminally ill and their carers are plaster saints; we felt that it was important to give a more realistic picture in this book. Tillie Olsen's 'Tell me a riddle' is a moving fictional account of another difficult relationship in which the couple must eventually confront the terminal illness of one partner. The elderly Russian Jewish immigrant couple whom Olsen describes with poetry and precision salvage some tenderness from their anger.

Another first-person account, Clare Williams's 'Learning the hard way', also expresses realism and acceptance. Clare Williams was diagnosed HIV-positive after rape. The theme of social death comes across clearly in her account: 'I'm "one of them". The sort of people who, if they admit to their condition, may lose their job, their partner, may watch friends disinfecting the cups they have drunk from and find their best friend suddenly won't let them into the same room as her newborn baby – "I feel awful, but you know how it is."' But she also expresses a heightened zest for life: 'My life is fuller now – I daren't waste a second. That sort of thing sounds a cliché until it applies to you.'

The first three articles in Part 2 show the enormous diversity of reaction from dying people to their terminal illness. The next two articles both concern how professionals can deal with dying people in ways which respect them as persons and allow that diversity to flourish. 'Professionalism and paternalism', by Dennis F. Thompson, and 'Paternalism and moral deficiency', by R.S. Downie and K.C. Calman, consider whether it is ever right to override dying people's wishes 'in their best interests'. If telling dying patients the truth about their condition and detailing the risks of various interventions could increase their anxiety and make them less willing to undergo treatment, is the health care professional justified in telling less than the whole truth?

Truth-telling and lying are also the themes of two articles written especially for this Reader: Basiro Davey's 'The nurse's dilemma: truthtelling or big white lies?' and Alan Ryan's 'Professional liars'. Davey studied communication procedures in a district general hospital in the south of England, using in-depth interviews with qualified and student nurses and with junior and senior doctors. She found that the majority of nurses were critical of the general standard of communication between staff and patients, and between doctors and nurses. All the nurses in the study identified an unspoken rule laid down by most doctors which required them either to evade patients' direct questions about their condition or to lie to patients. Doctors, however, varied considerably in their willingness to allow nurses to be 'straight' with patients; but even those who favoured truth-telling by nurses had often failed to tell the nurses that they had no objection. Davey found that a model of benevolent paternalism was still operating in this fairly typical hospital, although most literature in medical ethics now treats paternalism as 'over the hill'.

Alan Ryan's 'Professional liars' is an innovative exploration of ways in which we could move beyond a simple truth-telling or lying dichotomy. Ryan suggests that professionals should help patients to construct the narrative of their own dying which fits their lives. This will entail a standard of truth-telling which is geared to their relationship with *this particular* patient, not with some generalized model patient. Thus Ryan's article slots in nicely with the three accounts at the start of this part, depicting very different reactions to imminent death from three very different patients. Each of those three – John Forsythe, the nameless dying woman in 'Tell me a riddle' and Clare Williams – could be seen as constructing their own version of what Ryan calls 'a narrative of endurance and death'.

'Organ transplants' by David Lamb and 'Dying to help: moral questions in organ procurement' by Martyn Evans – two more articles commissioned especially for this Reader – are also concerned with valuing the uniqueness of the dying person. Lamb looks in some detail at the practices and beliefs of particular religious and cultural communities regarding organ transplants, and considers the morality of some procedures of organ procurement, particularly the buying and selling of organs. Evans focuses on the difficult question of how nurses and other care-givers should respond to a 'potential' donor, that is, a brainstem-dead person being maintained on a ventilator. Uncomfortable issues arise because the person continues to look alive but is clinically dead. And how should health care professionals balance the interests of the potential recipient against those of their ostensible patient, the donor?

The next four articles all concern the difficult questions surrounding letting die or terminating care. 'The living will in clinical practice', written for this Reader by Ursula Gallagher, who has a background in primary care nursing, suggests ways in which advance directives might be used to give effect to dying people's previously expressed wishes about refusing painful or burdensome interventions, even when patients are no longer legally 'competent'. The living will, an information directive, and the enduring power of attorney, a directive by which people nominate a proxy to take decisions for them if they become incompetent, are said by their proponents to enhance the autonomy of dying people. Respect for dying people is also the concern of Henk ten Have's scepticism about the Dutch system in his factual report 'Euthanasia in the Netherlands'. But the discussion paper by the Institute of Medical Ethics Working Party on Prolonging Life and Assisting Death, which follows it, concludes that assisting death would actually *enhance* the autonomy of dying people. The debate continues in a reply to the Institute Working Party's discussion paper by a hospice physician, Dr Robert G. Twycross.

The great ethical uncertainties such as whether it is ever right to assist death sometimes cause understandable moral distress in carers and conflict on care teams. 'A student's story', an anonymous first-person account, was written for a workshop in which nurses were encouraged to share stories about such difficult moral problems in their own experience. The incident, which occurred sixteen years beforehand, still causes the author guilt and moral grief. This powerful account underlines how important it is to take ethical issues and carers' moral qualms seriously, along with those of dying people.

This part ends with an article written especially for the Reader by a doctor, Gwen Adshead, and a health care ethicist, Donna Dickenson, 'Why do doctors and nurses disagree?' The article explores the issue of why doctors and nurses, in particular, often disagree about ethical issues in caring for the terminally ill. Adshead and Dickenson suggest that nurses have a different kind of relationship with the patient from doctors; that the two professions have very different role models and training procedures; that the female role model in nursing and the male model in medicine could be expected to cause conflict, according to recent work in developmental psychology; and that the caring–curing distinction both reflects and engenders conflict between the professions. Only by acknowledging such potential disagreements in the face of the massive uncertainties surrounding death can professionals create reflective practice which serves the real needs of dying people.

20

My husband the stranger

Elizabeth Forsythe

Large parts of John's life were always secret; I believe they remained hidden even from himself. Since his death, in 1986, I have come to see his illness and its conclusion as a development of the sort of person he was. [. . .]

I think that he was by nature a solitary person, although at times, on the surface, he seemed to enjoy being with people. During the war his talent for languages was of use in the intelligence service, and his attachment to various embassies helped him develop a role of easy sociability and charm which became useful later when he returned to business life. His inner solitariness seemed to need the protection of a superficial gregariousness. By the end of his life his solitariness was uppermost and in his dementia he became totally isolated and unreachable.

When we married, he was 45 and I was 28. To me he remained extraordinarily remote, in many ways essentially a stranger. He was a successful businessman and esteemed by his colleagues; yet there was always the sense that he was acting a role. He had expensive and immaculate business suits but would then wear a shabby tweed coat over the top and a rather battered felt hat. [. . .]

He had the expatriate Scot's longing to return to his homeland. In 1969 we bought some land and ruins in the far north-east of Scotland, and in due course built a beautiful house overlooking a harbour and the Moray Firth. I moved up there with our three children in 1973 and John should have retired and come to live there the following year; but sadly many things happened, including changes in his firm. He did not retire until five years later, though this was apparently not his decision.

It is difficult, looking back on the life of somebody who develops Alzheimer's disease, to be able to say, 'Yes, it started at such and such a time.' This was so in John's life. Hindsight makes it easy to say that John was not at all the same person outwardly when he retired in 1978 as he was when we made the decision to move to the far north of Scotland in 1969. Looking back now, I am sure that by 1978 his

---

Extract from *Alzheimer's Disease: The Long Bereavement*, London: Faber & Faber, 1990.

'normal' solitariness had tipped into an abnormal sort of isolation which progressed into dementia.

Early that year, while John was still working in London and living in our earlier home near Cambridge, he suddenly developed a severe pain in his back. He stayed on his own in bed for a number of days before deciding to make the long journey north. He arrived on the night sleeper in Inverness and was exhausted, in a lot of pain and very depressed. He was admitted to an orthopaedic ward for diagnosis and treatment. After a week he was discharged in more or less the same state and came home to Caithness for a period of rest. Certainly he was in pain and in great distress; but he was also, quite uncharacteristically, depressed and tearful. He did not want me out of his sight and kept saying that he had spent all his life worrying about possessions and ignoring people. He seemed very sad that he had had so little time for his family during his working life. [. . .]

I shall never know whether these months prior to his return to London were the onset of Alzheimer's disease or a depressive illness; perhaps the distinction is unimportant. Certainly something profound and disturbing was occurring in John's mind. Although he was depressed while he was at home with his painful back, he had hopes and aspirations for his retirement which were different from his previous way of living. For many weeks we were extraordinarily close. It really did seem to be a turning point in his life and in our relationship.

I did not see John for several weeks after his return to London; when we did meet, he was once again a distant stranger and there was no more talk of spending time together.

In retrospect, some indication of his worsening condition might have been given by his attitude to money. John had had a substantial 'golden handshake' from his firm on his retirement. Early in 1978, during his week of 'depression', he had told me about the money and said that he intended to make two trusts: one to pay for the university education of our children and the other for an annuity for me because his work pension did not make provision for his widow, and with our age difference it was likely that I should outlive him.

After his return to London he spoke no more about these provisions. When two of the children started at university in the autumn of 1978, he said that he did not have enough money to help them and did not mention his capital sum or his earlier plans. He had always been secretive about money, and I had never known what his financial position was or how much he earned. From the time of the move to Caithness I had always been short of money and did some part-time work to help with household bills. His sudden announcement that he was not able to make any contribution to our son and daughter's upkeep at university came as an amazing blow and I could think of no way of supporting them. [. . .]

The stranger with some sense of familiarity had gone and a stranger with a chilling feel of remoteness seemed to have arrived in his place. I found myself alone, very far from relatives and friends of long standing, with somebody who apparently wished to be entirely isolated both physically and emotionally. I became full of fear, for him, for the children, for myself and for the future. John now believed that I was responsible for any problems that he had in his retirement and this was because I was English.

Had he really changed, or was I different, and was there any way out of this nightmare? I could not find out, and at the end of 1980 I had a severe breakdown and went into hospital. John said that he wanted a divorce and did not want me to come home. I returned to the south on my own without job, money, home, husband, family, possessions or any understanding of what had been happening.

It was a time of great confusion and it did not then occur to me that John might be mentally disturbed, because I had been so obviously mentally ill myself.

From then on John made no contact with me. The following year he sold the house and moved to a London suburb to be near a cousin; but he did not send me money from the sale of the house, as he had previously agreed to do. I managed to get part-time work, rented a cottage, and the children continued at university without any financial support from John. He would not let me know his new address or his telephone number. I had no understanding of what had happened and in the end I tried not to think too much about him. I had to struggle with my own depression and work.

Two years later our son graduated from Edinburgh University and wanted both his parents to be at the ceremony. Peter had seen John at various times and found him a bit difficult and demanding. I had a shock when I met John that day. He looked a lot older: he was very preoccupied with his poor eyesight, and seemed convinced that he was going blind (he had always had very healthy eyes). John and I spent the afternoon together. Walking back to the hotel where I was staying, I realized that he was totally preoccupied with himself. These hours together had the sense of being in a dream and I seemed able to enter into his world and see it as he saw it.

It was a very frightening world. John believed that he was being pestered with people demanding money from him and sending him bills for things which he had never had. I do not know if I thought that this was the truth but I took everything he said as such because it was clearly what he believed to be true at that time. I had felt threatened by his strange view of reality but now I was no longer dependent upon him, and the physical and emotional distance made my understanding greater. [. . .]

A year after the meeting in Edinburgh, Peter was trying to equip a flat and asked John if he had any surplus household equipment. John said that he could take a van and meet him outside his flat. When Peter arrived, John said that he could only give him very little because all his possessions had been stolen. We thought that he was not being very generous and possibly even a little devious; now I realize that these delusions were an essential part of his dementia.

The 'crisis', the point at which some sort of intervention was unavoidable, came in the summer of 1985. He was still driving his car, and caused an accident. The police went to his flat to interview him but probably realized that he was not able to give evidence and finally dropped any charges against him. His driving licence was confiscated. His cousin kept in touch with me and finally wanted me to go and see him. I had not previously been to John's flat but it was immediately identifiable by all the locks, spy-holes on the door and strange signs and messages about where to put things. I could hear John walking about inside but it was about ten minutes before he came to the door. I could see him looking through one of the spy-holes and then he finally opened the door a crack while it was still chained. He did not appear to recognize me and was very suspicious. I just kept talking and eventually he let me in.

It was the middle of a rather hot afternoon, but all the curtains were drawn, some of the windows were shuttered and the heating was on. He was partly dressed and took me all the way through the flat to the furthest room, which was his bedroom. It was blacked out, the electric lights were on and it was overpoweringly hot. The room was in a chaotic state, the bed unmade and the sheets filthy. He told me to sit down and indicated one of the two large director-type chairs in the room. Then he told me not to sit down but to put a towel on the seat first. He sat down and kept talking in a distracted way and looking at me with a puzzled expression but without recognition. I could not believe that this sad and mad old man was really my husband.

Eventually he went to a shelf, picked up a photograph of me, brought it over and thrust it at me, rather as a small child would, and told me that it was Elizabeth. I tried to explain that certainly it was a photograph of Elizabeth and that was me, his wife. He did not seem able to put these two ideas together. [. . .]

We walked the short distance to his cousin's together, but what two years previously had been a slow walk was now a shuffle. It was devastating.

John was obviously in need of help. His cousin was alone, following a series of bereavements, and wanted him to stay near her in his own flat, although his condition was deteriorating; but she did not want to have full responsibility for him. No one knew if he had any money, so that we were not able to employ help or begin to investigate the possibility of moving him to a home. I felt overwhelmed by the horror of the situation.

John had continued to go for private annual medical check-ups and always told his cousin that he was 100 per cent fit. He refused, however, to see his general practitioner. When I got home I telephoned the GP to see if he could suggest any solution. At first it was impossible to speak to him. I wrote and received no answer.

In September 1985 I spent a few days with one of my wisest friends, whose mother had had dementia. It was three days before I could bring myself to speak about John because I felt so distressed and guilty about the whole problem. She helped enormously by telling me, among other things, about power of attorney and the Court of Protection.

I had still not managed to speak to John's doctor. Apart from my own judgement that his mind was disturbed, I had no medical or any other professional support.

Eventually I managed to make an appointment to see John's GP. I discovered that at each medical check-up there had been comments about John's deteriorating mental state, but his doctor said that as there was nothing he could do to help he had not contacted him. He was not enthusiastic about getting a psychogeriatrician to him. Nothing was settled.

John began wandering at night. The police brought him back to his cousin, who telephoned me. I suggested that it might be better if, instead of having him back in his flat, he might be persuaded to go into a nursing home. She refused to say to anybody apart from myself that she could not cope.

Finally I consulted a very compassionate solicitor, the first professional person I had met who actually knew what he was doing and could bring all the relevant problems together and begin to resolve them. John's doctor had to sign a form to say that John was not capable of managing his own affairs. This he would not do and the delay ran into months. I telephoned and wrote to him but he continued to procrastinate.

The legal profession cannot act until the medical profession commits itself to a diagnosis and signs forms to that effect. Eventually I did persuade John's general practitioner to arrange a home visit from a psychogeriatrician. It was confirmed that John had some sort of dementia. The question of whether he should be temporarily admitted to a mental hospital was discussed with the consultant, but no decision was taken.

It became clear that John could no longer live on his own. After a visit from a social worker, it was arranged that he should be taken to a mental hospital. The GP had finally been persuaded to sign the papers for the Court of Protection. While John was in hospital I managed to get down to his flat and, with the help of a social worker, go through some of his things and begin to get his financial affairs into some semblance of order. We realized that he could afford to go into a comfortable nursing home. I decided that as John's cousin wanted him to be near her, we should look for a nursing home in that area. We found one which appeared to be good and comfortable. He could have a large, ground-floor room with his own furniture, bathroom and a door into a walled garden.

Three weeks after John had been admitted, the agreed fee which I was paying rose sharply without any prior information. I felt an unease which later showed itself to be justified. I contacted the nursing home and discovered it had changed hands. A medical friend told me about a recently opened mental nursing home in Norfolk which had an excellent reputation. I went and saw it and was most impressed with the staff and the general atmosphere.

Suddenly I knew what had to be done in John's best interests and I had a great sense of urgency. It is a pity that I had not had the confidence to make John's interests of paramount importance long before this. I arranged for a medical agency to move him from one nursing home to the other – a considerable distance. The director thought that an ambulance might frighten John and sent his own car with two nurses, one of whom was a trained mental nurse; the other acted as driver. I went down with them. When I went into the nursing home I did not recognize John. He was totally rigid, could barely shuffle, was unable to swallow, so that his saliva was running down his face, and he was a strange sallow colour. He looked like a living corpse. [. . .]

The journey took about four hours but it seemed never-ending. He was so rigid that we had to bend him quite hard to get him into the car. I sat beside him on the back seat and kept looking at him to see if he was still breathing. It was very difficult to see if he was or not. His face was expressionless and the only signs of life was the slightest flicker of his eyelids from time to time.

In previous years we had spent a lot of time in Norfolk on holiday. As we started driving through Thetford Forest, I was aware of some sort of increased life in John. He did not move his head but his eyes seemed to be looking through the windows and I told him where we were and reminded him of all the previous times when we had driven along that road. We arrived at the nursing home and he was welcomed and made comfortable. The matron was horrified by the state he was in and thought that he had probably had too many drugs. This was later confirmed by their doctor. He had drug-induced Parkinsonism.

John lived for another six months. I think that for much of that time he was reasonably happy and at times I caught glimpses of a smile of recognition. Three years later I wish that I had abandoned every other activity and just spent as much time as possible with him during those months. I think that it is important to spend time with somebody who is dementing – for your own sake, if not for theirs. It is easy to say that John did not know who I was. I understand now that every small thing I did for him during those last months helped me sort out my own confused feelings about him. In the simple acts of feeding him or helping him dress or just sitting and holding his hand, I could rekindle some of the love and tenderness I had once felt for him.

One problem was that he became very spiteful as he became more active. Sometimes he would do nothing but hit, punch and pinch. Obviously I found this very distressing. He did talk a little, but it was almost impossible to understand anything of what he was saying, although at times a few words were clear.

His physical deterioration accelerated, and in October 1986 he died. Although he had not known who I was for more than a year, during his dying I know that he knew who I was, and could understand something that I wanted to say to him before we parted. His dying brought us back together again after many years of difficulty and much distress.

Three years later, I am better able to understand the damage that was done to John, to me, to our family and friends through ignorance about dementia – my own ignorance, and also that of John's GP. That ignorance perpetuated my own confusion, guilt and inability to believe that I was capable of doing anything positive. John's disintegration was a threat to my own integrity: accepting that this was so has brought the opportunity to understand a great deal about myself,and in so doing to improve my relationships with those around me. Watching the disintegration of somebody close and experiencing it within yourself is painful, but in the end all the anguish need not be a waste.

21

Tell me a riddle

Tillie Olsen

For forty-seven years they had been married. How deep back the stubborn, gnarled roots of the quarrel reached, no one could say – but only now, when tending to the needs of others no longer shackled them together, the roots welled up visible, split the earth between them, and the tearing shook even to the children, long since grown.

Why now, why now? wailed Hannah.

As if when we grew up weren't enough, said Paul.

Poor Ma. Poor Dad. It hurts so for both of them, said Vivi. They never had very much; at least in old age they should be happy.

Knock their heads together, insisted Sammy; tell 'em: you're too old for this kind of thing; no reason not to get along now.

Lennie wrote to Clara: They've lived over so much together; what could possibly tear them apart?

Something tangible enough.

Arthritic hands, and such work as he got, occasional. Poverty all his life, and there was little breath left for running. He could not, could not turn away from this desire: to have the troubling of responsibility, the fretting with money, over and done with; to be free, to be *care*free where success was not measured by accumulation, and there was use for the vitality still in him.

There was a way. They could sell the house, and with the money join his lodge's Haven, co-operative for the aged. Happy communal life, and was he not already an official; had he not helped organize it, raise funds, served as a trustee?

But she – would not consider it. [. . .]

Over the dishes, coaxingly: 'For once in your life, to be free, to have everything done for you, like a queen.'

'I never liked queens.'

'No dishes, no garbage, no towel to sop, no worry what to buy, what to eat.'

'And what else would I do with my empty hands? Better to eat at my own table when I want, and to cook and eat how I want.'

Extract from *Tell Me a Riddle*, London: Virago, 1971, pp. 76-90 (abridged).

'In the cottages they buy what you ask, and cook it how you like. *You* are the one who always used to say, better humankind born without mouths and stomachs than always to worry for money to buy, to shop, to fix, to cook, to wash, to clean.' [. . .]

'Let me alone about money. Was there ever enough? Seven little ones – for every penny I had to ask – and sometimes, remember, there was nothing. But always *I* had to manage. Now *you* manage. Rub your nose in it good.'

But from those years she had had to manage, old humiliations and terrors rose up, lived again, and forced her to relive them. The children's needings; the grocer's face or this merchant's wife she had had to beg credit from when credit was a disgrace, the scenery of the long blocks walked around when she could not pay; school coming, and the desperate going over the old to see what could yet be remade; the soups of meat bones begged 'for-the-dog' one winter. . . .

Enough. Now they had no children. Let *him* wrack his head for how they would live. She would not exchange her solitude for anything. *Never again to be forced to move to the rhythms of others.* [. . .]

And it came to where every happening lashed up a quarrel.

'I will sell the house anyway,' he flung at her one night. 'I am putting it up for sale. There will be a way to make you sign.'

The television blared, as always it did on the evenings he stayed home, and as always it reached her only as noise. She did not know if the tumult was in her or outside. Snap! she turned the sound off. 'Shadows,' she whispered to him, pointing to the screen, 'look, it is only shadows.' And in a scream: 'Did you say that you will sell the house? Look at me, not at that. I am no shadow. You cannot sell without me.' [. . .]

She did not know if the tumult was outside, or in her. Always a ravening inside, a pull to the bed, to lie down, to succumb.

'Have you thought maybe Ma should let a doctor have a look at her?' asked their son Paul after Sunday dinner, regarding his mother crumpled on the couch, instead of, as was her custom, busying herself in Nancy's kitchen.

'Why not the President too?'

'Seriously, Dad. This is the third Sunday she's lain down like that after dinner. Is she that way at home?'

'A regular love affair with the bed. Every time I start to talk to her.'

Good protective reaction, observed Nancy to herself. The workings of hos-til-ity.

'Nancy could take her. I just don't like how she looks. Let's have Nancy arrange an appointment.' [. . .]

'It's all of a piece when you think of it,' said Nancy, 'the way she attacks my kitchen, scrubbing under every cup hook, doing the inside of the oven so I can't enjoy Sunday dinner, knowing that half-blind or not, she's going to find every speck of dirt. . . .'

'Don't, Nancy, I've told you – it's the only way she knows to be useful. What did the *doctor* say?'

'A real fatherly lecture. Sixty-nine is young these days. Go out, enjoy life, find interests. Get a new hearing aid, this one is antiquated. Old age is sickness only if one makes it so. Geriatrics, Inc.'

'So there was nothing physical.'

'Of course there was. How can you live to yourself like she does without there being? Evidence of a kidney disorder; and her blood count is low. He gave her a diet, and she's to come back for follow-up and lab work. . . . But he was clear enough: Number One prescription – start living like a human being. When I think of your dad, who could really play the invalid with that arthritis of his as active as a teenager, and twice as much fun. . . .'

'You didn't tell me the doctor says your sickness is in you, how you live.' He pushed his advantage. 'Life and enjoyments you need better than medicine. And this diet, how can you keep it? To weigh each morsel and scrape away the bits of fat to make this soup, that pudding. There, at the Haven, they have a dietician, they would do it for you.'

She is silent.

'You would feel better there, I know it,' he says gently. 'There there is life and enjoyments all around.'

'What is the matter, Mr Important-and-busy, you have no card game or meeting you can go to?' – turning her face to the pillow. [. . .]

A bellyful of bitterness and every day the same quarrel in a new way and a different old grievance the quarrel forced her to enter and relive. And the new torment: I am not really sick, the doctor said it, then why do I feel so sick?

One night she asked him: 'You have a meeting tonight? Do not go. Stay . . . with me.'

He had planned to watch *This Is Your Life* anyway, but half sick himself from the heavy heat, and sickening therefore the more after the brooks and woods of the Haven, with satisfaction he grated:

'Hah, Mrs Live Alone And Like It wants company all of a sudden. [. . .] "Do not go. Stay with me." A new song for Mrs Free As A Bird. Yes, I am going out, and while I am gone chew this aloneness good, and think how you keep us both from where if you want people you do not need to be alone.'

'Go, go. All your life you have gone without me.' [. . .]

She was not in their bed when he came back. She lay on the cot on the sun-porch. All week she did not speak or come near him; nor did he try to make peace or care for her.

He slept badly, so used to her next to him. After all the years, old harmonies and dependencies deep in their bodies; she curled to him, or he coiled to her, each warmed, warming, turning as the other turned, the nights a long embrace.

It was not the empty bed or the storm that woke him, but a faint singing. *She* was singing. Shaking off the drops of rain, the lightning riving her lifted face, he saw her so; the cot covers on the floor.

'This a private concert?' he asked. 'Come in, you are wet.'

'I can breathe now,' she answered; 'my lungs are rich.' Though indeed the sound was hardly a breath.

'Come in, come in.' Loosing the bamboo shades.

'Look how wet you are.' Half helping, half carrying her, still faint-breathing her song.

A Russian love song of fifty years ago. [. . .]

'There was something after all,' Paul told Nancy in a colourless voice. 'That was Hannah's Phil calling. Her gall bladder. . . . Surgery.'

'Her *gall* bladder. If that isn't classic. "Bitter as gall" - talk of psychosom — '

He stepped closer, put his hand over her mouth and said in the same colourless, plodding voice. 'We have to get Dad. They operated at once. The cancer was everywhere, surrounding the liver, everywhere. They did what they could . . . at best she has a year. Dad . . . we have to tell him.' [. . .]

22

Learning the hard way

Clare Williams

I still have that photo of myself, taken eleven months ago. Taken moments before my life changed irrevocably. I'd been standing in the street with a friend who wanted to finish his film. There I am, dressed in jeans and a scarlet teeshirt, with my hair falling over my face.

I haven't changed. I still have that shirt, those jeans. My hair still falls over my face. But now I am fundamentally different. Minutes after that photo was taken, I walked into the clinic outside which I had been standing, where I was told that I had the HIV virus. And now things will never be the same again. Not only am I a year older – I'm 23 now – but I'm 'one of them'. The sort of people who, if they admit to their condition, may lose their job, their partner, may watch friends disinfecting the cups they have drunk from and find their best friend suddenly won't let them into the same room as her newborn baby – 'I feel awful, but you know how it is.'

Then there are the friends who make sure they phone every couple of weeks; who ask you to godmother their children; who will cuddle you for hours while you cry at the sheer unfairness of it all.

I don't know how I picked up the virus, why my life is now full of catch phrases like 'T-helper cells' or why I am now a threat to some of my oldest friends. I look the same as I did eleven months ago, I still fall in love, I still enjoy long suppers with friends over a bottle or three of wine. I'm still the same person. It is your society, my society, that sees me as different, as a threat to your cosy way of life. I'm a 23-year-old, heterosexual, non-drug-using, safe sex practitioner.

I'm a child of the AIDS age, you see. I know the dangers. I had unprotected sex once – I was raped and I didn't really get the chance to ask my attacker if he'd be so kind as to wear a condom. So henceforth my blood will test sero-positive; I have HIV.

Obviously things are no longer straightforward. I meet someone I like, we have dinner a few times, then the inevitable suggestion comes – 'Bacon and eggs or just toast for breakfast?' So do I tell him, or trust to the safety of the condom? So far, I've always been honest. In fact, the ignorance and complacency of people terrifies me. When will

From *The Guardian*, 'First Person', 29 May 1991.

people realize that we are all at risk? If I can get HIV, then everyone can.

And then, of course, there is the big question: how to tell people. At first I told no one, not even my partner, and my family still have no idea, but I want my friends to know, even though actually telling them is so difficult. I find myself sounding out their views; how much they know about AIDS, whether they would realize I am no threat to them, how discreet they will be.

Yet it isn't all bad news. My life is fuller now - I daren't waste a second. That sort of thing sounds like a cliché until it applies to you. Losing my job was a blessing; I decided to go to college. My relationships are far more intense now. I go to the theatre, the cinema, the ballet as often as I can - I've a lifetime of happiness to fit into maybe ten years. I surround myself with the people I love and feel a new freedom to ignore those I don't. I now make the most of everything.

You don't appreciate life until you think it's going to be taken away. I feel that I've been given a second chance to live as wonderful a life as I can. In so many ways, I'm very lucky.

23

Professionalism and paternalism

Dennis F. Thompson

It may be argued that the relationship between a professional and a client is justifiable paternalism if it is paternalism at all. By enlisting the help of a professional, the client demonstrates that he lacks essential knowledge that only the professional can provide; the professional intervenes in limited and foreseen ways, and promotes a good, such as health or legal redress, that the client obviously accepts. Since a client voluntarily chooses the professional, can refuse his advice, and can go to another professional, we may suppose that the client, in effect, consents to whatever restrictions on his liberty the professional may impose.

This voluntaristic portrait of the relationship between a client and a professional neglects some features of professionalism that can give rise to paternalism. A profession is characterized, inter alia, by claims to a body of knowledge and specialized training; a monopoly over the training and practice of the profession (including self-regulation); and a social prestige that further enhances the authority of its members (Greenwood, 1966: 12–16; Wasserstrom, 1975: 2n; Larson, 1977: x). The client's ignorance that sometimes justifies paternalism also restricts the ability to choose among professionals, and to decide whether to follow professional advice. Abetted by the profession's claim to superior knowledge, a professional may be inclined to intervene in ways less limited than are actually called for by the client's circumstances. Professionals, for what they believe to be their client's own good, may, for example, withhold certain information, prescribe treatment, or provide services without the client's knowledge (Greenwood, 1966: 12; Larson, 1977: 220–5; Hughes, 1963: 2–3). Although the client usually agrees with the general goal promoted by the profession (health, justice, welfare), professionals pursue these goals in many different ways, some of which a particular client may not accept, but is powerless to defy. To seek a second opinion, to engage another professional, or to charge malpractice is often very difficult. The client must challenge not merely an individual

Extract from 'Paternalism in medicine, law and public policy', in Daniel Callahan and Sissela Bok (eds), *Ethics Teaching in Higher Education*, New York: Plenum Press, Hastings Center Publication, 1980, pp. 256–60 (abridged).

professional, but an institutionalized profession that in principle claims to be the exclusive arbiter of its members' competence, and in practice rallies to protect its members from criticism. Given the unequal roles of the professional and the client, it is not surprising that professionals restrict their client's liberty sometimes in ways that go beyond the limits and purposes of justifiable paternalism. This excessive paternalism is not a logically necessary consequence of professionalism, however, and in recent years many people, including professionals themselves, have urged changes in the relationship between professionals and their clients, to reduce or eliminate paternalism (Cumont, 1970: 26–31).

The salient feature of the traditional model of the relationship between doctor and patient is, according to many writers, 'paternalistic benevolence' (Barber, 1976; *Yale Law Journal*, 1972). The doctor's superior professional knowledge and altruistic intentions, on this view, warrant acting in a patient's interest without fully informing the patient of the nature of the diagnosis or the treatment, if the doctor believes that the health of the patient is best served in this way. In extreme cases, the doctor may use deception and even subtle forms of coercion to secure a patient's compliance. [. . .] A doctor who adopts a paternalistic attitude may violate a patient's liberty by restricting the range of choices that he can make. Although the doctor may know best what treatment is most appropriate for a specific pathology, he or she does not necessarily know best how information or treatment will affect a patient's whole well-being. Although the doctor may find it difficult to explain to a patient the diagnosis and the options for treatment, he can usually give much more complete and honest explanations than the traditional model demands (Bok, 1978: 220–41; Reiser et al., 1977). Similarly, the notion that the relationship between doctor and patient rests on a contract in which the patient at least temporarily surrenders his autonomy to the doctor has been criticized for, among other things, implying that the doctor is accountable to no one but himself and the standards of the profession (Masters, 1975: 26–8; May, 1975: 36). Furthermore, several empirical studies have shown that, the more fully a doctor explains a diagnosis and treatment, the more likely the patient is to comply with the doctor's instructions, and to be satisfied with the treatment (Schmidt, 1977; Duff and Hollingshead, 1968: 280ff.; Plaut, 1975). Proponents of a more participatory model of the doctor–patient relationship propose measures such as a Patient's Bill of Rights, a Patient Rights Advocate and changes in professional education and standards to encourage doctors to consult more openly with their patients, and recognize their professional ethics to be part of a universal ethics that creates a presumption against paternalism (Margolis, 1978; Annas and Healey, 1974; Veatch, 1972). [. . .] All of these proposals seek to foster a doctor–patient relationship in which a patient's ignorance and a doctor's unilateral actions and neglect of a patient's own views about his welfare are kept to a minimum – in short, a relationship that is as little paternalistic as possible. [. . .]

Yet another kind of professional relationship – between social worker and client – has been criticized for excessive paternalism (Miller, 1968; Haug and Sussman, 1969: 156–9; Glasser, 1978: 107–8, 118–9). Added to the paternalistic tendencies of professionalism are further effects that flow from the social worker's position as an agent of the government. Because the social worker must follow general policies set by government, he or she may not be able to define the client's good exclusively as the client might (Piliavin, 1968: 35–7). In the process of helping the client, the social worker may also change 'the client's attitudes and conduct so that he conforms more closely to expected and accepted patterns of behavior' (Toren, 1974: 343). The process bristles with the dangers of self-justifying paternalism. Furthermore, because clients are typically poor, and members of minority groups, the inequalities of class and race exacerbate the inequalities of professionalism. To counter what has been called 'welfare paternalism', reformers have urged greater participation by clients in the agencies that social workers and other professionals now dominate, stronger statements of the rights of clients, various legal protections, including welfare rights advocates, and the separation of income maintenance from the other services, so that a citizen may obtain the former without the latter (Paull, 1967: 104ff.; Ad Hoc Committee on Advocacy, 1969: 19–20; Miller, 1968: 30–1, 33; Glasser, 1978: 146ff.). [. . .] Others have warned that these reforms may go too far. In their efforts to exorcize the baleful aspect of paternalism, the reformers have forgotten that the paternalism of social work has a benign side. At least ideally, the social worker brings professional skills and a sense of caring that can genuinely benefit clients. [. . .] Here, as in other professional relationships, the problem is not to embrace or eradicate paternalism totally, but to locate its justifiable limits.

References

Ad Hoc Committee on Advocacy (1969) 'The social worker as advocate', *Social Work*, 14.
Annas, George J. and Healey, Joseph M. (1974) 'The Patient Rights Advocate: redefining the doctor-patient relationship in the hospital context', *Vanderbilt Law Review*, 27: 243–69.
Barber, Bernard (1976) 'Compassion in medicine: toward new definitions and new institutions', *New England Journal of Medicine*, 295: 939–40.
Bok, Sissela (1978) *Lying: Moral Choice in Public and Private Life*. Hassocks, Sussex: Harvester Press.
Cumont, Matthew P. (1970) 'The changing face of professionalism', *Social Policy*, 1: 26–31.
Duff, R. and Hollingshead, A. (1968) *Sickness and Society*. New York: Harper & Row.
Glasser, Ira (1978) 'Prisoners of benevolence: power versus liberty in the welfare state',

in Willard Gaylin et al. (eds), *Doing Good: the Limits of Benevolence*. New York: Pantheon Books.

Greenwood, Ernest (1966) 'The elements of professionalization', in H.M. Vollmer and D.L. Mills (eds), *Professionalization*. Englewood Cliffs, NJ: Prentice-Hall. pp. 12-16.

Haug, Marie R. and Sussman, Marvin E. (1969) 'Professional autonomy and the revolt of the client', *Social Problems*, 71: 156-9.

Hughes, Everett C. (1963) 'Professions', in Kenneth Lynn et al. (eds), *The Professions in America*. Boston, MA: Beacon Press. pp. 2-3.

Larson, Magali S. (1977) *The Rise of Professionalization*. Berkeley: University of California Press.

Margolis, Joseph (1978) 'Conceptual aspects of a Patient's Bill of Rights', *Journal of Value Inquiry*, 12: 126-35.

Masters, Roger D. (1975) 'Is contract an adequate basis for medical ethics?', *Hastings Center Report*, 6.

May, William F. (1975) 'Code, covenant, contract, or philanthropy', *Hastings Center Report*, 6.

Miller, Henry (1968) 'Value dilemmas in social casework', *Social Work*, 13: 32-3.

Paull, Joseph E. (1967) 'Recipients aroused: the new welfare rights movement', *Social Work*, 12.

Piliavin, Irving (1968) 'Restructuring the provision of social services', *Social Work*, 13.

Plaut, Thomas F. (1975) 'Doctor's order and patient compliance', *New England Journal of Medicine*, 292: 1043.

Reiser, Stanley Joel et al. (1977) *Ethics in Medicine*. Cambridge, MA: MIT Press. pp. 201-40.

Schmidt, David D. (1977) 'Patient compliance: the effect of the doctor as therapeutic agent', *Journal of Family Practice*, 4: 853-6.

Toren, Nina (1974) 'The structure of social casework and behavioral change', *Journal of Social Policy*, 3.

Veatch, Robert (1972) 'Medical ethics: professional or universal?', *Harvard Theological Review*, 65.

Wasserstrom, Richard (1975) 'Lawyers as professionals: some moral issues', *Human Rights*, 5.

Yale Law Journal (1972) 'Note: restructuring informed consent: legal therapy for the doctor-patient relationship', 79: 1535-7.

24

Paternalism and moral deficiency

R.S. Downie and K.C. Calman

One type of attitude to which health care workers are prone is that of paternalism. We are not here thinking of a failure in applying legal requirements of informed consent to treatment, but rather of a more subtle form of the same; namely the failure to explain to a patient what is happening, why certain activities are taking place and what effects are to be expected. Instead of doing these things as appropriate the paternalistic professional will smile benignly and say, 'Don't you worry, everything is going fine.' This kind of attitude is patronizing and hurtful, because it conveys that the patient is not capable of under-standing anything, or that the patient is too unimportant to be worth the trouble of an explanation. It must be remembered also that patients are in a vulnerable position, because the professional is at home in the care setting and has power over the patient or client. The power of the professional can be conveyed in all sorts of ways, as for example by standing over the patient, or speaking about him to others in his presence. This is irresponsible behaviour in that it shows a lack of respect for the autonomy or dignity of the person who happens to be a particular client. [. . .]

A second form of this morally irresponsible attitude is shown when a professional implies that the patient's wants, fears and anxieties are all to be construed as causally produced by the illness or related psychological factors, and therefore to be treated as symptoms rather than as expressions of genuine purpose or rational desires. For exam-ple, a doctor, nurse or social worker might say, 'You will see things differently when you are well again.' Or a doctor might say to a nurse about a patient, 'Don't worry about the patient's complaints. He's angry because that's one of the stages which dying patients go through.' In both cases the effect is to undercut the reasons which the patient himself would give for his actions or thoughts, and replace them by mechanisms on which the doctor, nurse or social worker would claim to be an expert. The motivation for doing this may be [. . .] the wish to avoid genuine encounters with people.

But just as often health care professionals have no such ulterior motive and may simply believe that they know more about what the

Extract from *Healthy Respect*, London: Faber & Faber, 1987, pp. 96–101 (abridged).

patient does, thinks or feels than the patient himself. In either case, the implication is that the patient is not to be regarded as an autonomous being who acts in pursuance of his own purposes and has genuine questions to ask. [. . .]

All this may seem unreasonable to some doctors and nurses. After all, they will say, we are dealing all the time with people who on any reckoning are governed to a more than average extent by non-rational factors. Even if we leave aside the cases of the mental illness, doctors and nurses are often dealing with people whose rationality is impaired by physical illness or pain, or who are affected by drugs. [. . .]

There is much truth in this objection [. . .], but two points must be borne in mind in mitigation of it. The first is that there is always a temptation, which must be guarded against, to extend this attitude beyond those patients, and those aspects of patients, which would justify it. The temptation exists because adopting a detached casual attitude to patients is often an easier option than taking them seriously. The second is that it may be therapeutic to express a genuine respect for a patient's autonomy even in cases which may not fully justify it. The policy of treating people as rational unless proved otherwise may have the effect of fostering rationality, which is not an all-or-nothing matter.

25

The nurse's dilemma: truth-telling or big white lies?

Basiro Davey

This article reports on part of a much wider study into communication in general hospital wards where cancer patients are nursed and treated in close proximity to many other categories of patients, including those with acute conditions or admissions for elective surgery. This is a very different environment from the specialist oncology (cancer) unit or hospital in which most of the research into communication with cancer patients in institutional settings has taken place, and it is also the setting in which most cancer patients find themselves at some stage in their illness.

The district general hospital chosen for the study is in the south of England. All medical and nursing staff are fully trained, there are no students on the wards, and the consultants are fairly young, mostly in their first consultancy appointment. The medical teams on the general wards are small (consultant, registrar *or* senior house officer and one junior house officer), so even the most senior doctors are in close contact with their patients. The nurses and doctors on these wards have no specialist training in oncology; there is no oncology unit or radiotherapy unit in the hospital. The wards are of the modern four-bay design and the nursing process style of patient management is in full operation. This means (among other responsibilities not dealt with here) that all the patients in a bay are allocated to the same nurse for all or most of her shift, ensuring more continuity of care.

Results and discussion

The nurses

Eighteen qualified nurses (all female) were interviewed in depth, using the same interview schedule, each interview lasting between one and three hours depending on the volubility of the respondent. The group consisted of five Ward Sisters, seven Staff Nurses and six State Enrolled

The author gratefully acknowledges research funding from the Cancer Research Campaign and Marks and Spencer plc.

Nurses (SENs), with twice as many working on surgical wards as on physical medicine (non-surgical) wards at the time of the study. This ratio reflects the ratio of admissions for cancers on these wards (i.e. twice as many cancer patients are treated surgically as non-surgically).

The majority of nurses in this study (15 out of 18) were critical of the general standard of communication between staff and cancer patients in the wards and six of these nurses were highly critical. Two of the most frequently emphasized reasons given for poor communication are the focus of this article: first, unspoken rules about what nurses can say to cancer patients, compounded by policy differences between doctors on the same ward; and second, poor exchange of information between members of staff (and particularly from doctors to nurses) about what has already been said to cancer patients. In addition, but not discussed further here, nurses mentioned the following reasons for poor communication: insufficient time available to spend simply talking with patients; insufficient training of nurses and doctors in communication skills; ambiguous or directly misleading terms used by doctors when talking to cancer patients (e.g. 'mischief', 'inflammation', 'blockage', 'growth'); failure of some doctors to appreciate that many cancer patients suffer less anxiety if told truthfully and sensitively about their diagnosis and prognosis; poor setting chosen by some doctors for communicating distressing information (nurses were especially critical of the ward round as a setting); patients' insecurity about asking questions leading to an assumption by doctors that the patient does not want more information (Davey, 1988); and restrictions placed by relatives and agreed to by doctors on what can be said to the patient.

All the nurses in this study believed that there is an unspoken rule laid down by most (though not all) doctors which either prohibits them totally from answering direct questions posed to them by cancer patients about diagnosis and prognosis, or requires them to be extremely cautious or evasive in their responses, or even to tell 'white lies' on occasion. This 'rule' is well recognized in nursing (Wells, 1988) and may be attributed in part at least to the tradition of training student nurses in hospital-run schools of nursing, where nurses are socialized early in their careers to accept the rules of the 'doctor–nurse game' (Stein et al., 1990). (The nurses in this study had all completed their training before the inception of the Project 2000 initiative in nurse education, which may have a significant impact on the status of nurses in the future.) Nurses in the study reported here were particularly eloquent about the constraints placed on them when talking to cancer patients and the effects on themselves and their patients:

> *N5*: I have seen a lot more people go through a lot of anguish because they wanted to know and no one's told them, and I have had to keep putting them off . . . which hurts me more I think, and I feel bad about it because you don't like not telling the truth do you? Or you know that the patient wants you to tell, but you know you're not allowed to, you've got to hang

on. . . . It is sort of inbred into you as a student that you mustn't say. . . .
There's hundreds of ways of getting round it without telling the truth.
(Staff Nurse)

> *N15*: I think there is probably an unwritten rule, I think, that you shouldn't
> give too much away. . . . I think a lot of nurses are frightened of giving
> over that sort of information in case perhaps the medical staff don't agree
> that it should be done, and also a lot are frightened of confronting the
> issue anyway. . . . I think it does put a strain on you if the patient says,
> 'And what did the result of this or that test show?', which is often the
> case, and then you have to say, 'I don't know, I haven't got it back yet'.
> . . . It is lying I admit, but I don't really feel you can do a great deal else
> in that situation. (Ward Sister)

The last quote reveals that even the most senior nurse on one ward
struggles with the issue of telling the truth or lying to patients.
Moreover, the kinds of questions that she evades are often quite subtle
openings which could rapidly lead her into difficulty. For example, a
patient might ask if the results of a test were back, knowing that the
news might be bad. The nurse is aware that if she confirms that the
result *has* arrived on the ward then the patient will ask her what the
test showed. The choices then open to her seem to be: tell the patient
the truth, even though fearing that certain doctors will consider that
this exceeds her responsibility and may lead to a reprimand; or
acknowledge that she has seen the report, but raise the patient's
anxiety by stating that she is not allowed to discuss it; or be evasive
or tell a lie to conceal what she knows and risk damaging her relationship with the patient. (In all cases she would then inform a doctor that
the patient has been asking about the test results.) Given these choices
it is not surprising that white lies are both commonplace and distressing for nurses and, in their view, also for the patient:

> *N2*: I think if you go away from somebody when they've asked you a direct
> question like that, you don't stand a chance, they never trust you again
> if you didn't answer them. And anyway by not answering them and walk-
> ing off and coming back you *have* answered their question. (SEN)

> *N21*: They take it for granted that the doctors will be truthful and the consul-
> tant couldn't possibly tell them a lie. He is not *directly* telling them lies but
> he is telling them a lie by implication. Then as the days go on you watch
> the fear in their eyes and the fading of hope and the terrible realization
> that 'I have been *had!*' And then *we* have to cope with it, not just their
> coping with this knowledge but their anger with *us* and their distrust of
> *us* after. (Staff Nurse)

Another fairly common question that poses the truth-telling dilemma
for nurses is when a patient asks for clarification of a euphemism for
cancer that has been used by a doctor, as in, 'He said I've got a growth
. . . does that mean it's cancer?'

> *N9*: We aren't really supposed to go up and say, 'Look, you have got cancer'
> – it is not really our place. That's the worst thing really, on here, because
> you don't really know how much you can always say to a patient or how

much you can reassure them because you don't know how much they know. (Staff Nurse)

It should be made clear that none of the nurses wanted the responsibility of telling a cancer patient their diagnosis in the first instance and all acknowledged that the most senior doctor was the best person to do this. Their difficulties stemmed from questions that patients asked if there was a prolonged period between staff learning the diagnosis and the patient being told, or when the patient had been told too little or ambiguously and later asked the nurse for clarification.

Not every nurse said that she wanted more freedom to answer cancer patients' questions. Three enrolled nurses acknowledged that they were frightened of confronting strong emotions and did not feel capable of taking on such a responsibility. These nurses were routinely evasive with cancer patients:

N22: I wouldn't feel able to do it personally, I have to say, 'If you want to know then you must ask a doctor because I am only a nurse and I am only here to see to your everyday needs.' If they leave it at that then that's fine, but if they ask more questions I feel very uncomfortable. (SEN)

The unspoken general rule that nurses should not discuss the diagnosis or prognosis with cancer patients is compounded by policy differences between different consultants on the same ward about appropriate levels of communication with 'their' patients.

N5: It does pose a lot of problems . . . you have never got one level to work on, you have always got to think, 'How much does he know?', and 'How much can I tell him?', and 'What will that consultant say if you told him?' (Staff Nurse)

Staff Nurse N5 in the extract quoted above touches on the second major source of difficulty for the nurse faced by a questioning cancer patient – how much does the patient know already?

N13: We have got a patient on the ward now with cancer. . . . I still don't know what he knows, what his wife knows and what is going on, and he has been here a long time, and everything seems to get distorted the further round it goes. (SEN)

On these wards, there was no agreed procedure for ensuring that doctors who saw the patient alone, outside the formal ward round, passed on relevant information to nurses about what had been said or what the patient was asking or hinting. Nurses complained that it was rare for doctors to tell them what had been said to cancer patients as the diagnostic sequence unfolded and many of the doctors themselves acknowledged during their interviews that they were bad at keeping nurses up to date. Nurses were forced to 'chase after' doctors and 'pester' them for information:

N12: [The consultants] will come round just out of the blue and they will go and talk to the patient and won't say anything to the nurses – then you will go and talk to the patient and you will find that the consultant has been and he has said this and that, and the junior doctors won't know until the next day. So all the time you are trying to pick up the threads and find out what is going on. And I suppose it does happen that the Sisters do tend to get more feedback because you have more access to the doctors and you tend to pester them more, whereas the junior nurses wouldn't ... they sometimes don't tend to pester the doctors enough for information, so they might not know exactly what is going on. It is a very common problem. (Ward Sister)

Uncertainty about what the patient knows leaves the nurse feeling ill at ease with the patient:

N9: If you don't know [what has been said] you are stumped, you have really nothing to say to them because you are so worried about what to say in case they *don't* know. That's one of the worst things on here, I find. (Staff Nurse)

There is a predictable tendency for the more senior nurses to be more confident about answering patients' questions, but it is noticeable that just over half the samples (10/18) state that they are evasive most or all of the time and some of these nurses lie to patients on occasion to protect themselves or the patients from distress and to avoid censure from doctors. Some of the nurses who say they want more freedom to answer patients' questions might, in reality, still be evasive even if encouraged by nursing management and doctors to be truthful. The weight of research into the verbal behaviour of nurses in communicating with cancer patients consistently shows that the majority block direct questions and ignore patients' cues to take the conversation into painful areas (e.g. Knight and Field, 1981; Macleod-Clark, 1983; Wilkinson, 1991). However, the culture of individual wards has a profound influence on the degree to which nurses facilitate communication with patients: wards in which the ability of nurses to answer questions about a cancer diagnosis or prognosis has been openly negotiated with doctors display a high level of facilitating verbal behaviour from nurses in interactions with patients (Field, 1984; Wilkinson, 1991). None of the wards in the study reported here had those characteristics.

The doctors

The next phase in unravelling the pressure on nurses to be evasive with cancer patients was to investigate the attitudes of doctors to their nursing colleagues. Nineteen doctors were interviewed, a sample which included seven Consultants, two Registrars, one Senior and nine Junior House Officers. Doctors were asked first for their general opinion about where the lines of responsibility for answering direct questions about a cancer diagnosis or prognosis should be drawn, and then asked about the two specific examples of 'dilemma' questions that nurses had raised (i.e. 'Does growth mean cancer?' and 'Are my lab results back yet?'). Doctors were not asked directly if nurses should tell white lies to patients; the three doctors who advocated lying did so spontaneously when talking about nurses' responsibility for answering cancer patients' questions:

> *D14*: I would expect them to lie and say 'I haven't seen the histology, sorry, but I'll find out for you.' (Senior House Officer)

> *D26*: Even though she has seen the lab report she should say 'I don't know, I will ask the doctor' . . . It's not her job to read histology reports, she's seen it in passing, it's nothing to do with her really. Now *I'll* sometimes tell a white lie and say to the patient 'The result's not back.' (Junior House Officer)

> *D22*: Even if she knows it [the biopsy report] has come back, I would rather she lied about that because the next question is, 'What did it show?' (Consultant)

The majority of doctors in this sample (13/19) displayed attitudes to truth-telling by nurses that were in agreement with nurses' perceptions, namely that the doctor would disapprove – often in strong terms – if a nurse answered a direct question about a cancer diagnosis or prognosis. However, a minority of doctors (6/19) accepted that nurses have a legitimate role in discussing this sort of information.

> *D27*: If she was asked the question I wouldn't expect her to lie about it. And if she was asked the question because she gained the trust of a patient who wanted the information at that point, then I think she should give it. (Consultant)

If almost a third of the doctors on these wards, including three consultants, say they would support nurses who answer patients' questions truthfully, then why do so many of the nurses perceive themselves to be at consistent risk of censure? One possibility not excluded by this study is that at least some of the doctors who report themselves as supportive of the nurses' role as communicators are, in practice, more restrictive than they acknowledged in the interview. Or mismatch may result partly from expectations about doctors that are embedded in nurse training, partly in the obvious gender divisions between nurses and doctors which encourage women to take up subservient roles in relation to men and vice versa, and partly in the extremely low levels of contact between junior nurses and senior doctors, which prevent the nurse from ever finding out that her truth-telling would be supported by a particular minority of the medical staff. Certainly, these supportive doctors had made no attempt to make their views known to the nurses.

> *N21*: Perhaps it is just the old thing that nurses are afraid of doctors and we don't see our role as being . . . we think we are perhaps under *their* jurisdiction. We forget that we went into nursing to look after patients and part of it all when we took on the role of a nurse was to speak for the *patient*, act for the *patient* – not the *doctor*. (Staff Nurse)

Interviews with the majority of doctors who felt that nurses should be evasive or even lie to patients in certain circumstances revealed a lack of trust by the doctors that nurses are sufficiently well trained to be able to answer direct questions about diagnosis and prognosis accurately:

> D20: I think they should be evasive or in the ideal world they should say 'I will get doctor and he will come and talk to you' ... because I think – and it sounds very arrogant and I'm sure nurses will say it *is* arrogant – nurses do not know as much in terms of what cancer actually involves ... she is in a whole morass of things that I don't think she can answer and if she does she is often inaccurate. (Consultant)

A rather more critical statement about the intellectual calibre of nurses was also made:

> D24: Some nurses are sufficiently able and skilled in this respect to be able to communicate information. All I would say is the same applies to doctors – some are better at it than others – but more of them are likely to be better at communicating that kind of information. I mean, it is to do with what is required intellectually, etcetera, to become a doctor and what is required to become a nurse. (Consultant)

One senior doctor (who claimed to support nurses who tell the truth) also had a rather poor view of the willingness of nurses to engage honestly with cancer patients who ask them direct questions:

> D27: Nurses are always hesitant to accept responsibility for anything very much and I wouldn't want them to feel that they *had* to answer a question like that. Many of them – the majority these days – wouldn't feel that they could take on that responsibility. Fine. (Consultant)

The Consultant's assumptions about his nursing colleagues are not supported by their responses at interview. Only 3/18 nurses in this study reported themselves to be unwilling to take on the responsibility of truthful communication, whereas 8/18 said they always answer truthfully if they are up to date with what the patient has already been told. This discrepancy may be another consequence of lack of communication between the two professions, but also raises issues about male perceptions of women.

The nurse's dilemma – truth-telling or big white lies – is summed up in this last extract from an interview with a senior doctor, which reveals the tightrope that she must walk without the safety net of explicit guidance from the doctor about what she can say:

> D24: It is perfectly acceptable to me for a nurse to communicate information to a patient provided she does it to my satisfaction and in a way that I think is appropriate. What I don't want is to come onto the ward and find a patient in tears because of inappropriate communication and bad handling of a delicate situation. (Consultant)

This statement is consistent with the dominant medical mode of *benevolent paternalism* (Davey, 1988) in which the senior doctor makes decisions about what the patient can safely know without negotiating this directly with the patient. Doctors who relate to the patient from this paternalistic position are also likely to view nurses as subordinate professionals who should defer to the doctor's better judgement. It will be interesting to watch the impact of Project 2000 nurses on the 'doctor–nurse game'. The rules may well be changed by a generation of nurse practitioners whose training gave precedence to their education needs instead of using students as part of the nursing establishment on wards where 'doctor knows best'.

References

Davey, B. (1988) 'The ethical framework of the consultation: doctors' assumptions about the patient's need to know'. Paper given at the International Conference 'When Doctors and Patients Meet' held in Churchill College, Cambridge, 6-9 July.

Field, D. (1984) 'We didn't want him to die on his own – nurses' accounts of nursing dying patients', *Journal of Advanced Nursing*, 9: 59–70.

Knight, M. and Field, D. (1981) 'A silent conspiracy: coping with dying patients on an acute surgical ward', *Journal of Advanced Nursing*, 6: 221-9.

Macleod-Clark, J. (1983) 'Nurse–patient communication – an analysis of conversations from cancer wards', in J. Wilson-Barnett (ed.), *Nursing Research: Ten Studies in Patient Care*. Chichester: Wiley.

Stein, L.I., Watts, D.T. and Howell, T. (1990) 'The doctor-nurse game revisited', *New England Journal of Medicine*, 322 (8): 546-9.

Wells, R. (1988) 'Ethics, informed consent and confidentiality', in V. Tschudin (ed.), *Nursing the Patient with Cancer*. Englewood Cliffs, NJ: Prentice-Hall.

Wilkinson, S. (1991) 'Factors which influence how nurses communicate with cancer patients', *Journal of Advanced Nursing*, 1 (6): 677-88.

26

Professional liars

Alan Ryan

The title of this article is something of a come-on, but I hope it suggests some of the issues it embraces. The notion of a professional liar involves the idea of telling lies for a living, or at any rate in the course of earning a living: perhaps that of telling lies *well*, with conviction, and with aplomb, that one's stock-in-trade includes a capacity to utter a well-judged falsehood. I shall rely on the thought that there *might* be such a thing as the well-told professional lie, in order to explore the obligation to tell the truth, and the obligation to lie under certain conditions as it attaches to certain professional roles.

In order to sort out our ideas of when lying is permissible or perhaps even mandatory, we need to understand *what kind of relationship the passing of information and dis-information is serving*. The familiar 'little white lie' passes the scrutiny of the non-severe moralist because the non-severe moralist accepts that holding together a marriage is an acceptable goal. 'Absolutely hideous' won't assist that, even if it is an honest answer to the question, 'What do you think of my new suit?' The severe moralist will deny it. But the severe moralist who takes a relational perspective differs from previous severe moralists in thinking that that sort of marriage is better demolished; the objection to the 'little white lie' is the paternalistic relationship it presupposes rather than the lie itself. At all events, what most of this article proposes is a *look at the connection between truth-telling (lie-telling therein included) and the relationship in which it is embedded*.

Lying and the duty to tell the truth

One problem with looking at the obligation to tell the truth in terms of what's right for our particular relationship is that I need to know a great deal about your values and preferences in order to get it right.

You ask me when the bus goes, and I reason that you'd be happier if you believed it went sooner and duly tell you that it goes in ten minutes when it actually goes in an hour. This might be a frightful error because you may feel angry at being lied to. Or I may make allowances for this and reason that you will be happiest if the bus goes sooner than you had expected – and duly tell you that it will go in an hour and a half, knowing that your irritation at being lied to will vanish in your pleasure at not having to wait. Of course, I may decide that it's too difficult to know what you will feel and tell you the truth as a compromise. The only point is that the right answer occupies (apparently) no special position in my thinking.

The obvious route by which one returns to solid ground here is by invoking the right of the enquirer to hear the truth. Most discussions of truth-telling and lying concentrate on the would-be liar. It is better to concentrate on the would-be hearer. You can't complain if the policeman takes away the car you have just stolen; you can't complain that you are lied to when you are trying to murder someone.

The question at stake, however, is the ground of the right to be told the truth. Many accounts of rights claim that human beings have a pressing need for security. *Trust* in the beneficence of doctors, and to a lesser degree of lawyers and politicians, is an element in security. Trust is fostered by knowledge of what their plans and actions are; for them to keep us in the dark threatens our security. Conversely, the duty corresponding to that right would be a duty to respect vulnerability; the liar renders others vulnerable to his or her schemes and their own anxieties.

If autonomy – the capacity to plan one's own life, to form and act on a scheme of one's own – is the basis of the right to be told the truth, then liars arrogate to themselves a manipulative control over their dupes and so violate the dupes' right to self-government. The notion of being an end in oneself is that nobody may exercise a control that treats others as means, even if it is as a means to their own well-being. The claim that it is the grossest tyranny to force others to be happy according to our conception of their happiness is only half the story; it is the same tyranny to make them happy even according to their own conception of their happiness.

Truth in relationships

The idea of a right to the truth based on autonomy gets us a long way, especially in combination with an attention to security. I want to go on from there to something much messier. We need an account of more than the duty not to lie, and the right to be told the truth; we need an account of what truths we ought to tell, how, and to whom. This is what I somewhat grandly term an account of 'truth in relationships'.

Ordinarily, we are capable of distinguishing between telling the truth and blurting it out; we distinguish between telling the truth and rubbing it in. We ordinarily distinguish between helpful and unhelpful truth-telling. We don't count as truthful someone who merely utters statements that don't diverge from literal accuracy. What we look to is their readiness to enter into their questioners' search for information, to steer by the enquirers' map so to speak and help them work out the landscape according to their own needs. It is that aspect of the subject that the rest of this article explores.

To begin with another platitude, with us doctors are treated as a curious mixture of priest and mechanic; conversely patients enter the relationship in a curious frame of mind in which guilt mingles with anger at the mechanical malfunctioning of their body. The maintenance of decorum and predictability demands of all of us the meticulous management of our bodies and their peculiarities. Control and management, our whole ability to deploy our bodies for social interaction, is threatened when they go seriously wrong. Hence the guilt: we feel embarrassed in anticipation for what may become failures to behave properly. Hence, too, a measure of anger at the culpable failure of the equipment on which we so intimately rely for the maintenance of our good opinion of ourselves.

Given this background, it becomes easier to make some headway with the questions of *what* truth to tell and where a certain 'economy of the truth' may be in order. A properly rich description of such situational strains illuminates the importance of autonomy and the kind of vulnerability on which we earlier thought the right to hear the truth might be based. If patients face the problems of reassembling their attitudes towards their bodies and themselves, as in difficult cases they must, the thought that the doctor must do better than brutally hand out 'the facts' is a very bare beginning of wisdom. What's wanted is more near co-conspiracy: the patient needs to be able to work out an appropriate schema for understanding and dealing with the unpleasantness she or he faces, though it is hard to say anything very definite about what this will be like in the abstract.

One thing we can say is that people will have very different views about it, according to how they see much else about themselves and the world. It is not enough to insist simply on the overwhelming value of autonomy, as if that meant the same thing to everyone. Freud's famously angry 'bei welchem Recht?' ('with what right?') when his doctor tried to give him a pain-killing dose of morphine towards the end of his final illness illustrates a certain heroic conception of illness as confrontation. The body might crumble, but the will remained. A patient with that firm a grasp on his own view of the matter presents few practical difficulties. Consequently, he is interesting because he violates the thought that the brutal handing out of facts is inappropriate; it is *his* wish that they should be brutally put and brutally understood. His understanding of the task of the patient is that he has a duty to face facts with a ruthless refusal to comfort himself with illusions. Few of us are quite like that and many of us are unsure quite how we are or might be. It is this that tempts doctors to utter verbal bromides; insecurity and uncertainty look like simple weakness.

The 'heroic' approach to illness, debility and death has been prominent in literature for 2,000 years and more. Freud was drawing on images that he would have come across in his childhood readings, images whose power partly depends on the way they permeate so much of our reading. It is certainly not the only approach that we might use in the face of illness. One that makes perhaps more sense in modern conditions, where pain can be managed (and many of us will spend quite a lot of our last months and years more in need of devoted nursing care than heroic medical intervention) is precisely to let go, to learn *not* to mind too much about always being in charge of our own fate. This is not an invitation to lapse into simple oblivion. It is to recognize that one way of handling our burdens is to yield them to someone else with gratitude. Freud was determined to be in charge of his own experience. It is an equally serious project to allow other people to gain the satisfaction that comes from caring for us. Hospice visitors talk movingly about the process of persuading terminally ill patients that there is still something that they can do for other people, even though that task is to accept the kindness and care that is offered to them and so allow their care-givers the satisfaction of doing their own job well.

It is right to concentrate on the relationship between doctor and patient. Still, it is not the only relationship involved in health care. One other is that of practitioners to one another. Here many truth-related issues rear their heads. The first is the way in which confidence in each other's capacities is maintained: one objection to lying to patients is that it is then hard for two practitioners – doctor and doctor, nurse and doctor, nurse and nurse – to talk to one another in front of the patient. More generally, there is the issue of the way in which professional etiquette may serve a valuable role in not reducing everyone to a state of anxiety – by encouraging us *not* to blurt out every doubt we feel about a diagnosis and prognosis – but may, if it goes wrong, kill off patients needlessly by making practitioners feel they cannot ventilate doubts abut one another's competence even when it is necessary.

If the main dramatis personae of the comedies of illness are patients and their immediate helpers, we ought not to neglect the wider society. A powerful argument for a professional ethic of scrupulous truth-telling even in the face of benevolent temptations to lie or palliate unpleasant truths is that the not-yet-ill hope for advances in medical science and, as in all walks of intellectual enquiry, honesty is almost always the only policy. Because medicine is both an applied science and an expensive one, the temptation to exaggerate one's successes and shove one's failures under the rug is strong, especially when outside agencies don't look kindly on doubt and hesitation.

For as long as medical technique did more to shorten life than prolong it – until about 1920 – a plausible way of looking at illness was to see it as a blow dealt by fate. Since doctors could not do much to relieve it or cure it, they could at best assist the patient through the process. In fact one might think that for the most part their assistance was not likely to do much good, either physically, or by way of assisting patients to reconcile themselves to their fate. Most descriptions of the pointless bloodletting and poisoning that medicine involved before the twentieth century suggest that patients did best simply to keep out of the way.

Models and narratives

Still, in the late twentieth century, we can keep patients comfortable, whether or not we can cure them, so that one minimal medical task is simply to do that. With that as a basis, two models of the medical role have some room for manoeuvre. One concentrates on teaching people to see themselves as managing a complex piece of machinery; the other concentrates on teaching people to work through the experience of illness, pain and dependency on medical attention. Both, be it noticed, find room for the idea of the good patient – *not* simply the cooperative patient – as well as the good doctor; the patient must contribute to the performance that makes one or another vision of illness, cure, failure and death 'official' for the wider society. Both emphasize that truth-telling is embedded in relationships.

American doctors, for instance, are prone to complain of the nihilism of British doctors, by which they mean the tendency of British doctors to tell their patients that they must learn to live (and sometimes to die) with whatever ailment they have diagnosed, and not to encourage them to try all possible means of redress. This is where the point about the selection of truths worth telling becomes very obvious. Suppose you have a 25 per cent chance of recovering after some grim treatment; it is equally true that you have a 75 per cent cent chance of not recovering. You may take the view that the glass is at any rate a quarter full or that it is at best three-quarters empty. Which you think is 'the truth' – by which you will mean what's worth saying in the circumstances – doesn't depend on the literal truth of the propositions you might utter but upon the entire surrounding context of beliefs about such matters as how great an evil death is, how endurable various sorts of pain are, what aspects of life do and what do not depend on perfect health, and so indefinitely on.

Evasion reflects a general uncertainty about what story the public at large is able to live with. My sense is that it is harder to establish any one story in a society like the USA where doctors, patients and the public at large are such a cultural mix. Nobody who has become sympathetic to the idea that all enquiry involves the negotiation of accounts of reality will have any less sympathy with the ideal that the negotiation of accounts of life and death will be exceedingly difficult across cultures and across groups with very different capacities to make their accounts stick. But the claim to be examined is that the aim of truth-telling is to allow people to *set their lives, ailments, recoveries and deaths in a satisfactory narrative structure.*

This brings me to my last thought about the truth-telling ethics of medicine. What I would like to be able to do is give a coherent account of the ideal of narrative adequacy. I cannot do that, but I can perhaps motivate the search for such an account. It is surely true that people have strong feelings about being allowed to enact their own version of the drama, whatever it might be.

Human beings want to act in a good story. The story is that of their life and eventually death. Neither the vision of doctor as mechanic nor the vision of doctor as priest quite does the trick – or, rather, they can work rather well some of the time, but they work rather badly in conjunction. Otherwise fit and healthy people who cheerfully take their malfunctioning bodies in for a bit of repair and then go home with a machine they no longer distrust may be thought of as deluding themselves, but on my account it's a perfectly adequate narrative *under those conditions*. The difficulty arises when the repairs won't work and we're faced with the fact that we can't throw this body away and get a new one. Then the fact that this body is also me is impossible to overlook. Then, what is needed is a narrative of endurance and death.

27

Organ transplants

David Lamb

Organ transplantation has given hope when formerly death was inevitable. But the replacement of vital organs highlights major moral problems in medicine concerning the role of physicians and nurses, patient autonomy, and respect for the dying and dead. These include the morality of excising organs from a healthy donor, and related problems regarding an individual's consent to have organs removed for the benefit of others. These problems are not restricted to live organ donation: cadaveric organ procurement raises further questions of fundamental moral concern over the authorization of organ removal. The time may be approaching when almost every part of a cadaver can be used for the benefit of organ recipients and experimental research. It is therefore important to ask whether there is a limit to what can be done to a dead body. Should appeals to the integrity of the human body outweigh the interests of those who have an urgent need for bodily parts?

A consensus has not yet emerged with regard to these questions, but one common feature of the problems is the tension between the potential benefit for an increasing number of patients requiring organs on the one hand and those who have reasons for not authorizing their release on the other hand. In some cases resistance might be due to religious or ethical beliefs concerning the integrity of the corpse; in other cases resistance might be out of fear that the donor's life might be shortened in order to maximize benefits for others.

Living donors

Living donors present a problem for the 'do no harm' imperative in medicine as they are said to be harmed by the loss of the relevant organ. This, of course, only applies to irreplaceable organs; blood and semen, for instance, are self-replenishing and under appropriate conditions can be collected without harm to the donor. There are, however, risks involved in the donation of solid organs such as kidneys, but the general consensus is that if the risk is not too great, an individual who freely wants to donate a kidney should not be prevented from doing so. If there are no undue pressures it is widely agreed that organ donation is one of the finest gestures of fraternity of which human beings are capable. Monsignor Angelini, Bishop of Messine, is reported to have said that 'organ donation . . . from a living donor . . . is the very highest expression of nobility, in which the Evangelic Commandments of love are concentrated' (Report of the Conference of European Health Ministers, 1987). This view is endorsed by many secular and religious belief systems, provided the donation is freely consented to and not motivated by suicidal or homicidal intentions, out of financial desperation or, in the case of prisoners, in the expectation of custodial relief.

In recent years there have been a number of scandals in Europe and the USA involving allegations of a commercial traffic in human parts. In several cases international agencies have been reported as brokers in an illegal organ market. There is one single feature common to every case where organs have been sold; the organs have been excised from the poor and sold to the wealthy. There are no recorded instances of traffic going the other way. This is not a new phenomenon. In the eighteenth century wealthy Europeans paid for unsuccessful tooth implants which were wrenched from the mouths of the poor. In the nineteenth century moral indignation focused on the entrepreneurial activities of the organ and body suppliers Messrs Burke and Hare. The buying and selling of organs is illegal throughout Europe and the USA and, despite the occasional argument in its favour, it is likely to remain illegal. The arguments against selling organs are that it represents a commodification of human bodies, a dilution of altruism, and that it fails to overcome both logical and economic objections. For example, voluntary consent to sale would be self-refuting as the organs would come from (a) those who were economically coerced, or (b) those who had a hopelessly misguided perception of the transaction, or (c) those who were reasonably wealthy but obsessively concerned with accumulating money at any price. None of these categories would meet requirements for a legally endorsed contract or provide an acceptable moral basis for the procurement and distribution of transplantable organs.

Cadaver donors

The most suitable cadaveric donors are brainstem-dead individuals who have died in intensive care units, who are younger than 35 (40 for women) and who have no history of organic heart disease. In the USA there are between 17,000 and 26,000 diagnoses of brain death each year. In the UK the estimated figure is 4,000. Improvements in immunosuppressive therapies, such as cyclosporin, and techniques of preserving and transporting cadaveric organs have emphasized how much the dead can contribute to the well-being of the living. Yet the need for transplantable organs is greater than the supply. In the UK the average waiting time for a kidney transplant is two years and there are approximately 4,000 people on dialysis awaiting surgery. If those awaiting hearts, lungs and livers are added the total urgent waiting list is over 4,500. A report in *The Guardian* (6 December 1988) quoted a director of a cardiopulmonary unit as saying that 'about 900 people under 55 on transplant waiting lists are dying every year because of an acute shortage of human donors'. Such figures give moral weight to proposals to increase the procurement rates of organs.

Guidelines in most transplant centres stress that up to the time of death, every effort should be maintained to save the potential donor's life, including emergency treatment of injuries, maintenance of blood pressure, blood transfusions, repeated attempts at resuscitation, and other appropriate therapy. By the time the transplant surgeon appears on the scene brain death should have been clearly determined by doctors who are not involved in the transplantation process. The diagnosis of brain death marks a shift in priorities from life-prolongation to the maintenance of organ viability. In the interests of both scientific accuracy and ethical propriety it is essential to separate questions relating to the need to obtain organs for transplantation from questions relating to the conceptual and factual aspects of determining death. Demand for more donors is sure to increase. Under these circumstances doctors can be subjected to conflicting moral pressures when the organs of one patient can be used to save the life of another. To avoid potential conflicts between the attending physician and the needs of the transplant team practices have been consolidated which ensure that the donor's physician should have no role in the transplantation procedure itself.

To avoid the need for transplant organs interfering with decisions concerning the diagnosis of death some countries have proposed tougher guidelines when transplantation is under consideration. Several European countries have considered legal requirements which specify that a whole team of doctors must agree over the diagnosis of death in the case of a potential organ donor. The reasons for these extra provisions is to allay public fears of a premature death for organ donors, but it is questionable whether these requirements reduce public suspicions as much as they create them. They certainly introduce an absurd suggestion that there is a special kind of death for organ donors, and perpetuate mistaken beliefs that diagnosing brain death is a hit-or-miss affair lacking precision. As a matter of consistency as well as respect for the deceased and the relatives, criteria for diagnosing the deaths of organ donors should be exactly the same as for those whom immediate burial or cremation is intended. The current UK practice of requesting agreement from two consultants over a diagnosis of brain death – whether or not transplantation is intended – is quite adequate.

The requirement for objective criteria for death, and hence cessation of therapy, must be shown to be quite independent of any external requirements (Lamb, 1985, 1990). If organ transplantation had never developed, or if it were prohibited, it would be necessary to seek reliable criteria to ascertain death. Any attempt to gerrymander the definition of death for the purpose of organ procurement is widely regarded as immoral. As a Report of the Conference of European Health Ministers (1987) noted: 'It would be preferable by far for man's future survival to have to abandon transplantation than to agree to remove vital organs from individuals who are not really dead.'

The views of various cultures

Respect for the body of the deceased is a feature of all religious and secular belief systems. The body represents the past memory of life which should be kept as close as possible to the image of the departed person. For this reason the idea of mutilation of the body is unacceptable. Although a cadaver is not a person, it merits respect because it was that person's body. To lose respect for the body of a dead human being would mean disrespect for the person, the next of kin, and ultimately other human beings.

Although respect for the deceased involves different practices in various cultures, for the most part violation of the body's integrity for therapeutic purposes such as transplantation is not regarded as disrespect. At least no major Western Church has adopted an unfavourable stance towards organ removal. Protestant, Roman Catholic and Buddhist countries, despite prohibitions against the mutilation of corpses, permit cadaveric transplants provided that prior consent of the deceased – or family consent – has been obtained. The issue of transplantation in Jewish culture is complex. The State of Israel was one of the first countries in the world to recognize brain death and organ transplants are common. Talmudic imperatives stress loss of breath which is compatible with evidence of irreversible apnoea (cessation of breathing) as part of the criteria for brainstem death. However, the Talmud forbids the mutilation of a corpse or the deriving of any benefit from a dead body. Nevertheless, these prohibitions can be overruled by the prescription of *pikuakh nefesh* ('the preservation of life'). Thus the Chief Rabbi of Israel was able to argue that, as a successful graft becomes part of the recipient, prohibitions related to deriving benefit from the dead do not, in the long term, apply.

The respect accorded to dead bodies in Islam rules out the study of anatomy on indigenous corpses. Post-mortems are rare in Islamic countries. There is considerable objection to organ transplantation among ordinary Muslims. This is partly based on familiar stories of mutilation of the dead during the time of the Prophet. The murder of the Prophet's uncle, Hamzah, by the heathen, Hind, who opened up the victim's belly and ate his liver, has a profound meaning in Muslim culture and partly explains resistance to liver transplants. However, post-mortem kidney transplantation should be less of a problem as the Hadith explicitly states that those entering the garden will never need to urinate. Despite widespread resistance to organ transplantation in

Islamic countries, post-mortem donation was declared 'halal' (permissible) in 1982 by the Senior 'Ulama' Commission, the highest religious authority in such matters, in Saudi Arabia. According to Islamic teachings a man is answerable to Allah for the good or bad use made of his organs during his life-time. If he makes a will donating his organs for the purpose of saving other lives he is eligible for a reward in the hereafter. If, as one Islamic expert points out, 'in Islam respect for the living is greater than respect for the dead', then cadaveric transplantation to save lives is acceptable (Moulavi, M.H. Babu Sahib, 1984).

There are cultural reasons for hostility in the Japanese community to brain death and organ transplants. In traditional Japanese thought it is the belly or the gut which symbolically represents the major organ. Hence the Samurai warrior commits harakiri by plunging the sword into his belly, not his heart or brain. Just as Europeans spoke of the heart as the seat of the emotions and virtue, thus reinforcing the attractiveness of cardio-centric definitions of death, Japanese refer to the gut: thus being 'good and honest' is having a 'clean gut'. Whilst the English have a 'heart to heart' talk, the Japanese refer to 'opening one's gut'. To say one thing but mean something else can be described as 'the gut and the mouth speak differently'. This does not mean that Japanese doctors and nurses believe that the gut actually is the master organ, but such symbolic beliefs stand as a barrier to the acceptance of a brain-related concept of death and the removal of organs after brainstem death.

One of the cornerstones of medical ethics is the principle of respect for the individual patient. In any multi-cultural society objective scientific knowledge must co-exist with respect for the individual's deeply held beliefs. If distress is to be avoided guidelines for the harvesting of organs will be modified by religious and cultural views concerning the integrity of the body.

References

Lamb, D. (1985) *Death, Brain Death and Ethics*. London: Routledge.
Lamb, D. (1990) *Organ Transplants and Ethics*. London: Routledge.
Moulavi, M.H., Babu Sahib (1984) 'Organ donation: an Islamic viewpoint', *Newsletter of the National Kidney Foundation* (Singapore), 1 (2): 1–5.
Report of the Conference of European Health Ministers (1987) Council for Europe, *Ethical and Socio-Cultural Problems Raised by Organ Transplantation*. Paris, 16–17 November.

28

Dying to help: moral questions in organ procurement

Martyn Evans

Given that we cannot tackle every moral issue to which kidney trans-plantation might give rise, let us focus on two aspects of this practice which require particular moral scrutiny. In each case we can bring out the moral problem in the form of a *choice* that has to be considered:

1 in connection with so-called 'cadaver' donors, there is the choice between emphasizing the *continuing care of the patient*, and subor-dinating this to the *maintenance of a source of donor organs*;
2 connected with this, there is the choice between searching for a definition of death which best fits the *values and experiences of our society*, and defining death in a way which has the *greatest practical usefulness*.

We can see at once that these choices are particular forms of a more general moral choice, and one we should continue to bear in mind: namely the choice between giving priority to the interests of the *donor* of an organ, and giving priority to the interests of the potential *recipient*.

The first choice

Some transplanted kidneys are obtained from living donors, but most come from patients who meet the criteria for brainstem death, and they are 'usually the victims of road traffic accidents or intracranial haemorrhage' (Diliner, 1991: 267). But the organs of those who die at the roadside will deteriorate beyond usability before they can be retrieved. Clearly the transplant team have a moral obligation to their *own* patients, namely those who are to receive transplanted kidneys, to provide them with new organs in the best possible condition. To be maintained in the best condition, it is necessary for the kidneys to be perfused *in situ* in the patient's body until immediately prior to their

I am particularly grateful for the comments and criticisms I have received from Neil Pickering in the preparation of this discussion.

removal, and this of course requires the maintenance of a suitable donor's general functions in the intensive therapy unit (ITU), from the moment of the donor's admission – as a patient – until immediately after the organ retrieval surgery.

Now there is obviously already something of a conflict between the idea of someone who is regarded as dead, and the idea of looking after such a person in the intensive 'therapy' unit: how can one give 'therapy' to the dead? This conflict has both moral and what we might call conceptual aspects to it: it is both troubling, and also intellectually puzzling. The troubling aspect concerns the moral question of the *right way to treat those people whom we do regard as dead*. The puzzle concerns the question of *whether we can really regard as dead* people who in many important respects actually resemble the living.

Most patients who are placed on life support are ventilated first of all in the hope that the intensive therapy will offer time and opportunity in which they themselves may to some extent recover. The tests which are carried out in order to diagnose brainstem death are generally carried out on patients who have already been placed on a ventilator. The ventilator is disconnected in order to allow the final test (for loss of breathing) to take place (Pallis, 1983: 21). By the time that the tests for brainstem death are carried out, the medical and nursing team involved will know whether organ donation is envisaged. If it is, then upon diagnosis of brainstem death, the patient is reconnected to the ventilator, and maintained in the ITU until the transplant surgery can be carried out.

During this period, every necessary step will be taken to ensure that the patient's relevant physiological functions continue in a controlled and integrated manner. The patient will continue to look more or less identical with the way he or she looked when first admitted to the intensive therapy unit. Yet ordinarily we expect someone who is declared dead to undergo a gradual change in visible appearance. Again we ordinarily expect that medical support will be withdrawn for someone who is declared dead. Yet since the care the patient is receiving is, in most significant respects, also very much the same as when first ventilated, it seems that the declaration of brainstem death may not mark a clinical change of the kind that 'death' usually signifies. The only obvious clinical change which the declaration of brainstem death signifies in the present case is a change in the *purpose* of continuing care. Declaring brainstem death in the potential organ donor shifts the purpose of continuing care away from the interests of the potential donor, and towards the interests of the potential recipient. The emphasis has changed from the care of a patient, to the maintenance of a source of donor organs.

The moral challenge of this change of emphasis is clear enough: given all the known benefits of using the donor's kidneys for transplantation, are we justified in subordinating the interests of the donor to the interests of the recipient in this way? Of course it is true that we may have no clear sense or meaning of the idea of 'the interests' of the dead. Yet we do have a clear notion of 'respect' for the dead, particularly regarding the way in which their bodies are treated. Partly this may be a matter of the donor's own wishes, of course: many people express a desire to become organ donors in the event of their death. But even here we should consider whether there is something morally disturbing in the way that the patient's *status* seems to change to that of a source of donor organs, when little if anything else has changed about their clinical condition and the external circumstances of their clinical management.

More challenging still is the suggestion that, beyond those patients who are admitted to the intensive therapy unit in their own interests, the demands of the transplantation programme require donors to be identified *before* they are admitted to the unit, and then admitted *in the interests of someone else*, expressly in order to become organ donors. One consultant anaesthetist has recently reported how he was approached and asked 'to ventilate a young girl dying of a brain tumour solely so that she should not die before arrangements could be made for her organs to be removed' (Hill et al., 1991: 312). Some institutions have explored making this practice routine (Feest et al., 1990; Salih et al., 1991). Mixed reactions to such a practice are recorded, in one case, thus:

> There is resistance to this from some doctors because a patient may be put on a ventilator and then not meet the criteria for brain stem death. Also intensive care units are busy places and staff do not like a bed being occupied by someone who is not going to get better. (Diliner, 1991)

It is true that the purpose of occupying this bed is certainly in order for someone to get better, albeit not the person occupying the bed. But there seems something repugnant about employing invasive methods of caring for someone who is not going to get better, when the purposes of employing that care have nothing whatever to do with the clinical interests of the patient receiving it. Again a response to this objection might hinge on the express desire of the patient to become an organ donor in the event of his or her death.

Whether we would find this a compelling response would largely depend on whether we thought such a consent could justify each and every aspect of the organ retrieval process, including the maintenance of the brainstem-dead patient on ventilation. After all, there are many things which are regarded as impermissible in themselves, *regardless* of whether consent has been given: think of the use of illegal drugs, or assisting a suicide attempt, for instance. Again, it would certainly be instructive to learn whether those people who give their consent to become organ donors realize that they will not be disconnected from ventilation until immediately *after* their organs have been removed.

(Indeed, given that few lay people have detailed knowledge of the clinical realities of the brainstem-dead organ donor, we might ask whether carrying an organ donor card represents anything like a meaningful consent.)

Part of our response to these challenges concerns our understanding of the very meaning of human death, and to this we must now turn.

The second choice

> The concept of death is multifarious, and to specify what death means might seem a hopeless task. . . . Thus we must take as our guide in establishing a concept of death the everyday experience of death common to the individuals of a particular culture. (Rix, 1990: 6)

With these words Dr B.A. Rix sums up the approach taken by the Danish Council for Ethics to the problem of adopting a morally appropriate understanding of human death, in Danish clinical practice. The Council's advice, that Denmark should persevere – virtually alone amongst European states – in affirming a cardiac standard for death – is of course incompatible with the claim that brain-dead organ donors are actually dead, a fact not lost on proponents of brain-centred conceptions of death, who have opposed the cardiac definition (Gillon, 1990; Lamb, 1990; and Pallis, 1990).

Traditionally the clinical question of when a human being dies has been straightforwardly answered by looking for certain agreed signs. It is because these signs – the loss of respiration and the loss of heartbeat – are hidden or masked by the effects of the life-support technology that medicine has turned its attention to what it regards as the patient's *underlying state*, and has conceived of this state essentially in terms of brain function. In this sense, life-support technology has appeared to generate the need for a new definition of human death (Pallis, 1983: 1).

However, is it really doctors alone who can tell us what 'death' ought to mean? In particular, must we accept the medical emphasis on the patient's underlying state, if this means taking no account of the significance of the patient's apparent state? Ventilated brainstem-dead patients look identical to how they looked prior to the declaration of brainstem death: their chests continue to rise and fall, and they are warm and pink. Indeed although a machine 'breathes' for them, they are perfused by the continuing *spontaneous* action of their hearts and of the body's feedback systems governing blood temperature and pressure. Medicine tends to regard the clinical emphasis upon the brain (and upon what this indicates concerning the patient's underlying state) as a matter of the dictates of science alone. But we cannot dissociate the facts about the patient's observable state from the *significance* that, for instance, breathing and circulation, warmth and body colour have for us in our everyday experience of life and death. Science can tell us that without the artificial maintenance of respiration the spontaneous heartbeat will soon cease. But science cannot tell us what cultural and moral importance we should attach to the spontaneous heartbeat whilst it still persists (Evans, 1990a and 1990b; Jonas, 1974; and Browne, 1991).

Again, since moral questions have no conveniently definitive answers, there may not be easy agreement on what are the relevant factors to ponder in relation to the definition of death. Consider again the way the question has arisen: it arose initially in connection merely with the sheer ability artificially to 'prolong life', but it is now greatly sharpened by the claims of organ transplantation, where the ability to sustain physiological function is intentionally harnessed to the practical purposes of obtaining donor organs. Should we, perhaps, be inclined to a cautious or sceptical view of the definition of death simply because the prime mover in the current debate is a straightforwardly practical need to obtain donor organs?

The role of our instinctive reactions is also something that we may feel it necessary to consider. If we feel a repugnance - as some transplant theatre staff are reputed to feel (Younger et al., 1989; Timmins and Hinds, 1991) - at the evisceration of a patient who at the very least *resembles* a living human being, does this repugnance have any moral force? Or is it simply a matter of overcoming our anxieties by rational explanation and education?

One helpful way of proceeding in moral enquiry is often by the use of *analogy*: we consider one situation where we feel uncertain alongside another which, in its most important respects, both resembles the original situation and appears to offer us clarity. The hope is that the second situation provides us with lessons regarding the first. One analogy we might consider in the present context is between two alternative procedures which the brainstem-dead might undergo. A serious definition of death must hold good for all circumstances, since someone could hardly be declared dead for some purposes yet alive for other purposes. If the brainstem conception of death is true in circumstances of organ retrieval, it must also be true in other circumstances such as cremation. Therefore someone who is prepared to remove a patient's organs when they meet the criteria for brainstem death ought to be prepared to allow someone to be cremated in precisely the same condition - a condition which includes the persistent, spontaneous beating of the patient's heart. By corollary, anyone who would shrink from regarding such a patient as dead enough for cremation ought to shrink from regarding them as dead enough to be an organ donor - if we are to take the concept of brainstem death seriously as an understanding of human death, rather than merely as a stage in the process of human dying.

The analogy effectively encapsulates the second choice: should a definition of death express our society's general experience of human life and death (which attaches great traditional and symbolic importance to the beating heart), or should we adopt a new definition, unfamiliar outside medicine, which subserves the practical usefulness of retrieving transplantable human organs? However unwelcome, even distasteful, this choice may be, it is forced upon us by the emergence of undeniably beneficial medical technology. So in this respect as well, kidney transplantation demands our moral scrutiny.

Conclusion

These two choices concern only the use of cadaver organs – if indeed society finally decides to accept such a description of them. But, uniquely among the major organ transplantation procedures, kidney transplantation can also make use of whole organs from living donors (indeed the procedure originally relied exclusively on living donors). The problem of balancing the interests of the donor with those of the potential recipient gives rise to further moral choices, for instance between ensuring that the donor is acting freely and in an informed way, and maximizing the availability of donor organs. A fuller consideration of that choice would take us outside our present concerns with death and dying, since the most prominent recent issues in medical consent have included the phenomenon of trafficking in human kidneys from living donors. Perhaps this reminds us that an activity such as transplantation, whose hallmarks have been generosity and self-sacrifice, may none the less require our moral scrutiny. There are many ways in which we can obtain that self-sacrifice, but they may not all be tolerable. We recall the more general challenge which underlies the particular moral choices we have been considering: should we, in a modern technological society that is capable of producing astounding benefits, give greater emphasis to the interests of the recipients who stand to gain from such benefits, or should we emphasize the interests of the donors whose generosity we need?

Put like this, of course, the challenge is the perennial one of how society can obtain the sacrifices of some of its members in the service of others. Organ transplantation presents this challenge to us afresh in a vivid and acute form.

References

Browne, A. (1991) 'Defining death', in B. Almond and D. Hill (eds), *Applied Philosophy: Morals and Metaphysics in Contemporary Debate*. London: Routledge. pp. 312-21.

Diliner, L. (1991) 'New kidneys for old', review of R. West, *Organ Transplantation, British Medical Journal*, 303, 3 August, 267.

Evans, M. (1990a) 'A plea for the heart', *Bioethics*, 4 (3): 227-31.

Evans, M. (1990b) 'Death in Denmark', *Journal of Medical Ethics*, 16 (4): 191-4.

Feest, T.G., Riad, H.N., Collins, C.H., Golby, M.G.S., Nichols, A.J. and Hamad, S.N. (1990) 'A protocol for increasing organ donation after cerebrovascular deaths in a district general hospital', *The Lancet*, 335, 12 May: 1133-5.

Gillon, R. (1990) 'Death' (editorial), *Journal of Medical Ethics*, 16: 5-7.

Hill, D.J., Evans, D.W. and Gresham, G.A. (1991) 'Availability of cadaver organs for transplantation' (correspondence), *British Medical Journal*, 303, 3 August, 312.

Jonas, H. (1974) 'Against the stream: comments on the definition and redefinition of death', in *Philosophical Essays: From Ancient Creed to Technological Man*. Englewood Cliffs, NJ: Prentice-Hall. pp. 132-40.

Lamb, D. (1990) 'Wanting it both ways', *Journal of Medical Ethics*, 16: 8-9.

Pallis, C. (1983) *ABC of Brainstem Death*. London: British Medical Journal.

Pallis, C. (1990) 'Return to Elsinore', *Journal of Medical Ethics*, 16: 10-13.

Rix, B.A. (1990) 'Danish Ethics Council rejects brain death as the criterion of death', *Journal of Medical Ethics*, 16: 6.

Salih, M.A.M., Harvey, I., Frankel, S., Coupe, D.J., Webb, M. and Cripps, H.A. (1991) 'Potential availability of cadaver organs for transplantation', *British Medical Journal*, 302, 4 May, 1053-5.

Timmins, A.C. and Hinds, C.J. (1991) 'Management of the multiple organ donor', *Current Opinion in Anaesthesiology*, 4: 287-92.

Younger, S.J., Landefield, C.S., Coulton, C.J., Juknialis, B.W. and Leary, M. (1989) '"Brain death" and organ retrieval: a cross-sectional survey of knowledge and concepts among health professionals', *Journal of the American Medical Association*, 261: 2205-10.

29

The living will in clinical practice

Ursula Gallagher

There has been much discussion recently about protecting dying people from what many see as the potential excesses of medical intervention and involving them in all decisions about their health and future treatment. This article aims to explore whether the existence of a living will, one suggested solution, would help to enhance clinical practice in this difficult area of decisions at the end of life.

What is a living will?

The living will, a type of advance information directive, was first proposed by Louis Ketner in an article entitled 'Due Process of Euthanasia: The Living Will, a Proposal' in 1969. It is not a will in the conventional sense. It does not dispose of any property. It does not appoint executors or guardians. It is a declaration made by a competent adult expressing the wish that if he or she becomes so seriously ill that there is absolutely no prospect of recovery, any extraordinary means designed to sustain or prolong life will be withheld or withdrawn. There is no defined format for a living will although several are in existence (an example is attached in the Appendix). The statement may be verbal but it is most commonly written and then lodged with a general practitioner or sometimes a solicitor.

At present the living will has no legal status in the United Kingdom, although several groups, including Age Concern (1988) and the Voluntary Euthanasia Society, advocate that it should. (A private member's bill legalizing living wills is before Parliament as this book goes to press, and the Law Commission has considered advance directives in a 1991 consultation paper.)

Although advance directives were first proposed over twenty years ago, they have only emerged as people have come to realize the extent to which modern medical technology can prolong life but at potentially poor quality which the individual might consider unacceptable. The living will is justified by the premise that although the individual has the right either to consent to or refuse treatment, where the patient is *in extremis* and incapable of giving consent, a constructive consent is assumed in law, that is, that patients would always consent to measures to save their lives. The living will aims to refute that assumption of consent, although the legal status of this remains untested.

The living will is probably going to be of more use outside a legal framework, that is, in the more informal decision-making in everyday clinical practice. Clinicians (and by that I mean all those involved with the care of patients – nurses, doctors, physiotherapists and others) are becoming increasingly comfortable with the concept that the patient is an autonomous individual capable of being involved in decisions about his or her disease and treatment. They now find it difficult when the patient is unable to participate either because of physical or mental incapacity. The existence of a living will would provide the team with some idea of the patient's clearly expressed wishes. This might also enable medical and nursing staff to discuss the issue with relatives of the patient, hopefully reducing some of the anger and guilt that can sometimes occur at these stressful moments, since it would help the family to know that they are complying with the expressed wishes of their loved one. But it would be wrong to give the impression that the existence of advance directives or living wills would solve all the problems faced by families, relatives, carers and health care professionals in this very difficult area of current practice.

The living will is not at present a recognized legal document in this country and there is no standard form of words, since it is difficult to draft a document that is clear and unambiguous. This means that there could be some difficulties over interpretation. Is the condition the patient is now in the one imagined when the living will was made? Also it is frequently difficult for clinicians to make predictions about the expected degree of recovery and prognosis especially in the early stages of illness, particularly with trauma and head injury.

There is a question of how long a living will could be considered valid. Is a living will signed at the age of 18 still applicable when the patient has a stroke at the age of 60? It is certainly very difficult to be sure that a level of handicap considered unacceptable to a young person would still be so to an older person who may have adjusted to a certain level of incapacity. The problem could be easily addressed by putting an expiry limit on the wills: in some states in the USA living wills have five- or seven-year limits. This often has to be clarified in the case of demented patients by confining it a period before the onset of the incapacity.

Euthanasia remains illegal in this country and therefore it should be remembered that a living will or advance directive can only give instructions about consent to treatment. It cannot request any health care professionals or other relatives to intervene actively in order to shorten the life of the patient.

Many people worry that allowing advance directives to be considered when caring for the incapacitated will reduce the quality of care and service provision. The Royal College of Nursing has produced *Living*

Wills: Guidance for Nurses (1991), which raises the concern that living wills may be used to compensate for poor provision of health care. For example, if nursing homes are of such a poor standard that people opt to die rather than be cared for in them, then good services might never be developed.

There is also the currently existing confusion between when a treatment is considered to be life-saving and when it is life-sustaining. Life-saving treatment would include such measures as cardiopulmonary resuscitation, emergency surgery and intravenous antibiotics. Life-sustaining treatment is generally considered to include such things as artificial provision of food and fluids, for example, drips and tubes.

Some commentators have concluded that life-sustaining measures are also medical interventions and can be withdrawn in the same way that a ventilator can. Allowing withdrawal of drips and tubes under the same conditions as ventilators is roughly the current legal position in the US, but not in England and Wales, where either withdrawal of the ventilator or of feeding tubes would probably expose health care workers to prosecution. The Scottish Procurator Fiscal has indicated that the position on artificial feeding and hydration might be different in Scotland, provided that withdrawal of feeding tubes had been agreed by two or more doctors and discussed with the family. But others think there *is* a distinction: some nurses, for example, might balk at running together life-saving *medical* interventions and life-sustaining *nursing* care.

The Royal College of Nursing guidelines are cautious in their advocacy of advance directives. They advise that nurses should avoid signing or drawing up living wills for patients and comment that they are no substitute for good communication or team decision-making. They also advise the development of local guidelines about when to initiate treatment for any patient.

It seems that the professionals are far from feeling comfortable about the possible uses and value of living wills in practice. However, there is an undeniable public demand to be involved in these decisions and a fear of what medical technology is now able to do which might prevent people dying on their own terms and 'with dignity'.

The problems and issues of advance directives cannot be ignored, and some safeguards would be necessary to ensure that the patient was clear about what he or she was signing and that families and carers were involved in the decision-making processes. Health care professionals need to keep up to date with legal developments about living wills and their roles and responsibilities with respect to them. Living wills and other forms of advance directives may have a significant role to play in allowing patients to have a say in decisions about their treatment even if they are incapacitated at the time the decision needs to be made.

References

Age Concern and the Institute of Law, Medicine and Ethics (1988) *The Living Will: Consent to Treatment at the End of Life*. London: Edward Arnold.

Ketner, L. (1969) 'Due process of euthanasia: the living will, a proposal', *Indiana Law Review*, 44 (4).

Royal College of Nursing (1991) *Living wills: guidance for nurses*, Issues for Nursing and Health, No. 4, May. London: Royal College of Nursing.

Appendix: New York living will

***INSTRUCTIONS*:**
This is an important legal document. It sets forth your directions regarding medical treatment. You have the right to refuse treatment you do not want, and you may request the care you do want. You may make changes in any of these directions, or add to them, to conform them to your personal wishes.

I. ———————————————————, being of sound mind, make this statement as a directive to be followed if I become permanently unable to participate in decisions regarding my medical care. These instructions reflect my firm and settled commitment to decline medical treatment under the circumstances indicated below:

I direct my attending physician to withhold or withdraw treatment that serves only to prolong the process of my dying, if I should be in an incurable or irreversible mental or physical condition with no reasonable expectation of recovery.

These instructions apply if I am a) in a terminal condition; b) permanently unconscious; or c) if I am conscious but have irreversible brain damage and will never regain the ability to make decisions and express my wishes.

I direct that treatment be limited to measures to keep me comfortable and to relieve pain, including any pain that might occur by withholding or withdrawing treatment.

While I understand that I am not legally required to be specific about future treatments, if I am in the condition(s) described above I feel especially strongly about the following forms of treatment:

I do not want cardiac resuscitation.
I do not want mechanical respiration.
I do not want tube feeding.
I do not want antibiotics.

I do want maximum pain relief.

Other directions (insert personal instructions): _____
_____
_____
_____

These directions express my legal right to refuse treatment, under the law of New York. I intend my instructions to be carried out, unless I have rescinded them in a new writing or by clearly indicating that I have changed my mind.

Sign and date here in the presence of two adult witnesses, who should also sign.

Signed: _____ Date: _____
Witness: _____
Address: _____
_____
Witness: _____
Address: _____
_____

Keep the signed original with your personal papers at home. Give copies of the signed original to your doctor, family, lawyer and others who might be involved in your care.

30

Euthanasia in the Netherlands

Henk ten Have

Central to the debate on active euthanasia are the moral principles of respect for the personal autonomy and sanctity of human life. Although euthanasia is prohibited by the Dutch Penal Code, many patients and physicians in the Netherlands agree that it is morally acceptable in cases of competent patients requesting a doctor to actively end their life. The emphasis on the persistent, conscious and freely made patient's request is reflected in the specific, value-laden definition of euthanasia widely accepted in the Netherlands: 'the active termination of a patient's life at his or her request by a physician'. The importance of self-determination, and thus voluntariness, is also stressed in the pattern of jurisprudence that has developed in the last two decades: a voluntary request is a necessary condition under which in practice physicians are not subject to criminal sanctions.

However, the growing consensus regarding the ethical and legal framework guiding the practice of euthanasia has become more complicated recently as a result of two events.

1. The report of the Committee on the Study of Medical Practice (published in September 1991) showed that current practice is clearly not in accordance with the conceptual consensus. Empirical research data indicate that the number of euthanasia cases in compliance with the definition was unexpectedly low (2,300 cases a year, or 1.8 per cent of all deaths). On the other hand, medical practice regarding decisions at the end of life appeared to be more diversified than expressed in the definition. Most important, in approximately 1,000 cases annually, a patient's life was ended without any request at all. In such cases, patients were no longer competent to make decisions, yet apparently suffered severely.

2. The government responded with new legislative proposals, issued in November 1991. The criminal law will not be changed (therefore, euthanasia in principle remains illegal), but through amendment of the Law on the Disposal of the Dead, several procedural criteria have been listed to be checked by the prosecution council (such as careful case documentation and reporting). The same procedure, however, is

From *Philosophy Today*, September 1992, 11: 1-2.

proposed to extend to nonvoluntary termination of life as well. It is argued that this is desirable in order to make such practices open to legal audit.

Both events have led to ambiguous situations. Political parties in favour of legalizing euthanasia want to hold a clear line between voluntary and nonvoluntary cases. On the other hand, the Christian Democrats, opposed to legislation permitting euthanasia, support the new proposals, including auditing of nonvoluntary termination of life. In April 1992, a parliamentary majority (Christian Democrats and Socialists) decided not to make a crucial distinction in the legislative proposals between voluntary and nonvoluntary termination of life, and not to prosecute nonvoluntary cases.

From a moral point of view, the present situation is confusing too. Empirical research and political debate show that in daily practice two moral considerations compete with each other: respect for autonomy and relief from suffering. From the doctor's standpoint, the latter consideration seems the most important: it is the major motive to act in cases of incompetent patients who, in the judgement of the doctors, suffer unbearably, but it is also a strong motive in cases of competent patients. The moral sensibility of the medical profession apparently is the only guarantee against abuses.

From the patient's point of view, requesting assistance in dying seems morally justified because it is a voluntary, competent decision. Precisely as an act of self-determination, such a request is safeguarded against abuse and medical power. And that is why it has all begun: the 'euthanasia movement' started as a protest against medicine's alienation of individuals from their own dying. Respecting a patient's autonomy should restore control over his or her own life and death. But finally, in most cases it is physicians who decide that suffering is unbearable, quality of life is too low, or life is no longer worth living, and that therefore it is appropriate to hasten death. Physicians now have even more power than before over the life and death of their patients. This is a paradoxical result for a protest movement against medical power.

31

Assisted death

*Institute of Medical Ethics Working Party on the Ethics of
Prolonging Life and Assisting Death*

The Institute of Medical Ethics has frequently been urged to address
the following issue:

> The lives of an increasing number of patients, predominantly but by no
> means all elderly, are now being prolonged by modern medicine in states of
> coma, severe incapacity, or pain they consider unrelievable and from which
> they seek release. Doctors in charge of such patients have to decide not only
> whether they are morally bound to continue with life-prolonging treatment,
> but also, if no such treatment is being given, whether and in what
> circumstances it is ethical to hasten their deaths by administration of
> narcotic drugs. [. . .]

When may a doctor assist death?

This discussion paper is concerned with the general question, 'in what
circumstances, if any, is a doctor ethically justified in assisting death?'
In its preparation, the working party has considered many papers on
euthanasia, especially the 1988 British Medical Association report
(Working Party to Review the British Medical Association's Guidance
on Euthanasia, 1988), and has also discussed the current practice in the
Netherlands of withholding prosecution from doctors admitting that
they have ended the lives of patients who, together with their families,
have asked that this should be done to cut short terminal physical and
mental distress (Ritger et al., 1988). The paper is concerned solely with
occasions when assisted death is requested – not the related issues of
ending the lives of infants, or of patients who are unconscious or
unable to make valid requests. Nor does it discuss the law, living wills
(or advance directives) or the actions of health professionals other than
doctors.

'Assisted death' is taken to mean an act by a doctor with the
deliberate intention of hastening the death of a patient with a terminal
illness. The word terminal here implies a progressive illness whose

From *The Lancet*, 'Viewpoint', 8 September 1990: 610–13 (abridged).

distressing symptoms cannot be eased by any alteration of treatment. Such patients are usually close to death, but there are some, such as those with disabling breathlessness or paralysis, who may have to face months or even years of increasing distress.

The act of assisting death, if asked for by the patient, may be described as 'assisted suicide' or 'homicide upon request' (Dunstan, 1972). These terms are not used here, lest their legal implications confuse the ethical issues. Nor is 'euthanasia' used, because it means different things to different people. More important is rejection of the word 'killing'. This word is generally used to indicate a violent act in war or crime, rather than to describe a gentle act of merciful clinical care.

Objections to assisting death

There are four commonly raised objections to assisting death.

First, if doctors were known to be allowed to assist the death of their patients on request, this might put pressure on frail, elderly patients (especially those with unscrupulous relatives) to feel that they ought to request death to save trouble for the family. If this is the reason for the request, however, it should not normally be difficult for the doctor to discern this and discuss it with the patient and family. Such a request may be due to clinical depression which could be relieved by suitable medication, counselling or psychotherapy. If this is not so, and the doctor is confident that the patient's disabilities, coupled with his genuine distress about the trouble and expense of the care he needs, make continued life devoid of any enjoyment, the doctor's response will depend on the more general question of how he regards his ethical responsibilities in relation to assisting death.

Second, an option for doctors to assist the death of patients with terminal illnesses might reduce the pressure for research into better methods of symptom control in such patients, or for provision of resources for their care. In the past, opposition to proposals for 'voluntary euthanasia' legislation provided an additional motivation to seek improvements in terminal care. The very success of such improvements, however, now means that a much smaller proportion of such patients are likely to ask for assistance in dying. Any failure to relieve terminal suffering, moreover, will maintain the demand for continued research.

Third, trust between patients and their doctors might be eroded. This does not seem to have happened as a consequence of what is now done in the Netherlands. At present many patients fear that their doctors, using modern technology, may prolong their lives against their wishes. This may erode their trust as much as any fear that their doctors might end patients' lives without being asked to do so.

Finally, assisting death on patients' request might lead to a slide down a moral slippery slope towards unrequested ending of the lives of unconscious, demented or mentally handicapped patients. Such a moral slide seems improbable. Except in cases of irreversible unconsciousness [. . .] disapproval of involuntary termination of patients' lives is strongly entrenched in the concepts of most doctors and laymen. Furthermore, despite the denials in the BMA euthanasia report, we know that many doctors have assisted and still assist the deaths of occasional patients in their own homes. These rare acts have been accepted as desirable without any consequent moral decline. Such acts are probably less frequent than they were, since more patients die in hospital, where many health professionals are involved in their care and where assistance of death can no longer be left to the private judgement of doctor and patient. Consequently more people now fear that they will not receive the curtailment of terminal distress which they may wish as they approach their deaths. This means that to permit doctors to assist death, but only in generally agreed and defined circumstances, may be seen as a moral advance rather than a moral decline.

The list of possible undesirable consequences, in addition, needs to be balanced against strong arguments for prevention of terminal suffering. Without this help, many patients would, as now, suffer persistent mental and physical distress while awaiting natural death. It would be unjust if only some doctors, as at present, continued to relieve terminal suffering by assisting death in the privacy of the home, while others, especially in hospital, did not do this. Continuing with the tacit agreement to overlook doctors' illegal actions might seem, to some, preferable to permitting them explicitly. But this would provide no safeguard for patients denied this kind of help by their doctors, nor legal safeguards for doctors who acquiesced with their wishes. Public, explicit agreements on the circumstances in which these acts of mercy were to be allowed would benefit and protect both patients and their doctors. It is possible indeed that a public, explicit agreement of this kind might lead fewer patients to ask for assisted death. If everyone knew that it was permissible, this could counter any fear that if they found themselves distressed *in extremis*, doctors would not be allowed to end their lives, however much they were suffering in mind or body. Abolition of such anxiety might enable both patient and doctor to concentrate on symptom relief, which might then become more effective (Higgs, 1983). Paradoxically, allowing doctors to assist death could be seen as a way of fulfilling their commitment to prolonging lives of satisfaction and dignity. [. . .]

Relief of suffering

Doctors hold relief of their patients' suffering to be their first and most rewarding duty. It is the main reason for their looking unfavourably on the useless prolongation of miserable life, and on assisting its termination. In fulfilling this aspect of their duty to relieve suffering, doctors have to bear the following six constraints in mind.

Respect for patients' autonomy

This constraint has only recently become accepted by many doctors. Previously, a paternalistic attitude was widely accepted and practised: patients were expected to follow 'doctor's orders' without question or demur. Now it is increasingly recognized that, under the principle of patient autonomy, doctors have an obligation to ensure that what they do for their patients is in accord with their patients' wishes. [. . .]

Duty to do no harm

Unfortunately, many forms of treatment that will ultimately relieve suffering involve some degree of harm, such as the side-effects of useful medicines or the painful and disabling consequences of surgical or diagnostic procedures. Doctors and their clinical colleagues, in discussion with their patients, must carefully consider the balance of good and harm, and do what will cause most good and least harm in terms of relieving suffering and prolonging life.

Justice

Nowadays much medical and surgical care is increasingly costly and doctors have to ensure a fair distribution of expensive investigations and treatment among all who need them. They may resent or even seek to dismiss this encroachment on their clinical freedom, but this is an increasing influence on decisions about prolonging life and refusing assistance of death, both of which may be costly in terms of medical resources.

Alternatives

If asked by a patient to end his life because of suffering, the doctor must first ensure that there is no doubt about the diagnosis of fatal disease, and that every possible means of cure and relief have been tried – in particular, methods for relief of pain and clinical depression. It is also essential to inquire about sources of distress in the patient's family or social circumstances which might be contributing to the wish to die.

Collaboration

All of the above should be done not only to the doctor's satisfaction, but also in full collaboration with others, particularly the nursing staff. Whom to involve, especially the patient's family or friends, and how to involve them in such discussions, needs sensitive judgement. [. . .]

Conscientious objections

There will inevitably be occasions when a doctor who has deep conscientious objections to the deliberate ending of human life is asked by one of his patients for assistance in dying. This situation is similar to that of a gynaecologist with conscientious objections being asked by a patient for an abortion. In both instances the right thing is for the first doctor to refer the patient to another doctor without such objections, with a request that he or she take over the patient's care.

Prolonging life

A doctor's duty to prolong life is not concerned with all forms of life, but only human life of a quality that the person concerned wishes to have prolonged. There are some patients whose lives are of a quality which they do not wish, at the time, to have prolonged, but for whose prolongation they may be grateful in the future – as in attempted suicide or clinical depression. With a patient who cannot express a wish, the doctor's duty is to prolong life only if it can be assumed to be such that this would be the patient's wish, or if, as in the case of infants or mentally handicapped patients, there is nothing to contradict the presumption in favour of prolonging life. But to prolong life which a person, being of sound mind, does not wish to have prolonged, contradicts the fundamental moral principle of respect for autonomy and, in some cases, the doctor's duty to relieve suffering. A patient's sustained wish to die is a sufficient reason for a doctor to allow him to do so.

An important and in hospital a common occasion for hesitating to prolong life is when a patient's heart stops beating. Formerly this was immediately fatal, but now cardiopulmonary resuscitation enables many hearts to be restarted so that the patient's life may be restored. If the patient is disabled by a chronic illness however, and resuscitation succeeds, his or her plight is often worsened. In such cases doctors have to decide whether the brief extra span of a gravely disabled life is worth the often unpleasant experience of being resuscitated. Doctors who decide against resuscitation place their duty to save terminal distress above their duty to prolong life. Thereby they allow the patient to die in circumstances where this is morally equivalent to assisting death. Decisions not to resuscitate are usually paternalistic since, in order to avoid alarm, they are taken without asking for the patient's consent (Gillon, 1989).

Conclusion

The majority view of the IME working party may be formulated as follows. A doctor, acting in good conscience, is ethically justified in assisting death if the need to relieve intense and unceasing pain or distress caused by an incurable illness greatly outweighs the benefit to the patient of further prolonging his life. This conclusion applies to patients whose sustained wishes on this matter are known to the doctor and should thus be respected as outweighing any contrary opinions expressed by others. Assistance of death, however, is not justified until the doctor and the clinical team are sure that the patient's pain and distress cannot be relieved by any other means – pharmacological, surgical, psychological or social. To this end the views of medical and other professional colleagues and of the patient's family must be ascertained as fully as is consistent with maintenance of the patient's trust.

References

Dunstan, G.R. (1972) 'Euthanasia: clarifying the issues', in A.V. Campbell (ed.), *The Problem of Euthanasia*. (Proceedings of a conference held at the Royal College of Physicians, London, by the London Medical Group and the Society for the Study of Medical Ethics.) Edinburgh: Contact (Pastoral). pp. 4–5.

Gillon, R. (1989) 'Deciding not to resuscitate', *Journal of Medical Ethics*, 15: 171–2.

Higgs, R. (1983) 'Cutting the thread and pulling the wool – a request for euthanasia in general practice', *Journal of Medical Ethics*, 9: 45–9.

Ritger, H., Borst-Eilers, E. and Leenen, H.J.J. (1988) 'Euthanasia across the North Sea', *British Medical Journal*, 297: 1593–5.

Working Party to Review the British Medical Association's Guidance on Euthanasia (1988) *The Euthanasia Report*. London: BMA.

32

Assisted death: a reply

Robert G. Twycross

In the Parliamentary debate on the Gulf Crisis on 6 September 1990, Paddy Ashdown, leader of the Liberal Democrat Party and former officer of the Royal Marines Special Boat Squadron, said:

> I have learned from bitter experience that when the armchair theorists and the Whitehall generals start talking of a surgical [i.e. locally contained and decisive] war, it is time to start to run for cover.

These words, applied to a different context, summarize the feelings of disquiet I experienced on reading the statement by a working party of the Institute of Medical Ethics on the ethics of prolonging life and assisting death [see the previous article in this volume].

My overriding impression is that it does not speak to the everyday situations that I meet in a hospice within the National Health Service. It seems to me that the working party's conclusion – namely, a doctor acting in good conscience is ethically justified in assisting death if the need to relieve intolerable intractable physical and/or mental suffering outweighs the benefit of further sustaining the patient's life – is based on a faulty weighing up of the facts of the matter, such as they are.

I have worked for nearly twenty years in palliative medicine/hospice care. During this time, my opinions on many issues both within and outwith clinical practice have changed. One that has not changed, however, is my belief that it would be a disaster for the medical profession to cross the Rubicon and to be permitted to use pharmacological means to precipitate death deliberately and specifically. When all the factors are taken into account, physical, psychological, social and spiritual, it is *not* the answer (Roy, 1990; Gaylin et al., 1988).

The end of life is death

I should stress that I am not in favour of 'meddlesome' or 'mindless' medical intervention at the end of life. I believe, for example, for an octogenarian to say 'I've lived a good life and I am ready to go' is neither immoral nor anti-life. It is merely a recognition of biological

From *The Lancet*, 'Viewpoint', 29 September 1990: 796–8 (abridged).

fact – namely, that eventually we must all die and that, with the onset of progressive senile decrepitude, the burden of living becomes increasingly demanding for many old people. Because death is ultimately inevitable, a doctor must practise his or her skills accordingly. Thus the claim made by some, tacitly or overtly, that a doctor must preserve life at all costs is biologically untenable.

In palliative medicine there are, perhaps, many occasions when, having weighed up the benefits and burdens of a proposed course of action, the right initial step seems to be 'to give death a chance'. In other words, not to prescribe an antibiotic in a terminally ill moribund patient with pneumonia or not to blood transfuse another patient whose dying is complicated by haematemesis [vomiting of blood] and/or melaena [passing of black, tarry stools, indicating bleeding from the upper gastro-intestinal tract]. I also believe that there are rare occasions when it is necessary to use benzodiazepine, phenothiazines, or barbiturates to sedate a patient in order to relieve intolerable distress in a patient whose dying is complicated by an agitated delirium or tracheal obstruction.

I still feel bound, however, by the cardinal medical ethical principle that I must achieve my treatment goal with the least risk to the patient's life. In this case, rendering the patient unconscious is clearly less of an immediate risk than deliberately killing the patient. Members of the working party will presumably say that I am splitting ethical and therapeutic hairs in as much as the end-points of my action and that of the doctor who would actively assist death are identical. I disagree; for me there is a fundamental difference. Even in these extreme and rare circumstances, my approach maintains a measure of humility in the face of the mystery of life and death. I am saying the dangers of crossing the Rubicon are so great that, even though I may have been forced by extreme circumstances to put one foot in the river, I will continue to respect the necessity of this ultimate barrier.

What are these dangers? The working party states that 'we know that many doctors have assisted and still assist the deaths of occasional patients in their own homes'. I accept this, for the moment, at its face value. Reading between the lines, however, the working party's statement seems to suggest that legalizing assisted death will not lead to a massive increase in such happenings. I beg to differ. In 1967, the law concerning induced abortion was changed. It was said by many at the time that it was a matter of recognizing what was now considered good medical practice, and that a statute was necessary to prevent a doctor who was acting in good conscience from the threat of prosecution. Yet the outcome is common knowledge – that abortion on demand is performed in considerable numbers year after year. (Note, I am *not* commenting on whether abortion on demand is right or wrong; I am simply pointing out that a statute designed to do one limited thing led in practice to another unlimited result.) [. . .]

Economic and other pressures

For me, perhaps the greatest danger is that of economic pressures. Here in Oxford, progressive health care cuts led to a reduction of beds at Sobell House from a norm of 18 to a norm of 14 in November 1989. In the current financial year, we are heading for an overspend on nursing costs of about £70,000. If this money is not found from outwith the NHS, it will mean a further reduction to 10 beds. It is already impossible to manage on 14 beds. Sobell House serves a population of about 0.5 million and concentrates on home care. Seven Macmillan nurses (5 based locally and 2 in the north of the county) are involved at any one time in the care of about 100 patients. In addition, another 30 patients attend the day centre. Yet we are having to face the impossible situation of being required to operate with only about *half* the number of back-up beds needed to supply the needs of such a group of patients. The temptation to move from voluntary assisted death to involuntary assisted death would be too great for some of us to resist, myself included, as patients clamour for admission to non-existent beds for symptom relief or respite.

I feel that the working party is naïve when it states, concerning possible pressures imposed on frail, elderly patients by unscrupulous relatives, 'It should not normally be difficult for the doctor to discern this and discuss it with the patient and family.' Pressure from unscrupulous relatives is a present reality and I, for one, need the protection of the law to assist me in resisting it at times.

Plain speech

I also wondered why the working party opted for narcotic drugs as the most appropriate means of assisting death. In the Netherlands, doctors do not rely on such a dubious means of achieving death. There, the usual method is to induce sleep with a barbiturate, followed by a lethal injection of curare (Angell, 1988). Why did the working party not opt for a similar approach? A bit too brazen? A bit too calculated? An echo of the Third Reich? Surely, if doctors are going to assist death, it is imperative that they use the most reliable means.

In my experience, however, there are many more patients who are fearful of an iatrogenic [doctor-induced] death (accidental or intentional) than there are patients who request euthanasia. To tarnish the public's image of narcotics by allowing them to be used as 'killer drugs' is irresponsible. Already some terminal cancer patients are reluctant to take morphine to control persistent severe pain because they believe that it will cause them to die sooner than otherwise. Intuition warns me that the number would increase substantially if there was a euthanasia statute. [. . .]

When all else fails?

The working party states that 'assistance of death is not justified until the doctor and the clinical team are sure that the patient's pain and distress cannot be relieved by any other means – pharmacological, surgical, psychological or social'. To expect this utopian criterion to be upheld in practice is naïve. Which doctor and which clinical team? In 1972 when a visiting medical officer at St Joseph's Hospice, London, an elderly terminally ill cancer patient was referred to me from the London Hospital. The referral letter said, 'We have tried everything but have failed to relieve his pain.' After two to three weeks at St Joseph's he was *completely* free of pain and returned to his daughter's home. He continued to take regular oral analgesics [. . .] He lived an active life until five months later when he was readmitted to St Joseph's with pneumonia and died two days later. I ask: will it be mandatory for the London Hospital to seek the assistance of St Joseph's Hospice in all potential cases of assisted death in cancer patients before proceeding?

It is time to remove the rose-tinted spectacles and to be realistic. The opportunity to opt out will probably *discourage* the patient and clinical staff from pursuing all other available avenues. [. . .]

Last words

In conclusion, I should like to say two things which I hope will show that I am neither unfeeling nor uncaring. First, a doctor who has never been tempted to kill a patient has probably had very limited clinical experience or is not able to empathize closely with those who suffer; second, the doctor who leaves a patient to suffer intolerably is morally more reprehensible than the doctor who opts for 'death assistance'.

The final word, however, must be that of Lord Raglan, who presented a euthanasia bill to the House of Lords in 1969. Inevitably, the proposed statute included proposals for obtaining and recording the patient's consent. The bill was defeated, and subsequently Lord Raglan concluded that the problem of drawing up a suitable declaration may well be insuperable: 'All the attempts that I've seen at drawing up a declaration had too many weaknesses for my liking, and had too many holes picked in them' (Raglan, 1972).

References

Angell, M. (1988) 'Euthanasia', *New England Journal of Medicine*, 319: 1348–50.
Gaylin, W., Kass, L.R., Pellegrino, E.D. and Siegler, M. (1988) 'Doctors must not kill', *Journal of the American Medical Association*, 259: 2139–40.
Raglan, Lord (1972) 'The case for voluntary euthanasia', *Contact*, 39: 9.
Roy, D.J. (1990) 'Euthanasia: taking a stand', *Journal of Palliative Care*, 6: 3–5.

33

A student's story

Anonymous

During my third year of training in a large city training hospital, I elected to do the obstetric module. I was placed on the special care baby unit (SCBU) for a period of about four weeks. On my second or third day on the unit, I was on a 'late shift', i.e. 12.25 p.m.–9 p.m.

During the day a very premature baby, estimated to be about twenty-eight weeks' gestation, was brought to the unit from the labour ward.

He was extremely tiny, I had never seen such a small baby before. There were three or four other babies nursed in cots on the unit and only this tiny premature baby was in an incubator.

During the afternoon I gradually became aware that I would be the only nurse on duty between 5 p.m. and 9 p.m. that evening. I was naturally terrified at the prospect of being left alone with this tiny baby and refused to tube feed him.

He was having hourly tube feeds of minute quantities.

It was arranged that the sister from the antenatal ward next door would come and feed him at 6 p.m. I was to continue his routine observations of respiratory rate, apex beat, etc. I had never measured a baby's apex beat before, but I was instructed during the afternoon how to do this.

Needless to say I hovered above the incubator watching him constantly and doing his observations far more frequently than instructed.

Six o'clock eventually came, but there was no sign of the sister who was to tube feed him. The minutes ticked by endlessly and by 6.10 p.m. I went to the antenatal ward to remind her. She assured me she hadn't forgotten and would be along in a minute, she still hadn't appeared at 6.15 p.m.

The baby appeared to change colour slightly and I felt he didn't look well. I took his apex beat and it had fallen quite dramatically. I was really frightened now, so I ran to get the sister.

From G. Fairbairn and D. Mead, 'Ethics and the loss of innocence', *Paediatric Nursing*, June 1990: 22–3. This extract is taken from an article discussing ethical dilemmas in nursing and the ways in which the effects such dilemmas have on nurses can be viewed as being akin to bereavement. It was written during a workshop on ethics. The authors of the article express their gratitude to the nurse who shared this experience with them.

She came in promptly, laughed at me saying he looked fine, but he certainly didn't to me. I asked her to check his heart rate, which she did very briefly and said it was quite normal and she promptly left without feeding him.

I was now terrified. He looked ghastly to me, so I did his observations again. His apex beat was now down to 60. I knew I was right, but I obviously couldn't get her back again, so I just ran into the corridor, grabbed a doctor and dragged her into the unit to look at the baby.

She immediately demanded resuscitation equipment. I hadn't a clue where it was kept. I frantically started searching cupboards, she was shouting, I was terrified. The baby died before I could find anything.

I reported the death to the senior sister on the labour ward and was instructed to prepare the baby for the mortuary.

Nobody came to see me or to help me, so I did what I thought was right. I found a little nightdress that appeared to be a shroud and I washed him and dressed him in the shroud and reported to the sister that he was ready to be checked before going to the mortuary.

When she came to the unit and found that I had neither weighed him nor checked his head circumference, she really laid into me.

I had no idea that preparing a baby would be different from an adult. She handled the baby quite roughly, removing his nightdress, weighing and measuring him, I found her actions very disturbing, and she really upset me. I was made to feel worse than useless.

I already felt the baby had died because of my actions. If I had known where the resuscitation equipment was kept he may have lived.

Perhaps I did his observations too often, and caused him to be cold. I felt responsible for his death for years.

This all happened sixteen years ago but I can remember it as if it happened yesterday. One thing that strikes me particularly about it all, is that even now when I remember and think about it, I can smell the unit. It had a very distinctive sort of smell about it.

34

Why do doctors and nurses disagree?

Gwen Adshead and Donna Dickenson

Why might doctors and nurses take contrasting approaches to ethical dilemmas in dealing with dying people? In this article we suggest four reasons. Beginning with the most empirical, and ascending towards the theoretical empyrean, they are:

1 the ways in which the relationship between doctor and patient differs from that between nurse and patient;
2 the contrasting training and socialization of the two professions;
3 gender issues arising from the female paradigm in nursing and a masculine paradigm in medicine; and
4 the model of medicine as 'curing' and nursing as 'caring'.

1 The relationship with the patient

If one begins by considering the doctor–patient relationship, one can see that it is a complex interaction. It is affected by a number of factors, of which the training and expectations of doctors are only two. (Medical training and socialization will be considered at greater length under the next heading.) The clinical state of the patient affects the relationship: the relationship of the comatose patient with his or her doctor differs from that of the alert and well-orientated patient seeking cosmetic surgery.

Patients' expectations, previous experiences and personalities have an influence on the doctor–patient relationship: there is a personal interaction as well as a professional one. The amount of time that is spent with the patient affects the quality of the doctor–patient relationship, as with any other relationship. This is an important issue: many doctors appear to think that time allocation is purely a clinical matter, not (as we argue) a potent medical resource, whose usage is not only an ethical but also a political issue. Similarly, third-party interests affect the doctor–patient relationship: the law has the most obvious claim, but families and friends may have an influence as well.

Viewing the doctor–patient relationship in purely clinical terms, as a process of diagnosis, management and (hopefully) cure, leaves little room for interaction with the patient, which *is* emphasized in the prevailing paradigm of nursing (Campbell, 1984). (Task-orientated nursing of the sort still found on some general surgical wards would be more mechanistic: see Field, 1989, for an account of the moral dilemmas which this just-get-through-the-work style of nursing raises for practitioners.) Doctors holding this model would stress the essentially scientific aspects of medicine, and would claim that their role is limited to a somewhat mechanistic intervention. This very particular view of medicine gives rise to a very particular view of the doctor's ethical duties. For example, such an outlook would support a very paternalistic type of ethics, in which the duty of beneficence (doing good) 'trumped' all other claims, such as patient autonomy, good communication or effective resource management.

How did this mechanistic and simplistic model of health care delivery manage to persist so long among doctors, until very recently? If the doctor has a limited interaction with the patient, it is easier to avoid empathizing too much. Empathy means that patients share their sense of pain, hopelessness and fear, if that is indeed what they are feeling. Because they are closer to patients in status terms, nursing staff may be more likely to empathize with patients. This can be very demanding, and requires explicitly tailored systems of management and support (Field, 1989; Katz, 1989). Far easier simply to avoid it altogether, as the more limited nature of doctor–patient interaction permits.

A scientific view of medicine also reinforces mechanistic interaction, because of the value placed on scientific endeavour. The stereotype of scientists popular among medical students and doctors depicts them as calculating, dispassionate, rational in the extreme and oblivious to all but the pursuit of knowledge. Respect for this image bolsters self-esteem in those who cultivate it, but again reinforces a very mechanistic model of the doctor–patient relationship.

2 Training and socialization

The positivistic model – which denies values and beliefs any place in science – is inculcated during medical training, or even earlier, during the education and socialization of prospective medical students. In England, Wales and Northern Ireland this begins at the age of 15, when pupils choose the three science A-levels necessary for medical school entry. Thus at an early stage trainee doctors are likely to be cut off, not only from study of the humanities, but from other people who have the same enthusiasm for non-scientific matters as the trainee doctor has for science. The prestige of medicine overrides any doubts about the narrowness of this preparation. Although prospective nurses may have a similar school background, nursing also continues to recruit numbers of mature entrants who may have quite a different school or university background, possibly even a humanities-based one.

In the first two years at medical school, when the basic medical sciences are studied, the focus is on the human body as possessing a 'normal' condition, which is made abnormal by defects, producing signs and symptoms. The mechanistic model is thus reinforced. Although medical sociology has been taught for some time, medical ethics teaching was generally absent from medical school curricula until its inclusion was recommended by the Pond Report (1987). At the medical school which one of us attended, papers involving less obviously scientific material, such as psychology and sociology, were known by students as 'the silly papers'.

It may be argued that things have changed considerably, and that this is too gloomy a view. The publication of the Pond Report, the launch of the Oxford Practice Skills project to develop an ethical and legal curriculum in medical teaching, and the involvement of many doctors in ethical teaching and research are certainly hopeful signs. But there are a great number of practitioners, teachers and students of medicine largely unaffected by such changes.

It is not surprising that junior doctors are ill-equipped psychologically when they first arrive on the wards. They are rarely trained to communicate with people, especially not people who want something very valuable from them: medical knowledge and skill. Very little in their training has prepared them for the reality of other people's misery.

The positivistic attitudes cultivated in doctors' training spill over into a particular ethical view, we speculate. From our own experience of teaching ethics to trainee and practising doctors and nurses, we have the impression that doctors tend to accept utilitarianism – which measures how good or bad moral choices are by quantifying how much welfare they produce – more readily than do nurses, who tend to think in terms of individual patients' immediate needs rather than the long-term welfare of whole classes of patients. Perhaps this is because a utilitarian view fits into doctors' positivist world picture. The model of the moral agent as a calculating machine appears quite foreign to many nurses, particularly those who deal frequently with weak or confused patients.

Added to this positivism in doctors' training is a cult of macho toughness. This is particularly stringent for women, we argue. In some senses, women in medicine are forced to take on a super-masculine role, as 'marginal men'. In our experience they compete to work longer and harder than their male colleagues and are quite nervous of showing their feelings. Doctors who express pain or distress at work are frowned upon by their colleagues, and women may be particularly under suspicion, as supposedly the 'more emotional' sex. One female junior doctor has complained that she was very much discouraged from admitting grief at her father's death: had she been a nurse, she wrote, a few tears would have been more acceptable (see 'Doctor's Mask on Pain', pp. 83–4 in this volume).

3 Gender differences

This last point, about the socialization of female medical students into a macho model of behaviour, leads into gender issues. Although approaching 50 per cent of the intake into UK medical schools is now female, and although men are well represented in nursing management and psychiatric nursing, the paradigm of medicine remains male, and that of nursing female. This is not simply because the most prestigious areas in medicine remain largely inaccessible to women: only ten of the 10,000 general surgeons in England are female, for example. It is also because the models of the two professions reflect very different values, and because gender issues underlie that split.

Why should the gender balance or image of the two professions matter, in terms of the ethical issues most relevant to each? Because some developmental psychologists have argued that girls and boys develop different and partly opposing moral outlooks; and, incidentally, because boys' view of the moral universe is regarded as more mature in most developmental tests, since these tests are skewed towards the male outlook. In a survey of 144 males and females matched for class, education, intelligence and age, at varying points throughout the life cycle, the psychologist Carol Gilligan (1982) suggested that boys were more likely to operate with a morality of *rights*, whereas girls were most swayed by considerations of *responsibilities*. Other psychologists have challenged Gilligan's empirical evidence (Greeno and Maccoby, 1986; Luria, 1986); she counters that 'the argument was not statistical – that is, not based on the representativeness of the women studied. ... Rather ... the examples presented illustrated a different way of seeing' (Gilligan, 1986: 326). Do nurses also have a different way of seeing from doctors – one based on a more intimate relationship with the patient?

Asked, 'When responsibility to oneself and responsibility to others conflicts, how should one choose?', an 11-year-old-boy in Gilligan's study, Jake, answered succinctly, 'You go about one-fourth to the others and three-fourths to yourself.' The point of Jake's answer is not his selfishness: it is that he was at ease with the question. Thinking in terms of his rights versus everybody else's posed few problems for him.

In contrast a girl of the same age, Amy, found the question unanswerable as it was, and appeared to dither in her reply. She wanted to know who the others were, what the situation was, what the relationships comprised. To Amy, morality was less to do with quantifiable *rights* and more dependent on the intricacies of *relationships*. Although the question was actually phrased in terms of relationships rather than rights, it was not written in her 'language'. It did not give her enough information about her responsibilities in particular relationships.

Lawrence Blum views Gilligan as trying to prove empirically that there can be a kind of moral outlook other than what he calls the 'impartialist' one, based on impartiality, justice, formal rationality and universal principles – like Beauchamp and Childress's (1978) four norms in medical ethics: autonomy, beneficence (doing good), non-maleficence (doing no harm) and justice. 'For Gilligan . . . the moral agent must understand the other person as the specific individual that he or she is, not merely as someone instantiating general moral categories such as friend or person in need. Moral action which fails to take account of this particularity is faulty and defective' (Blum, 1988: 474–5).

The four principles were devised entirely for medical cases. They may apply quite differently for nurses. For example, issues about patient autonomy in nursing do not focus on invasive procedures, but on the possible affront to autonomy which can come from the very intimate nature of nursing care.

Conventional definitions of 'autonomy' may merge too readily into 'acting rationally'. If so, too many patients will be thought incapable of acting autonomously: children, people with dementia, perhaps even all people in hospital – since a few days in hospital much diminishes anyone's independence of mind and thought. In a discussion of justifications for limiting autonomy, Meta and Hatti Hayry (1991) include the case in which the patient possesses insufficient information of knowledge about a procedure, compared with the doctor. This, they say, shows limited autonomy.

But actually it only shows possible limitations on rational choice: the possession of full information about the alternatives is a first condition of rationality (Brandt, 1979). We all lack sufficient information to make any choice whose outcome is only probabilistic: we can never be sure whether the side effect with a .01 probability of occurrence will occur in our particular case – as it did for poor Mrs Amy Sidaway, left severely disabled after an elective operation which carried a 1 per cent risk of damage to the spinal cord (*Sidaway* v *Board of Governors of Bethlem Royal Hospital*, 1984). In that sense we all lack perfect rationality. Do we all therefore lack full autonomy?

Focusing on a different model of autonomy might be consistent with the approach to ethics which Gilligan argues – controversially – to be more typical of girls and women. Such a model requires not just projection of one's own preferences onto the patient, but genuine recognition of her as autonomous. This entails more than simply letting her alone – rather, trying to understand her as another mind. Is this the sort of knowledge of a patient which a nurse is more likely to obtain than a doctor? 'Empathy, not sympathy', is after all a catch phrase in nurse training. This leads into our fourth area of consideration, the supposed distinction between the nurse's caring function and the doctor's curing role.

4 Caring and curing

The distinction between medicine as concerned with 'curing' and nursing as being about 'caring' has been accepted surprisingly widely, given how simplistic it is. Perhaps this is because it overlaps with other distinctions which many find comfortable and familiar. The caring–curing distinction also fits in with the mechanistic model in medicine – fixing what's broken – and the emotion-tending duties in nursing. Part of the nurse's job is seen – by outsiders and by nurses themselves – as maintaining the patient's emotional well-being, just as women are supposed to take care of relationships generally.

Clearly the caring–curing contrast cannot cope with palliative medicine, which does not aim to cure. As Ian Johnson (1991), director of Leicester Hospice, puts it, the 'liberating' effect of palliative medicine is the recognition that curing is no longer a requirement, only caring. Nor is the contrast consistent with the rise of holistic medicine in fields other than palliative care and in areas other than the hospice movement; for example, the use of complementary medicine in some geriatric nursing. Holistic care is whole-person care, of both the body and the emotions.

Nevertheless, some who would argue for nursing ethics as a separate domain do so on the grounds that it concerns questions about caring (Noddings, 1984, 1989), and that medical ethics has failed to deal with these in its headlong rush to concentrate on new technologies of curing. This links back to Gilligan's assertion that men and women develop separate moral outlooks, and to the implication that moral philosophy has wrongly read men's concerns as universal.

> The moral imperative . . . [for] women is an injunction *to care*, a responsibility to discern and alleviate the 'real and recognizable trouble' of this world. For men, the moral imperative appears rather as an injunction to respect the rights of others and thus to protect from interference the right to life and self-fulfillment. (Gilligan, 1982: 100)

Of course there are chicken-and-egg questions here. Are women born caring, do they achieve caring, or is caring thrust upon them? But wherever the caring concern comes from, it cannot be generated from principle alone: you can't simply *will* a caring attitude into being because you think it right on principle. So again, if there really is a distinction between women's and men's moral approaches, a principle-centred approach to ethics may ignore women's outlook and needs. If their concern *is* caring, caring will always be second-best to curing, and .their concerns less important.

> The wish for cure dominates medicine and the routine tasks of caring are delegated to nurses, who are regarded as more appropriate hourly companions for the patient. We might say that doctors tend to serve the male God of interventionist medicine, Asclepius. The more tranquil, nurturing role of Hygeia, the goddess of well-being, is seen as a lesser task, suitable for the womanly patience of nurses. (Campbell, 1984: 31)

But Campbell means this criticism to sound the death knell of what he sees as a stereotyped and sexist distinction between curing and caring. Against the view that caring and curing reflect genuine differences in women's and men's moral outlooks, writ large in the gendered roles of the two professions, is the argument that stereotypes of caring and curing are just that: stereotypes.

Although Gilligan is careful to assert that the male and female moral outlooks are equally valid, there is also a risk that accepting her arguments – or those about curing as medicine's province and caring as nursing's concern – will redound against women. 'Separate but equal' was pronounced a chimera in relation to race by US Supreme Court judgement in the *Brown* case in 1954: separate inherently means unequal. If nursing is defined as being about caring, and medicine about curing, medicine will continue to be seen as more important. If the role of the female paradigm profession of nursing is seen as caring, the old stereotype of the nurse as the doctor's 'helpmeet' will be revived. Caring is likely to be seen as less important than curing because we fear death, and wrongly attribute to medicine the power to cure us of mortality.

We would also suggest that caring will be seen as less important than curing precisely because caring is traditionally perceived as a woman's job. When a job begins to be done exclusively by women, its value declines: the most potent example is the denigration of male clerking – which could lead into partnership in the firm in Nicholas Nickleby's time – into the typing pool. Similarly, the view of women as possessing a separate and more emotional nature from men has been used to exclude them from participation and power (Okin, 1989).

There is also a risk to men and medicine, as well as to women and nursing, in separating out curing from caring, because curing is impossible without caring, without immersion in relationships. As Alasdair Campbell puts it, the true (curing) power of medicine is only found 'when the doctor genuinely listens to the patient and to the message of the illness'. As he describes it, this sound very much like 'caring':

> This is the love which is appropriately described as 'brotherly' and 'sisterly', a love which fosters friendship (*philia*). The power of medicine then becomes the power of *letting go* control, using knowledge of the limitations of medical work to encourage the patient to take part in the shared task of trying to understand and deal with the illness as it affects his or her personal being. (Campbell, 1984: 28)

If the split between caring and curing is wrong-minded – and we believe it is – then we want not a separate ethics of caring for nurses, but rather the integration of the requirements of caring into doctors' moral universe. And we want those requirements of caring to be expressed in terms of 'being with' rather than 'doing to', as Campbell puts it: in terms of genuine projection into the patient's mind as a moral virtue. We do need to consider the adequacy of a principle-based approach, as against one which is rooted in relationships. Even if we decide to remain within the Beauchamp–Childress framework, we need to rethink the four principles quite radically in order to accommodate everyday nursing dilemmas and feminist critiques about justice or autonomy. We may need something like a division of labour within a single ethical framework, to accommodate differences by speciality *within* medicine and nursing, not simply between the professions. But we should not be fooled into thinking that different health care professionals need different systems of ethics – if only because sticking together may mean, as the patients' advocate Jean Robinson has put it, 'that way doctors can learn something from nurses'.

References

Beauchamp, Tom L. and Childress, James F. (1978) *Principles of Biomedical Ethics* (2nd edn, 1983; 3rd edn, 1989). Oxford: Oxford University Press.

Blum, Lawrence A. (1988) 'Gilligan and Kohlberg: implications for moral theory', *Ethics*, 98 (3), April: 472–91.

Brandt, Richard (1979) *A Theory of the Good and the Right*. Oxford: Clarendon Press.

Campbell, Alasdair (1984) *Moderated Love*. London: SPCK.

Field, David (1989) *Nursing the Dying*. London: Tavistock/Routledge.

Gilligan, Carol (1982) *In a Different Voice*. Cambridge, MA: Harvard University Press.

Gilligan, Carol (1986) Reply to 'On *In a Different Voice*: an interdisciplinary forum', *Signs: Journal of Women in Culture and Society*, 11 (2): 324–33.

Greeno, Catherine G. and Maccoby, Eleanor E. (1986) 'How different is the different voice?', *Signs: Journal of Women in Culture and Society*, 11 (2): 310–6.

Hayry, Meta and Hayry, Hatti (1991) Paper delivered at the Society for Applied Philosophy annual conference, Isle of Thorns, Sussex, May.

Johnson, Ian (1991) Personal communication.

Katz, Jeanne (1989) 'Context and care: nurses' accounts of stress and support on a cancer ward'. Unpublished PhD thesis, University of Warwick.

Luria, Zella (1986) 'A methodological critique', *Signs: Journal of Women in Culture and Society*, 11 (2): 316–21.

Noddings, Nel (1984) *Caring: A Feminine Approach to Ethics and Moral Education*. Berkeley: University of California Press.

Noddings, Nel (1989) *Women and Evil*. Berkeley: University of California Press.

Okin, Susan Moller (1989) 'Reason and feeling in thinking about justice', *Ethics*, 99 (2) (January).

Pond, Sir Desmond (chair) (1987) *Report of a Working Party on the Teaching of Medical Ethics*, ed. K.M. Boyd. London: Institute of Medical Ethics.

Sidaway v. *Board of Governors of Bethlem Royal Hospital*, [1984] QB 493; [1984] 1 All ER 1018; [1985] AC 871; [1985] 1 All ER 643.

PART 3   CARING FOR DYING PEOPLE

Introduction

Palliative medicine or palliative care are the labels given to the modern package of skills, procedures and practices that have been sponsored and refined mainly within the hospice movement. Its application is not – and should not be – restricted to people who are dying. In practice, however, its combination of pain relief and the reduction of fear and distress tends to be reserved for those at the terminal stage of illness.

Much attention is given to the physical treatments which enable physicians to control pain and disturbing symptoms. But these are only a small, if vitally important, element of the growing repertoire of actions which can aid people to contemplate and cope positively with their imminent death. By far the greatest part of the range of measures which comprise palliative care is good and sensitive communication. So, whilst treatments and procedures have a proper place in this part of the volume, the focus is on how human beings relate to each other.

As we have seen in earlier parts of the book, the historical legacy of ways of dealing with the end of life and the diseases which hasten people to it has heightened guilt, fear and anguish. The iconography of death depicts constant images of the grim reaper and souls in torment on the one hand and poetic representations of the afterlife on the other. The timeless elusiveness of death and the dismaying notion of mortality have driven human interpreters over the ages to the creation of metaphysical and religious explanations which comfort some but terrify many. Against the background of this cultural heritage, most modern societies have developed defences which make talking openly about death when it is close at hand difficult for all concerned. Here we offer a selection of articles and accounts which provide both scientifically tested and experiential accounts of the therapeutic power of good communication.

Robert Buckman addresses the first, important stage of opening up, the breaking of bad news. Originally published in the *British Medical Journal*, before Buckman gained widespread recognition in the media, this piece speaks directly to doctors, Buckman's own ill-prepared profession. But much of what he has to say applies to all health and social care professions. He identifies the problem as lying deep within the professional socialization of doctors which requires them to be authoritative and omniscient. Arising from these characteristics he observes deep-seated fears – of emotional inadequacy, of not knowing the answers, of being blamed, of the patient's anger and of personal inability to cope with the frailty of life. The analysis is a thoughtful melding of professional and personal experience and the guidelines for change are clear and well grounded.

The themes set up by Buckman are further developed by Peter Maguire, a psychiatrist, and Ann Faulkner, a nurse academic, who have researched professional–patient interactions involving different subjects and handling bad news. Through the use of dialogues scripted from their own study material, they articulate a set of principles and strategies which gain specificity in their second piece. The authors wisely describe these statements as guidelines, but many practitioners will find them both authoritative and practical.

Communicating unwelcome information to adults is difficult enough, but engaging with dying children is a challenge with extra dimensions. Dorothy Judd integrates practitioner experience with the psychological literature on cognitive processes in children. Her writing is hallmarked with a deep personal concern for a better understanding of how to relate to terminally ill young people. Like the preceding contributors, she provides clear guidelines for adults, both professional and lay.

Human beings, whether adult or child, are not part of an undifferentiated mass. One of the significant differences, at the macro-level, is the set of religious and cultural rules which surround the individual. These dimensions are reflected throughout the book, but in this section we examine Jewish perspectives. In her article Jeanne Katz seeks to inform readers about the requirements and practices of Judaism, rather than to advocate any particular approach. In doing so she makes two distinct contributions. The first is a clear exposition of law and custom, mapping out the ways in which the separation of the sexes applies even in death. It is law that Jews shall not be cremated but convention dictates how the rules of mourning are interpreted. In differentiating the core elements, she provides a case study which illuminates the ways non-Jews should approach dying Jewish people – and a paradigm for working with anyone from a non-indigenous culture or religion.

Dr Patrick Pietroni is well known as the founder of the Marylebone Centre Trust which combines traditional allopathic medicine with a wide range of complementary therapies. In his article he describes a number of approaches to the relief of pain and anxiety, ranging from breathing exercises and meditation to massage, aromatherapy and acupuncture. These are presented not as new in themselves, for many of them have long histories, but so as to lodge them firmly in the palliative care toolbox. We include the piece to ensure that readers are aware of these therapies, whilst recognizing that there are others which also deserve attention.

In his book *Anguish*, Anselm Strauss reports in close detail the 'dying trajectory' of a single case study – Mrs Abel. The study carries further the celebrated research he did with Barney Glaser, which produced the concept of 'awareness contexts' in ward situations and established an empirical description of how patients continually negotiate with nurses over information about their condition. The short extract here explores what Strauss calls the temporal aspects of dying which influence the shape of the pathway (the dying trajectory) to death. It provides sociological research evidence about how staff, their expectations and regimes, prefigure the way their patients proceed towards death.

Spiritual care, the subject of Alyson Peberdy's article, is in the same territory as Strauss's analysis, because it highlights the personal search for meaning and for hope. In the face of death this search is inevitably heightened and is likely to be discussed with carers of every kind. The enquiry is not confined to those with religious beliefs and the article makes clear the dangers of assumptions about individuals on the basis of minimal knowledge of their religious and cultural affiliations. As she concludes, Alyson Peberdy makes a plea for spiritual care to become part of institutional character and not just be left to individual staff.

The last four contributions are first-person accounts of care for a dying person. The first is from an anonymous old woman who speaks through Elizabeth Dean, a nurse in an old people's home. Its matter-of-fact description of the routines of Sunnyside Lodge tells a story of finitude in an unimaginative care situation. Simone de Beauvoir's emotionally loaded recollection is the last chapter of her book about her mother's death. In *A Very Easy Death* the reader follows Maman's last months after a fall, and all the evocative biographical reflection it generated in this distinguished writer. Rosemary and Victor Zorza's book about their involvement in the protracted and painful death of their daughter, Jane, though contrasting in style, none the less shares with de Beauvoir a common humanity, as they exercise care, devotion and love to allow Jane to die in her own way and in a natural way. This extract provides a dramatic picture of how all the tools of palliative care can work together at the point of death. It serves as a synthesis of the themes in this part. Lastly, Susan Leifer's graphic and honest reporting of being a somewhat unwilling family carer has a contemporary resonance with which many will identify.

35

Breaking bad news: why is it still so difficult?

Robert Buckman

No one seems to find it easy to talk about bad news with a patient and, although little has been published about patients' reactions, there is very little written (other than in specialist journals) about doctors' reactions and feelings. In this article, I try to identify some of the major difficulties and show that they may arise partly because we are (properly) taught to deal systematically with organic medical states in a way that makes it difficult to know how to behave when different services are required by our patients. I venture to suggest that, with relatively minor changes in the medical school curriculum, we can in future produce junior doctors who are better at coping with this awkward (but important) part of clinical medicine.

By 'bad news' I mean any information likely to alter drastically a patient's view of his or her future (whether at the time of diagnosis or when facing the failure of curative intention). Naturally, how bad the news is will depend to some extent on the patients' expectations at the time, on how ill they actually feel, and on whether or not they already know or suspect their diagnosis or current state. I have based many of the ideas on my own reactions and experiences as a medical student and junior doctor. In the past four years I have given and participated in many tutorials and seminars with nurses, students and doctors. From their reactions I have begun to think that the fears and feelings I describe below are fairly common, though not often talked about.

I consider under two headings the major problems that face us as doctors in breaking bad news: the anxieties and fears that we have, which make it difficult for us to start the conversation; and those factors that drive us into taking responsibility for the disease itself, making it even more difficult once the conversation has been started.

From *British Medical Journal*, 1984, 288(1): 1597–9.

Some of the fears that doctors may have

Fear of being blamed

The worst fear for doctors – particularly junior doctors – is that the patient will blame them personally for the bad news that they bring. Of course, the phenomenon of identifying the bad news with the bearer of it is not new, nor is it unique to doctors (after all, the execution of bad news messengers was quite common in ancient times). At the heart of it is the identification of the target for the blame: the easier it is to identify the official authority by which means the news arrives, the easier it is to fix the anger aroused by the news itself on to the bearer. That's why it's so easy, for example, to get angry with a traffic warden – the real anger is at getting the ticket, but with a rapid bit of spurious rationalizing it is very easily transferred to that particular warden (who is quite obviously enjoying it, or who doesn't seem to care at all, or who could just as easily have gone around the block again or waited just two minutes – 'That's all I ask . . .').

Perhaps it is generally easier to personalize bad news to help deal with it. Whatever the prime cause, my point is that the transferring of a reaction on to the bearer is not uncommon or aberrant behaviour. This means that as doctors we can naturally expect (and thus fear) this kind of reaction from our patients when it's our turn to wear the badge of authority and hand out the bad news.

Worse still, the closer we are to our patients the easier we make it for them to blame us – we are (usually) easily identifiable, often in uniform, and we hand out the essential day to day information that actually makes an enormous difference to our patients ('. . . The bone scan is booked for Tuesday, we've fixed the marrow sample for Wednesday, and we should have the results by the ward round on Friday'). It's easy to see how patients come to regard doctors as the source and origin of everything that happens to them and not just of the scans and the blood tests. The more authority we have the more we select ourselves as targets.

Not every patient responds to bad news by blaming the doctor, but it is clearly common and well known enough for many doctors to fear it before they start the conversation and possibly to avoid the conversation because of it. Even doctors with many years of experience may find themselves relieved when a patient says 'Actually I knew it was cancer anyway' and they realize that the moment has passed without blame.

I don't wish to make too much of the sense of blame, but I believe that it is very off-putting to doctors and nurses early in their training and that it requires a great deal of care and attention to remind them (and often ourselves) that the patient's disease is not our fault and therefore that the act of blaming is a reaction (to be taken into account as we would inflammation or haemorrhage) and not to be taken personally. This is easier said than done, but perhaps it needs saying more often even so.

Fear of the unknown and untaught

By the time of qualification all doctors should have been trained (in theory at least) in the management of common medical crises. Nevertheless, unless they qualified in the past few years (and in only certain medical schools, even then) they will not have had any specific training in communication skills in general, nor in talking to dying patients in particular. Plainly it is vital that the doctor should be able to cope efficiently with a diabetic coma or cardiac arrest, and it is in the patients' interests that doctors should know the standard routine approach so that things get done properly and in the right order. That way, if the resuscitation attempt fails at least the doctor may be reasonably certain that he did his best and that nobody else could have done much better.

As we get better at doing the things that we have been trained for, however, the more awkward we feel in situations that we have not been trained for (such as talking to dying patients) and the more we will avoid them. Not only do we miss the comfort and the security of following the course of action that we've been taught but if it all seems to go wrong we have no idea whether it is because we were peculiarly crass or whether this is what happens all the time. This simply means that areas that are out of bounds whilst we are being trained tend to stay out of bounds once we are trained. It is as if a subject that is not on the curriculum is not a 'proper' subject, and the feeling of venturing out beyond the pale of standard medical practice into an uncharted and unfamiliar area adds to the insecurity and anxiety.

Fear of unleashing a reaction

There is also the problem of what may happen once the conversation actually starts – what happens if the patient has a 'bad reaction'? What happens if the patient starts crying – right in the middle of the ward, or in a busy clinic while the nurses are trying to get the next patient into a cubicle and the clinic is fifty minutes behind already?

Not knowing how to deal with the consequences of what we do breaks one of the most important rules of accepted medical behaviour. It makes us inadequate in our own eyes and those of others. There is also the embarrassment of being known as the doctor who goes around making the patients cry. It is generally regarded as better for all concerned if dealings with patients go 'smoothly'; and if patients burst into tears many doctors feel that it is because they failed to do the right things to prevent it. It is not easy to suggest that a patient's crying is not in itself a disaster (for the doctor or the patient) or that the tears may actually have done the patient some good, when confronted by nurses or other doctors who, from the kindest motives, don't want the patients to be 'disturbed'.

Fear of expressing emotion

We are trained to behave calmly in emergencies, to suppress any panic that we may be feeling, and also to suppress any antagonism that we may occasionally feel towards any individual patient. These principles are plainly unarguable and fit in with the accepted idea of proper professional conduct. Adopting the model of the calm and composed efficient doctor, however, does make it difficult to learn how to express sympathy and other emotions that might be helpful to the patient at the right moment. I do not wish to imply that doctors are unsympathetic – but merely that having learnt how not to show panic or anger it is necessary to relearn, as a conscious effort, a way of showing human sympathy. I've often heard doctors say how much easier it is to talk to a friend or a neighbour about the way a disease is affecting them than it is to talk to a hospital patient with the same condition. Perhaps in the clinical setting it's easy to get bogged down by the weight of clinical responsibility and to use authoritative language that disguises both therapeutic failure and underlying sympathy.

There is also a most unfortunate semantic quirk that makes this difficulty even worse – and that is the ambiguity of the word 'sorry'. In general use it has two quite distinct meanings. It may be used as in 'I am sorry *that I did this*', which implies responsibility; or it may be used as in 'I am sorry *for you*' to express sympathy. This makes it even harder to express sympathy, for even if he overcomes his medical reserve the doctor will feel that in saying sorry in the usual way he is inviting the patient to blame him. The knack of expressing sympathy clearly without covertly accepting responsibility is difficult and needs to be taught and demonstrated.

Fear of not knowing all the answers

The more junior the doctor the more difficult it is to maintain self-confidence while saying, 'I don't know'. Perhaps it's to do with the way we are taught to behave in exams early in our careers, when 'I don't know' is expected to earn failure. In practice, it seems as if only the most senior and respected doctors are able to earn applause for confessing ignorance. It is a common enough sight at a symposium or case conference. The consultant is asked for his opinion after the juniors have staggered through a morass of guesses and theories, and his reply 'I simply don't know' is so redolent of experience and authority that it gets the audience muttering 'Of course, that's it – the diagnosis is not known'. I would suggest that it is almost a universal law that you must be seen to know a very great deal before you are allowed to confess to not knowing it all.

At first, talking to dying patients does seem a bit like taking an exam, and it's only after some experience that it becomes apparent that many patients may not want The Answer (and may already know that there isn't one) but may simply want someone to listen to the problem.

Personal fear of illness and death

The personal fear of illness and death is too large a subject to deal with in detail here, and in any case I am not qualified to talk about it in depth. There seem, however, to be two very important factors that come into play. One is the general taboo of death (and talking about death), which is a fairly recent and much discussed social phenomenon and needs no further comment. The other concerns the denial of illness and death by the doctor. Some psychiatrists suggest that among the many reasons for which people want to become doctors is the feeling of invulnerability that comes from working among the sick while being healthy. Whether this is a major or a minor motive, it is much easier to defend the illusion of invulnerability by keeping at a distance from the patient and avoiding the discovery that patients are often very similar to us ('There but for fortune . . .').

I don't know how important this factor is. From the many articles written by doctors about their personal experience of illness and from the descriptions of how surprised and even affronted they were, I would guess that doctors are just a little more inclined than the general public to believe that It can't happen to them. It's easier to keep this illusion alive by staying at a distance from someone to whom It clearly can happen and has happened.

Taking responsibility for the bad news itself

If (despite all the anxieties and fears) a doctor begins to talk about the bad news, other factors begin to operate which push him into assuming responsibility for the disease itself, making him more and more identifiable as the target for blame, rather than as the ally and supporter of the patient.

Shielding

Some people are more inclined than others to pat a seriously ill patient on the shoulder and reassure him that all will be well. Those who do this most readily are not uncaring or insensitive or unaware of the patient's true state – in fact, the opposite is more likely to be so. Usually they simply want the news to be good – all the more if they have begun to identify with the patient in any way – and think that an optimistic picture, by heartening the patient, is a self-fulfilling prophecy.

Wishing for a successful outcome, however, doesn't produce it; and by shielding the patient the doctor removes the opportunity for him to react and behave in his own way to the news or take any intelligent part in his own care. That may seem like a rather trifling and insignificant aspect of being ill, but I believe that it's actually very important, although difficult for healthy people to understand. A man who was not told that he had multiple sclerosis until after seven years of symptoms put it very well to me. He said that it was like worrying about his bank balance and then going to the bank to find the cashier in whispered conference with the manager, who comes forward and refuses to give the current balance but smilingly reassures him that the balance isn't anything to worry about, really.

I do not say that shielding should never take place (roughly half of the patients in two studies indicated that they would rather not be told the exact diagnosis and would prefer to be shielded), nor do I believe that every gloomy detail and possible horror must be spelt out. But I do think that shielding should not go on by default, as a matter of course and without even considering the possibility that the patient may want to make up his own mind. If it does then at least half of the patients will (justifiably) see the doctor as assuming total command of things, and they will identify him with the disease instead of with the fight against it.

Taking the credit for remission

Talking about the possibility of future relapse (for instance, in the common solid tumours) is an unpleasant experience and there is always a great temptation to dismiss it altogether ('We got it in time'; 'It's all gone'). This is one of the most common examples of shielding and patients often overtly encourage us in it, making it difficult not to go along with it. They may be just recovering from primary surgery or treatment and be feeling well and optimistic for the first time since diagnosis and ask us for encouragement to speed their recovery. It seems churlish and cruel to sound a cautious note at that time, and it's very easy to agree, even tacitly, that the patient is cured. Doctors pushed into that position find that their ward rounds and clinics go smoothly and quickly and that their patients are happier – for a time. The problem is that if a cure is promised (when it's not possible) any future relapse will be seen as the personal failure of the doctor. The patient will (probably) see it that way, and the doctor may also feel – even subconsciously – that the relapse is a failure to fulfil the promise and may subsequently avoid contact with the patient for this reason. Ward rounds at that stage tend to be much stickier, with a great deal of hedging round the subject and much anxiety in the patient.

Exerting control over the information

We are trained to try to control disease processes, and it's very frustrating when that can't be achieved. This frustration may lead to a search for some aspect that can be controlled – and often this is the information given to the patient and relatives. Exerting control over this information may not alter things clinically, but it does offer the chance of behaving in a sort of doctorly way. This disguised therapeutic impotence originates from the very best of motives, and it's very difficult to realize while you are doing it that you may not be helping the patient and family at all.

What can be done?

Training in oncology, I have met many doctors who are good at talking to seriously ill or dying patients and a few who are absolutely superb at it and from whose example I have learnt a great deal. Only one or two of them, however, had the time, opportunity and motivation to teach formally or informally on the skills needed and the principles that guide them. This is sad because a great amount of accumulated experience goes to waste and it seems almost as if every trainee must learn all the lessons afresh for himself [sic].

I should like to make a case for medical students receiving more detailed instruction and demonstrations in the subject than they do at present. Only by introducing the subject at an early stage (for instance, using lectures, videos, interviews with patients and role play) will it be seen as part of the orthodox medical curriculum rather than as the esoteric obsession of one or two medical philosophers.

From my extramural activities I have two further points to support my case. First, my experience as a patient has made me much more aware of the very great benefit that a little well-expressed sympathy brings. Secondly, from many interviews with members of the public about medical matters I have a very strong impression that doctors are no longer expected to be omniscient and omnipotent and that our patients genuinely want to be trusted with more knowledge of their conditions and to have the opportunity of discussing their feelings. If they do not get that opportunity from us, then there are many alternative practitioners who will give it – if nothing else.

Conclusion

I do not suggest that there should be any major change in medical attitudes or teaching, but simply that talking to seriously ill patients is a subject in need of greater emphasis in the curriculum. It is a skill (not a divine gift) and it can be taught like any other aspect of medical care.

It can be done well by doctors (and can give satisfaction when well done), but above all it should be seen by all of us as a vital and appreciated part of the job of looking after sick people.

Further reading

Ahmedzai, S. (1982) 'Dying in hospital: the resident's viewpoint', *British Medical Journal*, 285: 712-14.

Bendix, T. (1982) *The Anxious Patient*. London: Livingstone.

Brewin, T.B. (1977) 'The cancer patient: communication and morale', *British Medical Journal*, ii: 1623-7.

Goldie, L. (1982) 'The ethics of telling the patient', *Journal of Medical Ethics*, 8: 126-33.

Hinton, J. (1972) *Dying*. London: Pelican Books.

Jones, S. (1981) 'Telling the right patient', *British Medical Journal*, 283: 291-2.

Konior, G.S. and Levine, A.S. (1975) 'Fear of dying: how patients and their doctors behave', *Semin Oncol*, 2: 311-16.

Moreland, C. (1982) 'Disabilities and how to live with them: testicular teratoma', *The Lancet*, ii: 203-5.

Novack, D.H., Clumer, R., Smith, R.L., et al. (1979) 'Changes in the physicians' attitudes towards telling the patient', *Journal of the American Medical Association*, 241: 897-900.

Parkes, C.M. (1978) 'Psychological aspects', in C.M. Saunders (ed.), *The Management of Terminal Disease*. London: Edward Arnold. pp. 44-64.

Sanson-Fisher, R. and Maguire, P. (1980) 'Should skills in communicating with patients be taught in medical schools?', *The Lancet*, ii: 523-6.

Souhami, R.L. (1978) 'Teaching what to say about cancer', *The Lancet*, ii: 935-6.

36

Communicating with cancer patients: 1. Handling bad news and difficult questions

Peter Maguire and Ann Faulkner

We suggest how to handle situations in communicating with patients with cancer which doctors and nurses commonly find difficult (Maguire and Faulkner, 1988).

Breaking bad news

It is important to accept that you cannot soften the impact of bad news since it is still bad news however it is broken. The key to breaking it is to try to slow down the speed of the transition from a patient's perception of himself as being well to a realization that he (or she) has a life-threatening disease. If you break the news too abruptly it will disorganize him psychologically and he will have difficulty adapting. Alternatively, it may provoke denial because the news is too painful to assimilate. Thus you should avoid stating baldly, 'I am afraid you've got cancer', and instead warn him that you are about to communicate serious information by saying, for example, 'I am afraid it looks more serious than an ulcer.'

While you may be tempted to soften this immediately by adding: 'Even so we should still be able to do something about it', resist this and pause to let your warning sink in. This will also allow you time to monitor how your patient is reacting. What you say next depends on his response. A question like: 'What do you mean not just an ulcer?' suggests that he wants more information. If, however, he [sic] says, 'That's all right, doctor, I'll leave it up to you', he is suggesting that he does not wish to learn more at this time. By using a hierarchy of euphemisms for the word cancer, such as a few odd cells, a kind of tumour, a bit cancerous, it is possible to manage the transition so that you can establish how far your patient wants to go at each stage.

From *British Medical Journal*, 1988, 297(2): 907-9.

Doctor: I'm afraid it's more than just an ulcer. . . .
Mr K: What do you mean more than just an ulcer?
Doctor: Some of the cells looked abnormal under the microscope. . . .
Mr K: Abnormal?
Doctor: They looked cancerous.
Mr K: You mean I've got cancer?
Doctor: I am afraid so, yes.

You should next explore how he feels about this information and why. This will usually reveal that there are good reasons for his responses.

Doctor: How does this news leave you feeling?
Mr K: Terrified! I've always had this thing about cancer. I've always been frightened of getting it. Two of my uncles died of it. They both had a bad time. Suffered terrible pain and wasted away . . . to nothing.
Doctor: So you're frightened you're going to go the same way?
Mr K: I'm bound to be scared, aren't I?
Doctor: Yes, you are in view of those experiences. It must be hard for you. Any other reasons you are terrified?
Mr K: I hate being a burden. My wife has enough to contend with.

Sometimes a patient's responses are better signalled by non-verbal behaviour. It then helps if you acknowledge this and invite him to discuss his feelings.

Doctor: I'm sorry I've had to give you this news. I can see you're distressed. Would you like to talk about it?
Mr C: It is so incredibly unfair. I have always been careful with what I eat. I've not been a drinker. I have exercised regularly. To get cancer now, just when we're getting on our feet as a family, seems so unfair. It makes me feel very bitter.

Having established his immediate responses you should establish any other concerns before attempting to give information about the treatment you propose and the likely outcome. Otherwise he will remain preoccupied with these concerns, will not heed your advice, and may misperceive what you say.

Doctor: We have explored why you feel so terrified at knowing you have cancer. Has it caused you to have any other worries?
Mr C: Yes.
Doctor: Would you like to tell me about them?
Mr C: I'm not sure whether I should go ahead with my plan to move house.
Doctor: Sounds as though you're worried that we may not be able to do anything for your cancer.
Mr C: Yes I am.
Doctor: I'll come back to that in a minute. Before I do, do you have any other concerns?
Mr C: Yes. Who will look after the children if I don't make it?
Doctor: So, you are concerned about whether or not to move house, about your children.
Mr C: Yes I am.
Doctor: Anything else you're concerned about?
Mr C: No.

Doctor: Are you sure?
Mr C: Yes.

Once you have established your patient's concerns you should be able to decide if they can be resolved. It is important that your statements about these concerns are realistic but maintain hope.

Mrs H: It is the prospect of pain that terrifies me.
Doctor: I can understand that.
Mrs H: Can you do anything?
Doctor: There is every chance that we can. So, it is very important you let me know if you have any pain, and we can see what we can do.

Similarly, efforts to foster and maintain hope about the outcome of treatment should be appropriate.

Doctor: When we removed your cancer we found that a few of the nodes under your arm were affected and removed those as well. To be sure we mop up all the cancer we ought to give you some chemotherapy. There is then a good chance you'll be OK.
Mrs M: You're not certain?
Doctor: No I can't be certain, but I do think there's every chance of a reasonable outcome in your case providing you have some chemotherapy.

When the prognosis is poor the doctor can usually indicate that something can be done.

Doctor: You're right, you have got lung cancer.
Mr S: That's what I thought. I keep coughing up blood and I've lost so much weight. Are you going to be able to do anything about it?
Doctor: Yes, I think so. I'm hopeful that we'll get some response with radiotherapy and that you will feel much less ill.
Mr S: Only some response?
Doctor: While we should be able to shrink it considerably, I'm not certain we'll be able to get it all.
Mr S: You mean there could be some left?
Doctor: There could be. But we would then consider giving you a course of strong drugs. I think we ought to start with radiotherapy first. I'm pretty certain we can get it under control and that will make you feel better.
Mr S: I suppose I have to be grateful for that.
Doctor: I can understand that you are disappointed that I can't guarantee getting rid of it all, but I think it likely you'll feel better once you start radiotherapy. Then maybe you won't be so worried. We will still have the drugs at our disposal should they be necessary.

Even when you cannot eradicate the disease it is still important to explore your patient's feelings and concerns since it is likely that you can still do something.

General practitioner: You remember that you came to see me because you were feeling so weak and were worried your cancer had come back and was spreading . . . and I sent you to the hospital for tests?
Mr F: Yes I do.
General practitioner: Good. The reason I came round this morning is to give you the results of those tests they did at the hospital.
Mr F: I guessed that. What did they find?

General practitioner: I am afraid your guess was right, the cancer has come back. That's the reason why you've been feeling so weak and tired.

Mr F: I thought so. Are you going to be able to do anything for me?

General practitioner: I'm afraid I do not feel that further treatment is going to make much difference to the cancer.

The general practitioner then explored Mr F's resulting concerns and an important issue emerged. He was worried that he might suffer severe pain.

General practitioner: I'm sorry to have to tell you this. It can't be easy for you. Do you have any particular worries?

Mr F: I'm terrified of getting bad pain.

General practitioner: If that happens I hope we will be able to control your pain with strong pain killers. Let me know if you're having any problems with pain, or any other symptoms, come to that. The sooner we know about it the sooner we should be able to do something.

Mr F: Yes I can see that.

General practitioner: Apart from getting pain, are there any other concerns?

Mr F: No.

General practitioner: I'm sorry it's worked out this way, but we certainly should be able to do something to help you if there are any problems with pain. It's very important we keep in close touch.

The doctor did not say that he could eliminate any pain, for this would be false reassurance. Instead, he indicated that there was every chance he could palliate the pain. He also showed that he was prepared to discuss other concerns.

This strategy of moving from acknowledging and exploring the nature and basis of any strong feelings to identifying key concerns is essential if the breaking of bad news is to be managed effectively. It allows the patient to be 'lifted' from being overwhelmed to feeling hopeful that something can be done.

Handling difficult questions

Many doctors and nurses fear that if they get into a dialogue with patients with cancer they will be asked difficult questions – for example, 'Is it cancer?' (Maguire, 1985). When such a question is asked it is difficult to know what response is wanted by the patient. Does he (or she) want reassurance that it isn't cancer (because he wants to deny the reality of his illness) or the truth? Only the patient can suggest the direction he wishes to follow. You can usually discover this by saying, 'I would be happy to answer your question' and then reflecting his question back to him by saying, 'But what makes you ask that question?' You should then explore if there are other reasons why he asked it. It will then become clear if the patient is asking the question because he has guessed what is going on and wants confirmation that he is right.

Mr M: Is it cancer?

Specialist nurse: I would be happy to answer your question, but can I first ask you why you're asking me?

Mr M: It's obvious isn't it?

Specialist nurse: Why obvious?

Mr M: I have lost two stones in weight. I'm feeling weaker day by day and still coughing up blood. It's got to be cancer.

Specialist nurse: Any other reasons why you are so sure that you've got cancer?

Mr M: I've been a heavy smoker all my life. The doctors want to give me radiotherapy. You only get radiotherapy for one thing and that's cancer.

Specialist nurse: Yes, I'm afraid you're right.

Mr M: I knew it. I'm not a fool. Why did they tell me they were just giving me radiotherapy as an insurance?

Specialist nurse: I honestly don't know. But look, would you like to talk more about it?

Mr M: Yes I would. What I really want to know – is radiotherapy going to make any difference?

Specialist nurse: We're hopeful that it will get the cancer under control and that some of the symptoms you're complaining about will improve considerably.

Mr M: That sounds better than I thought, I thought I was a goner.

Specialist nurse: A goner?

Mr M: I thought I'd only a few days to live at the most.

Specialist nurse: That's not the case. There is a real prospect that the treatment will help you feel better and keep you going for some time.

Some patients indicate that they wish to deny what is happening.

Mrs R: I'm going to get better aren't I?

Medical oncologist: What makes you ask that?

Mrs R: You and your team tell me that I have some kind of lymphoma. I can't accept that. I'm certain it is an infection I picked up when I was out in the tropics.

Medical oncologist: I don't want to argue with you about that. The key thing is that you continue with our treatment.

Mrs R: I'm happy to do that.

Conclusion

You may have noticed that the strategies we advise are determined by the patient's responses and not decided unilaterally by the doctor or nurse. We do not expect you to accept them unquestioningly but hope that you will try them out with patients in your care.

References

Maguire, P. (1985) 'Barriers to psychological care of the dying', *British Medical Journal*, 291: 1711–13.

Maguire, P. and Faulkner, A. (1988) 'Communicate with cancer patients: 2 Handling uncertainty, collusion and denial', *British Medical Journal*, 297: 972–4.

37

Communicating with cancer patients: 2. Handling uncertainty, collusion and denial

Peter Maguire and Ann Faulkner

Breaking bad news often prompts patients to ask questions about their future like: 'How long have I got?' You then have to help them cope with uncertainty without them becoming demoralized.

Handling uncertainty

When asked: 'How long have I got?', it is tempting to give a finite [time] ('Oh, three months') or a range [of time] ('Anything from a month to six months'). But such predictions are usually inaccurate, tend to err on the optimistic side, and cause problems for patients and their families. Patients then pace themselves according to the time they believe is left. If they deteriorate earlier than expected and are prevented from achieving planned goals they will feel cheated and bitter. Relatives can find an unexpectedly prolonged survival ('borrowed time') hard to cope with because they have used up their physical and emotional resources. So it is better to acknowledge your uncertainty and the difficulties that this will cause.

> *Doctor*: You asked me how long he has. The trouble is, I don't know. I realize this uncertainty must be difficult for you.
> *Mrs W*: It is. It is terrible knowing that he is going to die, but not knowing when. I mean it could be in one month's time or next Christmas.
> *Doctor*: That's the trouble, I just don't know how long it will be.

You should next check if she would like to know the signs and symptoms that would herald further deterioration.

> *Doctor*: What I can do, but only if you would like me to, is tell you what changes would suggest he is beginning to deteriorate further.
> *Mrs W*: Yes, I think that would help me.
> *Doctor*: He will probably complain of feeling breathless, weak, and start going off his food.

From *British Medical Journal*, 1988, 297(2): 972-4.

You can then encourage her to try to use the intervening time.

> *Doctor*: But as long as there are no signs like that I think you can take it that he is relatively OK. So, you should try to make the most of this time if you can. Is there anything you would particularly like to do?

Later, add that you are prepared to check him regularly, and show a willingness to negotiate the frequency of such check-ups.

> *Doctor*: I think it would help if I saw him from time to time to monitor how he is doing. How often would you like me to do that?
> *Mrs W*: Would every month be OK?
> *Doctor*: Yes, fine.

You should explain that if anything unforeseen occurs between these assessments you should be contacted immediately. This gives patients and relatives confidence that they have a 'life line'.

> *Doctor*: If you are worried at any stage between his appointments you must get in touch with me. I can then assess him and decide what needs to be done.

Few patients or relatives abuse this offer.

When some patients or relatives face uncertainty they show that they do not want any markers.

> *Doctor*: Would you like me to tell you how you might recognize if Peter's health is deteriorating?
> *Mrs B*: No, I'll leave it to you. You're the expert.

Sometimes the uncertainty concerns issues other than 'how long'. Again you should acknowledge the uncertainty and establish any resulting worries.

> *Doctor*: I sense that this uncertainty is a major problem for you.
> *Mr J*: It is. I feel helpless not knowing what's going to happen or how it's going to happen.
> *Doctor*: What are you worried about in particular?
> *Mr J*: I'm worried about how I'm going to die. I don't want to be a burden on my family, and I'm not sure what to expect after death.
> *Doctor*: Any other concerns?
> *Mr J*: Isn't that enough?
> *Doctor*: Yes, it is, but I just want to make sure I establish all your concerns before we discuss them in detail.

By separating out and exploring each concern the patient begins to see that there is some prospect that they can be tackled.

Breaking collusion

It is commonly alleged that relatives withhold the truth because they cannot face the pain of what is happening and wish to deny it. More commonly, however, it is an act of love. They cannot bear to cause anguish to their loved one. Approaching collusion from this perspective makes it possible to respect relatives' reasons and work positively with them. The first step is to acknowledge the collusion and then explore and validate the reasons for it.

Doctor: You've told me that you don't feel Richard ought to know what is going on. Why do you feel that?

Mrs P: I'm terrified that if he's told he'll simply fall apart. I wouldn't want that, I couldn't bear it.

Doctor: Well you know him best and you could be right. It could be that if he's told he will fall apart. Have you any other reasons why you feel he shouldn't be told?

Mrs P: I think he'd just give up and turn his face to the wall.

Doctor: Any other reasons?

Mrs P: No.

Doctor: So you have good reason for him not being told.

Mrs P: Yes.

It is then important to establish the emotional cost of the collusion.

Doctor: I now understand why you have kept the information from him, but what effect has this been having on you?

Mrs P: It's been a terrible strain. I'm feeling extremely tense, I'm not sleeping as well as I should, I'm getting nightmares.

Doctor: Would you like to tell me about your nightmares?

Mrs P: He seems to be getting smaller and smaller, he seems to be wasting away.

Doctor: That's, I suppose, what could happen, isn't it, given that he is dying?

Mrs P: [In tears] Yes, it is, and I'm very worried about it.

Doctor: So it sounds as if you are finding it a strain!

Mrs P: It is. It's a big strain. I worry that he will begin to guess. He's already commented that I seem quieter than usual.

Doctor: Just how tense have you been?

Mrs P: At times I feel at screaming point and I'm taking it out on the children. I feel bad about that, but I just can't see how I can tell him without him falling apart.

Doctor: Are you experiencing any other problems because of not telling him?

Mrs P: Yes, we're not talking together like we used to. I'd like to be extra loving to him, but if I am he'll guess. He says I'm backing off. But I can't explain to him why. It's horrible. Just when I want to be close to him a barrier is growing between us.

Doctor: So, there are two good reasons for trying to consider whether there's some way round this, the strain on you and the effect on your relationship with your husband.

Mrs P: Yes.

Doctor: So would you like me to suggest how we might be able to do something about it?

Mrs P: But you're not going to tell him are you?

Doctor: No, what I'm going to discuss doesn't involve telling him, would you like me to go into it?

Mrs P: Yes, I would.

You should now indicate that you would like to chat with her partner to check whether he has any idea of what is happening to him. You should reinforce that you have no intention of telling him and enter into a contract to this effect.

Doctor: Let me emphasize that I have no intention of telling him. What I'd like to do is to chat to him to see what he's thinking about the present situation. It may be that he will reveal that he knows he has cancer. If that's the case there will be no reason to maintain the pretence.

Mrs P: But you're not going to tell him are you?

Doctor: No I'm not, I will simply check whether he knows. If your hunch that he doesn't have any idea is correct, that's the end of the matter. I won't say anything.

Mrs P: [Reluctantly] All right then.

Your next task is to establish her partner's level of awareness. You should ask an appropriate directive question which elicits his view of what is happening and then explore the cues he give.

Doctor: I wanted to have a chat to see how you feel things are going.

Mr P: Not very well.

Doctor: Not very well?

Mr P: Isn't it obvious? I'm not having any more treatment. The hospital don't want to see me again but I'm still getting the pain. I'm losing weight and I haven't much energy. I'm in bed all the time now.

Doctor: So what are you making of this?

Mr P: I think it's the end, isn't it?

Doctor: Are there any other reasons why you're beginning to feel it's the end?

Mr P: I've always known that what they've told me was a precancerous ulcer was a cancer. Now what's happening is confirming that I was right. I'm lying here just wondering why no one has levelled with me.

Doctor: It sounds as though you've known for some time what's happening.

Mr P: Yes, I have, but I didn't want to upset my wife. She has enough on her plate with me being ill, and having to run around all the time.

You should now confirm that he is right ('I'm afraid you are right') and then seek permission to convey his awareness to his wife, indicating that she knows the diagnosis. Then negotiate with the couple to see if they are prepared to talk with you to establish their concerns.

As you help the couple talk you may notice that the patient is angry with you. This usually indicates that he feels talking is a waste of time because it will not change the outcome of his disease. If you get this feeling acknowledge it.

Doctor: Would you like to say how this leaves you feeling?

Mr P: What's the point? It's not going to be of much use.

Doctor: It sounds as if you might be feeling that it's no use because it won't make any difference to your situation.

Mr P: That's right; it's not going to stop me dying is it?

Doctor: No, you're absolutely right. That's the one thing I can't do and I'm sorry about that. But it may help if we talk about how you're feeling and what you're worried about. It is quite likely there is something I can do to help you both. However, I will understand if you decide not to talk to me.

Mr P: I suppose I've nothing to lose by talking.

Breaking collusion is painful for the doctor because he witnesses the love between a couple and the effects of imminent loss. But it is important to break it as soon as it becomes a problem. Otherwise important unfinished business will be left unresolved. The patient is then likely to be distressed and may become morbidly anxious and depressed. This mental suffering will lower the threshold at which the patient experiences physical symptoms like pain and sickness and cause problems with symptom relief. Failing to deal with important practical and emotional unfinished business also makes it difficult for relatives to resolve their grief.

Challenging denial

Patients use denial when the truth is too painful to bear. So denial should not be challenged unless it is creating serious problems for the patient or relative. In challenging denial it is important to do it gently so that fragile defences are not disrupted but firmly enough so that any awareness can be explored and developed.

It is first worth asking the patient to give an account of what has happened since his (or her) illness was first discovered and explore how he felt at each key point – for example, when he first developed the symptoms, saw a specialist, was investigated, and was told about his illness. He can then explain what he perceives is wrong, and this may provide glimpses of doubt: 'I'm certain it's an ulcer, at least I'm pretty sure it is.' By repeating 'Pretty sure?' you may prompt him to say, 'Well I suppose these could be some doubt.' The cue 'some doubt' can next be explored to see if he owns up to the possibility that the ulcer could be cancer. It is then important to interpret what is happening by saying, 'Part of you prefers to believe that it's an ulcer, but another part of you is willing to consider that it is more serious.' The patient can then retreat to denial or develop his awareness further ('I've been trying to kid myself that it's an ulcer, but deep down I realize it's cancer'.)

If this strategy fails look for and challenge any inconsistencies between the patient's experiences and perceptions.

> *Doctor*: You say you were far bigger in this pregnancy than in your two previous ones. Did you consider why that might be?
> *Mrs J*: I thought it was just one of those things. I didn't think anything more about it.
> *Doctor*: Are you sure?
> *Mrs J*: Yes I am sure it was a normal pregnancy. The reason I'm still feeling so weak is because I didn't take it too well.

The patient had developed ovarian cancer which was so advanced that little treatment could be offered. She preferred to deny this and insisted that her symptoms represented normal sequelae of pregnancy.

If challenging inconsistencies fails to dent denial check if there is 'a window'. Do this by asking: 'I can understand that you feel it is an infection. But is there any time, even a moment, when you consider that it may not be so simple?' The patient may say 'No', in which case you have to accept that the patient finds it too painful to look at what is happening. Alternatively, the patient may admit, 'Yes, there is. Sometimes I feel it could be something much more sinister.' Exploring what the patient means by 'sinister' may help him [sic] acknowledge that he has something much more serious than an ulcer. This then helps him shift from denial into relative or full awareness of his illness or prognosis.

He may then oscillate between denial and awareness. So, do not assume what stance he is going to take but explore it each time by asking: 'How do you feel things are going?'

Conclusion

The best way to validate our guidelines is to try them out in practice. Either they will work and promote confidence or they will prompt you to develop other strategies.

38

Communicating with dying children

Dorothy Judd

Look, the dying, –
surely they must suspect how full of pretext
is all that we accomplish here, where nothing
is what it really is.
(Rilke, 'Fourth Duino Elegy')

Children with a life-threatening illness sense that it is serious, and that they might die or are dying, even if not explicitly told. Recent research has challenged the 'protective' approach in relation to whether to talk to the child about his or her impending death. It seems from the weight of evidence that children need to be given the opportunity to speak 'about their concerns so that they can receive support in their struggles' (Spinetta, 1982).

Background

Before we can approach how, when and why we might talk to dying children about their situation, we need to think about children's understanding of the concept of death. This varies according to age, intelligence, life experience, environment, the seriousness of their illness, and their 'inner world' of fantasies and dreams.

Kane (1979) gives a useful summary of children's concepts of death. She writes that children from approximately 6 years of age have a more-or-less mature grasp of the concept of death, including its irrevocability and universality, whereas younger children do not generally understand these and other more subtle qualities, such as that dead people or creatures cannot *feel*. The most clear and feared implication for younger children is of the implied separation from those who are loved and needed, as well as that dead people/creatures cannot move. Generally it is not until the age of 12 that children grasp all the complex implications of death: for example, that the dead person may, or may not, look as though he were alive.

These cognitive findings, although useful as broad categories, do not adequately reflect the vicissitudes of the child's inner world and unconscious fantasies which colour and inform the perceptions of the outer world, including thoughts about death. In other words, we cannot simply look at a child's intellectual grasp of a concept without paying adequate attention to the fantasies and emotions which abound.

The developing child's response to separation and death reflects his or her ability to have an inner representation, idea or memory of the mother/main care-taker in a way which is hopeful, sustaining and promises its return. This capacity develops as a result of the mother's repeated sensitive management of the infant's anxieties, in conjunction with the infant's ability to 'take in' and hold onto the image of a good mother.

Rochlin (1959, 1967) has focused on the influence of emotional states on children's attitudes to death. He writes that children clearly know about death as the extinction of all life at a very early age, but that they then utilize a range of defences in order to avoid the full implications of this awareness. As Orbach (1988) so clearly summarizes, children 'reflect the duality of knowing and denying the existence of death'. The child's use of denial, omnipotence, magical thinking and actual independence all influence the extent of his/her fear or acceptance of the subject. Of course all this is set against the influential background of adult's oscillation between acceptance and denial of death. Adults' protective concern for children over issues around death clearly reflect their own fears and use of denial, in a society where the taboo may be lifting in a widespread social and intellectual sense, but not necessarily in a personal or private sense (Judd, 1989: 4–16).

If children have had to negotiate the concept of death through the actual death of someone close, or of a pet, their understanding may well be enhanced. However, if the death is too overwhelming, the child may recede to an earlier stage of 'not knowing'. Similarly, if they are fatally ill, they are more aware of their own mortality, but may hide defensively behind denial. This has been shown in studies where the fatally ill child's level of anxiety is markedly higher than that of the chronically ill, even if undergoing the same number and duration of hospital treatments (Spinetta et al., 1973). This anxiety, as well as a sense of isolation, persists when they are not in hospital, and even during remission in the case of leukaemic children (Spinetta, 1975).

The hospitalized dying child's awareness of death is more sharply focused when another child dies on the ward. If the child has the same illness, of course the link between that event and the dying child's imminent death is made more immediate. Fortunately nowadays there is a more open and truthful attitude on children's wards in most hospitals, where the event is often discussed openly in response to parents' questions, and sometimes with children, depending on the ethos of the unit. This is not always the case, however. Some hospitals have not altered much since this account by a consultant paediatrician of the approach to the death of a child on the ward, about twenty-five years ago:

> Our present method of dealing with the solemn situation that arises when a child dies in a children's ward is both ugly and obscene. There is a

whispering and a scuffling behind the screens, a furtive moving of white-covered trolleys out of the ward, usually during the night. Nurses and doctors are preoccupied and don't answer questions and are unduly irritable. Above all, there is a stupid pretence that nothing at all unusual is happening. . . . But do we really think that the 'secret' is not known to every child on the ward? (Yudkin, 1967: 40)

This account is a useful reflection not only of ways of handling actual deaths, but of the days or weeks or months of illness preceding a death, when the 'pretence that nothing at all unusual is happening' is adopted by some parents and some professionals. Yudkin writes that this furtive behaviour was an affront to children's intelligence. Instead of helping them to regard death as a 'very sad but solemn and dignified event', it characterized death as something fearful and secretive, depriving the child of the opportunity to talk about his or her fears.

Richard Lansdown (1987) of the Hospital for Sick Children, London, has usefully summarized the stages of understanding their own death that a dying child goes through:

I am very sick
I have an illness that can kill people
I have an illness that can kill children
I may not get better
I am dying

However, as stated earlier, the child's age, anxiety level, cognitive development, inner world and environment would all influence the course of that understanding. For a child under 3 years of age, the 'I am dying' concept would probably not embody a real understanding of dying, with its irreversibility, but may be a feeling of not understanding what is happening to his body and an anxiety about this unpleasant state of being unwell separating him from his parents.

Communicating with the dying child

It is clear that dying children need to be given an age- and development-appropriate opportunity to share and explore their fears and concerns. This does not mean imposing a discussion, but involves attempting to be open to the child's willingness – or otherwise – to talk. For example, 9-year-old Helena (recently diagnosed with a very large osteosarcoma below her knee) said she was 'fine' when first meeting the hospital child psychotherapist, whilst lifting her long skirt to reveal the conspicuous tumour. The psychotherapist took up the non-verbal cue, saying, 'Well, you're letting me know that you're not altogether "fine"'. Helena then talked openly about her cancer: about her worries that it had been caused by falling over and about whether her mum was 'sick with worry'.

Laura, a 10-year-old with another type of bone tumour in her leg, carefully drew the branch of a tree, delineating each leaf and their veins, during a session with the child psychotherapist. Laura had previously readily shared her feelings about having cancer being 'scary'. Now, in this drawing, she abruptly drew the branch as not being attached to a tree, but appearing cut off. The psychotherapist asked, 'What happens if a branch is no longer joined to the tree?' Laura replied, 'It dies', glancing up into the therapist's eyes meaningfully. This was an opportunity to begin to explore Laura's fears of dying and of being cut off from her mother to whom she was very close. On later occasions, she discussed her not unrealistic fears of amputation of her leg being like the branch of a tree being cut off. However, all these developments towards a sharing of her anxieties required the right moment and an appropriate setting of reasonable privacy and calm.

Laura's mother had given permission for her child to be seen by the psychotherapist. Although the mother was not able to talk to her daughter about the possibility of dying, she was willing for someone else to 'hear' her daughter's concerns. Without this permission, the professionals or other adults involved need to try to explain their reasons for believing in the helpfulness of open communication. If the parents have a first-hand experience of *their* fears being listened to, they may gain the confidence to explore the child's fears, or to allow someone else to begin the process. With adolescents, where their understanding is usually more mature and close to that of adults, it is usually easier for the professionals to explain to the parents that they cannot lie about the situation and will aim to foster the patient's trust by answering questions truthfully and letting them know the situation.

Adolescents tackling death have specific problems. Unlike younger children, adolescents are caught in a more polarized struggle: they are often powerfully attempting to stake out their independence and identity and to *live* life fully, all of which greatly conflicts with having a terminal illness. Therefore, in this most difficult task, there is often an impressive determination to continue to live their life despite the limitations and constraints brought by the illness. The alternative to this attitude would be to regress to an earlier more infantile state of dependence on nurses or parents. Therefore, in communicating with a dying adolescent we need to respect the denial – or as it may be viewed, the living for a future, albeit a limited one, and the struggle for a sense of identity and control.

The idea of 'stages' of understanding is useful to have at the back of one's mind when talking to children who are dying, but should not be the main guide. Receptivity to the young person's willingness or need to talk is paramount, as well as *their* level of understanding. These discussions need repeated opportunities for the information to be digested, as well as for further exploration. The adult may simply spend a few meaningful minutes with a child or young person, but may end by saying, 'I will come back tomorrow and we can talk some more if you want.' The child may well then save up some thoughts to share the next day. A useful introductory approach may be, 'Would you like to talk about anything that's bothering you?' and, in a follow-up discussion, 'I wonder what thoughts you've had about our last discussion?' Of course the child's age is very relevant to the type of verbal exchange, and with younger children the communication may well be symbolic, through their play with toys, or plasticine, or drawing with the provision of coloured crayons. A set of hospital play dolls can be useful, but again the toys are the child's vehicle for communication, and the adult's ability to observe, listen and not pre-empt is important. However, there are times when the child has used a symbolic communication and may feel uncomfortable, or interrogated, with the externalization of the unconscious into words. In this case the drawings or play-sequence may have to be 'received' unconditionally. The child may need to cling to the unspoken conspiracy of mutual protectiveness between child and parents, especially if the parents are very repressed in their expression of pain. With symbolic, non-verbal communication the adult might simply describe what the child seems to be 'saying', thus acknowledging the child's fantasies and, possibly, fears. A child will usually say if the response is wrong, and usually gives several opportunities to get the message before finally giving up trying to communicate.

Usually hopelessness in the face of impending death is interspersed with hopefulness. Indeed, it seems there is always some hope, even if not for cure, then for some last wish or achievement to be fulfilled, or for a comfortable last phase, or for a death that is peaceful. Children may need to overcome a fear of being buried before they can express their own wishes about how they would like to die, where, with whom, and even about the content of the funeral service. Where the family has strong religious or spiritual beliefs the child may be helped by optimistic images of an afterlife. This, however, does not usually remove the pain of loss and separation from those he or she loves.

What can seem like unrealistic hopefulness on the part of the dying child needs sensitive responses on the part of the adults. The dying child's fluctuating awareness of his or her reality deserves a flexible response which encourages a dialogue, rather than alienating the patient with a reminder of a reality which may be intolerable for the time being. If the child seems to be more hopeless than hopeful, and withdraws into a state of depression, or of psychic closing off, they may be helped by someone close simply acknowledging this very process: 'It seems you're giving up . . . you don't want to live whatever time is left . . . this must be very hard for you. . . .' If the child seems to be 'somewhere else' emotionally, but not depressed, this may be a very understandable separating from the world around. It is important for the child's choice, or decision, to withdraw to be tolerated – difficult though that may be for those involved – rather than pressurizing the child to be jolly, or to 'hang on' for others. This may in part be the one area of control the child has: to choose to withdraw, in the face of so much he or she cannot control.

Ultimately, the dying child *is* alone. We can accompany the child some of the way on that journey, and physically be with the child hopefully until death and after cessation of bodily functions, but emotionally, and, some would say, spiritually, we can never really fully accompany the child. This truth is part of the painfulness for the parents and others who love the child: the pain of loss and separation often begins some time before death. For many it begins at diagnosis, and then re-occurs repeatedly in many bursts. The parents and others may like to share with the child some of their happy memories of when the child was well, just as the child may like to do the same, or look at photographs. Thus the shared past and shared joys can have a strengthening effect: an understanding that the many memories live on in those who survive, and that the child, the whole child, includes the pre-illness state.

Where parents and the dying child have time to face the impending death gradually, and the child's condition does not cause unmanageable pain, all involved can feel that the time which is available is precious and a privilege. Alongside this awareness there may be anger at the child's life being cut short, at the death of a child being unnatural and unacceptable. Just as hopefulness and despair oscillate, so an appreciation of the time left oscillates with anger at how little of it there is. These polarities seem to exemplify the extremes of life and death itself: without one we could not have the other, and by attempting to embrace this polarity we are more able to receive the fluctuating feelings and awareness of the dying child.

References

Judd, D. (1989) *Give Sorrow Words - Working with a Dying Child*. London: Free Association Books.

Kane, B. (1979) 'Children's concepts of death', *Journal of Genetic Psychology*, 134: 141-53.

Lansdown, R. (1987) *Personal Communication*.

Orbach, I. (1988) *Children who Don't want to Live*. San Francisco, CA: Jossey-Bass.

Rochlin, G. (1959) 'The loss complex: a contribution to the etiology of depression', *Journal of the American Psychoanalytical Association*, 7: 299-316.

Rochlin, G. (1967) 'How younger children view death and themselves', in E. Grollman (ed.), *Explaining Death to Children*. Boston, MA: Beacon.

Spinetta, J.J. (1975) 'Death anxiety in the outpatient leukaemic child', *Paediatrics*, 56 (6): 1034-7.

Spinetta, J.J. (1982) 'Behavioural and psychological research in childhood cancer: an overview', *Cancer*, 50: 1939-43.

Spinetta, J.J., Rigler, D. and Karon, M. (1973) 'Anxiety in the dying child', *Paediatrics*, 52 (6): 841-5.

Yudkin, S. (1967) 'Children and death', *The Lancet* 1: 37-40.

Some suggested books for dying children

Varley, S. (1984) *Badger's Parting Gift*. Picture Lions.
Meltonie, B. and Ingpen, R. (1983) *Beginnings and Endings with Lifetimes in Between*. Surrey: Paper Tiger, Dragon's World Ltd.

39

Jewish perspectives on death, dying and bereavement

Jeanne Samson Katz

Many theological, philosophical and practical texts have described Jewish practices regarding death and bereavement (Lamm, 1969; Rabinowicz, 1989; Goldberg, 1991; Weiss, 1991; Green and Green, 1992). These practices are based on the Old Testament texts, rabbinic literature and other precedents. This article will present those aspects which may be of help when caring for dying Jewish people who may vary in the degree of their religious observance. Although Jewish law specifies regulations and requirements with regard to death and dying, not all Jewish people will want to observe all or some of these. Jews in the UK and Europe are either of Western (Ashkenazi) or Middle Eastern (Sephardi) origin and there are considerable differences in liturgy and practices. Those British Jews who practice Judaism belong to synagogues which are affiliated to the Orthodox (amongst which there are several groups as well as independent communities), Reform, Conservative, Progressive and Liberal movements. Traditions vary amongst these movements and even amongst members of each community. Even observant Jews may choose not to observe all the rules, and may not be familiar with the intricacies of specific Jewish laws, such as the variations dictated by the calendar when festivals occur shortly after death or during the mourning period.

The obligation to visit the sick

'Where there is life, there is hope', is central to Jewish teachings and visiting the sick is a religious duty (*mitzvah*). This is to prevent the alienation and isolation of the sick as well as to pray for their complete recovery (*refuah shlaymah*). According to Maimonides, the mediaeval rabbinic codifier, one should refrain from visiting the sick only if the illness is a source of embarrassment to the sick person.

The concept of *retention of hope* applies even to dying people, for whom

I should like to thank Rabbi Dr Louis Jacobs for helpful comments and discussion on an earlier draft.

all avenues towards recovery should be explored (Schindler, 1982). These include several religious acts such as giving charitable donations, changing one's actions and adding a new name to the sick person (so that the Angel of Death will not recognize the person). Prayers for the sick person's recovery are offered. However, some commentators hold that it is permissible and even laudatory to pray that a dying person in great pain should be granted a merciful release (Jacobs, personal communication).

Jewish beliefs about life and death

Jewish practices centre on the seasons of the year. Death itself is also seen as the inevitable consequence of life: 'To everything there is a season: a time to be born, and a time to die'.

Teachings emphasize the sanctity of human life, which cannot be judged on the basis of length or quality. From this principle numerous obligations are derived, including the duty to heal the sick and the instruction to preserve human life even if this conflicts with other religious obligations, such as the observance of the Sabbath.

Traditional Jewish teachings oppose any measures which could be interpreted as hastening death, preferring life-extending measures, as long as these measures do not prolong the act of dying. The code of Jewish law (the Shulchan Aruch) states: 'A patient on his death bed is considered a living person in every respect . . . and it is forbidden to cause him to die quickly' (Yoreh De'ah, a compendium of law, 339: 1).

Any act which might precipitate death is forbidden by Jewish law, including shutting eyes, removing the pillow or oiling the body (Goldberg, 1991). Steps should be taken to make the dying person (*goses*) comfortable, for example by giving water, and reducing levels of noise.

The concept of 'preparing for death' therefore is alien to the Jewish tradition (Jakobovits and Philipp in Byrne et al., 1991: 190-1). Psalm 71 emphasizes retention of hope: 'cast me not off in my old age when my strength faileth, forsake me not. . . . But as for me, I will hope continually.' Hence many sources suggest that it is not in the dying person's interest to disclose the nearness of death.

When death is imminent

When approaching death, many Jewish people would like to see a rabbi. Members of a specific congregation might welcome a visit from their own rabbi. Where this is not feasible, many institutions have an associated Jewish chaplain who is willing to visit. The dying person may then be helped to recite certain psalms and prayers and, if sufficiently conscious, the 'confessional prayer on the deathbed'. In Judaism the concept of confession through an intermediary does not exist, it is solely between the individual and God. This prayer enables the dying person to participate in his/her own future. It is usually recited in Hebrew and is translated as follows:

Confession on a Deathbed

I acknowledge unto Thee, O Lord my God and God of my fathers, that both my cure and my death are in Thy hands. May it be Thy will to send me a perfect healing. Yet if my death be fully determined by Thee I will in love accept it at Thy hand. O may my death be an atonement for all sins, iniquities and transgressions of which I have been guilty against Thee. Bestow upon me the abounding happiness that is treasured up for the righteous. Make known to me the path of life: in Thy presence is fulness of joy; at Thy right hand, bliss for evermore.

Thou who art the father of the fatherless and judge of the widow, protect my beloved kindred with whose souls my own is knit. Into thy hand I commend my spirit; Thou hast redeemed me, O Lord God of truth. Amen and Amen. (Singer's Daily Prayer Book)

The commentary that accompanies this confession indicates the importance of maintaining the morale of the dying person:

If a sick person is near death, Heaven forbid, someone should recite the confession with him. However, it is required that this be done in such a way that his morale not be broken because this may even hasten death. He should be told, 'Many have confessed and did not die and many who did not confess died anyway. In reward for having confessed, may you live, but everyone who confesses has a share in the World to come.' If the patient cannot speak, he should confess in his heart. One who is unsophisticated should not be asked to confess because it may break his spirit and cause him to weep. (Art scroll commentary to confession on deathbed)

Rabbinic commentators were concerned how the relatives of the dying person might react to these prayers and suggested that the above not be said in front of children in case they became upset and consequently distressed the dying person (Schindler, 1982). If the dying person is unable to recite these prayers they can be said on his or her behalf.

Where possible, relatives or friends should maintain a presence at the deathbed. This reassures the dying person and ensures that he or she is not alone when the soul departs (Goldberg, 1991). As death approaches relatives should recite Psalms 90, 121 and 130 very quietly and when death occurs recite the Sh'ma (the basic prayer of Judaism). In some communities it is customary to open the windows when the soul departs (Goldberg, 1991). Water that is standing near the body or in jugs in the home where death has taken place should be discarded.

The body

The treatment of the Jewish body is seen as a religious act and strict rules must be observed. Weiss (1991: 27) suggests that: 'In keeping with the life-affirming nature of Judaism, the human body becomes the chief source of ritual impurity when it is bereft of life.' The body should not be moved until death has been established, when the eyes should be closed, all tubes removed and the body covered with a white sheet, the arms and legs straightened with the feet pointed towards the door (Abeles, 1991). The body should be handled as little as possible (Green and Green, 1992) and not left alone until the burial society (*Chevra Kaddisha*) come to collect it. Volunteers from the *Chevra Kaddisha* will take the body to their own premises where trained persons of the same sex as the dead person will perform *tahara*, the ritual cleansing of the body. Although embalming is generally forbidden in Judaism, to conform with international health regulations certain forms of embalming are permitted to enable bodies to be transported across international boundaries. Rabbinic advice should be sought to establish which forms of embalming are permitted.

Autopsies (post-mortems)

The Jewish view is that although the human body is no longer usable it was once a person and should not be violated. The body is compared with the Torah scroll (the Pentateuch handwritten on parchment and used in synagogue services). Both the body and the scroll should be allowed to decompose naturally and not be burnt. Deuteronomy 21: 22–3 forbids the desecration of the body, encouraging speedy burial. Post-mortems and any disfigurement of the corpse are thus forbidden in Jewish law except where civil law requires it (Green and Green, 1992) or it is viewed that the autopsy might save the life of another when it may be permitted; in any event all the organs should be returned and buried with the corpse.

The funeral

Burial should take place as quickly as possible after death and not more than three days later. Funerals do not take place on the Sabbath nor on Jewish major festivals, and may also be delayed to enable principal mourners to attend. Some secular, Reform, Liberal and Progressive Jews opt for cremation and these communities have recently evolved a range of services to be used at crematoria. Jewish law, however, *strictly forbids cremation* for the reasons cited above. Consequently there are no traditional Jewish mourning rites following cremation.

Jews are buried in simple, undecorated, wooden coffins to comply with the 'dust unto dust' principle. No differentiation may be made between rich and poor. Jews are buried in designated burial grounds which are separated from other cemeteries and rarely surround synagogue buildings. Where cemeteries are some distance from the residential areas, parts of the funeral ceremony may take place in halls or in the home of the deceased.

The 'mourners' are delineated by Jewish law. These are sons and daughters (who have the most extensive obligations), mother, father, brothers, sisters and spouse of the deceased. Before the service begins (sometimes at the deathbed) the mourners tear an outer garment (usually a cardigan or tie) which they wear for the 'week' of mourning (*shiva*, meaning seven). This outward symbol of grief permits 'the mourner to give vent to pent-up anguish by means of a controlled, religiously sanctioned act of destruction' (Lamm, 1969: 38).

In the UK and Europe, where cemeteries are fairly accessible, the funeral service usually begins in the chapel at the gates to the cemetery. The chapel is not decorated, but stark and simple. Flowers are not customary at Jewish funerals; a more appropriate token of esteem is a donation in the name of the deceased to a worthy charity.

In keeping with the separation of sexes in all Jewish services, men and women stand apart at the funeral service. This is conducted in a mixture of biblical Hebrew and Aramaic and is a sombre, 'but emotionally meaningful, farewell to the deceased' (Lamm, 1969: 36). The service is usually divided into four parts, but this may vary according to local custom. This includes a collage of various psalms, the memorial prayer and an eulogy recited in the local tongue, and in some communities a recitation from the Book of Psalms (usually Psalm 23).

> The twenty-third Psalm is the quintessential expression of faith: 'Yea, though I walk through the valley of the shadow of death, I shall fear not evil, for Thou art with me. Thy rod and staff, they comfort me.' It brings consolation, comfort and serene reassurance to the broken-hearted bereaved. The collage has been aptly titled: 'What is Man?' Its purpose is to remind the mourners of the essential brevity of life, so that they may resolve to fill their days with meaningful activity. (Weiss, 1991: 74)

The memorial prayer asks God to embrace the soul of the deceased and grant him/her spiritual reward. The eulogy (*hesped*) has two aims, to arouse the emotions of the listeners, and to focus on the worthy characteristics and attainments of the deceased. The eulogy should be truthful, but not hurtful – in Dr Johnson's words, 'in Lapidary inscriptions a man is not upon oath'! Eulogies are not recited on occasions such as minor festivals when expressions of sadness are not appropriate.

After the service in the chapel the coffin is wheeled or carried to the grave in a ritual procession which includes several stops during which Psalm 91 is recited. The coffin is lowered into the grave with the body facing upwards and the feet facing the gate of the cemetery and 'may he (or she) come to his (her) place in peace' is said. In some communities the male mourners (the women are present throughout the service) then recite the Burial Kaddish (others wait till they return to the chapel). This praises the Almighty:

> May His great name be magnified and sanctified in the world that is to be created anew, where He will revive the dead and raise them up unto life eternal.

The men attending the funeral fill the grave with soil, covering it completely. The shovel should not be passed from hand to hand, but replaced in the soil in order to express the view that death is not contagious (Weiss, 1991). The participants return to the chapel, ritually washing their hands on leaving the burial grounds and reciting the verse from Isaiah 25: 8: 'He hath swallowed up death forever, and the Lord hath wiped tears from all the faces.' On re-entering the chapel the focus shifts from the deceased to the bereaved and the traditional consolation is recited: 'May the Lord comfort you among all the other mourners of Zion.' All the participants greet the mourners individually. The mourners then return to where they have elected to spend the week of *shiva* (usually the house of the deceased) and mourning rituals start immediately with a special meal of 'recovery' which must be prepared by non-mourners (often neighbours). The custom includes eating food which is round, for example hard-boiled eggs, round cakes, which symbolize the circular nature of life – death comes to all.

Laws and customs in the house of mourning

A candle is lit for the benefit of the deceased, preferably in the room in which death took place. If this is not possible, a candle is lit in the place where the mourners will remain for the week of *shiva*. Twenty-six-hour candles (or one-week candles in the USA) are lit and relit ensuring continuous light for the week. Mirrors are covered in the house of mourning because (a) they cause joy and the mourner is forbidden to rejoice, and (b) it is forbidden to pray in front of mirrors and prayers are recited in the house of mourning (Goldberg, 1991). In some communities, it is customary to cover all pictures.

The consolation of mourners is a scriptural precept, cited in Genesis 25: 11: 'After the death of Abraham, God blessed Isaac' (Goldberg, 1991). Jews are expected to make condolence calls and help the bereaved: for example, by taking food to the house of mourning. Mourners usually do not leave the house, except to attend services if they cannot arrange this at home, and to go to the synagogue on Sabbath, where they are greeted formally by the community.

Adult (over 13) male mourners recite the Mourner's Kaddish three times a day (morning, afternoon and evening prayers) for eleven months for children of the deceased and a month for other mourners. Wherever it is said, the Mourner's Kaddish must be recited in the presence of at least ten men (*minyan*) to ensure that the mourner is not isolated (Goldberg, 1991). This prayer is an ancient hymn of worship to God, does not refer to death, yet is said for the benefit of the soul of the deceased. As the Mourner's Kaddish developed in mediaeval Germany where women rarely attended synagogue services, it is not customary for women to recite this. However, it is not forbidden and some women mourners choose to attend thrice-daily services to recite the Kaddish.

The Jewish rites of mourning are believed to be of therapeutic effect, enabling expression rather than repression of grief (Lamm, 1969; Goldberg, 1991; Weiss, 1991). Mourners move through graduated stages of obligations until they are fully resocialized into society. Relatives and friends are central to this process, ensuring that mourners are cared for and not isolated and that enough men are present at the daily prayers to enable the mourner to say Kaddish. The mourner's sense of community solidarity is reinforced by daily attendance at services where other mourners are likely to be present.

Judaism has five graduated periods of mourning, each with its own laws governing the expression of grief and the process of return to the normal affairs of society. The first stage of mourning, (*aninut*), is between death and burial. The mourner's despair is recognized and he (or she) is relieved of all religious obligations. Immediately after burial, the period of real mourning (*avelut*) begins, with its attendant obligations. In the *shiva* week mourners remain in the house of mourning, sit on low chairs, wear slippers rather than shoes, wear the torn clothing and receive condolence calls. Where possible the thrice-daily prayers are recited in the house of mourning with at least ten men attending to enable the mourner to recite Kaddish. Men do not shave during this time. For the first three days, the mourner is expected to be distressed and not return greetings. For the rest of *shiva* mourners move from the state of intense grief to the point of talking about the deceased with those offering condolences.

The next stage is the *shloshim* (thirty days from burial), during which the mourner returns to work. Many men continue not to shave nor have their hair cut, but are permitted to do so should this cause them embarrassment. Except where parents have died, the mourning period ends at thirty days. The obligation to mourn is terminated by the beginning of any major Jewish festival during this period. Mourning for parents continues to be observed for twelve lunar calendar months, although Kaddish is only recited for eleven.

From the time of burial till the end of the mourning period (thirty days or a year) mourners do not attend festive functions or public places, especially if music is played. This restriction aims at limiting pleasure (Goldberg, 1991). If the mourner is a professional who subsists on providing entertainment, taking photographs at functions, etc., this restriction is lifted.

A memorial stone is erected on the grave to honour the deceased usually between thirty days and a year after burial. The biblical precedent for this is the tomb Jacob placed on Rachel's grave (Genesis 35: 20). The stone should be unostentatious; if one wants to commemorate over and above that, charitable donations are encouraged. The timing of the tombstone unveiling (sometimes called consecration) varies in different communities; the UK custom is after eleven months. On the stone are engraved the name of the deceased, his (or her) dates of birth and death as well as a Hebrew abbreviation for 'May his/her soul be bound up in the Bond of Life'. The consecration of the stone is a short service either at the graveside or in the chapel. A further eulogy might be said. Thereafter mourners mark the Hebrew date annually by lighting the twenty-six-hour candle, attending services three times that day to recite the Mourner's Kaddish, and avoiding 'pleasurable' outings. One continues to commemorate this date (the *Yarzheit*) for the rest of one's life. Memorial prayers are also said on certain holy days.

Life after death

Little mention was made of life after death in the Old Testament, which emphasizes the value of life on earth. However, during the Rabbinic period the two concepts, that of the immortality of the soul and the resurrection of the dead, became combined so that 'when a man dies his soul lives on in Heaven until the time of the resurrection when soul and body are reunited' (Jacobs, 1973: 158). These concepts have continued to be accepted belief and were reinforced by the reference to life after death in Maimonides' thirteen principles of faith, which may be regarded as the essence of Judaism. The practical details of life after death are not specified in Jewish teachings:

> The doctrine of the immortality of the soul is affirmed not only by Judaism and other religions but by many secular philosophers as well. Judaism, however, also believes in the eventual resurrection of the body, which will be reunited with the soul at a later time. ... The human form of the righteous men of all ages, buried and long since decomposed, will be resurrected at God's will. (Lamm, 1969: 228)

Judaism delineates bodily death as a consequence of life:

> Death is defined as the irreversible separation of body and soul. No longer required by the soul, the body degenerates and decays. The soul, however, continues to exist in a non-physical dimension which we call 'heaven'. Free of the limitations of the body, but enriched by its earthly experiences, it is conscious of its attainments and earthly associations. Death is merely one's passage into a higher, more meaningful, more spiritual, more satisfying realm of existence. (Weiss, 1991: 14)

Judaism must be viewed as both this-worldly and other-worldly (Jacobs, 1973). Jacobs quotes the second-century Rabbi Jacob who illustrates this paradox:

> Better is one hour of repentance and good deeds in this world than the whole life of the world to come; yet better is one hour of blissfulness of spirit in the world to come than the whole life of this world. (Pirkei Avot 4: 17, quoted in Jacobs, 1973: 164)

Thus Jewish customs emphasize behaviour on earth, value the human body even after death and consider that the expression of grief is a normal human response to bereavement.

References

Abeles, Margaret (1991) 'Features of Judaism for carers when looking after Jewish patients', *Palliative Medicine*, 5: 201–5.

Byrne, P., Dunstan, J.R., Jakobovits, Lord I., Jayaweera, R.L.A., Marshall, J., Philipp, E., Saunders, Dame C. and Seller, M.J. (1991) 'Hospice care: Jewish reservations considered in a comparative ethical study', *Palliative Medicine*, 5: 187–200.

Goldberg, Chaim B. (1991) *Mourning in Halachah*. New York: Mesorah Publications.

Green, M. and Green, J. (1992) *Dealing with Death*. London: Chapman & Hall.

Jacobs, Louis (1973) *What Does Judaism Say About?* Jerusalem: Keter.

Lamm, Maurice (1969) *The Jewish Way in Death and Mourning*. New York: Jonathan David.

Rabinowicz, Tzvi (1989) *A Guide to Life: Jewish Laws and Customs of Mourning*. London: Jason Aronson.

Schindler, Ruben (1982) 'Confronting terminal illness and death in religious Jewish society', *Advances in Thanatology*, 5: 2.

Weiss, Abner (1991) *Death and Bereavement: A Halakhic Guide*. New York: Ktav Publishing House.

40

Complementary medicine – its place in the care of dying people

Patrick C. Pietroni

Probably there is no greater factor which determines the nature of our health care system than our attitude towards death, and indeed whether we believe in life after death. Different cultures have different concepts of death in the same way as there are different attitudes towards courtship, marriage and birth. Medical practice that is linked to these 'rites of passage' is influenced profoundly by the cultural attitudes and beliefs associated with these life events. In the nineteenth century, with the increasing influence of science in medicine, the use of powerful drugs and anaesthesia, we begin to see a separation between natural death and abnormal death.

Natural death was seen to come without previous sickness or obvious cause. It is very rare to find a picture of a doctor or nurse at a deathbed scene before the nineteenth century. After the First World War, pictures depict doctors fighting valiantly against death, tearing a young woman from the arms of a skeleton – locking a skeleton in the cupboard. And as our own modern culture has developed we have become adept not only at denying the possibility of death but at seeking ways to delay the ageing process. The consequence of this cultural shift is that our own Health Service has assumed a role more akin to a 'death prevention service'. Medical practice in most Western cultures developed an impressive array of drugs, surgical procedures, heroic interventions, to ward off and delay the time of death. Many of these initiatives are now considered to be good medical practice, but have in the last thirty years been influenced by the pioneers of palliative care, including Elisabeth Kübler-Ross and Cicely Saunders.

Complementary medicine is a 'pot-pourri' of approaches to health care that are not, as yet, taught in Western undergraduate medical schools. Some of these approaches, for example osteopathy, require four to five years' rigorous training and draw upon a Western framework of illness and disease. Others, such as spiritual healing, have no formal training and operate from a belief system that has no place in Western medicine and is rejected by most scientific doctors. Many, if not all, of those therapies that have found a place in the care of dying patients have arisen from non-Western cultures whose attitudes and approaches to death are at variance with the traditional views we are familiar with, that is, death is to be denied, death is to be feared, death is to be delayed and death is the end.

Although Socrates felt that philosophy – the love of wisdom – was 'simply and solely the practice of dying – the practice of death', this view has not taken root firmly in Western civilizations. However, it is found to form the basis of much Eastern philosophy from which many health care practices in complementary medicine are derived. In the Tibetan Book of the Dead, which is a treatise on how to die, it is considered that it is not possible to judge the value of a person's life until one has witnessed his or her manner of dying. Shavasana – the corpse posture – is one of the first postures taught in Yoga as a preparation for death. The aspirant Yogi is then taught Udana Prana – the control of breath during the last few hours of life – and Yoga Nidra – dreamless sleep – which is a practice to help students experience the 'state of death'. These exercises would be unacceptable to the majority of Western patients if expressed in the language and belief systems of Yoga. However, these have been adapted by many practitioners and are now finding favour in many hospitals, including hospice centres.

Breathing exercises and progressive muscular relaxation

The vicious cycle of anxiety, muscle tension, pain is not uncommon in patients dying with terminal cancer. Even when the terminal phase of someone's life does not involve physical pain, the fear and mental anguish often linked to dying may ensure that the last few days or hours are made far worse for both the dying person and his or her family. Breathing and relaxation exercises which can be taught and learnt before the event can provide great solace for all concerned. In the same way as a pregnant woman can learn to moderate and modulate the pain of childbirth through breathing exercises, many patients can learn to reduce the level of distress following surgery and during painful procedures.

Most of us develop a pattern of *chest breathing* during anxiety-laden situations. Breathing tends to be shallow and fast with an emphasis on inhalation and increased muscle tension. This pattern of breathing can be prolonged after the frightening or painful event is over and become the regular and 'normal' breathing pattern. *Diaphragmatic breathing,* which does not involve the movement of the chest muscles, leads to a deeper, more prolonged breathing pattern with an emphasis on exhalation and is the pattern observed in people who are relaxed and whose metabolism is in a restful state. Teaching individuals how to shift from chest to diaphragmatic breathing in classes or through the use of cassette tapes when they can practice at home is both simple and easy. It provides for a self-help 'tool' to be used in difficult and stressful situations as well as a health-promoting exercise to enhance well-being.

This simple skill is often taught alongside a muscular relaxation exercise which can help to undo physical tension present in the face, back of the neck, hands or other muscle groupings. There are several techniques described from a systematic and progressive muscular 'tensing and releasing' exercise through to one where each muscle group in turn is encouraged to relax using a count of one to five: 'On the count of one, allow your arm to feel heavier and relaxed. On the count of two . . . etc.' Once individuals have mastered these simple skills which allow them to obtain some mastery and control over their bodies, it is possible to introduce more complex skills which allow them to have some control over their thoughts, feelings and imaginative processes.

Meditation

This 'skill' of calming the mind is associated with many Eastern spiritual traditions. It received a boost in the 1960s when the Beatles were photographed sitting at the feet of Maharishi Mahesh Yogi. The practice of meditation is, however, well-founded in Christian mystical texts as well: for example, the spiritual exercises of Ignatius Loyola. In the last forty years it has achieved scientific respectability after many research studies identified the effect it had on blood pressure, heart rate, brain-wave patterns, anxiety levels and performance under stressful conditions. It has now been used as a 'complementary therapy' in such diverse conditions as high blood pressure, migraine, asthma, breast cancer and coronary prevention. There are several different techniques used in meditation, some focusing the mind on an object (picture, flame) or sound (mantra), others which encourage the mind to 'open up' and transcend normal human consciousness. The aim of all such processes is to achieve a state of mental calmness where troubled thoughts, worries and anxieties no longer intrude and the individual is freed for a while from painful, emotional experiences.

Individuals who meditate regularly find there is a 'carry-over' effect, that is, the state of calmness persists during the remaining 24-hour period and not only whilst the individual is meditating. Learning to meditate may require a few lessons from a teacher, although some people can learn from a cassette tape. Some individuals find learning in a group much easier, although others can be too self-conscious to join a group. Learning the basics of diaphragmatic breathing and muscular relaxation is an important first step as the distractions that come from a physical body that is in pain or uncomfortable can make the meditative state difficult to obtain.

Meditation is most often taught sitting upright in a chair, although there is no reason why someone who is bedridden cannot be taught it. It is important to explain to 'students' that meditation taught within a caring or medical context need not carry any spiritual connotations, whether Christian, Buddhist, agnostic or atheist. That some people who meditate regularly find a re-awakening of their own spirituality may be a by-product which, for some, will be welcome. Many dying patients have found the peace and inner calmness that regular meditation brings of particular help in their last few weeks of life. Unfortunately, many patients in the West will only learn how to meditate when they know they are approaching death. If they are in physical pain as well, this may make it impossible for them to achieve the state of 'physiological non-arousal' (the scientific term for the meditative state). The inability to learn how to meditate in such circumstances is unfortunately all too common and enthusiasts and teachers of meditation must guard against this and caution patients whose distress is too great from attempting to learn. All too often the wholesale application of self-help techniques to vulnerable individuals who are unable to make use of these techniques only helps to increase their burden and, at times, their guilt – 'It's my fault I can't meditate. . . .'

Visualization

Visualization, or guided imagery, like meditation, is a self-help and therapeutic technique that is well described in Eastern spiritual and medical texts and has become increasingly popular in the West, although, as yet, it is not well-integrated with more orthodox approaches. The technique involves the imagining of 'mental pictures', 'a calm sea' or a 'beautiful garden rose', for a period of time whilst in a state of deep relaxation. In the same way that imagining cutting a lemon will produce physiological changes (salivation), it is believed that visualizing peaceful and calm scenes will decrease the level of stress hormone and effect cellular changes in the immune system that play a part in warding off infection and destroying cancer cells.

It is in the treatment of cancer that visualization has made most public impact. In the Simonton technique, the patient is encouraged to imagine his/her white blood cells eating/destroying the cancer cells in his/her body. In the initial study, the Simontons claimed that those patients who were able to visualize in this way were able to make their cancers regress and thereby live longer. Subsequent studies have failed to support this initial claim, although it has been shown that less aggressive images (a peaceful scene) can significantly affect the mood of patients with cancer and reduce their level of depression. Visualization is more difficult to learn than meditation, and if attempted as a 'last resort' can be of little or no value.

It is interesting to observe how techniques which arose out of an Eastern cultural attitude to death, that is, 'expect and accept', when used by many Western therapists and patients become altered and are used as a way to prolong life and avoid death. The *positive health* movement that has taken over many of these therapies is, at times, responsible for deluding not only itself but many vulnerable and distressed patients that these techniques are another form of the 'magic bullet'. That they can help to reduce unnecessary suffering and pain and ease the process of dying there is no doubt, but they must not be sold as some form of do-it-yourself radiotherapy which can dissolve away all cancerous and diseased tissue.

Massage and aromatherapy

So far we have discussed 'self-help' techniques. Massage and aroma-therapy (the use of essential oils) are particularly good examples of complementary therapy in the care of dying patients. Massage is one of the oldest healing interventions. It was written about in 3000 BC and Hippocrates himself wrote: 'The way to health is to have a scented bath and an oiled massage each day.' Until the nineteenth century, massage was commonly referred to in medical textbooks, but with the advent of drug therapy it lost its appeal and it is only fairly recently that it has regained a respectability within the medical and nursing professions. There is nothing more natural or human than the use of touch to relieve pain and distress, whether it is a hug, a hand on the shoulder or a mother rubbing around the injured knee of her young child.

Massage is a form of 'structured touch' or 'therapeutic touch' which has been and can be used systematically to relieve muscle pain and tension, bring about a sense of relaxation, and for those isolated and lonely, re-affirm their humanity with contact from another human being. In the care of the dying, it can be most powerfully used to help with the sense of hopelessness and despair that surrounds the deathbed. Many relatives who sit helplessly round the hospital bed can be taught to massage the foot or hand of their wife, husband, father or mother, which will reduce the anxiety and bring pleasure to both the giver and the recipient. For unlike many other therapies, massage can be used as a form of communication between therapist and patient as well as a specific intervention for the relief of pain and muscle tension. Apart from simple common-sense caveats of avoiding open wounds, vein thromboses and areas of extreme sensitivity, massage for the dying patient is of particular use.

Most modern Western massage techniques are derived from the work of Per Henrik Ling, who devised what is now called Swedish massage, which involves one of four main techniques: percussion – short, sharp, fast rhythmic movements; effleurage – slow, rhythmic strokes usually performed with the hands close together; petrissage – involving grasping and squeezing sections of the skin such as those close to the waist or stomach; and friction – a series of small circular movements made by one or more fingers, the heel of the hand or the pads of the thumbs. Many weekend courses teaching massage now exist and it is not uncommon to find massage therapists attached to hospital wards, working in hospices or linked to a general practice.

The use of oils in massage is important to avoid unnecessary pain and friction and aromatherapy takes this practice further by using aromatic, highly concentrated essential oils during massage. This is not always necessary and inhalation and scented baths are additional ways of obtaining the benefit of these oils. The oils are produced by the tiny glands in the petals, leaves, stems, bark and wood of many plants and trees. They are extracted through a process of distillation and concentration. Their modern use was pioneered by a French chemist, Professor Renie Gattefosse, who accidentally discovered the power of lavender essence when he plunged his hand into it after receiving a bad burn. Qualified aromatherapists will use different oils for different conditions: for example, cedarwood, because of its sedative effect, will be used for anxiety and for troublesome coughs, and rosemary, which has an invigorating and refreshing effect, will be used for someone who is depressed, tired and has lost his or her memory.

Acupuncture

The placing of sterile needles in the skin forms one element of traditional Chinese medicine (TCM). It has received much interest recently in the care of the dying because of its ability to reduce pain, enhance muscular relaxation and induce anaesthesia. TCM, like many approaches to healing derived from Eastern traditions, is based on the concept of 'Chi' or life force. Chinese practitioners believe that in addition to a circulatory and nervous system in the body there is an equivalent energetic system. Illness, disease, well-being and ultimately death are dependent on the harmonious and balanced flow of energy through the channels known as meridians.

Acupuncture needles are placed along points in this energetic system to help unblock and release the flow of 'Chi', thus restoring health. This model of understanding traditional Chinese medicine and acupuncture was disregarded by Western-trained doctors. In the last twenty years, as a result of a number of serious studies, it has become evident that not only can acupuncture help in pain relief but that its mode of action can be easily understood in Western terms. Several studies have demonstrated that during acupuncture, the body releases endorphines, a class of chemicals known to relieve pain and decrease muscle arousal. In clinical settings, acupuncture is now frequently used for pain relief and in the care of the dying patient this can be of particular benefit, especially when the use of oral or parenteral [not absorbed through the digestive tract] analgesia produces sedation. This specialized use of acupuncture requires a skilled practitioner.

Spiritual healing

By far the most common complementary therapy sought for and used by dying patients is spiritual healing, according to the most recent survey of complementary therapists in the UK. The laying on of hands and blessings have always formed part of spiritual practice and derive their authority from the Scriptures. European royalty, who claimed to rule by Divine Right, took on this power – 'The King's Touch' – but by 1600 itinerant healers were common all over England. Modern science, notwithstanding some rather elegant research studies, dismisses this approach as a 'placebo effect', and regards the 'miraculous' cures occasionally reported as examples of spontaneous remission only. Whether or not healing works does not belie the fact that many dying patients receive enormous comfort and hope after being visited by a healer. Healing is generally considered to be a two-way process. The first thing a healer will do is to talk soothingly and generally calm the patient. A state of deep relaxation is then encouraged and the healer will then focus on his or her powers and allow them to flow through his/her hands to the patient. The patient may also be instructed to visualize projections of white or coloured light which are thought to aid the healing process. Sessions are usually undertaken once a week and many healers will visit patients in their own homes – a decided advantage. Indeed, many healers will not charge for their services. A register of practitioners willing to visit patients in hospital as well as in their home is available from the Confederation of Healing Organizations (CHO). Several Christian Churches now hold regular healing services where the 'laying on of hands' and anointment with oils is carried out within the context of receiving the sacrament. But in orthodox medicine, doctors are justifiably concerned that false hopes may be raised and that patients may not seek orthodox treatments for complaints because they are seeking a spiritual healer.

Conclusion

A range of complementary therapies are now in widespread use in European countries and in North America, both through independent practitioners and within established health systems. They are most notably present in the care of dying people and have been welcomed more in hospices and within the developing specialism of palliative care than within mainstream curative medicine.

41

Dying trajectories, the organization of work and expectations of dying

Anselm Strauss

Before commencing the case history, it is important to locate Mrs Abel's own type of dying trajectory – lingering – within a general picture of types of dying trajectories as they relate to the temporal organizations of hospital work, the accountable features of terminal care and the progressive change of the staff's expectations of dying.

Temporal features of terminal care

While not entirely medical or technical, most writings about terminal care focus on the psychological or ethical aspects of behaviour toward dying persons. These emphases flow from generalized considerations of death as a philosophical problem, and the psychological and often ethical difficulties accompanying death and dying. Just as legitimately, however, the behaviour of people toward the dying may be viewed as involving 'work'. This is just as true when a person dies at home as when he [sic] dies in the hospital. Usually during the course of his dying he is unable to fulfil all his physiological and psychological needs. He may need to be fed, bathed, taken to the toilet, given drugs, brought desired objects when too feeble to get them himself, and near the end of his life, even 'cared for' totally. Whether the people who are in attendance on him enjoy or suffer these tasks, they are undeniably 'work'. Wealthier families sometimes hire private nurses to do all or some of this work. In the hospital, there is no question that terminal care, whether regarded distastefully or as satisfying, is viewed as work. Mrs Abel required considerable physiological and psychological care which became progressively distasteful to the staff.

This work has important temporal features. For instance, there are prescribed schedules governing when the patient must be fed, bathed, turned in bed, given drugs. There are periodic moments when tests must be administered. There are crucial periods when the patient must be closely observed, or even when crucial treatments must be given or

---

Extract from *Anguish: the Case History of a Dying Trajectory*, San Francisco, CA: Sociology Press, 1971, pp. 5–13 (abridged).

actions taken to prevent immediate deterioration – even immediate death. Since there is a division of labour, it must be temporally organized. For instance, the nurse must have the patient awake in time for the laboratory technician to administer tests, and the physician's visit must not coincide with the patient's bath or even perhaps the visiting hours of relatives. [. . .]

On Mrs Abel's ward nurses preferred to focus care and attention on recovering and less troublesome dying patients. The temporal ordering of work on given services is also related to the predominant types of death in relation to normal types of recovery. As an example, we may look at intensive care units: some patients there may be expected to die quickly, if they are to die at all; others need close attention for several days because death is a touch-and-go matter; while others are not likely to die but do need temporary round-the-clock nursing. Most who will die here are either so heavily drugged as to be temporarily comatose or are actually past self-consciousness. Consequently, there is little need for nurses or physicians to converse with those patients, as there is on lingering wards, where we find Mrs Abel. She continually wished to talk to nursing staff and her doctor no matter how pressed they were to keep working.

Each type of service tends to have a characteristic incidence of death, and speed of dying, which together affect the staff's organization of work. Thus, on emergency services, patients tend to die quickly (they are accident cases, or victims of violence, or people suddenly stricken). The staff on emergency services therefore is geared to give immediate emergency service to prevent death whenever possible. Many emergency services, especially in large cities, are also organized for frequent deaths, especially on weekends. At such times, the recovering (or non-sick) patients sometimes tend to receive scant attention, unless the service is flexibly organized for handling both types of patients. This patient competition also occurs on wards where patients die slowly. On the cancer ward, for example, when a patient nears death, sometimes he may unwittingly compete with other patients for nurses' or physicians' attention, several of whom may give care to the critically ill patient. When the emergency is over, or the patient dies, then the nurses may return to less immediately critical patients, reading their vital signs, managing treatments and carrying out other important tasks. Mrs Abel fared poorly in such competition with other patients during her long stay in the hospital, and especially during her last days.

All these temporal features of terminal care make for a complex organization of professional activity. The required organization is rendered even more complex by certain other matters involving temporality. Thus, what may be conveniently termed the 'experiential careers' of patients, families and staff members are very relevant to the action around dying patients. Some patients are very familiar with their diseases, but even then are encountering symptoms for the first time, such as Mrs Abel confronting her intense pain. What a patient knows about the course of his disease, from previous experience with it, is very relevant to what will happen as he lies dying in the hospital. The same may be said about personnel in attendance upon him. Some personnel may be well acquainted with the predominant disease patterns found on their particular wards; but some may be newcomers to these diseases, although quite possibly old hands with other illnesses. The newcomers may be quite unprepared for sudden changes of symptoms and vital signs, hence may be taken quite by surprise at crucial junctures: that is, they make bad errors in timing their actions. More experienced personnel are less likely to be caught unprepared, and are readier with appropriate care at each phase of the illness. [. . .]

Dying trajectories

The dying trajectory of each patient has at least two outstanding properties. First, it takes place over time: it has *duration*. There can be much variation in duration among specific trajectories, ranging from instant death to months, as for Mrs Abel. Second, a trajectory has *shape*: it can be graphed. It plunges straight down; it moves slowly downward (Mrs Abel); it vacillates slowly, moving slightly up and down before diving radically downward; it moves slowly down at first, then hits a long plateau, then plunges abruptly to death.

Neither duration nor shape is a purely objective psychological property. They are perceived properties; their dimensions depend on *when* the perceiver initially *defines* someone as dying and on his expectations of how that dying will proceed. Dying trajectories are, then, *perceived courses of dying*, rather than the actual courses themselves. This distinction is readily evident in the type of trajectory which involves a short reprieve from death. This reprieve represents an unexpected deferment of death. On the other hand, a lingering death may mean that bystanders expect faster dying, as in Mrs Abel's trajectory.

Since dying patients enter hospitals at varying distances from death, and are defined in terms of when and how they will die, various types of trajectories are commonly recognized by the hospital personnel. For instance, there is the trajectory that is a complete surprise: a patient who is expected to recover suddenly dies. A frequently found trajectory on emergency wards is the expected swift death. Many patients are brought in because of fatal accidents, and nothing can be done to prevent their deaths. Expected lingering while dying is another type of trajectory; it is characteristic, for example, of cancer patients like Mrs Abel. Besides the short-term reprieve, there may also be the suspended-sentence trajectory. Another commonly recognized pattern is entry–re-entry: the patient, slowly going downhill, returns home several times between stays in the hospital. All these generalized types of trajectories rest upon the perceivers' expectations of 'duration' and 'shape'.

Regardless of the particular attributes of a specific patient's trajectory, there are ordinarily certain events - we shall term them 'critical junctures' - which appear along the dying trajectory and are directly handled by the temporal organization of hospital work. These occur either in full or truncated form: (1) The patient is defined as dying; (2) Staff and family then make preparations for his death, as he may himself if he knows he is dying; (3) At some point, there seems to be 'nothing more to do' to prevent death; (4) The final descent may take weeks, or days, or merely hours, ending in (5) the 'last hours', (6) the death watch and (7) death itself. Somewhere along his course of dying, there may be announcements that the patient is dying, or that he is entering or leaving a phase of dying. After death, death itself must be legally pronounced, and then publicly announced.

When these critical junctures occur as expected, on schedule, then all participants - including the patient, sometimes - are prepared for their occurrence - the work involved is provided for and integrated by the temporal order of the hospital. For instance, the nurses are ready for a death watch when they can anticipate approximately when the patient will be very near death. When, however, critical junctures are not expected or are off schedule, staff members and family alike are caught off guard, or at least somewhat unprepared. This case will offer many examples of both anticipated and unanticipated junctures. The point we wish to emphasize here is that expectations are crucial to the way critical junctures are handled by all involved. [. . .]

42

Spiritual care of dying people

Alyson Peberdy

Current approaches to caring for dying people acknowledge the need to pay attention to the person as a whole, not just the physical symptoms. An English Nursing Board course, for example, ambitiously speaks of aiming to produce 'a competent practitioner in all aspects of care, one who recognizes the total needs of the dying patient and the family' (ENB 931, Sir Michael Sobell House, Churchill Hospital, Oxford). It goes on to describe these needs as physical, psychological, social and spiritual. Most people have a clear picture of what is meant by the first three terms but there is much less certainty about the meaning of the word 'spiritual' and of how it relates to the others.

It is sometimes assumed that spiritual care is straightforwardly the province of religion in general and of the clergy in particular. In this view the role of carers is primarily one of contacting the appropriate religious representative, such as the priest or Imam, or ensuring that family and friends are enabled to perform the necessary rituals before and immediately after death. Carers who are themselves believers may perhaps want to offer more direct support, though some clergy wish to be entirely in control of religious care. One hospice chaplain, for instance, takes the view that it is inappropriate 'for a nurse to assess and attempt to meet effectively the spiritual/religious needs of a patient or family' (Hoy, 1983: 178).

In our society the words spiritual and religious are not necessarily synonymous. This becomes obvious when we consider how for many people religion either has negative associations or feels irrelevant. Yet few have an entirely materialistic view of themselves and others. People commonly say 'I am not religious', they do not say, 'I am not spiritual' (Working Party . . ., 1991: 152). Without giving it formal religious expression there is a spiritual dimension to their living and dying. Perhaps it may help to see spirituality as a search for meaning, and religion as a particular expression of that (one that usually involves God-language).

Much nursing or hospice literature that discusses spirituality focuses on this concept of a search for meaning. An American community

---

The thinking underlying this article has been influenced greatly by an unpublished paper written by Janet Mayer (1989).

liaison nurse, for instance, writes that spiritual care 'entails a putting together of the broken pieces, the meaningless pieces. It involves a mending, a healing and a search for new meaning and purpose that has always been the challenge of what it means to be human' (Granstom, 1985: 39). 'Spiritual distress', writes Burnard, 'is the result of total inability to invest life with meaning' (1987: 377).

Sometimes this search for meaning is expressed in the form of questions about the cause or purpose of the suffering the dying person is experiencing, especially when a death seems premature. 'What have I done to deserve this?' 'Why now?' Or, more widely, like Job in the Hebrew scriptures who expressed a powerful sense of anger towards God:

> Why was I not still born,
> Why did I not perish when I came from the womb? . . .
> Why is life given to those who find it bitter? (Job 3: 11, 20)

The question of whether there is an existence beyond death may also be put into words. 'What happens after death?' 'Will I meet loved ones again?' For people from religious traditions involving the idea of judgement after death considerable anxiety may underlie their thoughts about the possibility of an afterlife.

Although the search for meaning forms the major element in the way in which spiritual need tends to be understood in the literature, also included is the need for identity and relatedness, which is sometimes expressed in terms of being loved or accepted and of having a sense of self-worth. McCavery, for instance, identifies four spiritual needs in acute illness: meaning, love, self-worth and hope (1985: 131).

In this context it is important to distinguish between the narrow meaning attached to 'hope' in clinical usage, where it refers to survival or recovery, and its much wider use in everyday language. It is the second and wider meaning which is crucial to spiritual care.

In the face of death the desire for life that fuelled a person's hope for recovery *may* become transformed into a wider sense of hope which continues to discover and affirm creative possibilities despite the prospect of death. According to Bruce Rumbold (1986) this happens when a person: (a) has a realistic knowledge of the situation; (b) focuses attention on the quality of life and is able to look beyond their immediate situation; (c) is able to live in the moment; and (d) affirms the value of life even in the face of their own death.

In practice what does it mean to recognize and try to meet the spiritual needs of a dying person? This question seems easiest to answer where a person definitely identifies with a faith community within which there will be a body of knowledge and experience to draw upon. For example, within the Christian tradition the story of the crucifixion and resurrection of Jesus may help give a dying believer a sense of purpose and future and rites of confession and absolution may help restore a sense of right relationship. Amongst Hindus the same sense of right relationship may be arrived at through the presence of the wider family carrying out the rituals that precede and surround death. Similar resources are to be found throughout the various religious traditions. But what of people who have found the tradition they know best unhelpful, harshly judgemental or plain irrelevant in their lives? And what of those who have never had any real connection with a religion? What might spiritual care mean in relation to them?

Nursing literature in the United States has attempted to provide guidelines to help carers gain some understanding of the perspective and needs of those dying people with whom they are not already familiar. So, for example, nurses have been advised to develop a spiritual history of their patients which involves asking four main questions (Stoll, 1979: 1574-7). What is the person's concept of God or duty? What is the person's source of hope or strength? What is the significance of religious practice or rituals to this person? What is the person's perceived relationship between spiritual beliefs and his/her state of health? The aim here is to identify areas of spiritual need and to plan appropriate support.

Whilst questioning may well be a good idea, an insensitive approach could do more harm than good. Any idea that spiritual needs can be identified, classified, recorded and responded to in much the same way as bowel dysfunction is obviously highly problematic and rejected by most people. Yet the notion that spiritual care can be delivered from active carer to passive patient tends to be present even in more nuanced and softer versions of what might be called an interventionist model of spiritual care. One of the few British nurses researching the area of spiritual care argues that the extent to which patients are able to find, experience or anticipate meaning is dependent on what she calls the 'skills' of knowing, hoping and trusting, and that these can be *taught* by nurses as a central part of spiritual care (Simsen, 1988: 41-2). But if we look at our own experience of life we find that hope and trust are not so much skills that can be taught as qualities that emerge out of, and are fostered by, certain kinds of relationship in which we have been valued, where life has felt trustworthy and reality can be faced.

The process by which hope may emerge in the face of the prospect of one's own death is complex but not random. Extending a model put forward by Avery Weisman, a psychiatrist interested in the defences used by dying people to protect themselves from the knowledge of their imminent death, Bruce Rumbold suggests that there is a recognizable shape or pattern to the development of hope.

People who are ill usually entertain a hope for recovery. This is usually shared by patient, carers and family who together tend to want to maintain this hope by limiting information that might challenge it. But if the possibility of dying cannot be faced and explored a hope which goes beyond insistence upon recovery cannot emerge.

When the possibility of death is acknowledged a person becomes free to choose to hope for death rather than life at any price, to hope for a certain kind of death and for certain circumstances to prevail. Often family and hospital staff fail to allow these hopes to be articulated or may hear them as expressions of despair, themselves insisting on an unrealistic hope for recovery. But it is only through acknowledging the imminence of death that it becomes possible for a person to look back over his or her life to affirm its value, take a wider perspective and allow a wider sense of hope and integration to emerge. The content of such hope may or may not be linked to an established system of belief (Rumbold, 1986: 64–6).

This understanding of the way in which hope develops suggests that spiritual care is the concern of all carers and it is perhaps as a force for integration that spiritual care may best be understood. 'The spiritual dimension transcends and holds together the physical, psychological and social dimensions. The spiritual integrates the other three dimensions into a "I"' (Working Party . . ., 1991: 152). Such integration will not be fostered where spiritual care is considered as simply another aspect of care alongside physical, social and psychological care. Attempts to classify, clarify, evaluate and categorize spiritual need and create interventionist spiritual care plans which are separate from and parallel to other care plans are likely to increase rather than reverse the disintegrating impact of suffering.

Hospital chaplain Janet Mayer concluded an extensive review of the nursing literature with the suggestion that spiritual care can best be seen as a quality pervading care as a whole. It is something we all give when we are fully attentive to another; something we all receive when someone gives us that same full attention. A nurse who expertly dresses a patient's wound while engaged in conversation with a colleague about her holidays is caring for the wound but not the person. The manner in which the nurse carries out her nursing tasks and relates to both dying people and other members of staff provides a vital basis to the spirituality of the dying person's experience. A nurse whose touch is gentle and whose observations are perceptive not only reduces physical pain but also provides evidence of a sensitivity on which a trusting relationship can be formed (Mayer, 1989). Conversely, a nurse who is too busy to sit with a lonely or anxious patient will further reduce that person's self-esteem. 'When asked what he most looked for in those caring for him, a patient replied "For someone to look as if they are trying to understand me." He did not ask for success, but only that someone should care enough to try' (Working Party . . ., 1991: 155).

Spiritual care is not just a question of relationships between individuals: the spirituality of institutions also needs to be considered. This involves thinking about a hospice or hospital's general atmosphere, rules and even furnishings and asking what impact they may have on the dying person. Even the fact of having china cups rather than disposable mugs may well influence people's ability to discover meaning and value in their lives and in the world in general. So too will the morale of carers. In this respect the employment conditions of paid carers and the amount of recognition and support available to informal carers are matters of profound spiritual significance.

References

Burnard, P. (1987) 'Spiritual distress and the nursing response: theoretical considerations and counselling skills', *Journal of Advanced Nursing*, 12: 377–82.

Carson, V. and Huss, K. (1979) 'Prayer – an effective therapeutic and teaching tool', *Journal of Psychiatric Nursing and Mental Health Service*, March: 34–7.

Granstom, S. (1985) 'Spiritual care for oncology patients', *Topics in Clinical Nursing*, April: 39–45.

Hoy, T. (1983) 'Hospice chaplaincy in the caregiving team', in C. Corr and D. Corr (eds), *Hospice Care Principles and Practice*. London: Faber & Faber. pp. 177–96.

McCavery, R. (1985) 'Spiritual care in acute illness', in F. McGilloway and P. Myco (eds), *Nursing and Spiritual Care*. New York: Harper & Row. pp. 129–42.

Mayer, J. (1989) 'Wholly responsible for a part or partly responsible for a whole? An evaluation of the nursing concept of spiritual care'. Unpublished paper.

Rumbold, B. (1986) *Helplessness and Hope*. London: Routledge.

Simsen, B. (1988) 'The spiritual dimension', *Nursing Times*, 26 November: 41–2.

Stoll, R. (1979) 'Guidelines for spiritual assessment', *American Journal of Nursing*, September: 1574–7.

Working Party on the Impact of Hospice Experience in the Church's Ministry of Healing (1991) *Mud and Stars*. Oxford: Sobell Publications.

43

Sitting it out

Elizabeth Dean

The writer has worked as a registered nurse in homes for the elderly. In this article, one of those for whom she has cared speaks through her about the diminishment - and hope - which old age brings.

My day begins around 5.30 when I'm woken by the night staff changing the sheets of the old men and women that have wet themselves during the night; my bed is dry, I am not at this stage yet.

I am 79 years old and of sound mind, at least I think I am. It's not my mind but my body that no longer functions reliably and I am termed 'unsafe' by my doctor, my daughter-in-law and my son, although for my son to say it causes him guilt and he somehow can't quite look me in the eye. Between them they arranged for my house to be sold and the money it provided has secured me a place here, in a 'home', where I can be well looked after. It's not so bad I suppose: beyond my window I can see a beautiful garden.

I never really expected my son and his wife to look after me, it was an unrealistic hope, they're busy with jobs and their children, I can remember what it was like bring up a family, there's very little time for anything else. I understand now but I felt very hurt and bitter at first, knowing they couldn't look after me, but like so many other things these days I find I accept it. They visit me most weekends and bring pictures of my grandchildren; I suppose it wouldn't be much fun for them coming to see their Granny in a place like this.

I miss my home; they call this place 'Sunnyside Lodge, Home for the Elderly', most people just call it 'The Home', to me it's just a place and there are many places like this one, large, old houses converted to take in old relics like me - storage houses really. They tend the garden well and have planted masses of flowers; sometimes, if my window is open, I can smell the scent on the breeze.

The nurses, or care assistants as they are called, are cheerful most of the time and do the best they can to ensure our physical well-being. They refer to us as 'residents', we are patients really but nobody uses that word, it smacks too much of hospitals and illness; it's all psychology jargon to try and kid you and it really doesn't matter, I suppose.

From *The Tablet*, 25 May 1991.

I think a lot these days and sometimes I find it hard to know if I'm saying what I'm thinking or just think I'm saying what I'm thinking and I become very confused but Louise seems to understand me, she's a nurse and she works here on Monday nights. I wish they were all like Louise, kind and comforting.

They give me pills, I lose count how many I take in a day. Some almost choke me, they're so big you see and my throat is very dry so they stick halfway down – it's frightening. It seems every part of me is drying up; skin, joints, hair, nails, I'm like an autumn leaf, all dry and brittle and about to disintegrate.

When I arrived at this place I could walk by myself, I could even help the others, like changing the channel on the TV or picking up a dropped newspaper, that sort of thing. Their helplessness made me feel better, now I'm just as helpless. I'm a prisoner trapped in a hard upright chair that I have to sit in all day long.

My best hours are between 11 o'clock and 1. The pain in my joints has eased by this time, with the help of the tablets. The nurses are busy making beds and cleaning medicine trolleys so we are left alone. I can still read the newspaper with a magnifying glass and I can read books as long as they are not too heavy to hold.

All things considered the food here isn't too bad. We are given our lunch at half past 12, if meat is served I have to ask someone to cut it up for me. Sometimes I try to do it for myself, but very often the knife slips and the food spills onto my lap and stains my clothes and then I've made more work for the nurses.

I try not to grumble, I never did like to hear people moaning but it's the frustration I find unbearable – the fact that my body is so useless and refuses to do what I want it to. If I was at home it wouldn't bother me, it wouldn't matter if I didn't wash my face one day or brush my hair another, these things seem unimportant but I can't tell the nurses that, they seem hurt if we complain, if we don't try and some of them can get quite cross. I'm too weary to resist their demands so I put up with their concern about washing me and dressing me and lifting me to rub my bottom so it doesn't become sore; and I let them put pills into my mouth to ease the pain and I put up with the side-effects they produce; the sickness, the constipation, and I suffer the indignity of the enemas to relieve the constipation and through all this I find myself saying 'Thank you' constantly and why? I should be clawing their eyes out for making me suffer in this way. There is no sense to any of it. Why can't they leave me alone? I know I shouldn't think this way, they are doing their best, it's not their fault I'm old.

After lunch we are toileted and arranged in chairs in a semi-circle in front of the television set and left for two hours; that's the average length of time it takes before we need the toilet again, or so the nurses say. We would all dearly love to go to bed but this is not allowed, 'It's not therapeutic' they say and we are denied our beds unless we are ill.

So I am forced to sit in front of a blaring TV set, my hearing remains good whilst most of the others are deaf, consequently the TV has to be set at full volume. I am imprisoned in my chair, watching ludicrous programmes that I can't understand, unable to sleep because of the noise and every muscle and every bone in my body is creaking with tiredness.

My voice, much weaker now, cannot be heard above the noise when I call for help. I can see the bell by the mantlepiece but I can't reach it and the fear of falling keeps me rooted to my seat. The sight of that bell, so tantalizingly close, plays cruelly on my nerves. Knowing I am forced to sit here until someone happens to look into the room agitates me to the point that I feel I need the toilet; fear of wetting the chair and my clothes increases the desire to wee.

The night staff put us to bed around 9 o'clock. I am one of the first to be undressed and eased between the cold, stiff sheets. They scratch my tender, papery-thin skin but this no longer bothers me, all I want is to lie down and never have to get out of bed again.

It's Monday and Louise is working tonight and she sits on my bed chatting quietly. She seems to understand the suffering and fear that ageing forces us to endure. She doesn't try to cajole me or make light of the effort required to keep myself going. She has a gentle humour and somehow makes me laugh at my infirmities, laughter is a fine medicine.

'One day nearer,' Louise says as she tucks me into bed and she says the words with such hope in her voice, not in a morbid way, as if she knows for sure that something better waits just ahead of me. And she makes it sound so natural, as if there is nothing to be frightened of and her words comfort me because I am frightened, but beyond the fear lies hope, beyond this dark tunnel of pain there is a wonderfully bright future and I just have to be patient.

Louise strokes my hair soothingly. 'God bless you,' she says as she switches off the light. And I wonder – is that what death will be like, as if someone has switched off the light and as I lie in bed I pray that God in His infinite mercy does just that but I pray that He does it gently, tenderly ... without pain, because I am bone weary and all that was once strong in me is crumbling and there is little left to support me. I am exhausted by this world.

44

A very easy death

Simone de Beauvoir

Why did my mother's death shake me so deeply? Since the time I left home I had felt little in the way of emotional impulse towards her. When she lost my father the intensity and the simplicity of her sorrow moved me, and so did her care for others – 'Think of yourself,' she said to me, supposing that I was holding back my tears so as not to make her suffering worse. A year later her mother's dying was a painful reminder of her husband's: on the day of the funeral a nervous breakdown compelled her to stay in bed. I spent the night beside her: forgetting my disgust for this marriage-bed in which I had been born and in which my father had died, I watched her sleeping; at fifty-five, with her eyes closed and her face calm, she was still beautiful; I wondered that the strength of her feelings should have overcome her will. Generally speaking I thought of her with no particular feeling. Yet in my sleep (although my father only made very rare and then insignificant appearances) she often played a most important part: she blended with Sartre, and we were happy together. And then the dream would turn into a nightmare: why was I living with her once more? How had I come to be in her power again? So our former relationship lived on in me in its double aspect – a subjection that I loved and hated. It revived with all its strength when Maman's accident, her illness and her death shattered the routine that then governed our contacts. Time vanishes behind those who leave this world, and the older I get the more my past years draw together. The 'Maman darling' of the days when I was ten can no longer be told from the inimical woman who oppressed my adolescence: I wept for them both when I wept for my old mother. I thought I had made up my mind about our failure and accepted it; but its sadness comes back to my heart. There are photographs of both of us, taken at about the same time: I am eighteen, she is nearly forty. Today I could almost be her mother and the grandmother of that sad-eyed girl. I am so sorry for them – for me because I am so young and I understand nothing; for her because her future is closed and she has never understood anything. But I would not know how to advise them. It was not in my power to wipe out the

Extract from *A Very Easy Death*, Harmondsworth: Penguin, 1969, pp. 89-92.

unhappiness in her childhood that condemned Maman to make me unhappy and to suffer in her turn for having done so. For if she embittered several years of my life, I certainly paid her back though I did not set out to do so. She was intensely anxious about my soul. As far as this world was concerned, she was pleased at my successes, but she was hurt by the scandal that I aroused among the people she knew. It was not pleasant for her to hear a cousin state, 'Simone is the family's disgrace.'

The changes in Maman during her illness made my sorrow all the greater. As I have already said, she was a woman of strong and eager temperament, and because of her renunciations she had grown confused and difficult. Confined to her bed, she decided to live for herself; and yet at the same time she retained an unvarying care for others – from her conflicts there arose a harmony. My father and his social character coincided exactly: his class and he spoke through his mouth with one identical voice. His last words, 'You began to earn your living very young, Simone: your sister cost me a great deal of money,' were not of a kind to encourage tears. My mother was awkwardly laced into a spiritualistic ideology; but she had an animal passion for life which was the source of her courage and which, once she was conscious of the weight of her body, brought her towards truth. She got rid of the ready-made notions that hid her sincere and lovable side. It was then that I felt the warmth of an affection that had often been distorted by jealousy and that she expressed so badly. In her papers I have found touching evidence of it. She had put aside two letters, the one written by a Jesuit and the other by a friend; they both assured her that one day I should come back to God. She had copied out a passage from Chamson in which he says in effect, 'If, when I was twenty, I had met an older, highly-regarded man who had talked to me about Nietzsche and Gide and freedom, I should have broken with home.' The file was completed by an article cut out of a paper – *Jean-Paul Sartre has saved a soul*. In this Rémy Roure said – quite untruthfully, by the way – that after *Bariona* had been acted at Stalag XII D an atheistical doctor was converted. I know very well what she wanted from these pieces – it was to be reassured about me; but she would never have felt the need if she had not been intensely anxious as to my salvation. 'Of course I should like to go to Heaven: but not all alone, not without my daughters,' she wrote to a young nun.

Sometimes, though very rarely, it happens that love, friendship or comradely feeling overcomes the loneliness of death: in spite of appearances, even when I was holding Maman's hand, I was not with her – I was lying to her. Because she had always been deceived, gulled, I found this ultimate deception revolting. I was making myself an accomplice of that fate which was so misusing her. Yet at the same time in every cell of my body I joined in her refusal, in her rebellion: and it was also because of that that her defeat overwhelmed me.

Although I was not with Maman when she died, and although I had been with three people when they were actually dying, it was when I was at her bedside that I saw Death, the Death of the dance of death, with its bantering grin, the Death of fireside tales that knocks on the door, a scythe in its hand, the Death that comes from elsewhere, strange and inhuman: it had the very face of Maman when she showed her gums in a wide smile of unknowingness.

'He is certainly of an age to die.' The sadness of the old; their banishment: most of them do not think that this age has yet come for them. I too made use of this cliché, and that when I was referring to my mother. I did not understand that one might sincerely weep for a relative, a grandfather aged seventy and more. If I met a woman of fifty overcome with sadness because she had just lost her mother, I thought her neurotic: we are all mortal; at eighty you are quite old enough to be one of the dead . . .

But it is not true. You do not die from being born, nor from having lived, nor from old age. You die from *something*. The knowledge that because of her age my mother's life must soon come to an end did not lessen the horrible surprise: she had sarcoma. Cancer, thrombosis, pneumonia: it is as violent and unforeseen as an engine stopping in the middle of the sky. My mother encouraged one to be optimistic when, crippled with arthritis and dying, she asserted the infinite value of each instant; but her vain tenaciousness also ripped and tore the reassuring curtain of everyday triviality. There is no such thing as a natural death: nothing that happens to a man is ever natural, since his presence calls the world into question. All men must die: but for every man his death is an accident and, even if he knows it and consents to it, an unjustifiable violation.

45

A way to die

Rosemary and Victor Zorza

In the late afternoon, Patricia went to see Jane on her way home. 'I just came in before I went off duty. You may not be here on Saturday . . . of course, I'd like you to be, but I know you'll be glad to get it over with . . . ' She stumbled slightly, not knowing quite how to put it into words. 'But I did want to say goodbye properly to you.'

Jane had always valued the affection of family and friends, even if she'd sometimes rebelled against the disciplines love imposes. But to be loved by people who had been, only a week before, absolute strangers was a constant source of wonder and happiness. She couldn't thank them enough; she wanted to give presents to express her own love and gratitude. She tried hard to make everyone understand how much it meant to her to be in a place so 'good'.

'Once I'd have found that a trite thing to say,' she said. 'In fact, all the things that have meant most to me these last months would have seemed corny or sentimental before I got ill.'

Her happiness was clearly apparent. She had no guilt about being helpless and dependent on others. She had always loved to give, but she seemed at last to accept that she could now only receive. Perhaps she realized she could only give by taking – with gratitude and without guilt. Her needs were fulfilled without question and without resentment. In return she lavished praise on everyone who served her, and did so with humility. Perhaps it was the first time in her life that she didn't feel she had to live up to someone else's expectations of behaviour or achievement. Absorbed in the most difficult task of her life, that of dying, she had no doubts left.

Rosemary said to David Murray, 'I know she's not religious, so I hesitate to use the words, but it's almost as if she were in a state of grace.'

'I think you could say that,' David agreed.

We no longer felt sickened by the cigarette smoke. All too soon there would be no more smoke; it seemed impossible that such a little thing could have upset us so much. But as Jane's weakness increased, her smoking became even more perilous. Someone always had to watch

---

Extract from *A Way to Die*, London: Sphere, 1980, pp. 234–41 (abridged).

the cigarette wobbling insecurely between her limp fingers, holding the ashtray ready to trap the blocks of burned ash. But if the sitter's attention was distracted for a moment, the cigarette might fall, singeing Jane's chest or shoulder. On one occasion it took several minutes to rescue a glowing stub.

Rosemary told David she was afraid they might burn the place down.

'We do have flame-proof sheets,' he said, unworried. 'But if you like, we can have a bucket of sand kept outside the door in case of emergency.'

Victor had another, more serious concern. He spoke to David privately about it. 'What about the death rattle? Isn't that very alarming? I've read about this horrible noise going on and on.' He feared that Jane, perhaps semi-conscious in her last moments, might hear her own death rattle and realize what was happening.

'That we can deal with,' David answered. 'The so-called rattle is the result of fluid in the back of the throat causing a bubbling, choking noise. An injection of hyoscene will dry up the secretions if necessary.'

At five o'clock on the day Jane had said goodbye to Michael, David went in to see her. Her periods of waking had been shorter, and further apart. It was many hours since she had last opened her eyes. She lay still, her breathing light but regular. Now she was deeply asleep, perhaps unconscious.

David signalled us to follow him out of the room on to the terrace.

He was clearly moved. 'She's going, isn't she?'

There seemed no doubt of it.

Victor asked unsteadily: 'How long do you think she has?'

'It's hard to say. Perhaps as little as two hours.'

Even now, when Jane gave no sign of hearing what was said, none of the hospice staff ever talked as if she were not in the room. They spoke to her and included her in every conversation. They told us that sick and dying people often hear quite clearly what is being said around them, even though they seem unconscious.

The promise that Jane wouldn't be left alone was easy to keep. Two old friends who had known her since she was a small child, and had opened their home to us all when she came back from Greece, sat with her for long periods. Sometimes we talked, sometimes we sat in silence, not because we felt we shouldn't or couldn't talk, but because silence was more natural than speech. The presence of these friends was a great comfort to us, helping Jane on her last journey. It was a link with all the bedside vigils of past centuries when relatives and friends silently watched and waited. It was a reminder that death was inevitable, a natural part of life's pattern, not an isolated event that was destroying Jane, but a universal experience.

David had warned us that, now her bowels were obstructed, she might start to vomit. This could precipitate her death, but would make it a horrible event.

'We must look out for any signs,' he said. 'Then we'll act to prevent it with injections.'

We watched Jane with this possibility always in our minds. Dr Brown, who had admitted her to the hospice, was back on duty again. 'She looks so peaceful,' he said; 'we must do our best to keep her this way.' But his words upset Rosemary. *They must succeed in this. There should be no question that Jane must die in peace.* She knew she was being unreasonable, that everything possible would be done. Dr Brown had not been expressing any doubt, merely re-affirming an intention.

Jane continued to lie still, peaceful.

That night Victor stayed with Jane while Rosemary slept in the visitor's room.

She woke suddenly in the middle of the night without apparent reason and, without thinking, got out of bed and walked down the corridor towards Jane's room. Outside the night was dark and still; inside, dim lights shone in the nursing station. Both night nurses must be busy.

There was a soft light in the room. Nora and Victor were bending over Jane.

He was surprised to see Rosemary. 'How extraordinary . . . Jane's just this minute woken for the first time. Can you hear what she's trying to say?'

Rosemary bent over her daughter, afraid that the terrible sickness was on its way. 'Darling,' she said. 'Are you all right?'

Jane mumbled something indistinct.

Rosemary spoke more urgently: 'Do you feel sick, Jane?'

Her answer was clearly heard by them all. 'Sick – pain,' she said.

These words were enough, and Nora was ready with the injection. Jane sank once again into a deep sleep.

The next morning her breathing had changed. There was no longer a continuous flow of air in and out of her body; one sharp intake of breath would be followed by silence lasting several seconds. Then she would exhale a long sigh. Although the period between inhalation and exhalation varied a few seconds each time, it always seemed interminable. The silence was a vacuum, a foretaste of death.

The nurses came regularly to give injections, to move her, to moisten her mouth. They talked to her even though she was unconscious, explaining what they were doing in low, calm voices. The halting breaths dragged on. But the pulse at her neck beat with surprising vigour. [. . .]

During the day Jane's breathing changed again, growing harsh and thick, wheezing in and out of her throat with apparent difficulty, making us wonder whether this might not be the beginning of the death rattle after all. Her face became red and congested, but her expression remained serene.

'She has pneumonia,' Dr Brown said. 'This will save her.' What he meant was that pneumonia would help her to die more quickly. He prescribed drugs to clear her congested lungs. The possibility of giving antibiotics to prolong her life was never mentioned. The pulse at her throat still beat strongly. He watched it with compassion. 'That's the penalty of being young. She has a strong body,' he said.

As we came out of Jane's room, Julia asked, 'Perhaps you'd like to be in with Jane? We're just going to turn her. It's possible that the fluid on her lungs will shift when we move her. She may go very suddenly.'

Jane lay as we had left her.

Her body was limp as they raised it in their arms. We watched while they laid her gently down in the bed. The heavy breathing went on, the pulse at her neck beat as strongly as before.

'It could come at any time,' said Julia.

It was Friday evening – twenty-four hours since David had said that she might have no more than two hours.

The bedroom door had developed a harsh squeak every time anyone came in or out. Rosemary whispered to Elizabeth: 'That door. Have you any oil?'

Elizabeth nodded and left the room. Again the door shrieked a hideous protest.

A few minutes later there was another squeak and Elizabeth returned with the familiar injection tray.

'Thank you, Elizabeth.' Julia held out her hand for the syringe.

'No, no!' The note of horror in Elizabeth's voice stopped Julia short, her hand outstretched. 'That's not for Jane. It's the oil for the door!'

Rosemary hoped that Jane was still able to hear what was going on. It was the odd spot – the moment of ridicule in the middle of tragedy – that her daughter would have appreciated.

Julia and Elizabeth were smiling. 'I hope you don't use the syringe on the patients after this?' Rosemary said.

'They're usually thrown away. This is an old one,' Elizabeth reassured her in case she really was worried.

Frank, the porter, asked if he could come in to say goodbye. He stood holding Jane's hand for several minutes, then turned to us. 'Thank you,' he said, and left the room in silence. [. . .]

About two o'clock on Saturday morning, Rosemary pressed the bell, and Emily, on night duty, was in the room in an instant.

'Her breathing has changed,' said Rosemary. 'Suddenly . . . now it's so quiet I can't hear anything unless I get very close.' She watched as Emily leaned over Jane. 'Does this mean it's nearly over?'

Jane lay like a marble statue of death on a medieval tomb, white and still. Her arms were crossed over her chest. Her hands bent at right angles to her wrists. Her breathing was almost inaudible.

Emily straightened her back and smiled quietly. 'She still has some way to go.'

As the day began, Jane's quiet breathing persisted. The pulse at her throat was calmer. It was a surprise to the doctors and nurses that she struggled on so long, but it wasn't a struggle, merely a continuing, a going on. There was no hint of pain or stress. Her face was serene; her limbs seemed completely relaxed.

During the day the outer rim of her lips began to show white. Then, slowly, this area of pallor increased until her mouth was as pale as the rest of her face. Only her hair, brows and lashes showed colour.

Julia suggested that from now on we should stay in the building. She arranged to have our lunch brought to the room.

The last rose of Jane's life was picked from the garden outside her window. [. . .] The bud was pure white, without a fault, a perfect rose. Too perfect, Jane would have said, almost too good to be true. Rosemary laid it on Jane's pillow, close to her face.

The signs of death were clear. Her flesh was shrinking into itself more rapidly. Hour by hour her body became softer, thinner, limper, more fragile; deep lines and white patches showed where it had rested against the bedding. Talking softly to her as they turned her over, the nurses rubbed her skin where the patches showed, soothing the bruised flesh.

The last time they turned her it was as if there was no life in her body, no resistance to the pressure of the arms that lifted her.

Victor was on the terrace when Jane's breathing suddenly changed to a high thin note, infinitely sad and far away. Rosemary felt she had heard this sound before somewhere. It carried an unmistakable warning. But she hesitated to call Victor.

Then the sound of Jane's breathing changed again. This time it was low and soft, each breath so light it could scarcely be heard. Rosemary called Victor.

We stood on either side of the bed, each holding one of her hands. As we listened, the breaths came lighter and lighter. Jane's head moved very slowly, as if reaching up for air, and her eyes were open a fraction, showing a slit of light.

Then everything was still. There was nothing more. The pulse at her throat had ceased.

We have seen pictures of the dead who died violently – victims of murder, accident, war. These are the terrible images etched into our minds: the distorted bodies of those who died in pain and fear.

For us, who watched Jane's quiet end, there is a memory of her still, peaceful face and the warmth of her skin beneath our lips as we kissed her goodbye. This slow, gentle death was a natural end to life. The waning of her body was easy to believe and to accept. Her retreat had been strangely beautiful to watch. We felt no fear.

46

Caring for mother

Susan Leifer

The incident – the diagnosis

In August 1989 my mother, aged 64, suffered a severe and damaging stroke. The fact that I was on a small Greek island with my two young children, didn't get the news for two days and then had to travel back without a ticket, in mid-season, via Athens airport represents graphically the disruption and distress that ensued and continues.

Prior to this occurrence, she had experienced twenty years of sad widowhood, had a propensity to become very 'worked-up' very fast, and had suffered small strokes of a mildly disabling nature leaving her with an unpleasant residue called 'thalamic syndrome' – intractable pain caused by a lesion in the brain.

She was discovered on the floor by a neighbour who called an ambulance and she was admitted to the Royal Free Hospital where she remained until November. I was told by the Consultant Geriatrician that she would never walk again and that the prognosis, although uncertain, was very poor. She was doubly incontinent, could not speak properly, was aware of her circumstances enough to be depressed and distressed. Her vision was affected and her quality of life was nil. In this state, I was her only representative towards the rest of the world, and her only child.

She and I had not been the best of friends since my adolescence. She was an elegant, houseproud, traditional middle-class lady. She didn't like my hair (unruly and wild), my clothes, my bad language, pseudo-intellectualism, lack of respect for the establishment, etc. In turn I was disappointed that she didn't help me with my children like a grandma should – play with them, read to them, have them for weekends. She couldn't. She was too ill, even before the stroke, because she was stroke-bound, but this was hard to accept.

The options after discharge from the hospital

(i) My home with a nurse

I would have wanted to do this if I knew it had a foreseeable end. I would have enjoyed trying to get closer to her and making her comfortable for 'the end' if this was the end. But it might not be. It could be months – years. Maybe this would have been a possibility if the relationship had been better, but I couldn't do it.

(ii) Residential care

Fortunately my mother's finances, quite unbeknown to me before, were sufficient to cover the indefinite cost of a nice residential home. Local to me, pretty curtains, constant Philippino ladies to care, but totally out of the question. My mother didn't even enjoy the company of the refined, educated lady in the next bed – let alone a house full of people.

(iii) Home to her flat with a nurse

I told myself that this is what she would want. I tried to talk to her to elicit a real response, but basically I put all I knew about her, gathered in forty years, together and pretended she'd decided. She is a very private, home-loving person; not sociable and hating strangers, strange places, strange routines, etc.

I advertised in the local paper and contacted agencies and hired a cheerful, resourceful New Zealander with great references and an air of confidence. My mother started eating again – she was informed of all the plans and met Karen *before* she was hired. I pretended she had helped to make the decisions.

Some spontaneous recovery occurred and Karen trained her (a) to be continent in the day and (b) to walk with two hands held in front. This took six months.

We had to find a *sub-structure of carers* to relieve Karen – who needed time off. I am not great as an employer so I found this an enormous strain.

At first, my mother attended the day centre twice a week. After a couple of months of the day centre there was *an incident*. My mother flung her tea at a care assistant. The member of staff flung it back. The former got evicted from the day centre; the latter got disciplined. I cried. We needed the day centre. Too bad, my mother was now a known risk to other attenders.

Daily routines and the effect on our life

From the beginning, I felt I had to visit every day. Her flat is only five minutes' drive away and, in spite of our history, I am the only person she is pleased to see. I punctuate her day. Also, the carer – no longer Karen, who left after eight months, but Belinda, from Australia – needs support. It is an isolated and depressing job.

This is a considerable burden and usually means I'm not helping with homework, or making the supper when I should be. Sometimes I get there earlier in the day and then it is 'done'.

Every Sunday since her return from hospital, my mother has come to lunch. This seems 'the right thing to do' and helps the Sunday relief carer who is a medical student.

Some of the problems

I want to show *my children* that you must care for your loved ones with respect and affection and make them comfortable and happy. I suspect they pick up that there is a good deal of resentment, bitterness and anger.

Why should I pull down her knickers, do everything for her, pull them up again and again and again, when she never looked after my children and didn't like my hair?

When she says, 'I want to go home', when she *is* at home, how can I help her feel at home, when her home inevitably feels like the annexe of an Antipodean party?

Her friends

She actually has some very nice friends, whom she was good to when she was well. She had many friends. They have deserted her to a man. And yet, when she dies and I ring and tell them, they will all come to the funeral. I am very upset about this and I do not want them to come. It will be too late.

My relationship with her

The animosity of my rather extended teenage years is gone. I now feel great pity. She was an upright, moral person, why should she suffer so much now? She is like my child, she often calls me 'Mummy' – but she is a huge burden which will not lighten.

I wish she would die

The Consultant, who gave her such a poor prognosis, told me at the last check-up that I had kept her alive. Terrific. To whom was I doing any favours? Her quality of life is still nil. The best things that happen to her are a bath, a nice meal, seeing me (with the hair) singing along with *Neighbours*. I think *she'd* rather be dead. I think; I don't know.

PART 4 BEREAVEMENT: PRIVATE GRIEF, COLLECTIVE RESPONSIBILITY

Introduction

This final part of the Reader contains first-person accounts, imaginative literature and practitioners' stories along with more conventionally academic articles. Throughout, the theme is responding to the needs of bereaved people in an open and open-minded manner.

This part begins with a classic exposition of reaction to loss: 'Bereavement as a psychosocial transition' by Colin Murray Parkes. Parkes extends the frequent explanation of why loss affects us deeply – John Bowlby's assertion that it throws us back into the profoundly disturbing separation anxiety which we first experienced as children – by adding that we must also consider how loss shakes the entire world-view of the bereaved person. This is the idea of loss as a 'psychosocial transition', one which typically affects many areas of the bereaved person's life. Loss is one aspect of the psychosocial transition, the psychological change that takes place whenever people are forced to change their assumptions about the world. Refusing to recognize change and other defence mechanisms against the transition may be temporarily useful, Parkes argues, but ultimately the transition must be made.

This view is balanced by an article which focuses on the social factors determining grief as well as the psychological ones: Lindsay Prior's 'The social distribution of sentiments'. Prior argues that the psychological approach alone is too individualistic: we must also understand grief in terms of what responses each society permits or encourages. In our own multi-cultural society, carers need to understand the bereavement practices of many communities, and in order to help them do this we have included an article by Shirley Firth, 'Cross-cultural perspectives on bereavement', specially commissioned for this Reader.

The meaning of loss is further explored in another article written for this Reader, Stella Ridley's 'Psychological defence mechanisms and coping strategies'. Ridley, a counsellor with many years of experience as a Samaritans volunteer, considers two case studies in which the bereaved person's grief seemed 'inappropriate' in conventional terms.

Drawing on Freudian theory, Ridley explores the deeper meanings behind the loss for each person in a sensitive and profound manner.

'Only connect', the epigraph to E.M. Forster's novel *Howards End*, emerges as a message from Ridley's article: the need for non-judgemental listening based on acceptance of our own unresolved pain. This idea is carried forward in other articles which urge practitioners not to impose set ideas of normality in bereavement or to expect standard stages and patterns of griefwork. These accounts are most moving when they come from bereaved practitioners whose grief has enabled them to see shortcomings in their own practice: George Castledine's 'When life moves on' and Sheila Awooner-Renner's 'I desperately needed to see my son', both first-person accounts. Awooner-Renner's account of the accidental death of her 17-year-old son, and, another first-person account, Evelyn Gillis's story of the death of her 22-year-old daughter ('A single parent confronting the loss of an only child') are followed by a brief epitaph about another early death: the inscription from the tomb of Libby Dickinson, 1798–1818. An article by D.W. Yates, G. Ellison and S. McGuiness, 'Care of the suddenly bereaved', illustrates reflective practice in action, changing the conventions of how bereaved or soon-to-be-bereaved parents are treated in accident and emergency rooms. Hospice principles are here extended to a very different sort of death: sudden, often accidental, and deeply traumatic for staff and bereaved alike.

Similar changes in hospital practice in relation to deaths of babies before the legal age of viability are detailed in Nancy Kohner's 'The loss of a baby', written for this Reader. Management of stillbirth after the legal age of viability (currently twenty-four weeks) has changed radically, Kohner notes, from a sense that parents should minimize the experience to emphasis on allowing the parents to hold the baby and on providing respectful burial or cremation. These changed procedures are now being extended to babies born earlier than the age of viability, partly through initiatives and input by bereaved parents themselves. A first-person account by one such parent, Gavin Fairbairn ('When a baby dies – a father's view'), reflects on the treatment which he and his wife Susan received following the death one hour after birth of their daughter Hesther Frances.

Another area of change is in relation to gay and lesbian bereavement, the subject of an article written for this Reader by Dudley Cave of the Gay Bereavement Project. The particular needs of bereaved gay and lesbian partners are considered, along with the inadequacy of current procedures involving only the family of origin – who may well be estranged from the surviving partner, or even unaware of his or her existence. The special needs of people with learning difficulties, another group whose feelings are sometimes ignored, are the subject of an article by Maureen Oswin, 'The grief that does not speak'. Using case studies illustrating the tendency to equate disturbed behaviour after bereavement with ordinary effects of learning disability, Oswin argues eloquently for a better response.

In encouraging reflective practice, the Reader articles do not ignore the stress on professional carers dealing with death and dying. Tom Heller's 'Personal and medical memories from Hillsborough' is a poignant account of one GP's experience at the scene of the catastrophe. Heller, also a member of the Department of Health and Social Welfare at the Open University, which produced this Reader, was one of the first doctors on the terrible scene. The subject of bereavement through violent death, accidental in the Hillsborough disaster, is extended to the case of murder in Lesley Moreland's 'Ruth: death by murder'. Her thoughts and experience following the murder of her daughter provide insight into a peculiarly traumatic form of sudden death.

The final four pieces all concern ways of remembering the dead: William Wordsworth's 'Essays upon epitaphs', from which we include excerpts; two previously unpublished poems by the Canadian-American poet Ellen Jaffe Bitz, one on the death of her grandmother and the other on the Navajo concept of ghosts; and one of the sequence of poems which Douglas Dunn wrote after the death of his wife, 'December'.

47

Bereavement as a psychosocial transition: processes of adaptation to change

Colin Murray Parkes

People are fascinating because of their individuality; no two problems are alike because no two people are alike. This tempts some people to reject theories of human behaviour. There are none that can be expected to predict or explain more than part of a person, and it seems mechanistic to attempt to force people into preconceived models. Yet we must have some frame of reference if we are to be of use to those who cannot cope with life's vicissitudes. It is not enough for us to stay close and to open our hearts to another person's suffering; valuable though this sympathy may sometimes be, we must have some way of stepping aside from the maze of emotion and sensation if we are to make sense of it.

One might say that our central nervous system has been designed to enable us to do just that. Human beings, to a greater extent than other species, have the capacity to organize the most complex impressions into internal models of the world, which enable us to recognize and understand the world that we experience and to predict the outcome of our own and others' behaviour. Psychological theories are one way of doing this, and the measure of their success is their usefulness.

This article describes a theory that the writer has found useful in explaining certain aspects of the human reaction to loss. Other theories are useful in explaining other aspects; these include theories about the nature of attachments, anxiety, family dynamics and the psychophysiology of stress. Each of these adds something to our understanding of loss, and *they do not conflict* with each other.

Reactions to life events

Bereavement by death is a major psychological trauma [. . .] but there are some bereavements that are not a cause for grief and many griefs that have causes other than bereavement by death.

From *Journal of Social Issues*, 1988, 44 (3): 53-65 (abridged).

What, then, defines a loss? How can we distinguish grief from the other emotions that arise in the face of life events? Why is it that some life events menace our sanity while others are an unmitigated blessing? These questions are more easily asked than answered.

Grief is essentially an emotion that draws us toward something or someone that is missing. It arises from awareness of a discrepancy between the world that is and the world that 'should be'. This raises a problem for researchers because, though it is not difficult to discover the world that is, the world that should be is an internal construct; hence each person's experience of grief is individual and unique. Two women who have lost husbands are not the same. One may miss her husband greatly, while the other's grief may arise less from her wish to have her husband back (for she never did like him as a person) than from loss of the status and power that she achieved in marrying an important man. Clearly, grief is not a unitary phenomenon. [. . .]

Psychosocial transitions

Studies of the life events that commonly precede the onset of mental illness (Brown and Harris, 1978; Caplan, 1961; Rahe, 1979) suggest the most dangerous life-change events are those that (a) require people to undertake a major revision of their assumptions about the world, (b) are lasting in their implications rather than transient, and (c) take place over a relatively short period of time so there is little opportunity for preparation. These three criteria are the defining characteristics for events that can be termed 'psychosocial transitions' (PSTs) and that provide us with boundaries for a reasonably discrete area of study (Parkes, 1971). They exclude events that may threaten but do not result in any lasting change (e.g. exposure to terrifying situations over short periods of time) because these seem essentially different in their psychological implications. Insofar as these events cause psychiatric problems (such as anxiety reactions or post-traumatic neuroses), these are likely to be different from the disorders associated with PSTs. The criteria also exclude gradual changes, such as those associated with maturation, unless these are associated with more rapid changes that 'bring home' implications of the more gradual change. Thus the physical changes associated with sexual maturation do not constitute a PST, but they may bring about rapid attachments or disappointments that are PSTs. [. . .]

The assumptive world

The internal world that must change in the course of a PST consists of all those expectations and assumptions invalidated by the change in our life space (that is, the part of the world that impinges upon us – Lewin, 1935). These expectations constitute part of an organized schema or 'assumptive world', which contains everything that we assume to be true on the basis of our previous experience. It is this internal model of the world that we are constantly matching against incoming sensory data in order to orient ourselves, recognize what is happening and plan our behaviour accordingly.

Waking in the morning, we can put on the light, get out of bed and walk to the bathroom because we have an assumptive world that includes assumptions about the presence and layout of the doors, windows, light switches and rooms in our home, and assumptions about the parts of the body that we must use in turning the light on, getting out of bed, walking across the floor, etc. If as a result of some life event we lose a limb, go blind, lose our memory, move to a new house or have the electricity cut off, we must revise our assumptive world in order to cope with the numerous discrepancies that arise.

The death of a spouse invalidates assumptions that penetrate many aspects of life, from the moment of rising to going to sleep in an empty bed. Habits of action (setting the table for two) and thought ('I must ask my husband about that') must be revised if the survivor is to live as a widow.

The pain of change

Such changes are easier said than done, for not only does a major PST require us to revise a great number of assumptions about the world, but most of these assumptions have become habits of thought and behaviour that are now virtually automatic. The amputee knows very well that he has lost a limb, but this knowledge does not prevent him from leaping out of bed in the morning and sprawling on the floor because he has tried to stand on a leg that is not there. Likewise, the blind person 'looks' toward a sudden noise, and the widow 'hears' her husband's key in the lock. Each is operating on a set of assumptions that have become habitual over many years. Grief following bereavement by death is aggravated if the person lost is the person to whom one would turn in times of trouble. Faced with the biggest trouble she has ever had, the widow repeatedly finds herself turning toward a person who is not there.

These examples begin to explain why PSTs are so painful and take so much time and energy. For a long time it is necessary to take care in everything we think, say or do; nothing can be taken for granted any more. The familiar world suddenly seems to have become unfamiliar, habits of thought and behaviour let us down, and we lose confidence in our own internal world.

Freud (1917) called the process of reviewing the internal world after bereavement 'the work of mourning', and in many ways each PST is a job of work that must be done if a person is to adapt to the requirements of the real world. But the mind that is doing the reviewing is also the object that is being reviewed. A person is literally lost in his or her own grief, and the more disorganized one's thinking the more difficult it is to step aside from the disorganization and to see clearly what is lost and what remains.

Since we rely on having an accurate assumptive world to keep us safe, people who have lost confidence in their world model feel very unsafe. And because anxiety and fear cloud our judgement and impair concentration and memory, our attempts to make sense of what has happened are likely to be fitful, poorly directed and inadequate.

Coping and defence

Of course, people are not completely helpless when the level of anxiety becomes disorganizing. We have a number of coping mechanisms that usually reduce the level of tension or at least prevent it from rising any higher. Hence people in transition often withdraw from the challenges of the outside world, shut themselves up at home and restrict their social contacts to a small group of trusted people. They may avoid situations and chains of thought that will bring home the discrepancies between inside and outside worlds; they may fill their lives with distracting activities, or deny the full reality of what has happened. The complete range of psychological defence mechanisms can be called into play to protect someone from too painful a realization of a loss. These defences will often succeed in preventing anxiety from becoming disorganizing, but they are also likely to delay the relearning process.

Taking stock

The magnitude of a PST is such that it includes simultaneous dysfunctions in several areas of functioning. Thus the loss of a spouse may produce any or all of the following: (1) loss of sexual partner, (2) loss of protection from danger, (3) loss of reassurance of worth, (4) loss of job, (5) loss of companionship, (6) loss of income, (7) loss of recreational partner, (8) loss of status, (9) loss of expectations, (10) loss of self-confidence, (11) loss of a home, (12) loss of a parent for one's children, and many other losses. It may also produce (a) relief from responsibilities, (b) entitlement to the care of others, (c) sympathy from others and an increase in tenderness (or at least inhibition of hostility and competition), (d) attributions of heroism, (e) financial gains, and (f) freedom to realize potentialities that have been inhibited. These latter consequences, too, involve change in the life space and require that assumptions be modified, but since they also serve to assist those modifications (e.g. by providing time and opportunity for introspection, and by keeping people safe from threat during that time), they are more likely to facilitate than to impair the transition.

PSTs thus emerge as a complex interweaving of psychological and social processes, whose implications are far from clear to the person who undergoes them and even less clear to the would-be helper. Only in the most general terms can anyone else be said to 'understand'. But this does not mean we cannot help. By encouraging those who are in transition to help us understand, by talking about their situation, we help them take stock, review and relearn their assumptive world.

Resistance to change

Although minor changes are often embraced, major changes are more usually resisted. Resistance to change is seen as an obstacle by planners, but it is not always so irrational or so harmful as it seems. We can bring to the appraisal of new situations only the assumptions that arise out of old situations. Our old model of the world may be imperfect, but it is the best we have, and if we abandon it we have nothing left. Our first effort, in the face of change, must therefore be to interpret the change in the light of our old assumptions. To throw over old models of the world the moment they appear discrepant with the new is dangerous and often unnecessary. Closer scrutiny will sometimes reveal that our initial appraisal of the situation was incorrect and that the discrepancy was more apparent than real. Thus, a person who is told by a doctor that he has a terminal illness may be wise to ask for a second opinion before preparing himself to die.

Refusing to accept change also gives us time to begin rehearsing in our minds the implication of the change, should it come about. Thus, the patient who refuses surgery may need time to talk through its implications with his doctor and his family before changing his mind. While he does this, he is preparing a new model of the world, which will help ensure that the transition proceeds smoothly when, eventually, it comes about.

On the other hand, there may come a time when it is more dangerous to resist change than to accept it. Because the person in transition has no models of thought and behaviour to meet the new situation, he or she will eventually feel helpless and in danger. Three things are needed: emotional support, protection through the period of helplessness, and assistance in discovering new models of the world appropriate to the emergent situation. The first two of these may need to be provided before the person can begin to feel safe enough to accept the third. Thus, people whose sight has failed often refuse to learn blind skills until they have been supported in their helplessness and reached a point where they feel safe enough to accept the help of guide dogs, white canes and all the other means by which blind people can rebuild their model of the world. [. . .]

Implications of transition theory for bereavement

The death of a loved person evokes a characteristic emotion – pining for the lost person (or 'separation anxiety') – which is largely independent of the magnitude of the life change that will result. Thus, the death of a child may lead to very little change in the mother's model of the world, whereas the death of a spouse inevitably leads to a major upheaval. Yet it has been claimed that the emotional reaction of a mother to the death of a child is as great or greater than the typical reaction to the loss of a spouse (Fulton and Owen, 1971). This suggests it is the nature and quality of the attachment that determines the intensity of grief, rather than the magnitude of the psychosocial transition that results. This does not mean the PST is unimportant, but it does seem overshadowed, during the early phase of bereavement, by the pangs of grief, which are more easily explained in terms of attachment theory than transition theory. John Bowlby (1982) has shown how the bonds between human beings arise out of deep-seated innate mechanisms, which have evolved in order to ensure survival. The child's tie to the mother and the mother's tie to the child are biologically determined, and their very strength is a reflection of their survival value. Although derived from an inborn tendency, the child's attachment to its mother is influenced by its experience of its parents, and thus attachments may become secure or insecure. Basic trust arises out of these early attachments and then influences all later attachments, including those the child will make to his or her own children in years to come.

From this point of view, it is reasonable to suppose one's reaction to loss of a person will be determined as much by the biological significance of that person as by the magnitude of the life change resulting from the loss. In other respects, however, loss of a person resembles [other losses such as that of a limb. . . .]

Conclusion

Societies have always had their elders, doctors, shamans, priests and counsellors. Most of these have a dual role – to provide wise counsel and to perform rituals. The rituals mark the rites of passage (Van Gennep, 1909). They identify people in transition, induct them into a temporary status (as 'client', 'mourner', 'initiate', 'patient', etc.), and then, after sufficient time has elapsed, mark the end of the transition to a new identity (as 'widow', 'adult', 'disabled person', etc.). The rites performed by doctors include the provision of sickness certificates, prescriptions and a range of other procedures (some of them bloody) through which patients pass on the way to their new life.

The success of scientific medicine in finding cures for many diseases has distracted many members of the caring professions from their traditional responsibility to care for people in transition. As a result, medicine and its allied professions find themselves faced with the need to change, to face a psychosocial transition of their own, whose implications penetrate all aspects of our work. We can expect similar difficulties in revising our models of the world, like those experienced by the bereaved, the disabled and the dying when faced with irreversible changes in their lives. Social workers and counsellors are likely to find it less difficult than medical personnel to make use of a theory of transition because much of their existing work is carried out from a similar viewpoint. Consequently, they may need to take the lead in educating doctors, nurses and other health care workers. It is hoped that the theory presented here will facilitate this transition.

References

Bowlby, J. (1982) *Attachment and Loss: Vol. 1. Attachment.* London: Hogarth.

Brown, G.W. and Harris, T. (1978) *Social Origins of Depression: A Study of Psychiatric Disorder in Women.* London: Tavistock.

Caplan, G. (1961) *An Approach to Community Mental Health.* London: Tavistock.

Freud, S. (1917) 'Mourning and melancholia', in *Standard Edition of the Complete Psychological Works of Sigmund Freud, Vol. 14,* ed. J. Strachey. New York: Norton, 1957.

Fulton, R. and Owen, G. (1971, October) *Adjustment to Loss through Death: A Sociological Analysis.* Center for Death Education and Research, University of Minnesota.

Lewin, K. (1935) *A Dynamic Theory of Personality.* New York: McGraw-Hill.

Parkes, C.M. (1971) 'Psycho-social transition: a field for study', *Social Science & Medicine,* 5: 101-5.

Rahe, R.H. (1979) 'Life events, mental illness: an overview', *Journal of Human Stress,* 5 (3): 2-10.

Van Gennep, A. (1909) *Les rites de passage* (English translation, *The Rites of Passage.* London: Routledge & Kegan Paul, 1960.)

48

The social distribution of sentiments

Lindsay Prior

> Mourning is not the spontaneous expression of individual emotions.
>
> (Durkheim, 1968: 567)

[. . .] In this [article] I intend to do [two] things. The first is to trace the routes by which grief and sorrow were normalized and medicalized during the twentieth century. The second is to examine the evidence for the claim that human grief is socially patterned and socially channelled. [. . .]

The normalization of grief

[. . .] Grief in the twentieth century is primarily understood and 'managed' on the basis of principles which were first elaborated within the context of a normalizing psychology. The starting point of normalization rests in Freud's 1917 essay on mourning and melancholia in which he drew distinctions between normal and pathological responses to loss. This theme of pathology was extended in 1940 by Klein who asserted that all grief is in a sense pathological insofar as it apes the manic-depressive state – though for most people the phase is transitory. Now, these ideas contrast quite markedly with those of the nineteenth century in which grief, although it was sometimes viewed as a cause of insanity, was never interpreted as itself pathological. Grief, if anything, was a condition of the human spirit or soul rather than of the body and in that sense it could be neither normalized nor medicalized. The work of the psychoanalysts, however, was only the first in a series of processes which sought to medicalize grief. The second stage was represented in the work of Lindemann (1944).

Lindemann's work was the first to place the study of grief on an empirical footing and the first to establish a 'symptomatology of grief'. His work was based on the reactions of 101 bereaved 'patients' and included a number of subjects involved with the notorious Cocoanut Grove fire. His primary aim was to establish the symptomatology of grief and the secondary aim was to discuss the management of grief.

Extract from *The Social Organization of Death*, London: Macmillan, 1989, pp. 133–52 (abridged).

The symptomatology was drawn in terms of five or six factors and the general conclusion which Lindemann arrived at was:

Acute grief is a definite syndrome with psychological and somatic [bodily] symptomatology. (Lindemann, 1944: 141)

Furthermore, and in addition to reducing grief to a somatic state. Lindemann sought to measure it, and he did so by dividing his patients into those who suffered from normal and those who suffered from morbid grief. The two variables along which such normalization was assessed were those of intensity and duration, and he further argued that the management of grief should be related to these forms and factors. Needless to say, grief management was discussed in terms of the principles of clinical medicine alone.

The 'pathological' features of grief were emphasized in a somewhat disturbing article by Anderson (1949), entitled, 'Aspects of pathological grief and mourning', but the most forceful attempt to reduce grief to a somatically sited disease was that proposed by Engel (1961) in his paper 'Is grief a disease?', in which he directly compares grief to pathogenic bacteria. Further developments in the attempt to characterize grief as a (double-edged) disease occurred with the publication of Parkes's work in the 1960s and 1970s, though, as the following quotations illustrate, the symptomatology of the proposed disease remains somewhat ambiguous.

Of all the functional mental disorders almost the only one whose cause is known, whose symptomatology is stereotyped and whose outcome is usually predictable is grief. That grief is a mental disorder there can be no doubt, since it is associated with all the discomfort and loss of function which characterizes such disorders. (Parkes, 1965: 1)

By 1972 [sic], however, the blanket assessment that grief is a mental disorder was somewhat modified and now only the abnormal forms took this symptomatology.

On the whole, grief resembles a physical injury more closely than any other type of illness. . . . But occasionally . . . abnormal forms arise, which may even be complicated by the onset of other types of illness. (Parkes, 1975: 19)

For all of these authors and investigators, then, grief was something in the body which could be measured and assessed. The intensity and duration of grief were factors whose origins could be located in the biochemistry of the body or in the infantile history of the subject, and the context in which grief was analysed was viewed in medical terms, or at best in psychotherapeutic terms. Furthermore, the medicalization and normalization of grief took place within a theory of developmental stages. [. . .] In this view, human behaviour is seen to involve an unfolding of human potential towards an ultimate stage of stability or 'reintegration'. This theme has dominated the study of many and varied facets of death. Kübler-Ross (1970), for example, analyses the responses of the dying in terms of five stages: denial and isolation, anger, bargaining, depression and acceptance. And Backer et al. (1982) invoke the concept of stages in order to account for attitudes to death among children and therapeutic responses of hospital staff, as well as the responses of the terminally ill. In like manner, most of those who discuss grief also use the developmental metaphor. Thus Parkes (1975) talks of phases of yearning and phases of despair. Backer et al. (1982) list three stages: yearning, anger and guilt, and disorganization. Kavanaugh (1972) lists seven stages: shock, disorganization, volatile emotions, loss, loneliness, relief and re-establishment. Attempts to categorize grief as it occurs in specific age groups and populations have also been made and probably the most notable of these was that of Bowlby (1961) in his study of bereaved children. Broadly speaking, however, it is in terms of stages and timescales that the normal is assessed and it is within this context that grief is seen to unfold within the human psyche.

Despite the fact that both Lindemann and Bowlby gave a hesitant nod in the direction of social factors when they were assessing the impact of grief on the bereaved individual, most authors seem to have remained quite ignorant of the work of Durkheim and Hertz. The Durkheimians [. . .] had sought, very early on in the twentieth century, to discuss and explore the fact that the intensity of grief was not the product of some inner unfolding, but of social processes which tended to channel grief in some directions whilst deflecting it away from others. The structural distribution of grief seems to have been more or less ignored until the publication of Peter Marris's work on widows (1958) and Gorer's work on the bereaved (1965), and though both of the latter authors continued to assess grief in terms of the 'normal', 'stages' and timetables, they did supplement the study of grief with the missing link of social structure.

Broadly speaking, however, it is clear that psychology and anthropology adopted incommensurable standpoints on the study of grief, so that whilst the first concentrated on the subjective experience of grief in different populations, the second concentrated on the outward expression of grief and utilized that outward expression as an indicator of inner sentiment. In Western culture, it was psychology which therefore dominated the study of grief and bereavement during the twentieth century and, overall, the problem of grief, like death before it, became medicalized and individualized and subsequently fell under the control of medical personnel. Thus, the priest was ousted from the aftermath of death in favour of the doctor and grief was treated (in all senses of that word) as a private and segmented emotion. It was this segmentation and individualization of grief which prompted Gorer to carry out his study of the phenomenon, and it was on the basis of that study that he theorized about the denial of death in Western culture. [. . .]

Sentiments and social structure

The attempts to normalize grief, in terms of the assumptions and theories of psychology, took a new turn, as we have seen, in the analysis undertaken by Lindemann. And this concern to trace out the nature and limits of grief in empirical populations was further developed in the work of Marris (1958) and Gorer (1965). Marris's work was based on a study of seventy-two London widows, whilst Gorer's work encompassed a far wider range of bereaved individuals drawn from a number of age, sex, class and regional groupings. In both cases the intensity and duration of grief were studied empirically and some estimate of the normal and the abnormal was made. Neither study, however, explored the Durkheimian hypothesis that grief is socially distributed and socially controlled. In fact, Gorer, an avowed anthropologist, reached the somewhat curious conclusion that contemporary mourning practices are marked by a total lack of ritual – the consequence of which is 'maladaptive behaviour'. In the England of the 1960s, he concluded, 'The most typical reaction [to death] is . . . the denial óf mourning' (1965: 113). Marris's work also rested on many of the prevailing assumptions of psychological theory, though he did recognize that sociological factors impinged on the intensity and duration of grief. Thus, in his 1974 work he asserted that:

> The severity of grief depends, then, on the degree of [social] disruption: and it can be at least crudely predicted from the emphasis which a society places upon different relationships. (Marris, 1974: 38)

In that sense, the loss of infants and of the old is, for example, less disruptive than the loss of those in the economically active age groups, or of the married.

The claim that grief is controlled and distributed in terms of social ritual, as I have suggested, can be traced back to the work of Durkheim and Hertz. Both men argued that the intensity of grief expended by any individual or group was dependent on a socially constructed formula, rather than on innate or natural feeling. Thus, the mourning of infants or strangers was always cursory, whilst the mourning of healthy and active adults was not. [. . .]

One of the strongest adaptations of the Durkheimian thesis was that advanced by Monica Wilson in her (1957) study of the Nyakyusa. This study had its precursor in Godfrey Wilson's (1939) analysis of Nyakyusa burial rites which emphasized a number of issues which are worth noting here. Most important from our point of view was his claim that a 'normal' emotional response could not be assessed in purely statistical terms but only in terms of what is regarded as obligatory by any given group. To obey the constraints of the group is normal, to ignore them is abnormal. Normality was, therefore, socially imposed.

Secondly, the emotions which were so imposed were often socially differentiated. Thus, whilst Nyakyusa burial 'is a lively event', there were still marked differences between the reactions of males and females. Broadly speaking 'the women wail and the men dance', and the funerary ritual emphasized male strength and courage as against female fear and trembling. The women wept all of the time; the chief mourners wept only once or twice and, according to Wilson, the latter were *obliged* to show grief. Finally, he noted that the length of the mourning period depended on the status of the deceased: high status, extended mourning; low status, truncated mourning. The clearest expression of such sociologism, however, was that given by Monica Wilson in her discussion of Nyakyusa *rites de passage*:

> The rituals heighten the emotions and canalize them. They both teach men to feel, and teach them what it is proper to feel. (Wilson, 1957: 232)

Other observations on this funerary theme have been provided by Goody (1962) in his study of the LoDagaa. Goody claimed two things in this connection. First, that different social relationships demanded different expressions of grief, and second, that the amount of grief displayed varied according to the social status of the deceased. Thus, he noted that among the LoDagaa physical restraint was used on the bereaved (either symbolically or physically), and that the differences in standardized restraints indicated a diminution of the grief expected in the three classes of kinsfolk affected by bereavement. Hence, conjugal and parental roles demanded the sharpest display, followed by siblings, followed in turn by those who fulfilled filial roles. Furthermore, he often implied that the elaborateness of the funerary ritual was a direct function of the amount of wealth to be redistributed at death, though that was not the only source of differentiation, and it was equally clear from the study that this was also dependent on the existence of a social personality. Thus, 'The LoDagaa display no public grief at the death of an unweaned child, for it is not yet accorded human status' (1962: 149). [. . .]

The most adventurous claims of social anthropology on this theme of public displays of sorrow, however, are undoubtedly those made by Radcliffe-Brown in his study of the Andaman Islanders (1922). In that work Radcliffe-Brown offered a theory of weeping. He noted that in Andamanese society there were seven occasions for ceremonial weeping, three of which involved reciprocal (interactive) weeping and four of which involved one-sided weeping (as, for example, in weeping for a dead person). In keeping with his broad functionalist position he sought to discover the purposes of such weeping both for the individuals involved and for the social structure as a whole. He concluded that for individuals, ceremonial weeping served to release emotional tension, but its wider, social purpose was more interesting and more fundamental. Thus, of weeping, he stated:

The purpose of the rite is to affirm the existence of a social bond between two or more persons. (Radcliffe-Brown, 1922: 240)

Social bonds were therefore asserted and emphasized in public declarations. Consequently, without the bond there could be no weeping. Thus, in Andamanese society children, who had not yet been awarded a social personality, were 'little mourned' and, 'a stranger who dies or is killed is buried unceremoniously or is cast into the sea' (1922: 109). My purpose in citing these various cases of anthropological and historical investigation is solely to illustrate the point that grief, at least in its public manifestations, is socially variable and that the social location of a deceased person has much to do with the manner in which grief is expressed. [. . .] It is enough to show that grief is distributed according to social principles and to suggest that the experience of grief is, in some part, reflected in its public expression. [. . .] All public expressions of grief act as a mirror in which private feelings are reflected, and as the public expressions wax and wane so does the social base of the sentiments behind them.

References

Anderson, C. (1949) 'Aspects of pathological grief and mourning', *International Journal of Psychoanalysis*, 30: 48-55.

Backer, B.A., Hannon, N. and Russell, N.A. (1982) *Death and Dying: Individuals and Institutions*. New York: Wiley.

Bowlby, J. (1961) 'Processes of mourning', *International Journal of Psychoanalysis*, 42: 4-5, 317-40.

Durkheim, E. (1968) *Les formes élémentaires de la vie religieuse*. Paris: PUF.

Engel, G. (1961) 'Is grief a disease?', *Psychosomatic Medicine*, 23: 18-22.

Freud, S. (1917) 'Mourning and melancholia', in *Standard Edition of the Complete Psychological Works of Sigmund Freud, Vol. 14*, ed. J. Strachey. London: Hogarth, 1957.

Goody, J. (1962) *Death, Property and the Ancestors: A Study of the Mortuary Customs of the LoDagaa of West Africa*. Stanford, CA: Stanford University Press.

Gorer, G. (1965) *Death, Grief and Mourning in Contemporary Britain*. London: Cresset.

Kavanaugh, R. (1972) *Facing Death*. Baltimore, MD: Penguin.

Klein, M. (1940) 'Mourning and its relationship to manic depressive states', *International Journal of Psycho-Analysis*, 21: 125-53.

Kübler-Ross, E. (1970) *On Death and Dying*. London: Tavistock.

Lindemann, E. (1944) 'Symptomatology and management of acute grief', *American Journal of Psychiatry*, 101: 141-8.

Marris, P. (1958) *Widows and their Families*. London: Routledge & Kegan Paul.

Marris, P. (1974) *Loss and Change*. London: Routledge & Kegan Paul.

Parkes, C.M. (1965) 'Bereavement and mental illness', *British Journal of Medical Psychology*, 38: 1-12.

Parkes, C.M. (1975) *Bereavement*. Harmondsworth: Penguin.

Radcliffe-Brown, A.R. (1922) *The Andaman Islanders*. Cambridge: Cambridge University Press.

Wilson, G. (1939) 'Nyakyusa conventions of burial', *Bantu Studies*, 13: 1-31.

Wilson, M. (1957) *Rituals of Kinship among the Nyakyusa*. London: Oxford University Press.

49

Cross-cultural perspectives on bereavement

Shirley Firth

Religious and cultural rituals

Religious and cultural rituals invest death with meaning from religious, psychological and social perspectives. All the major religions of the world teach that there is some sort of continuity or survival after death. They also comfort and re-assure the mourners by helping to make sense of death and personal loss. Thirdly, they provide shape and meaning to the process of mourning, which lasts for a clearly defined period in different cultures, providing 'milestones' during the period of mourning, allowing the bereaved a gradual time to let go of the deceased and adjust to the changes in their lives psychologically, as well as to changes of status socially. Buddhists, Hindus, Muslims and Sikhs may come from very different religious traditions, yet in their countries of origin they share some common presuppositions about the nature of family life and marriage, and the role of the wider community. They tend to live in extended families and maintain closely knit communities, although this may change as new generations move elsewhere to find work.

It is important for carers to understand the religious beliefs and cultural traditions of members of these communities, and be aware of the problems they face when they are unable to follow them because of changes in medical practice, bureaucracy or lack of adequate religious or social support.

Preparing the body

For most cultures the laying-out of the body is an important part of the final care of the deceased person (cf. David Clark, 'Death in Staithes', in Part 1 of this Reader, pp. 4–10). For Hindus there are caste and family traditions concerning the washing and dressing procedures,

I would like to acknowledge my gratitude to the following who helped in preparing this paper: Rahim Bashir, Parveen Damani, Ven. Vajiragnana, Piara Singh Sambhi, and members of the Indian community who shared their experiences with me.

which are done by relatives of the same sex. Ganges water is usually
used to purify the body. A man is dressed in the type of clothes he
normally wears, and a woman in a sari, or *salvar kameze*. If she pre-
deceases her husband she will wear a wedding sari. Sikhs follow
similar procedures, dressing the deceased in the five Ks as in life
(cf. Shirley Firth, 'Approaches to Death in Hindu and Sikh Communities in Britain' in Part 1 of this Reader, pp. 26–32. The body is
then placed in a coffin and taken by hearse to the family home.

Among Buddhists family members wash the body, sometimes using
scented lotions, dress it in traditional clothes, which may either be
what is normally worn, or in white, the colour of mourning, and place
it in the coffin. Flowers are not used normally in Sri Lanka. Some Vietnamese cover the face with white cloth or paper to provide a symbolic
barrier between the living and the dead (Pearson, 1982: 480).

Muslims prepare the body in the local mosque if there are suitable
facilities, or at the local undertakers, according to strict rules. This
should be done immediately after the death, because until it is done
the body is impure, and those performing the ablutions will not be able
to say their prayers until they too have bathed. The body has to be
washed three times, the first two times with soap and water, and
finally with camphor or scented materials, starting with the parts of the
body which have to be washed before prayer, carefully observing the
modesty of the person at all times. It is then placed in a shroud, or
kafan, and now the family can have their last viewing. The strict rule
which applies in life to the mingling of the sexes still applies in death;
a woman who belongs to one of the prohibited relationships for social
contact may attend the funeral but cannot look upon the face of the
deceased, if male, and vice versa.

Funerals

In India the Hindu cremation is usually the same day as the death, or
the following day if death occurred during the previous evening.
Because of the limited time in the crematorium, part of the service,
which would normally take place at the pyre in India, takes place in
shortened or adapted form at home in Britain. While the *pandit* (priest)
chants from the scriptures the chief mourner (normally the eldest son)
performs the rituals according to caste and family traditions. Herbs,
sandalwood, clarified butter (which purifies the body and helps it burn)
and flowers may be placed on the body. Ganges water and *tulsi* (basil)
are put in the mouth, along with a coin, symbolizing payment of the
ferryman crossing the river of death. Then the family and mourners
circumambulate the coffin to bid farewell. The coffin is closed and
taken to the crematorium. All the friends, neighbours and community
members follow, except, among the Gujaratis, women. After a few
prayers and a homily by the pandit or a senior community member,

the eldest son or sons go down into the crematorium and press the button, or may actually push the coffin in.

Mourners and friends then return to the deceased's home, and sit quietly with the family. The principal mourners may bathe at a friend's house before returning home. Many Panjabis return to the house for a *havan*, the sacred fire ceremony, followed by the giving of a *pagri*, turban, to the eldest son to signify that he is now head of the household.

Children are not normally cremated under the age of 3 or 4, as they have unformed personalities and are too pure to require the ritual purification of fire. They do not have a normal funeral and may be buried with little ceremony in a special corner of the cemetery, or with a pandit saying some prayers.

Sikhs follow a similar pattern to Hindus, although the content of ritual is different and much simpler. The body is usually brought back to the house for a last viewing, and the *granthi* may attend and say prayers. The family, female friends and neighbours circumambulate the coffin which is then taken to the *gurdwara* (place of worship) where the *granthi* says prayers, and the family, male friends and neighbours pass around the coffin. At the crematorium there is a short service with prayers, and a homily. The evening hymn, *Kirtan Sohila*, may be sung before the final conclusion with prayers. The mourners return to the *gurdwara* for a service with a eulogy and prayers, and then the family and close friends return to the family home for a meal. Many Sikhs traditionally bury children, although according to Cole and Sambhi (1978: 177), infants should be cremated where the facilities exist. Sikh infants have a simplified ceremony but no meal is offered afterwards.

Muslims must bury the dead immediately, according to the *Hadith* (the traditional sayings of the Prophet Mohammed). The body, in a coffin, is carried on the shoulders of male relatives or friends either to the mosque or directly to the cemetery, where the funeral prayer (*salat-ul-janazah*) is said. (Women are not allowed to go.) In the mosque it is placed in front of the Imam, who faces Mecca. Prayers are said without the bowing and prostration accompanying normal prayer (Prickett, 1980: 95).

At the cemetery the body is addressed by a reciter who

> addresses him by name, gently shaking the shoulders, and reminds him of the fundamental beliefs of the faith. The underlying philosophy is that the person is not dead but merely in transition to the hereafter. (Sashir Rahim, personal communication)

The body should be buried in a deep grave facing Mecca. The Imam or a leading community member recites verses from the Qur'an, including Surah 20:55: 'From the [earth] did We create you, and into it shall We return you, and from it shall We bring you out once again.' In bigger cities there are special areas for Muslim burials, and in some they are permitted to bury the shrouded body without a coffin.

Buddhist teaching is directed towards a recognition that death comes to everybody and is part of the changing flux and continuity of existence (cf. Neuberger, 1987: 44). The time for the burial or cremation depends on the tradition of the country of origin. The service may take place in the house prior to going to the cemetery or crematorium. Monks are invited to remind the mourners of the impermanence and fleeting nature of life. Then one monk will make a funeral oration explaining Buddhist teaching and talk about the deceased, his or her family and achievements. The whole funeral is geared towards the comforting and education of the mourners.

Mourning

All four religions discourage too much weeping. Hindus say weeping creates a river which the soul has to cross. Sikh Gurus discourage too much grief, because the deceased has gone to God. The *Hadith* says that weeping is permitted for three days, but not beyond that, and wailing is forbidden, although it still occurs in villages on the Indian subcontinent, and the expression of grief is less inhibited than among native Britons. This can cause problems in hospitals, especially in large wards.

For Hindus in India the period of mourning lasts between ten to sixteen days. The family are regarded as extremely impure, and no other Hindu will receive food or drink from them. Furniture is removed from the living room, white sheets spread on the floor, and friends and neighbours drop in throughout the day to condole and listen to the readings from the *Bhagavad Gita* or other books, and to sing hymns. The family live austerely on simple food, without radio or television. On the tenth to twelfth days a series of rituals enable the soul (*atman*) to form a new 'celestial' body and join the ancestors. In Britain these rituals are usually done on the same day, and are considered by many Hindus to be the most important rituals they can do for the deceased. Gifts of money, food and clothing, which the deceased would normally need, are given to the Brahmin priests or to charity.

There are further rituals at one, three and six months. Widows used to be in mourning for at least a year, but here it is reduced to three months, after which they can go out and gradually resume normal life. In addition there is an annual ceremony, called *shraddha*, in which further offerings are made to the deceased relatives on the anniversary of the death and to all the ancestors during a period in the autumn called *pitr paksha*, maintaining a continuous link between the living and the dead. Gifts are made to Brahmins and to charity.

Sikhs follow a similar pattern in the home, without the severe restrictions of Hindus. It is the custom to read the holy book, the *Guru Granth Sahib*, either continuously for three days (*akhand path*) or over eight to ten days (*sadharan path*). This should normally begin after the funeral, but if there is a long delay because of an inquest, it may be started sooner. At the conclusion of the reading and prayers, if the deceased was head of the household, there is a *pagri* ceremony, followed by a feast in celebration of a long life if the deceased was elderly.

Islamic law requires friends and relatives to feed mourners for three days. After this the family should return to normal, and no one should talk about death or the deceased, unless the family is grieving too much or brings the subject up. The only greeting given at this time is 'From God we come, to God we return'. Wailing is still very common, and one young woman who was reminded that it was forbidden pointed out that if she did not wail the rest of the community would criticize her for not having enough feeling. Unofficial mourning often continues until the fortieth day with Qur'anic readings. At the end of this period the family may call their relatives and friends and have further readings and a meal to signal the end of mourning. At the end of Ramadan, during the festival of Eid, graves are visited.

Among Sri Lankan Buddhists mourners may return to work in three or four days. There are no religious restrictions for widows, although they may withdraw from social life for a time. Chinese Vietnamese Buddhists call the monks again on the seventh day to give the spirit a 'send-off', when all the relatives and friends come, and money is given to the temple. Other Vietnamese have a series of rituals which enable the spirit of the deceased to join the realm of the ancestors, and they will be especially honoured during the anniversary of the death and the lunar new year. Mourning lasts for 100 days, during which time no one wears bright colours or flowers. The wives and children of a man must mourn for three years, but the immediate family only mourns for one year on the death of a woman (Pearson, 1982: 480).

Finding meaning

Hindus believe that after death most people are reborn in a better or worse state, depending on how they have fulfilled their *dharma* (cf. Firth, 'Approaches' above). A common explanation for premature or untimely death is *karma*. The death of a child may be conceived of as either the parent's or child's *karma*, or both, as one Hindu explained:

> The child has a certain period fixed with you. [Understanding this] helps the parents to come to terms with the death . . . the only way you can explain to the mother is that this child was only going to live with you for five years, and you have to accept it, because now the child has gone for its betterment.

Sikhs also accept the concept of *karma* and rebirth, but believe these are under God's control. Physical death is not to be feared – only spiritual death – and those who are close to God will be united with God after death.

Buddhists also believe in rebirth, although it is not the soul that is reborn, but a collection of five aggregates containing patterns created by *karma*. At popular level this may be seen as fate, so that if a person dies young it is seen as being ordained. Buddhist teaching emphasizes the ephemeral nature of life and provides the way to overcome the suffering inherent in it.

Muslims believe that everything that happens is the will of Allah (God). At death the soul awaits the Day of Judgement, when the righteous will be resurrected and go to heaven and the wicked and unbelievers will go to hell. The belief that everything is in the hands of God brings great comfort at the time of bereavement. A Muslim woman who lost a much-wanted baby boy prematurely said that she found great comfort from her faith and from a visit to Mecca:

> We have three days' strict mourning, when the neighbours and friends come to help with food, and you talk about the death, and read the Qur'an, and you remember that this is God's will, that everything that happens happens according to His will. He is gracious and merciful, and never sends you a trial that you can't handle, he always gives you the strength you need. And because I know it was God's will, I feel I can cope, I have made a good adjustment, even though I miss my son, because I know he and I are in God's hands.

Problems of change

With hospital deaths in the United Kingdom several problems can arise. Muslims do not want anyone of a different faith – or of the opposite sex – to touch a body, although some will accept medical staff touching it if there is no one else to do it and rubber gloves are worn. No non-Muslim can give the ritual bath. A Muslim nurse pointed out that discretion must be used:

> I went to see this young Muslim who had died vomiting a lot of stale blood and had been left with his face in it. You need to have common sense. Can you imagine coming in to see your father or husband like that and remembering it for the rest of your life? Generally people don't mind having the tubes removed and the body straightened, but the important thing is to communicate with the family so that you know beforehand what you can do.

Great distress may be caused if a post-mortem is needed, especially for Muslims, whose belief in resurrection of the body makes the idea of mutilation abhorrent. (It also means that amputated limbs or organs or aborted foetuses must be buried and not disposed of in any other way.) To open the body to find out why death occurred seems to deny that death is God's will. The thought of the head being opened is particularly horrifying, and the Muslim insistence on modestly covering the private parts will also be violated, especially if passages have to be blocked. It is believed that the body still has a level of consciousness that enables the person to feel pain and to know what is happening.

Delays in timing before burial or cremation can also cause problems, as there are religious as well as practical reasons why disposal should be immediate in the countries of origin. For Muslims, burial should take place immediately, where the person has died (so the custom of returning the body to the country of origin is a matter of recent tradition – a need to return to one's roots, and to ensure the burial is properly done).

Buddhists are less concerned about timing. Tibetan Buddhists believe that consciousness may remain for as long as three days and even longer for accomplished meditators. To cremate prematurely before death of consciousness is absolutely certain, is tantamount to murder.

For Hindus delay in cremating the body, in theory, could disturb the proper progress of the soul and prevent it from becoming an ancestor or being reborn. It can also upset the mourning procedures which would normally begin immediately after the funeral, but which, if there is a delay, may have to be set in motion beforehand. Since one of the functions of mourning is to adjust to the absence of the deceased, these delays can disturb the customary pattern.

The notion of professional people who are paid to arrange things for them is regarded by some Asians as a complete denial of the community aspect they are used to, even though funeral directors are often perceived as more sympathetic than some medical staff. A Sikh man said:

> Whoever heard of funeral directors in the Punjab? Here funerals are administered by third parties who take money for this purpose, whereas in the Punjab a funeral is very properly a community affair.

He spoke of his shock, when his little boy died in England, at having to carry the little coffin by hearse instead of on his own shoulder, as he would have done in India.

Young Asians who have been brought up in Britain may never experience a death in the family until their late teens, and may be expected to mourn for relatives in India or East Africa whom they have rarely or never met. Even if it is a close relative who has died, young people may have difficulty coping with the expectations of relatives or other community members. One young girl said:

> They used to cry loudly, so loudly, but what they were doing really was impressing everybody around them that they were feeling the grief, but what you really feel inside is something different.

Traditional extended family structures may change in Britain. A young Asian professional man who marries a professional woman and sets up a nuclear household may find it very difficult, on the death of a parent, to find that he is expected to have the surviving parent live with him for the first time, particularly if it is a widowed mother who may have quite different ideas and expectations from his wife over matters of diet and child-rearing. However, he could be criticized by the community if he failed to follow the traditional pattern and make a home for his parent.

Conclusion

As can be seen, Asians bring with them a rich heritage of religious and cultural traditions. The changes required to assimilate are perhaps the most radical for Hindus because the very lengthy rituals depended on specialist priests, and there is neither the time nor the expertise readily available in Britain. However, provided that they can preserve those traditions which are really important, such as being present at the death, giving Ganges water and performing the *shraddha*, Hindus are pragmatic about the changes.

It is at the time of death that communal solidarity is strongest, and members from all communities support one another. Despite the pressures of visitors during the mourning period, the support is perceived to be of very real help and comfort. The insistence on weeping, judging from recent bereavement studies, is a valuable expression of grief, and the alternation between talking about the dead person, weeping and scripture readings provides a gradual period of adjustment to his/her absence. The regular gatherings of family and friends reinforce social and religious bonds. The psychological value of the legitimated mourning period warrants close attention, as the absence of proper mourning procedures, rituals and an acceptable way of dealing with grief may make adjustments more difficult. In the Asian communities, it is at the time of crisis that the great strengths of the community appear; cultural and religious beliefs give help and support and prove of great value.

References

Cole, W.O. and Sambhi, P.S. (1978) *The Sikhs, their Religious Beliefs and Practices*. London: Routledge.

Neuberger, J. (1987) *Caring for Dying People of Different Faiths*. London: Lisa Sainsbury.

Pearson, R. (1982) 'Understanding the Vietnamese in Britain, Part II: Marriage, Death and Religion', *Health Visitor*, Vol. 55 (Sept.).

Prickett, J. (ed.) (1980) *Death in Living Faiths Series*. London and Guildford: Lutterworth Educational.

50

Psychological defence mechanisms and coping strategies

Stella Ridley

Our lives are made up of many losses: among them the security of the womb, the comfort of the breast, our dependency and right to be cared for as children, our childish illusions about the power and security of adulthood, our first love or loves as we enter into sexual relationships, our children as they in turn grow up, and our independence as we fall ill or grow old. Most of these losses bring psychic pain, and the support we find at the time and the way we face and adjust to each loss is a fundamental part of our growth as individuals. Each step in our lives can only be seen in the context of our own history; losses today can echo and revive unresolved pain from unfinished business of the past. In the same way, our own past determines the way in which each of us can face the awareness of another's grief and pain, and the degree to which we can afford to empathize with this.

The loss of another person whose life was in some way interwoven with ours brings its own particular meanings to bear. Some of these meanings are clear, others are at a deeper level and may only be seen by their effects, such as inappropriate levels of anxiety, guilt, depression or intense activity in defence against something seemingly unknown. Painful and puzzling as these effects may be, they have a psychic function in terms of holding at bay truths that might themselves seem even more hurtful and unacceptable at a conscious level. Often these reactions have roots deep in the past, and many events have combined to produce the effect that is catalysed by loss. This complex combination of reasons makes it hard for an individual to simply 'piece together' the truth behind pain; often this can only be achieved at further emotional cost and time spent exploring the ways in which previous needs have been frustrated or only partially met.

Mary found herself apparently able to cope fairly well with the sudden loss of her husband in middle age when he suffered a heart attack and died. She experienced shock and grief, but busied herself initially with funeral arrangements and family matters, being a 'tower of strength' to everyone else. The following months were spent doing all the things in the house and garden that she had wanted to do for years - her husband had resisted change and she was enjoying the freedom to do as she pleased with her home. She returned to work part-time and was proud to find that the skills she had used many years ago before she had children were still of value. She was quietly aware of coping well with the bereavement, and of fitting in with a circle of widowed friends for a new pattern of social life. After nearly a year of this apparent adjustment to her loss, Mary's subjective world collapsed about her; it was meaningless, empty, and she became profoundly depressed.

It took many months of steady and often painful psychotherapy for Mary to begin to understand the nature of her feelings and the real meaning of her loss in the context of other events through her lifetime. As a child she had been aware of being held in low esteem by her parents and brothers for being a girl; she compensated for this by learning to cover her vulnerability wherever possible. The war intervened and as an evacuee she coped bravely for a few months, eventually returning to her mother withdrawn and depressed, having suffered great loneliness within the family in which she had been placed – a louder echo of her own loneliness within the parental home. She grew up to a successful career and a love affair which was crushed by parental disapproval. On the rebound she found a husband who met their requirements: he seemed a worthy choice and a good father to her sons. Prosperous and reliable he may have been, but in marriage and domesticity Mary was effectively back in the same role in which she had always found herself – lonely, constrained, but with the added frustration of having glimpsed the possibilities of a different life in which her own desires were given credence. There was an ever widening gulf within the marriage, and when her husband died she was in one way genuinely relieved and released; there was sadness for her in the loss of his life, but the possibilities of a future for herself were opening.

The depression which overtook her encompassed many features: a mourning for the loss of her parents whose deaths some years previously had been unrecognized at a psychic level; fear and guilt at her pleasure in her new-found independence both from her husband and from parental expectations which had in part tied her to him; grief at the loss of her own life to date as well as the loss of her children's father; pain at the loss of hope of recognition for herself within the family itself; and loss of hope of sexual fulfilment. This last loss became apparent in therapy when Mary's sexual feelings began to surface, and she became aware of a chain – the denial of her own feelings, desires and attractiveness as a child, where being a girl was of no value and she felt little interest from her father; the denial of her desires as an adolescent when her lover was sent packing by her parents; the denial of her sexuality by her unresponsive husband; and the denial of the emergence of her sexual desires again now – faced with the disapproval of a social circle of widows who held a preexistent tacit agreement to support each other in friendship and to stay outside any further relationships with men. When this chain was accessed and understood Mary felt better able to accept and experience her deeper feelings and needs, to work through her grief and despair over her many losses, and to recognize and make informed choices about her own particular desires for the future.

The above abbreviated case study shows a way of interpreting the meaning of one individual's feelings and defences in relation to a bereavement, and how depression set in once denial was no longer adequate as a defence against the many losses in her life; this was shown from a general psychodynamic perspective, within the framework of Freud's theories that allows examination of unconscious desires and their effect upon conscious feelings. Freud (1917) offers a view of mourning that suggests that inner attachments formed to those we are close to carry an 'investment' of emotional energy that is no longer appropriate when we know that they are absent and unable to receive or respond to this. This 'investment' needs to be detached from those we have lost, and held by the self again in readiness to 're-invest' in new emotional bonds when the right opportunity arises. Until this process takes place the loved ones are still 'out there' – lost; with the return to the self of the emotional energies also comes the internalization, the inner holding of the lost; they too then become part of the self and seem closer, not further away. The process of the return of these energies to the self and their place in mourning is illustrated in C.S. Lewis's description (1961: 38–9) of his feelings a while after the death of his partner:

> Something quite unexpected has happened. For various reasons, not in themselves at all mysterious, my heart was lighter than it had been for many weeks. For one thing I suppose I am recovering from a good deal of mere exhaustion, and after ten days of low hung grey skies and motionless warm dampness, the sun was shining and there was a light breeze. And suddenly, at the very moment when so far, I mourned H least, I remembered her best. Indeed it was something almost better than memory: an instantaneous unanswerable impression. To say it was like a meeting would go too far. Yet there was that in it which tempts one to use those words. It was as if the lifting of the sorrow removed a barrier. Why has no-one told me these things? How easily I might have misjudged another man in the same situation. I might have said, 'He's got over it. He's forgotten his wife', when the truth was, 'He remembers her better because he has partly got over it.'

This description gives an insight into a moment when, for C.S. Lewis, acute grieving was just beginning to move toward its resolution into an acknowledgement and acceptance of his loss.

Denial of loss at a psychic level removes the immediate and painful necessity of the task of mourning, but leaves emotional energy tied up uselessly with lost objects. Disavowal, reluctance to accept all aspects of a loss – to experience anger as well as affection – also blocks the re-integration and reinvestment of emotional energy. Sometimes 'unacceptable' feelings such as anger that rightly belong with the person who has been lost are instead projected outward towards others: a doctor may seem to be a safer and less vulnerable target for fury than a partner who has fallen ill and died. Sometimes feelings of anger or regret are turned inward and lead to agonies of 'soul-searching' and guilt.

Sarah had lost her 10-year-old-son when he was hit by a lorry while running across the road on the way home from school; her grief was intense and compounded by a terrible resignation – fatalism – about the loss. As the weeks passed she sank into a deeper and deeper depression, slowly losing touch with rational values until it became clear that she was somehow taking upon herself the blame for all the ills in the world; every war, famine and disaster was somehow linked to her, appropriated by her as part of the tragedy that was her life. Awareness of her terrible pain and fears that she would harm herself brought requests from relatives for professional help; therapy eventually reached feelings of intense pain and guilt at the death of her mother some years previously. Sarah had seen herself as being unhappy and demanding through adolescence; her mother's death from cancer following this had weighed on her conscience and she had always felt to blame, while hiding from herself the resentment she had felt at her mother's lack of availability to her at the time she had felt she needed her most. It was not until some of these feelings were to be unravelled that Sarah managed to reveal the additional burden of guilt that she was carrying – that she had caused her son's death also, by her insistence that he should always hurry home from school each day, and by arguments that had ensued when he had played with his friends and been late. In blaming herself she had hidden from herself the immense personal power that she assumed in 'being able' to bring about the death of both her mother and her son; but this power had started to show itself in her assumption of responsibility for all other ills in the world. Understanding and insight into these facets of her emotions and exploration of the meanings behind them led eventually to a more balanced and bearable acceptance of the awful losses she had sustained.

There are developments of Freudian theory, the psychology of perception and information-processing theories, which offer different but broadly compatible explanations of the ways in which areas of awareness can be separated from each other within one individual being, and suggest that one purpose of mourning is to bring about an integration of different 'awarenesses' whereby the individual can eventually accept the reality of a loss, its major implications, and look realistically again to the present and the future.

Information-processing theory describes the cognitive basis upon which we perceive the world. If our attention were to be spread over all the detailed incoming stimuli in our surroundings we would be swamped and unable to attend to anything effectively; instead we learn to attend only to certain aspects of our world at any one time. Processes within us but beyond our levels of conscious awareness decide what is salient and what is to be ignored at any one time. However, continued exclusion of certain features of the world can lead to distortions in perception; when something is excluded because of the painful or unpleasant nature of the feelings it evokes, the reality experienced by the individual is out of keeping with the general consensus of 'reality' of those about him or her.

Theories of memory give us an insight into how these 'exclusions' and conflicts may occur. Tulving (1972: 385) divided human memory into two classes: episodic memory consists of an individual's auto-biographical memories of specific events in a context of chronological time and place; semantic memory is not context-dependent in the same way, but is primarily a generalization of the meaning and implication of learned knowledge about the world. Although there is interaction between these two aspects of memory, they may not always be logically consistent with one another. An example might be an individual's own experience of a particular holiday as tiring travel, a half-built hotel, sunburn and expense, which is barely aligned with the same individual's semantic concept of 'holiday' as a peaceful rest in a sun-soaked tropical location, for example. Disappointment with the particular holiday may soon be forgotten or disregarded in the making of future plans for a holiday that will be anticipated again in terms of the ideal carried in semantic storage.

Bowlby (1980) offers an approach to the psychology of mourning encompassing these perspectives, in which he suggests that ways of dealing with relationships in infancy and childhood can become over-learned and continue to operate at a level below conscious awareness throughout life, sometimes inappropriately. In particular he sees this in relation to attachment behaviour, the way in which infants respond to the many pains of separation from the primary care-givers during the early period of childhood. When, for example, the generalizations stored about mother, father and self conflict with the experiences that have occurred, patterns of response may develop that exclude areas of conflict from awareness. This segregation can have implications in terms of the exclusion of incoming information at a later date. Response systems such as grieving may be de-activated; other responses and feelings may be disconnected cognitively from the event and give rise to diversionary alternatives. Rationalizations can often cover the inappropriateness of responses for a time, but they are sometimes seen even by the individual concerned as inexplicable or beyond control.

The title of Freud's paper of 1914, 'Remembering, repeating and working through', though applicable to psychoanalysis in general, is a useful description of the process of mourning, the way in which the individual reflects upon all aspects of the lost relationship until it is possible to assimilate it into a reconstructed view of the world. The inclination of the bereaved individual at the time of loss is often to go over and over the details of the relationship, and it would seem that this has the function of initiating the search for the deeper meanings behind the loss. In isolation it would appear to be a daunting task. In the company of others with an interest in maintaining a shared framework of meanings, as for example family members may do, it is all the harder to explore contradictory feelings.

Turning the other way, changing the subject, colluding with denial, may be the easier way out when witnessing grief; it is our own form of defence. This difficulty and embarrassment when faced with another's bereavement is an indicator of the unresolved pain we each carry within us at our own earlier losses. It is only to the extent that we can recognize this that we can extend real acceptance and non-judgemental listening to someone else in distress.

References

Bowlby, J. (1980) *Attachment and Loss: Vol. 3. Loss: Sadness and Depression*. London: Hogarth.

Freud, S. (1917) 'Mourning and melancholia' in *Standard Edition of the Complete Psychological Works of Sigmund Freud, Vol. 14*, ed. J. Strachey. London: Hogarth, 1957.

Lewis, C.S. (1961) *A Grief Observed*. London: Faber & Faber.

Tulving, E. (1972) 'Episodic and semantic memory', in E. Tulving and W. Donaldson (eds), *Organization of Memory*. New York: Academic Press.

51

When life moves on

George Castledine

I have heard it said that you get used to death when you practise nursing for long enough, that each experience hardens you and makes you more able to deal with the next. To some degree I have never been happy with the way I have dealt with dying patients or grieving relatives and friends – that is, until my recent experience.

My parents died within a year of each other, and like all such major experiences in life I feel I have learned something from that event. My mother greatly influenced my nursing career, and as a child taught me the rudiments of caring, including such practical skills as bandaging and taking temperatures. Finally, during the last few days of her life, I feel she taught me perhaps the most difficult aspect of all nursing situations – how to deal with death and dying.

I have seen patients die before and have tried to appreciate what it was that they, and their close ones, were experiencing. Nothing, however, could compare with the feelings I was going through when it actually happened to me.

There was a numbness and a silence, which built up a feeling of immense pressure followed by an emotional ache which started in my chest and filtered into every part of my body so that my eyes felt heavy, tears came easily, my voice laboured and my actions became uncoordinated. I drifted in and out of this ultimate emotional experience according to the intensity of the 'death situation'.

At times it was made worse by the shock of seeing my mother change from what I had become accustomed to. Her face lost that familiarity of expression, but on two occasions communicated something to me which I shall never forget.

The first time it happened was when she appeared to notice that I was starting to cry. We were holding hands and she looked up from her pillow for the first time, smiled and with tears in her eyes moved her lips as if to say something and then squeezed my hand. It was then I knew she was going to die, and it was from then onwards that she seemed to teach me how to come to terms with it all.

My mother never believed that anyone should be kept alive unnecessarily, that the quality of life was more important than the

From *Nursing Mirror*, 25 April 1984, 158: 22.

quantity. As an engineer, my father's philosophy was that he always wanted to 'wear out, rather than rust away'.

What used to concern me about both of them, was that they never seemed to care for themselves, but always for others. I suppose because of this and their strong beliefs, life was in many ways what they wanted it to be. It is thoughts like these, and many more which one recalls and reminisces about, which occupy your mind before and after someone's death.

I have read and heard people say that it is good to have people with you during an experience like this, but I wanted to be alone, uninterrupted and unfettered.

When it was all over, there was no final drama to be held or last-minute dash for a priest. My brother stood up rather embarrassed by the silence of it all, and I held my mother's hand for the last time. We went to see her body laid out properly a few days later – not because of a morbid wish to dwell on what had happened – and we both found it helped us.

In exactly what way is too difficult to say, but the body looked different, better in a way, and this made us both feel much easier, content and satisfied that life had moved on.

I hope I have not given the impression that this experience depressed and deflated me so much that I was unable to function and return to nursing. In fact, it has helped me. And, as if to put my knowledge and feelings to the test, fate presented me with a unique opportunity.

This happened shortly after I returned from compassionate leave and involved a young man, probably the same age as myself, having to come to terms with the fact that his father was dying.

His father had just been transferred to the ward from the coronary care unit, and it was obvious that the chances of his recovery were very slight indeed. There was a large number of relatives and friends, all wanting to be present at the death. One certain close friend of the family was demanding to know every piece of detailed information about the patient. He was questioning every medical and nursing action, which may have caused more than a little friction in some wards.

The anxiety he generated also precipitated further stress in the patient's son, which could easily have become out of control. I was thus faced with tactfully dealing with an awkward friend of the patient and the rapidly deteriorating emotional state of the son.

My immediate response was to say, 'Look, I know what you're going through, it's just happened to me!' But I decided not to use this approach and carefully separated the two men, using a more firm and understanding method, trying to put into words their feelings and experiences, encouraging them to talk about the hurt or anxieties they were going through.

This technique seemed to work well, and eventually I extended this approach to the whole family. When the patient eventually died, I felt I was further able to give them emotional support.

There is a real value in experiencing certain clinical events but, of course, such occasions are impossible to conjure up. Or are they? Perhaps we should be exploring more the value of role plays and learning through experience.

It certainly makes us better nurses the closer we get to the patient's situation, as long as we are guided, instructed and taught by someone who is also there and knows what it is we, as nurses, are looking for.

52

I desperately needed to see my son

Sheila Awoonor-Renner

Recently my child was killed in a road accident. He was 17. The journey had begun at 1 p.m. and he died at 3.28 p.m. I was told at 7.10 p.m. I couldn't quite understand why they had travelled such a short distance in six hours. My mind must have thought that it happened just before I was told. As the policeman who came to tell me of my son's death said that they were unable to take me to the hospital it took me some time to find someone to take me to him. The police at first seemed relieved that I had a car and could drive, but in the circumstances that was impossible. They were then anxious for me to find a relative to take me, and when I failed then a friend. I failed at friends, too. By now they were getting desperate – what about neighbours? I didn't know them either. In fact, there was a huge gulf between my reality and their understanding. My reality was that I needed someone close enough to be able to reveal myself safely who would not take over and do the right thing and say the right words and with whom I would have to behave as they were projecting I should behave. The people I needed are rare and were away. Therefore what I wanted was someone impersonal, a stranger – someone with no expectations of me. The police would have done nicely. I also needed someone with a good reliable car and without children who could just drop everything to take me to a place 50 to 60 miles away in the middle of an ordinary evening. Eventually, though shocked and barely able to function, I found somebody able to take me. The police were to tell the hospital of our intended arrival.

On arrival at the hospital just after 10.15 p.m. no one was expecting us. 'Everybody has gone now, and I should have gone too by now,' a social worker said. My friend and I were put in a small anteroom and the door was closed. We had been put in a box with the lid closed to spare us the sight of panicky people rushing to and fro, telephone calls being made, etc., while the system was being re-assembled for us. I wouldn't have that. I behaved myself for three to four minutes, then I opened the door. I still couldn't see anything but felt better. What would have made me feel much better was to have seen and shared

From *British Medical Journal*, 1991, 302: 356.

the panic. That would have been human: being put in a small, quiet, impersonal room behind a closed door was not.

Eventually the system assembled itself again. It seemed that I had not after all come to see my son but to identify him. The hospital manager was kind and caring with a woman's warmth. She knew what I needed or nearly knew. What I desperately needed was to see my son. But it was explained that I couldn't see him until I had been interviewed by the coroner's officer, who, not knowing I was to arrive, was somewhere else. Eventually he arrived. By now I was getting nicely institutionalized. I was behaving myself. I put him at his ease when he asked his questions – well, I tried to. He, poor man, knew the formula and knew each question had to be put with a sympathetic preamble. He was unctuous. He was sorrowful. And I wanted to see my son. He knew what to do with grieving relatives. He knew the formula, so he did it – to the end. He had no idea who, in reality, I was. I said that I wanted to see my son alone – no, I asked permission to see my son alone. Permission was granted on condition that I 'didn't do anything silly'.

With no idea what 'anything silly' was I acquiesced, imagining he meant 'don't touch and don't disturb anything'. He disappeared. Apparently there was great rushing about preparing Timothy for viewing. Putting a piece of gauze over a graze on his forehead was regarded as important so that I should not be offended or frightened or disgusted. We walked along a corridor. We arrived at a door. It was opened. No more hope; no more thinking it might not be Timothy. Incredibly, it was my Timothy. It was him, my lovely boy.

He was lying on an altar covered by a purple cloth, which was edged with gold braid and tassels. Only his head was visible. Such was the atmosphere of constraint I either asked permission or was given permission to enter. I can't remember. I entered, alone. The others stayed watching through the open door. I reached him and stroked his cheek. He was cold.

Timothy was my child; he had not ceased to be my child. I desperately needed to hold him, to look at him, to find out where he was hurting. These instincts don't die immediately with the child. The instinct to comfort and cuddle, to examine and inspect the wounds, to try to understand, most of all, to hold. But I had been told 'not to do anything silly'. And they were watching me to see that I didn't. So I couldn't move the purple cloth. I couldn't find his hand by lifting the cloth. I couldn't do anything. I betrayed my instincts and my son by standing there 'not doing anything silly'. Because I knew that if I did my watchers would come in immediately, constrain me, and lead me away.

Why did they do this? No doubt they thought that they were acting for the best. We, as a society, have lost contact with our most basic instincts. The instincts we share with other mammals. We marvel at cats washing and caring for their kittens. We admire the protection an elephant gives to her sick calf, and we are tearful and sympathetic when she refuses to leave her offspring when he dies, when she examines him, and nuzzles him, and wills him to breathe again. And we have forgotten that that is exactly what the human mother's most basic instinct tells her to do. And we deny her. If a human mother is not able to examine, hold and nuzzle her child she is being denied her motherhood when *in extremis.*

We have come to think that we are protecting her when we are really protecting ourselves. We have forgotten that this is the mother who has cleaned up the vomit, who has washed his nappies, who has dealt with and cleared away his diarrhoea. She has cleaned the blood from his wounds, she has kissed him better, and she has held him in his distress. She has done all of this since the day he was born. If he has been a patient in hospital she has possibly fed him by tube, she may have changed his dressings, she may have given him his injections. She will certainly have washed him and helped him to dress and combed his hair. And she will have held him.

Again I ask, who are we protecting when we deny her this last service which she can do for her child? We are not protecting the child. There is nothing she can do to harm her child. We are not protecting her: the fact of her child's death is not altered by the denial of her instincts.

Having nursed my mother through her last illness at home I was privileged to bathe her after death, to redress her wounds with clean dressings, to remove her catheter and drainage. It was a tearful and loving last service that my sister and I were privileged to perform for her. And it helped to heal our grief.

But my lovely boy was draped on an altar, covered with a purple robe, and all expressions of love and care which I had were denied to me. And I don't know when that wound will heal.

The time has come when we in the caring services should think again about how we serve the bereaved. A cup of tea and an aseptic look at the body does not serve. If it is their wish and instinct to wash the body, to hold the body, and to talk to the dead loved one then they should be helped to do this. They will be distressed and they may frequently need to stop to wipe the tears. But they will be helped in their healing. How ironic that we will have to retrain ourselves to help in this most basic service, but this is something which we must do.

53

A single parent confronting the loss of an only child

Evelyn Gillis

> My daughter, Lorena Mary Main, age 22,
> died with my sister, Mary, in an auto accident,
> April 26, 1981.
>
> Good night, sweet Lorena.
> I'll see you in the morning.
> Mom.

The word 'alone' screams at a single parent. Those of us who become single parents - either through death or divorce - find most physical, emotional and financial support severed. We must learn to accept independence from our spouse and assume full responsibility for our child. Daily life for our broken family must be maintained and sustained. It becomes necessary to live as normal a family lifestyle as possible.

After we recover from the emotional trauma of death or divorce, we create a new family unit of parent and child. As the child ages, and if we do not remarry, our relationship evolves beyond that of parent and child. Our lives become closely entwined. The child becomes a companion and helpmate. All of our parental love and caring is given to this one child.

Upon the death of the child, we face the absence of support from another adult who would share the same feelings of loss and grief. After being told of the child's death, we alone carry the responsibility of the funeral arrangements. Even when help is offered by friends and family, we must face those difficult final decisions alone.

After the funeral, when other people return to their own homes and families, we are left to face the reality of the child's death, alone in a house that offers nothing but silence. In the first few months we may charge into a whirlwind of activity. Dinner invitations, nights of visiting, weekends away, and even a movie alone - we'll try anything to get away from the emptiness and silence at home. Eventually, physical exhaustion limits such activity. And what is left? Nights alone in a silent house.

From A.T. Rando (ed.), *Parental Loss of a Child*, Glencoe, IL: Research Press Co., 1986, pp. 315–19.

We cry out to have another person alongside who knows, really knows, what the death of the child means, someone who shares those special memories of how our family once was. And that person could be anyone. We reach out to family, friends, and sometimes even strangers, only to find that it isn't enough. They did not know the child as we did. They cannot understand and return the depth of feeling. They cannot because they do not feel it. We are alone, trying to cope with the insane madness of grief and unable to share our emotions or remembrances with another. During those terrible times when we lose control of our mind and body there is no one to touch us, hold us, and re-assure us that we are not crazy. In the midst of this madness there is just silence. From somewhere we have to find the strength to regain self-control. We are totally responsible for ourselves.

Within a week or two after the death we must return to our job and profession. For eight hours a day or more we are confined with co-workers who expect us to produce and be as normal as possible. During these hours we must suppress our intense feelings of sadness, anger, hate, despair and fear, for society will not accept our expressing such negative emotions. And we ourselves consider this unacceptable public behaviour. These emotions are intense. When they grab hold of the body, most of us cannot control our reactions. The flowing tears, the shaking, nausea, vomiting, and the inexplicable pain through the body erupt as though they had a will of their own.

Conditions in the home change as well. There is no desire to clean house, shop for and cook food, entertain. Doing these things for one person is not enough. What does it matter if the refrigerator's bare insides all but echo? Food sustains life, and life is now a burden. Within us, a storm of fear and self-doubt rages. Why am I unable to function? Why can't I maintain my job and home? Why did my child die? Was it my fault? Am I a bad person? Am I being punished? Who will help me in all of this? No one. We must totally shoulder the feelings of doubt, guilt and blame. If we had custody of the child, we may be blamed by the other parent, thereby increasing the feeling 'I am to blame'. An ugliness and hatred for the other parent may grow, especially if that parent has remarried and has other children. At night, at home, the hours crawl until it is time to sleep.

Perhaps we have one glass of wine to help us sleep. Sleep does not come. One more glass. Still sleep eludes us, as exhausted as we are, and we are alone. Be it one glass of wine or enough wine to bring us to the point of insensibility, hoping to deaden the pain, there is no one to help. There is no one to say, 'You don't need that', 'Come to bed', or 'We can talk.' And most times there is not even the strength to make a phone call to ask for help. And who to call at this time of night? Friends and family would understand a call for help once or twice, but certainly not for the many months that these conditions exist. We are part of an exclusive club that all members wish they had never joined.

After hours of raging pain perhaps there is some sleep, but sleep, in its lack of mercy, does not last long. There are nights when we awake screaming from nightmares and we are in the dark alone, too frightened to try to return to sleep for fear the nightmare will return. In the morning, in this condition, we must present ourselves at our place of business, knowing that we must maintain the standards of our profession. Anything less may put us in jeopardy of losing our income, and this cannot happen because we are responsible for ourselves.

Having been responsible single parents and realizing that we are no longer can be devastating. Our need to be comforted by another adult is great. This realization takes time. It could be months before we are aware we are not coping as well as we could. For this reason we must not always be alone. We must reach out to family and friends. Best of all we should join a self-help group of bereaved parents. They alone will be there for us in the many months and perhaps years that are needed to learn to cope with the death of a child. We need understanding adult companionship to help us become strong, secure, childless, single adults.

Our children are our roots of family. With the death of an only child we know that this is the end of any family life. One day we were parenting, the next – nothing. We will never again hear those words 'Hi, Mom'; we no longer have a person who is truly ours. Where once was a happy family now exists a solitary person. What was once 'we' is now 'I'. In a family-oriented society we find ourself personless, with no one to share the joys and sorrows of life as do a child and parent. We feel the absence in our homes of any activity concerning children. There is nothing to do for our child; we are no longer needed. We begin to feel a sense of aloneness. How different this feeling is from feeling lonesome or lonely. Those feelings can be corrected just by being social with family or friends. I became so affected by this feeling of aloneness that when ordering carry-out food from a restaurant I was unable to order just one dinner, I had to order at least two. A feeling would come over me that if I ordered one dinner everyone in the restaurant would know that I was truly alone. It is difficult to be a family of one.

Gone are the graduations, birthday parties, proms and the dream of my child's wedding. Those once wonderful holidays, Thanksgiving and Christmas, will never be celebrated again as a family, if indeed celebrated at all. The thought of Christmas in my home with a tree, decorations, gifts and a turkey, without this precious person, is unbearable. My grief on normal days was so intense that with the approach of these holidays I feared for my sanity. How would I ever pass these days without becoming insane? Not having other children for whom a pretence of holidays would have to be made, my home was barren at Christmas. I also was unable to accept invitations from family and friends to share these holidays in their homes. I could not face being in the presence of their children knowing that my child was dead.

I will never become a grandparent, never see my family grow through my daughter and her family, never have anyone to whom I can pass on my family china. What will happen to me as I grow old? Who will come to me on holidays? If I become ill or infirm, who will care about and for me? Yes, I know there are people who care for me, but I also know they have families of their own, and that makes the difference. All these things and more contribute to that feeling of aloneness. Never again in social situations will I be able to say 'This is my daughter, Lorena' and know the love and pride I felt in having her. Instead, when asked that cruellest of questions, 'How many children do you have?' I know the answer: 'I had a daughter; she's deceased.' Before the death of my daughter I did not realize how much that question was part of life. Being childless, learning to answer that question became one of the most difficult adjustments. And saying it reinforced that feeling of aloneness.

My visits to the cemetery were overly long. Sometimes I sat by her grave for five to six hours. Although I knew I should leave, being alone, I could not find the strength to go to my car and drive away. Nor did I want to. This became the place where I felt I belonged. I would trace my fingers along the indentations in the newly laid grass, digging little holes to see how far down into the earth I could dig, all the while telling Lorena, 'Don't be afraid, I'll get you out of here. I'll take you home with me.' During this period my thoughts of suicide surfaced. At first it was just a strong urge to follow her. I could not accept on blind faith that she was safe and free from harm. I had loved and protected her in life and I wanted to love and protect her in death. Some spark of self-preservation brought me to a suicide counsellor. She called me daily. Hour after hour she would listen to me talk about Lorena, how agonizing the pain was and how I could not bear it one more minute. She helped me to understand I really did not want to die. I just wanted the pain to stop, and suicide seemed the way to become free from this pain. It is because of her day-after-day patience and understanding that I am alive today.

For my life to change, I had to give to someone the love and caring I had for my child. But I felt it was better not to love, not to give, to protect myself from pain. It was many months before I could reach out to others. Later I became the chapter leader of a sibling group in the Compassionate Friends' organization. If I had not learned to love and give again, I would always have had that feeling of aloneness.

54

Epitaph of Libby Dickinson, 1798–1818

Anonymous

Uncertain life, how swift it flies –
Dream of an hour, how brief our bloom –
Like the gay verdure soon we rise
Cut down ere night to fill the tomb.

———

From an abandoned graveyard in Avon, Connecticut.

55

Care of the suddenly bereaved

D.W. Yates, G. Ellison and S. McGuiness

The hospice movement was established over twenty years ago to care for and support the dying and their relatives and now makes an important contribution to the management of patients with terminal illnesses. Over one-third of people who die in hospital, however, do so within a few hours of arrival, often in the accident and emergency department and usually after a brief illness or an accident. Many of them are young, and most die outside normal working hours.

Medical staff are not trained to manage the suddenly bereaved. Nursing staff, who usually have more experience in this, are often working under considerable pressure. The first contact relatives have with hospital staff is just before or at the time of the patient's death, and there is rarely any subsequent support of the type recommended by the hospice movement. Yet the impact of a sudden death on relatives is often more pronounced than that of a death after a prolonged illness, during which the relatives have had time to prepare themselves.

We describe some of the problems encountered by the suddenly bereaved and present the experience of a counselling support service that has been developed in this accident and emergency department [at Hope Hospital, Salford] over six years.

Evolution of the service

Interest in providing support for distressed relatives within this department was stimulated by the experiences of Lapwood (1982), and in 1983 a bereavement counsellor was temporarily appointed. The appointment was generally welcomed, but problems were encountered; one nurse was lost from the resuscitation team, and the service was available only when the counsellor was on duty. The work was restricted to the department, but follow-up in the community was clearly needed.

In 1986 this temporary post was established as a formal part of the nursing service. When not counselling or teaching, the counsellor worked as a nurse in the department. Visits were made to relatives'

From *British Medical Journal*, 1990, 301: 29-31 (abridged).

homes on one day a week, and a network of community support was developed. Close liaison with the hospital's social work department was established so that the new service complemented and extended the work already being done by the social worker in the accident and emergency department.

All medical and nursing staff working in the accident and emergency department now receive training from the counsellor in the initial support of suddenly bereaved relatives when they are appointed. The working hours of a group of senior nurses have been coordinated so that the service is available at all times. This has allowed the counsellor more time to develop community support. The demands on the service, however, continue to outstrip the available resources, and conflict continues between the need to support isolated relatives in the community and the need to be present in the accident and emergency department. The counsellor must spend time working alongside the resuscitation team so that she can understand the stresses of the full-time nurses.

The emotional demands on those providing support are considerable. The counsellor helps the staff of the accident and emergency department but also needs support herself; this is achieved by monthly informal discussions with a professional counsellor based in an adjacent (non-medical) postgraduate institution.

Support in the accident and emergency department

On arrival in the department, friends and relatives of critically ill or injured patients are taken to a specially furnished relatives' room by a nurse, who stays with them and provides an honest interpretation of the patients' progress. All staff are taught the importance of continuous support and communication with non-technical language. The relatives' room is adjacent to the resuscitation area but opens on to a quiet corridor with toilets nearby. It contains sofas and easy chairs, facilities for making tea, a mirror, a box of tissues and a direct dial telephone. Carpets, wallpaper, curtains and a table lamp create a warm, domestic environment. Some relatives ask to witness the resuscitation, and this is encouraged after explanation by the nurse. Frequent reports of developments are essential. News of deterioration or death is given by the most senior members of staff managing the patient. Repeated, simple explanations and listening and sharing are important. Spiritual support is immediately available, but a priest is not approached without the relatives agreeing.

If the patient dies the body is moved into a private room. Relatives and friends, including children, are encouraged to visit and stay in the room for as long as they wish. If the patient was a child or baby the relatives are encouraged to hold the body. Subsequent communication

Table 55.1 *Factors that may complicate bereavement*

Loss of practical and emotional support and companionship
Loss of or anxiety about financial provision
Loss of or anxiety about the family home
Children or adolescents in the immediate family
Dependent family members (handicapped, elderly or sick)
A parent surviving his or her child
Inability to share feelings with the family
Reluctance to acknowledge the death
Marital or family discord
Difficulty in dealing with previous losses
Lack of spiritual support
Lack of community support
History of mental illness

Source: Based on Parkes and Weiss, 1983

with the coroner's officer, general practitioner, health visitor, social services and clergy follows standard practice.

When the patient's relatives and friends have left, the medical and nursing staff are given support. They are encouraged to take a few minutes for quiet discussion and to share feelings, and this time is considered invaluable.

Support in the community

The bereavement counsellor is told about all deaths and decides, in consultation with staff present at the time of death, whether she needs to give community support. The risk factors listed in [Table 55.1] are considered. Occasionally staff may think that a particular family is in need of support despite none of the risk factors being evident. Whenever possible the first visit is made without an appointment within seventy-two hours of the death. The extended family is usually together at this time, and a spontaneous conversation is considered to be more valuable than a pre-arranged formal consultation. The visit lasts about one hour, a non-directive counselling technique being used. The need for and the timing of further visits are then decided.

Results

Records of all deaths in the department over twelve months and the support provided for relatives were reviewed. A total of 338 patients died, of whom six were infants and seven were children under the age of 16. The support provided in the department seemed to be welcomed. Comments were made about the value of the relatives' room and the constant availability of the support nurse.

The success of the community work was more difficult to determine. The counsellor visited 109 families living within 100 km of the hospital. Follow-up visits were arranged in ninety-eight cases; a mean of five visits were made to each household. In eighty-five cases some of the family were at home when the unannounced visit was made. Sixty-eight families requested information and explanation about the cause of death, certification and funeral arrangements. Although the next of kin in seventy-four cases stated that they had good support from extended family, neighbours or the church, in five cases they were totally alone and admitted that the visiting counsellor was their first contact since they had been bereaved. Twenty-one people displayed grief reactions such as denial and anger, and one person rejected help.

The typical problems encountered by the suddenly bereaved and the value of continued support from this department in the community may be judged from the following case reports.

Case 1 – A 5-year-old boy had been given 20p by the tooth fairy and on the way to school dashed across the road to the sweet shop. He was knocked down by a car and sustained multiple injuries to the head and trunk. His parents quickly followed him to hospital and were present during the unsuccessful attempt to resuscitate him. Subsequently they found it helpful to talk to an outsider about their feelings of guilt and anger.

Case 2 – A woman was called to a hospital 80 km from her home after her husband had had a myocardial infarction and died on a motorway. Her initial reaction was complete denial, anger and agitation. Follow-up telephone conversations indicated that she had not adjusted to her loss, felt isolated and suicidal, and had little local support. After a visit from the counsellor and discussions with her general practitioner she received support from the community psychiatric nurse and the local branch of the Samaritans.

Case 3 – Before going out to play squash a mother had encouraged her 15-year-old only son to join his friends for a game of football. He was knocked down while crossing the road to the field. She arrived in the accident and emergency department to find her son dying in the resuscitation room. The bereavement counsellor drove home with her and maintained contact over many weeks. The mother had an overwhelming feeling of guilt and was keen to talk about her actions and her relationship with her son.

Case 4 – A 59-year-old widow whose pregnant daughter and 7-year-old grandchild died in a house fire had no surviving relatives. A bunch of flowers (paid for by the hospital's social work department) was a useful introduction to the first home visit. Further visits followed. She said that the knowledge that someone at the hospital cared had given her renewed determination to come to terms with her grief. She particularly appreciated the opportunity to talk over the events surrounding the deaths.

Discussion

[. . .] A person's personality and social circumstances will influence his or her response to the sudden death of a relative. It is therefore generally acknowledged that non-directive counselling is most appropriate (Rogers, 1951). We used this person-centred approach and tried to help by listening and empathizing as advocated by Egan (1986). This approach can take many months.

Woodward et al. (1985) suggested that early skilled counselling after the sudden death of an infant was particularly valuable when initiated in the accident and emergency department. Support offered in the hospital, however, is of limited value if it is not continued and developed in the community over the following weeks. This is time-consuming, and it would be impossible and inappropriate for counselling to be undertaken solely by a bereavement counsellor based in the accident and emergency department. The counsellor is more effective when showing the bereaved how to use the available resources than when trying to solve every problem personally. Integration with the work of the hospital's social work department and the bereaved relative's general practitioner is essential, and self-help groups are invaluable. The Compassionate Friends, CRUSE (for the widowed and their children), the Samaritans, and the Foundation for the Study of Sudden Infant Death have extensive local networks.

The bereavement counsellor trained a group of senior nurses, one of whom was available to support relatives and friends of critically ill patients at all times. We found that there were usually enough nurses available at the time of the resuscitation for one of them to be spared to support the relatives. Indeed, this was considered as important as many of the other aspects of resuscitation and is now an integral part of the resuscitation team's work.

Teaching medical, nursing and administrative staff in this department to care for the suddenly bereaved has been successful. The work has assumed a high profile, and there was no difficulty in establishing liaison with other professional groups, both within the hospital and within the community. Indeed, the enthusiasm to develop such liaison brings an increasing workload.

The counsellor was employed as a clinical nurse specialist (grade H), which was considered to be the minimum for the responsibilities entailed. This, together with the use of a hospital car, clearly has important cost implications for the health authority. Only a quarter of the counsellor's time is spent supporting her clinical colleagues in the department. The cost must be set against the long-term expense of supporting relatives in the community who have no initial support and subsequently present with major psychiatric problems and unresolved grief reactions.

A few courses are now available for those wishing to study

bereavement counselling, but they are usually designed by and intended for people with a specific interest in the hospice movement. An exception is the six-week training session run by CRUSE for voluntary bereavement counsellors.

Conclusion

Sudden death robs the relatives of preparatory grief, is more common in young people, and usually occurs either in the clinical environment of the resuscitation room or in an unfamiliar high dependency or intensive care unit. People who are suddenly bereaved may require more support and counselling than those who have known for some time that their relative is dying, yet they usually receive less. All accident and emergency departments should review their arrangements for providing help for the bereaved and integrate their services with those available in the community. A similar system should be developed in intensive care, coronary care and neurosurgical units, where many patients die shortly after admission. If such support were widely available it might reduce the number of people presenting with unresolved grief reactions.

References

Egan, G. (1986) *The Skilled Helper* (2nd edn). Pacific Grove, CA: Brooks & Cole.
Lapwood, R. (1982) 'Chaplain to casualty', *British Medical Journal*, 285: 194-5.
Parkes, C.M. and Weiss, R.S. (1983) *Recovery from Bereavement*. New York: Basic Books.
Rogers, C. (1951) *Client Centered Therapy*. Boston, MA: Houghton Mifflin.
Woodward, S., Pope, A., Robson, W.J. and Hagan, O. (1985) 'Bereavement counselling after sudden infant death', *British Medical Journal*, 290: 360-5.

56

The loss of a baby: parents' needs and professional practice after early loss

Nancy Kohner

It is now time to take stock and listen to the silent grief of [the] mother who do[es] not dare to rock the boat by a seemingly silly request that society should view the pre-viable fetus as her own special baby. (*The Lancet,* editorial, 10 December 1988)

The law and hospital practice

In the UK at present, at least one baby in every hundred is either stillborn (that is, born dead after the 24th week of pregnancy, according to the Stillbirth (Definition) Act of 1992) or dies shortly after the birth. Figures for the UK in 1990 (when the legal definition of stillbirth was a baby born dead after 28 weeks' gestation) show that 3,721 babies were stillborn, and 3,616 died within the first four weeks of life.

After a stillbirth, the law requires certain procedures: the stillbirth must be certified and registered, and the baby's body must be buried or cremated. It is also usual practice to obtain parents' consent for a post-mortem. These requirements, though basic, provide a practical framework for managing the death and its aftermath. They also imply certain moral obligations which are the result of recognizing the status of the body.

But in the case of the baby born dead before the legal age of viability there are no legal requirements, no official statistics and no generally accepted practice. So professionals caring for parents after an earlier loss have to devise their own form of management and their own procedures. For while a baby born dead at, say, twenty weeks' gestation is, to the parents and to the professionals involved, a baby that could have lived, it remains a non-viable foetus in the eyes of the law and is without legal status.

In recent years, many British hospitals have recognized the need to amend policy and practice to fit the reality of parents' experiences. In

This article is based on an extract from *Miscarriage, Stillbirth and Neonatal Death: Guidelines for Professionals*, London: SANDS (The Stillbirth and Neonatal Death Society), 1991.

consequence, many have now extended and, where necessary, adapted their policies for the management of stillbirth to include deaths at earlier gestations when the baby, had he or she been born alive, might perhaps have survived.

For example, just as after a stillbirth, parents are now helped to see and hold their baby, to care for the body perhaps by bathing and dressing the baby, and, above all, to take time to say goodbye. A medical certificate is given which, although not legally required, is still of great value to the parents as an official acknowledgement of their baby's existence. Other mementoes will also be given: a wrist band, a lock of hair, hand and foot prints. The hospital will suggest a funeral, and either cremation or burial, and will help the parents to organize for their baby and for themselves what they want and feel to be right.

In these ways, British hospitals now acknowledge the similarities in the experiences of all parents whose babies die when they might perhaps have lived, regardless of the dividing line which the current law imposes.

Deaths at earlier gestations

But what, then, should be done for parents whose babies are born dead (miscarry) at still earlier gestations, when there can be no realistic expectation of the baby's survival?

Such earlier loss is not necessarily less traumatic. Most women, from the beginning, think of their pregnancy in terms of a baby. If their pregnancy fails, it means, for them, the loss of that baby and of all that that baby meant to them. This is true whether the loss occurs early or late in pregnancy. It is the personal significance of the loss, not the gestational age of the baby, which determines the extent of parents' bereavement and their need to grieve.

It follows from this that the care and support which are offered should be determined not so much by the stage of pregnancy at which the loss occurs as by an understanding of *what the loss means to the parents*. For many parents, an early miscarriage means a great deal, and supportive, sensitive care is badly needed.

So, for example, even after an early miscarriage, parents are often helped by seeing what they have lost and, if there is no identifiable body, being given the information and explanations they need to understand why this is. They can be helped by staff who are prepared to talk with them, answer their questions and express some shared sorrow. They can be helped by mementoes (a scan photograph, a certificate, their hospital appointments card) which they can keep and which will later re-assure them that their loss, and so their feelings, are real. They can be helped by explicit acknowledgement of the significance of what has happened – by, for example, a memorial service, or an entry in a remembrance book.

When there is a body, no matter how tiny, then care may be in many ways like that for later loss. Even a tiny body may be held in the palm of the hand, and for some parents this contact with their baby later becomes a treasured memory. Even when a body is damaged or abnormal, parents can gain much from seeing their baby, perhaps well wrapped, and with the support of staff to help them.

This is not to suggest that early miscarriage is the same as later miscarriage or stillbirth, or that it should be handled in the same way. Clearly it is a different physical experience, and its management will differ accordingly. It is also true to say that although early miscarriage can be devastating, it is on the whole less likely to be so than later miscarriage and stillbirth.

But distinctions between one kind of loss and another should be treated with great caution. An early miscarriage may have a meaning which is not immediately apparent. It may, for example, not be the first but the second or third such event for a couple who long for a child. It may cause particular distress because it follows the death of a parent, or because it re-opens an older grief or some other unhappiness. Equally, a *later* miscarriage may be *less* significant than it appears. A woman who has not invested a great deal in her pregnancy, and who has felt from the start that the pregnancy 'wasn't right' may not feel her loss so acutely. There may even be an element of relief. There is, in other words, infinite variety of experience and many possible concealed meanings. No easy assumptions can be made about what the loss of a pregnancy means to individual parents.

Comparisons, too, should be avoided. For while professionals are in a position to compare one loss with another and may as a result judge later loss to be greater or 'worse', parents themselves have neither means nor reason to make such comparisons. Each parent experiences, quite simply, the loss of *their* baby. It is not helpful to parents to categorize their experience, or grade it in relation to the experience of others.

This means that to provide good care after loss at any stage in pregnancy, professionals must be able to listen and respond, as sensitively as they are able, to the feelings and needs of individual parents' experiences of loss and grief; the care and support they give should be determined by parents' *particular* needs. This means they must be prepared to work openly and flexibly, to communicate honestly with parents, to avoid assumptions and judgements, and, sometimes, to risk making mistakes.

To give care in this way is often challenging and always demanding, and professionals themselves have a need – not always recognized – for training and support.

The status of the body: implications for management

Babies born dead before the legal age of viability have no legal status and consequently the law does not prescribe what may or may not be done with their bodies. But these babies have a special status in moral terms, having been potential human life. And they have an undeniable status in the minds of their parents.

The respectful treatment of their baby's body is of the greatest importance to parents. Many simply assume that the body will be respectfully handled, and are then acutely distressed to learn, some time later, that this has not been so. Professionals, too, are often disturbed by hospital procedures. Two areas of practice are particularly implicated: pathology and disposal of the body.

If respect is to be shown, and the moral status of the baby's body is to be recognized, then it is essential that parental consent should always be sought before any pathological investigation is carried out. Equally, although there are at the time of writing no legal requirements concerning the disposal of the body or remains of a miscarried baby (that is, no requirement to bury or cremate, as is the case with stillborn and live-born babies), there should be provision for respectful disposal.

What constitutes respectful disposal may vary according to what is lost (especially whether or not there is a body) and, more importantly, what is appropriate for and needed by the parents. But the parents should be given the opportunity to express their wishes about the disposal of their baby's body and their wishes should, wherever possible, be fulfilled. A few hospitals are now providing cremation or burial for all identified babies' bodies, regardless of gestation. A few offer all parents the chance to participate in some kind of simple funeral or ceremony, and many parents are comforted and helped by this.

Progress and change

Ten years ago, it was felt that parents of a stillborn baby would be best helped if their experience was minimized as much as possible. As a result, many parents did not see or hold their baby, and many were not told what was done with the body. The radical change which has taken place in the management of stillbirth came about because professionals began to acquire a better understanding of what the experience of stillbirth is like and what it means to parents. Equipped with that understanding they could begin to respond in quite different and supportive ways.

Understanding of earlier loss is now also improving. And with it, there is a growing awareness of the common elements which exist in the loss of a baby at any stage of pregnancy. Gradually, professionals are acquiring more confidence about what kind of care is needed and what is possible. What has, in the past, seemed to many to be inappropriate, or impractical, or even, perhaps, wrong (such as the viewing of very tiny or abnormal babies) is now being reassessed and increasingly accepted. There are perceptible changes in attitudes and, most important, a more thoughtful, flexible approach to practice.

Much has been achieved by bereaved parents themselves who have found, through self-help organizations such as SANDS (The Stillbirth and Neonatal Death Society), The Miscarriage Association and others, not only support but also a means of publicly articulating and explaining their needs. Many professionals are now willing and anxious to listen to what parents can tell them, and to work with bereavement organizations and groups to develop improved practice. Given the rapid improvement in the management of stillbirth, it seems fair to expect that an equally rapid improvement will now take place in the management of early pregnancy.

Addresses

The Miscarriage Association, c/o Clayton Hospital, Northgate, Wakefield, West Yorks WF1 3JS. Tel: (0924) 200799. Support after miscarriage.
SANDS (The Stillbirth and Neonatal Death Society), 28 Portland Place, London W1N 4DE. Tel: (071) 436 5881.
SATFA (Support After Termination for Abnormality), 29–30 Soho Square, London W1V 6JB. Tel: (071) 439 6124.

57

When a baby dies – a father's view

Gavin Fairbairn

When my wife had our baby girl, Hesther Frances, by caesarian section, I was told pretty soon that she was unlikely to live. The paediatrician who was sticking tubes down her throat in an effort to help her breathe asked me whether I wanted him to continue doing so, or whether I would rather that he stopped, since it was unlikely to do any good. He explained that he was sure that Hesther was suffering from a chromosomal disorder called Edward's syndrome which made it very unlikely that she could live. I decided that he should stop and that we should allow Hesther to die rather than continuing this undignified attempt to make her live for a few extra hours.

They took Hesther out of her special care cot and gave her to me. I was in great emotional upheaval. This was my first child and I had agreed that she should be allowed to die. I had taken the word of the paediatric senior registrar that my child was unlikely to live and agreed that he should stop trying to make her live.

I was left holding Hesther while people, as it seemed to me, backed off into the corners of the room. I spoke to her and cried with her. As I welcomed her into the world and said I was sorry she would not be able to stay with us, I held out my hand towards the retreating figures and asked for help. They retreated further and further away. They seemed to vanish into every available corner of the special care room and into the adjoining office – safe behind psychological or glass partitions, able to deceive themselves into thinking that what I wanted was to be left alone with my baby, able to ignore my outstretched hands and eyes. These caring and committed professionals abandoned me when I needed them to stay with me and help me to be with my child.

Very soon I remembered Susan, whose emergency caesarian had come after an attempt to induce labour because of pre-eclampsia: rupturing the membranes at the neck of her cervix had resulted in a cord prolapse. I wanted to take Hesther to her. I wanted to know that she was going to be all right: I wanted us to be a family for a while before Hesther died.

I went to Susan and showed Hesther to her: I told her she was very beautiful but she was not going to live, the doctors had told me so.

From *Nursing Practice*, 1986, 1: 167–8 (slightly abridged).

Susan was very dozy, although she managed to come through the fog briefly to say hello to our daughter. It was a very sad time for us. It was a turbulent time for me – what to do? – stay with my wife or stay with my baby? In my mixed-up state it did not occur to me that I could stay with both.

After a few minutes I took Hesther back to the special care room and left her to die in a cot. I went back to Susan: I had begun to believe that she too would die and I wanted to be with her if she was going to do so. She was my love, she was my long-standing friend, she and I shared the world together. I left my baby to die with people who would not hold my hand while I cried and I went to be with my wife.

My continuing concern, my guilt, my regret, is that I left my baby to die with strangers and went and sat with my wife. I remember now how I admired my father many years ago when he sat and held his dog while the vet 'put her to sleep' and I wondered what possessed me to let my baby die in a room full of strangers while I ran off and hid from her.

The paediatrician who looked after Hesther during her few minutes of life after birth said two things to me before she died. The first was that he asked whether I wanted him to continue trying to get her to breathe properly. The second was a request that I give him permission to do a post-mortem. How was it possible that he could ask me such a thing while my baby was still alive in the next room? How was it possible that he could think it appropriate to back off from me in my anguish and yet ask me that minutes later? How was it possible that it could be an important part of his job to be aware of the 'need' to gain permission to perform a post-mortem, while failing to be aware of the need to care for parents in their bereavement, of the need that I had to have someone to be my friend while my baby died?

During the days that followed Hesther's death, Susan and I received very kind and caring nursing from the nurses and midwives at the hospital. They became important figures in our lives as we began to get to know one another in our grief. But during the ten days or so that she stayed and became gradually physically stronger again very few people with whom we came in contact ever actually referred to the fact that Susan was in hospital to have a baby who had died, rather than because she had had an operation the after-effects of which she was still suffering. Perhaps it was good that she suffered from high blood pressure and Bell's Palsy for a long time after Hesther's death – it gave the nurses and doctors something to worry about other than the fact that she and I were grieving the death of our baby.

Several good things happened in our grief. One occurred when we asked a few days after Hesther's death whether Susan could go to the mortuary to see her. She could not remember what Hesther looked like and needed to see her. At first she was told that she was very ill, that she was not well enough to go downstairs. Then someone came up with a solution – if Susan could not go to Hesther, why not bring Hesther to Susan. She was brought up in a carrycot and we sat and cried together with our baby. The second good thing that happened was that one day a student midwife asked Susan whether the photograph by her bedside was her baby, could she look and what was its name? The third was when the mortuary attendant apologized because he was aware enough to notice me wince when he referred to my child as 'it': he was a nice man – at least he referred to her, at least he acknowledged her existence.

Folk who have babies who die at birth, or are born dead or who die shortly after birth, are parents. They have lived with the idea, and the reality, of their baby for a long time. Perhaps they lived with the idea of their child for many years before it was conceived. Like the parents of babies who survive, they have, in all probability, laid plans. They have probably bought baby clothes and carrycots and nappies and all the other paraphernalia that babies require. They have probably given their baby a variety of names to choose from depending on its sex. They have carried it in their bodies and minds and hearts and souls since conception and perhaps for a good time before that. Because of this they need to be treated as bereaved parents. Women who have given birth to babies who are dead, or who die, need to be treated as mothers who have lost a baby, not as patients who have suffered a physical illness. Men whose babies are born dead or die after birth need to be treated as fathers who have lost a baby, not as men whose womenfolk are a bit unwell just now. All of this is true also for men and women who lose babies through miscarriage – they also are parents, they also are bereaved. [. . .]

Postscript. Hesther Frances lived for one hour in 1983. Her brother Thomas was born in 1986.

58

Gay and lesbian bereavement

Dudley Cave

When Lord Alfred Douglas wrote about the love that dare not speak its name, it was an exaggeration, and it is even less true today when we have had gay characters in soap operas like *Brookside* and *EastEnders*. Today 20,000 lesbians and gay men can march through London with banners proclaiming their sexual orientation. However they, like me, are a part of the tiny minority of homosexuals who are able to come out and speak for themselves and for the others. Most lesbians and gay men have to be discreet, secretive. Some have to be discreet if they are to keep their jobs. For every gay person you can see, there are dozens out of sight.

Estimating the number of gay men is not easy. According to the figures of Kinsey and Martin (1948: 651) it is as low as 4 per cent (1 in 25) if we are only considering totally and exclusively homosexual men – those who have never had an erotic thought about a woman. But, if we include every man who has ever had sex to orgasm with another man, the figure rises to 34 per cent (more than 1 in 3). With women it is even more difficult to calculate as so many lesbians are, or have been, married. Many have children. Kinsey's later studies suggest that there are about half as many lesbians as there are gay men. We at the Gay Bereavement Project think that 5 per cent (1 in 20) is the absolute minimum figure for those who identify themselves as homosexual. The London boroughs of Camden, Hackney and Islington estimate that 10 per cent of their residents are lesbians or gay men, and those are not particularly gay areas.

'Coming out' – that is, being visibly gay – can damage career prospects. We can be sacked just for being homosexual, although such sacking is illegal, and most of us keep our heads down, play possum, stay in the closet, live a lie and pray that the secret is safe. 'Staying in the closet' isn't just a matter of not 'coming out', it requires a programme of deceit. It means finding suitable escorts for functions, it means inventing a convincing opposite-sex partner and keeping secret all gay associations.

Some lesbians and gay men may 'play the field' but many settle into relationships which are as loving and long-lasting as any marriage. (My friend Bernard and I have been together for thirty-seven years.) For those who love in secret, the tangled web of lies will cause problems, and when one partner dies will cause far greater problems. Grief must be hidden. There won't be any of those letters of sympathy which mean so much, and there can be no talking about the loss to colleagues at work or with neighbours. We heard of a bereaved man whose cover was so good that the neighbours' only reaction to his friend's death was to ask if there was a room to let. Those who love in secret must mourn alone.

Funerals can be disasters with the real 'chief mourner', if not excluded by the blood relatives, probably sitting at the back, shrouded in private grief while all the sympathy is being directed to the blood family at the front. Clergy conducting services may be unaware of the real relationship. However, if they do know, they may have negative feelings about homosexual love and communicate this during the service – even if they do not go as far as one priest who prayed for forgiveness of the deceased's deviant lifestyle. Even when the relationship is fairly open and families appear to regard the partner as another son or daughter, they may well want the relationship concealed at the funeral. Partners are sometimes asked not to attend in case people should talk, or to attend but only as acquaintances.

Such a funeral is a poor starting point for good grieving. Lazare (1979) tells us that complicated grief can be expected when the loss is socially unacceptable, socially negated or if there is no support network. For surviving partners of a secret love the loss is socially unacceptable, is socially negated and, for most, there is no support network.

The Gay Bereavement Project offers support and advice, someone to turn to, someone to talk to – but if the bereaved partner does not know of us or where to find us we can't help. Sadly, most older people do not read the gay press or go to gay clubs or social activities but all too often 'keep themselves to themselves' and mourn in isolation.

The Gay Bereavement Project arose from a Unitarian Church bereavement initiative. It was a self-help group – bereaved people meeting to support each other. The group was publicized in the gay press, and people rang and asked for advice. They expressed distress, anger and worries, but very few came to meetings of the group. It was some time before it was realized that what people really wanted, needed, was someone to talk to rather than organized meetings. So the group changed to a Samaritan-type telephone service.

From talking with bereaved lesbians and gay men, Project members found that many doctors, nurses, members of the clergy and others dealing with death and dying seemed unaware that same-sex partners would be as bereaved as spouses or families. It just had not struck them. To help in that area of concern the Project started sending speakers to talk to groups of such people. The Lyndhurst Settlement gave a grant to cover travelling costs for these outreach trips.

Project members also found that many lesbians and gay men were dying intestate and all too often the surviving partner lost the shared home and possessions on the death of the lover: the estate going to blood relations or, if there were none, to the state. Without a valid will a same-sex partner cannot inherit anything. They then mounted a 'Write a Will' campaign and published a will form which anyone can have.

The Gay Bereavement Project is small: it has one part-time worker and twenty lesbian and gay men volunteers. One volunteer is on call from 7 to midnight every evening, ready to talk, ready to listen – and there is double-staffing over the Christmas holiday. There is someone there, someone to talk to, someone to turn to.

Volunteers work from their own homes but there is a strong support network. Volunteers must share 'heavy' calls with a colleague as soon as the call ends, whatever the hour of day or night, and there is always the supervisor and the convenor available if needed. All calls are briefly reported to the convenor.

There are regular case conferences, in-service training sessions and team-building days when all the volunteers and their lovers and life-partners come together for a social occasion. These occasions help to build up the trusting, supporting group.

The Gay Bereavement Project has three main aims:

1 to help, support and advise lesbians and gay men bereaved by the death of a life-partner;
2 to educate all who deal with death and dying to the particular problems of same-sex loss;
3 to educate lesbians and gay men to the facts of death – that, like it or not, we and those we love are mortal and a properly written will is a loving gift.

The name and phone number of the Gay Bereavement Project member on duty any evening is on a recording on (081) 455 8894.

The office is staffed from 2.30 to 5.00, weekday afternoons on (081) 200 0511.

The Outreach Officer, responsible for arranging speakers and discussion leaders, is on (081) 455 6844.

References

Kinsey, P. and Martin (1948) *Sexual Behaviour in the Human Male*. Philadelphia, PA, and London: W.G. Saunders & Co.

Lazare, A. (1979) 'Unresolved grief', in A. Lazare (ed.), *Outpatient Psychiatry: Diagnosis and Treatment*. Baltimore, MD: Williams & Wilkins. pp. 498–512.

59

The grief that does not speak

Maureen Oswin

An art therapist working in a long-stay mental handicap hospital became concerned when one of the residents attending her class seemed very depressed. He then suddenly said he was worried because his parents, who usually came each Sunday, had not visited him for several weeks. The therapist went up to his ward but could not find anyone on the staff to give her any information, so she looked in his case notes for any clues to explain why his parents' visits had ceased.

She discovered that his father had died. This meant that his frail mother, who was unable to use public transport, could no longer visit him. Nobody had told the young man what had happened. All that was recorded in his case notes was the bare fact of his father's death.

No recommendation was made that anything should be done about breaking the news of the death to him, let alone helping him with his bereavement or arranging that he should be in contact with his mother. Nobody had made a deliberate decision not to tell him; but everyone on the staff had somehow assumed that he knew, that somebody had told him. In that impersonal institution, the bereaved resident as a sensitive, worried son had been quietly forgotten.

Thirty-year old Miss A had very severe learning difficulties and additional physical disabilities. She had always lived at home. She could not walk or speak. She needed help with all ordinary tasks such as dressing, eating, washing, going to the lavatory. Her father had died when she was in her twenties but her mother had continued to care for her on her own. Once a week Miss A went to a local day centre, and on other outings when her mother and a neighbour pushed her round the park or to the supermarket in her wheel-chair.

When her very robust mother suddenly died, Miss A lost everything – not only her mother and her mother's loving care, but every vestige of family life and routine and the security of her home and the neighbourhood where she had lived all her life. The same day that her mother died the social services department arranged that Miss A should go into the care of a mental handicap hospital. She was lifted, washed and fed and clothed by strangers who knew nothing about her

From *Search*, Winter 1990, 4: 5-7 (slightly abridged).

or her previous life. She was unable to ask questions because she could not speak. Without any speech it was almost impossible for her to relate to the strangers who were now caring for her, especially when she was also grief-stricken for her mother.

For many months Miss A pined and grieved. The kindly staff worried about her wan condition and deterioration: 'We feel so helpless when people as handicapped as her come into hospital after a parent dies: we don't know them, they don't know us, and they must feel so unhappy.'

After Mrs Z was widowed, the doctor advised: 'Don't tell your son.' She had enough problems. 'He might make more problems for you, and anyway he won't understand.' Acting on his advice Mrs Z kept the death of her husband a secret for several months and merely told her mentally handicapped son that father had 'gone away'. It was a dreadful strain for her, grieving for her husband and at the same time having to keep the death a secret from her adult son who was sharing the same house.

When she did finally tell him, she discovered that he had known for some weeks, and felt very resentful that she had not talked about it to him before. He had somehow found out from things he had overheard at his day centre. The doctor's advice to his mother had set the widow and her son apart at a time when they had both needed to be emotionally close and supporting each other.

Why did he give such crazy advice? Was it because he did not know any people with learning difficulties and had a stereotyped image of them as being disruptive and troublesome, and not having any emotional needs? It is sometimes said by thoughtless professionals working in the health services that 'people with mental handicaps don't have the same feelings as other people'.

The majority of professionals are not callous or insensitive: so how do these things happen? Perhaps, in the grey area of emotions and grief, with the double taboo of death and a learning difficulty, it is very easy for bereaved people to be lost in a muddle of misconceptions and a panic of reorganizing their lives – so their needs as grieving people are quite forgotten.

People with learning difficulties have a right to grieve; they need opportunities to mourn, they need time to recover, and sensitive support as they go through the normal reactions of grief such as anger, weeping and depression. Their emotional care is just as important as their need for continuing care at home or appropriate residential care, and any plans made for them should consider their emotional needs as grieving people. Unfortunately, when people with learning difficulties do react in normal ways to loss, some professionals perceive the reaction only in terms of the primary learning difficulty.

For example, a young man who was usually quiet and placid began to get into very anger tempers at his day centre during the months following his father's death. The staff knew that he was bereaved but saw his behaviour only as part of his learning difficulty; they did not recognize that he was reacting normally to his loss; they did not allow that he needed time to recover from his father's death and that he wanted to express his grief in anger, nor that he required support and understanding in the same way as any other grieving person. After having a staff meeting to discuss his 'problem behaviour' they called in a psychologist to put him onto a behaviour modification programme. Their failure to recognize his needs as a grieving person was partly because nobody on the staff understood normal grief; their training had largely been concentrated on looking for abnormalities amongst persons with learning difficulties.

Nobody intends to be deliberately unkind to people with learning difficulties when they are bereaved, but unkindness seems to creep in because of the way that services are organized, or because of short-comings in staff training. One young man, on being told that his father had died, asked: 'Am I allowed to cry?' His tentative question sums up how vulnerable some people with learning difficulties feel when they are bereaved. It is also a question about the quality of services organized for such people and the attitudes of some people providing them. If social policy does not allow for tears, then what sort of services do we have?

A local support service for bereaved people with learning difficulties might help to prevent some of the sadness and misunderstanding described here. It would not require elaborate organization. Its members might be interested professionals already working with people with learning difficulties, and representatives of parent groups. One of its functions might be to alert other local professionals to instances of bereavement amongst people with learning difficulties and to help in the planning of sensitive and appropriate services for them in the months following the bereavement. Another function might be to draw staff's attention to the norms of bereavement, so that people with learning difficulties would have their grief reactions recognized as normal and be given opportunities to grieve.

Three issues should be of concern to all people who have an interest in bereavement problems.

First, *forward planning*: when a single carer dies, leaving a severely multiply handicapped person like Miss A, that person should not be removed from her home immediately. Somebody could stay with her for a few days or weeks until she can be carefully introduced to a residential care placement which is appropriate for her. She should feel that she has some choice about her future, a chance to grieve for the dead parent in her own home and a chance to say her last good-byes to that home.

Second, *honesty*: people with learning difficulties ought to be kept in the picture all the time about a death having occurred, whether within their own family or amongst their friends. This might mean making sure that somebody is named as being responsible for breaking bad news and then helping the bereaved person through the following months. Honesty also means giving the person an opportunity to attend the funeral if they wish to, listening to them when they want to talk about what has happened, ensuring that they have mementoes of the dead person, letting them know what has happened to the house, their belongings, any pets, clothes and books. In other words, keeping the person with a learning difficulty in the picture the whole time and respecting their need to be a normal grieving person.

Third, *in-service training* courses on bereavement could be arranged for all staff working with people who have learning difficulties, in day centres, schools, in residential care and as field social workers. Such courses would cover normal grief reactions to a death in the family or the death of a close friend, and would alert staff at all levels to what they might expect with regard to supporting bereaved people. [. . .]

60

Personal and medical memories from Hillsborough

Tom Heller

Outside every public house and on every verge on my way home there were relaxed groups of young men chatting and joking in their 'uniforms' of tight faded jeans, off colour teeshirts, and something red and white. Were these the people whom later I saw laid out on the floor with life just pushed out of them? There were so many I didn't dare count them. They looked as they had in life, not disfigured; they were just lying there, not quite the right colour. Not much to identify them on that sports hall floor. Who were they? What had gone wrong? Who was to blame for all this?

Call for help

I was on call for a practice adjacent to the Hillsborough ground for the weekend of Saturday 15 April. On Saturdays when there is a home match at the stadium I avoid passing the ground when crowds are coming and going. My home is one side of the ground and the practice is on the other. On the 15th the atmosphere was special for the semifinal; people were parking their cars miles away from the stadium and walking to the ground many hours earlier than the crowds usually do for home games. I remember being especially cheerful (despite being on duty) and proud that Sheffield was the centre of the sporting world that day. The snooker world championship was on just down the road, and at Hillsborough the semifinal that many people thought should have been the final of the FA Cup was being held. Both sets of supporters wear red and white; I wonder who was who on those verges and which of them now live to tell their tale of the day when such a terrible tragedy happened out of a relaxed and gentle sunny moment?

I switched on the television just after 3 p.m. and saw the coverage of the snooker being interrupted by scenes from Hillsborough. Like almost everyone else, I imagine, I thought that there had been a pitch

From *British Medical Journal*, 1989, 299: 1596-8.

invasion and worried about how this might affect the chances of English clubs being allowed back into Europe. I then got into my car and took my daughter to a party that she was due to attend. At about 3.30 p.m. I heard on Radio Sheffield the call for doctors to go to Hillsborough, so I hurried to drop off my daughter and go to the ground. The party was about 2 km from Hillsborough, and on my way to the ground I followed a fire engine with flashing lights and siren that was going through red traffic lights and on the wrong side of keep left signs. I kept my car glued to the back of the fire engine and was at the ground within a few minutes of hearing the announcement. I parked in Leppings Lane, about 20 m from the blue gate that became such a focus of attention later. I had no notion of the significance of the gate at the time.

As I was parking on the forecourt of a garage that fitted tyres I was approached by some policemen. I told them that there had been a call for doctors on the radio. One of them immediately used his radio to find out where doctors were being asked to go, and we set off, running through the corridors, round the stadium, and towards the sports hall. The stadium was familiar to me as I had often been to matches there. The concrete beneath the grandstands is unusual: it is stained grey, cold and unyielding; the light is always poor beneath the stands, even on sunny afternoons like that one. As we rushed along the atmosphere was all wrong: there were lots of people but there was no noise. We got to the sports hall in about two minutes, and I entered by stepping through a cordon of police officers who were holding back people who were crowding around the outside of the door.

Bodies everywhere

Nothing could have prepared me for the scenes inside. I had thought vaguely that there might be a couple of members of St John Ambulance standing over a man with his head between his knees, telling him to take deep breaths. I had thought that they might have been over-whelmed because four people fainting was more than they could cope with and that I'd join in their exhortations and be back at my daughter's party in time for the second round of the Marmite sandwiches. This was not normal though. There were bodies everywhere. Who was alive and who was dead? They couldn't all be dead. It had to be a mistake; this just didn't happen on sunny afternoons. Blotchy faces against the floor, not disfigured but apparently peaceful. Bodies higgledy-piggledy just inside the door, the line stretching over to the far wall. I asked a policeman what was to be done. Thankfully he pointed away from the bodies to a section of the hall that was separated from them by a long, low screen of the type used to divide sports halls when two different sports are being played at the same time. There were more bodies here though. My God, what could I do? Who was going to tell me what to do?

Without directions I ran along the line of crumpled bodies. At least this lot were alive. I stopped between two bodies, took out my stethoscope, and lifted up a teeshirt and listened, grateful to have the time at last to do something that I knew how to do. I often use 'stethoscope on the chest time' to think during consultations. It's a good ploy really; the patient thinks that I am being ever so thoughtful and thorough, and I have time to think about what the hell to do next. Panic overtook me on this occasion. How could I be sure that this person was the one who needed help most? What was going to happen to all of the others if I stayed with this bloke? I could hear his heartbeat and breath sounds. For some reason I took my stethoscope out of my ears and crawled up to his face.

'What's your name, mate?' I asked.

'Terry' was the reply.

'OK Terry. How are you feeling?'

No answer. Silly question really.

How could I help?

His leg was at the wrong angle somehow, and so was one of his arms; he looked terrible, and where I had rested my stethoscope earlier was obviously not all right at all: it was moving wrongly and was not the right colour either. Although I could hear breath sounds, they were hard to interpret. I think I was just panicking. I remembered how to do a tracheotomy with a Biro. Would this be my opportunity? I turned him over on to his side and pushed my fingers on to the top of his tongue to establish an airway. This seemed to help, and his breathing started again. I had pulled him over on to his bad leg though – there didn't seem much alternative. His face was against the floor, so I reached out and found a leather jacket on the floor and picked up his head and rested it on the jacket. What medical equipment could enable this man to survive? If only someone would arrive who knew what to do. What did I know about anything? I turned around and looked at the man behind me; he was immobile and a terrible blue-grey colour . . . and so it went on.

I had taken my bags full of the equipment and drugs that I usually use. Not much call for antibiotics or infant paracetamol this afternoon. After some time – how long? – I became aware of a friend of mine going between the bodies doing the same as I was. Another general practitioner. We had worked together in the past but not on anything like this, nor are we likely to again. A smile of recognition. I wonder if I looked as lost as he did.

The first large-scale equipment arrived, and we started working together, putting up drips on everyone. We intubated as many patients and established as many airways as we possibly could. We needed scissors to cut through clothes. Why didn't I carry them in my bags?

We started giving intravenous diamorphine, and some sort of routine and organization began to be established. I'm quite proud in a funny sort of way to be able to put up so many intravenous drips so quickly without missing a vein. More doctors had arrived by now, and around every body there was a little huddle of workers. Someone said that he was an anaesthetist – a man of gold dust. Come over here and look at Terry for me, mate. He's still alive, but he keeps stopping breathing. 'Hang on, Terry.' The anaesthetist took out the airway, and it was blocked with blood. Not a good sign. One rib seemed to be almost through the chest and was certainly at the wrong angle. The ambulance stretchers arrived, and we put in a passionate bid for Terry to be taken off first. By now six people were around him, holding the drip bottle, his head, and his legs, which were at all angles. He was rested on to a low trolley. I checked that the ambulance was waiting and could get through to the hospital. The anaesthetist went with Terry to the ambulance. Thank God for anaesthetists. I'll never tell an anti-anaesthetist joke again.

Comradeship amid the horror

Now that I had no one to work on I wandered around and could see the dead bodies again at the other side of the sports hall. Among the doctors I recognized many of my friends and colleagues who had also answered the call of duty. One of them gave me a hug, bless him – a friend for life after what we went through that day. The police were much in evidence, but nobody was in charge of the medical tasks. What should I do next? Where would I be most useful? I decided to use my newly refound skills to put up drips on everybody who was going to be transferred to hospital. I somehow remembered that this was the thing to do in case the patients suffered more collapse on the way to hospital. It was also a sign to the hospital doctors that we general practitioners could do something right after all. I used up all of my diamorphine on those in need. By this time the routines were more established. Someone was writing down the obvious major damage to each person and what he or she had received in the way of drugs, etc. Then suddenly there was nobody left in the hall who was in need of attention and who wasn't dead.

I noticed a close friend amid the sea of dead faces. He was comforting someone who was leaning over a body. I stepped over some bodies to speak to him and offer some help; there weren't any words, just a look of rare empathy and comradeship.

Not knowing how to react

The doctors in the hall grouped together, almost silent, all wondering what to do next. I left the hall and walked through the silent crowds back to my car. I went home stunned and numbed. My children were playing in the garden; it was all so lovely and normal. Sandpits and skipping ropes. I had not known any of the dead or injured. Why is a major disaster so important for the people who participate as helpers? I meet death almost every day of my working life. Was this worse or was it just larger numbers? Everyone sort of expects that an event like this will be upsetting. But why is it that more attention is focused on the feelings of helpers in such disasters than on those of people concerned with upsetting events that happen every day? For me it seems to have been a major shock to my system in a general sort of way. I was grumpy, washed out and flat for a couple of weeks. Passing Hillsborough shocked me again when I had nearly rebuilt my professional defences.

All of us general practitioners who were there met a few times to talk about our experiences and to support each other. Why are all the others so articulate about how they are feeling whereas I'm just sort of non-specifically upset? I can't remember what I felt like at the ground and can't describe to the helpful counsellor how I'm feeling during the group sessions. I know all the theory, but I can't get it together for myself – the plight of the modern professional. It's three weeks since the disaster now, and I'm feeling OK again; I make jokes at work and have lots to be thankful for. I've been enormously well supported through all this by family, friends and colleagues. Time has passed and lessons to be learnt are being thought about. Perhaps British football has changed because of these events, and perhaps major disasters will be better dealt with in the future.

I'd like to tell the official inquiry in a systematic way what I think went right with the medical response that day and what I think could be done better next time. I don't know what training should be given to general practitioners and why none of us took charge of the medical happenings in the sports hall and was prepared to be the coordinator. I've got strong views about the counselling that is necessary and appropriate after the event for helpers at disasters. I'd like to do physical damage to the person who took the pictures for the *Daily Mirror* and reserve a special act of aggression for the person who allowed them to be published. But most of all I'd like to find out what happened to Terry.

61

Ruth: Death by murder

Lesley Moreland

As the New Year 1990 started our family life seemed to have entered on a new and welcome stage. Our eldest daughter had married happily and moved to Knebworth in 1988 when she was 24 and our youngest daughter, then 22, had moved to share a rented house with friends in Enfield in the same year.

I had left my job as Director of the Stillbirth and Neonatal Death Society (SANDS) early in 1989 and had taken a big leap into working freelance, partly as a management consultant in the voluntary sector and also starting a very small business in holding craft workshops. We felt, maybe somewhat smugly, pride in our daughters and that our relationship with them and with each other was strong and loving and life looked very good indeed.

On 2 February, just as we had finished eating our evening meal, the doorbell rang. What happened after that was like a nightmare except that it was real. The callers were police officers who came to let us know that our youngest daughter, Ruth, was dead. She had been murdered and a young man was held in custody. The police were and have remained very certain that he is the person who killed her. We had never heard his name before Ruth died. Her 24th birthday was on 6 February and we had been expecting to see her over the weekend.

My years at SANDS had given me a wider than average background in the theory of bereavement and a great deal of contact with people in the various stages of grieving. In some ways this was helpful, in others it seemed to hamper the free expression of feelings.

Forgiveness

The Greek philosopher Aristotle said that there was one loss from which a person could never recover, and that was the loss of a child. It struck too deeply, he thought, at the foundations of a life for there ever to be a chance of rebuilding.

Since Ruth died there has been a constant struggle to survive rather than become a victim of her loss. I have always been aware that the issue of forgiveness of the person who killed her would need to be faced but this was difficult to even begin as our family had never even heard the name of the young man who was charged with her murder until after her death. Many people asked how I felt about him and I found it impossible to answer, although I had no problem with how I felt about what he had done.

Ralph Hetherington wrote a commentary about forgiveness in *The Friend* in January 1991 which was published in the week before the trial of the young man charged with Ruth's murder. The article considered whether repentance was a prerequisite for forgiveness and stressed the need to recognize the dangers of judging people who have harmed us. It seems to me that passing judgement on others is difficult partly because we cannot understand why someone has behaved in a way which has hurt us or those we love and partly because we have to recognize our own failings in our behaviour towards other people.

I was shocked that the evidence given during the trial seemed to reveal no remorse or insight into the suffering caused to Ruth and all those who loved her. One of my nieces, who also attended the trial, said 'I needed to see that he was sorry and he wasn't.'

But life takes many unexpected turns. When the trial was over I contacted a friend who is a probation officer. It hadn't occurred to me that the young man would be sent to the prison where she works. With our agreement, she saw him and he asked that a message should be sent to us to say how sorry he was, how much he admired and respected Ruth and that she had always been very kind to him. I was also able to send a message to him in which I hoped that he would accept any help offered to him to help him understand why he had done what he had done, to use any opportunities to extend his skills and education and to resolve to use the rest of his life in positive ways both for himself and for others. However, I couldn't bring myself to send a message of forgiveness.

Those affected and involved in the aftermath of murder

A month after Ruth was murdered her employers held a gathering of her colleagues and many of the people who had attended the courses that she had arranged for women returners. The event was guided by a man who described those present in terms of having been affected by an 'earthquake' and spoke of those in Ruth's family as being at the 'epicentre'.

Figure 61.1 is not intended to make distinctions between the depth of people's feelings – we were very aware that many who were involved professionally were also emotionally affected. Rather it is intended to give Victim Support volunteers a framework so that they can be aware of the numbers and kinds of people who are affected or involved in the aftermath of a murder.

Those included in the Figure will vary with each murder. We were spared any direct press or media involvement; for other families this will be a major aspect.

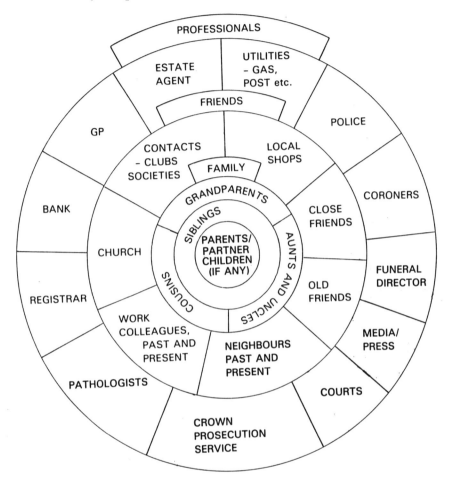

Note: Based on work done by Birmingham and Surrey SANDS, 1987.

Figure 61.1 *Circles of support*

Reference

Hetherington, R. (1991) 'Commentary', *The Friend*, 149(3): 67–8.

62

Essays upon epitaphs

William Wordsworth

> Yet even these bones from insult to protect
> Some frail memorial still erected nigh,
> With uncouth rhymes and shapeless sculpture deck'd,
> Implores the passing tribute of a sigh.
>
> Their name, their years, spelt by the unletter'd Muse,
> The place of fame and elegy supply,
> And many a holy text around she strews,
> That teach the rustic moralist to die.

When a Stranger has walked round a Country Church-yard and glanced his eye over so many brief Chronicles, as the tomb-stones usually contain, of faithful Wives, tender Husbands, dutiful Children, and good Men of all classes; he will be tempted to exclaim, in the language of one of the Characters of a modern Tale in a similar situation, 'Where are all the *bad* People buried?' He may smile to himself an answer to this question, and may regret that it has intruded upon him so soon. For my own part such has been my lot. And, indeed, a Man, who is in the habit of suffering his mind to be carried passively towards truth as well as of going with conscious effort in search of it, may be forgiven, if he has sometimes insensibly yielded to the delusion of those flattering recitals, and found a pleasure in believing that the prospect of real life had been as fair as it was in that picture represented. And such a transitory oversight will without difficulty be forgiven by those who have observed a trivial fact in daily life, namely, how apt, in a series of calm weather, we are to forget that rain and storms have been, and will return, to interrupt any scheme of business or pleasure which our minds are occupied in arranging. Amid the quiet of a Church-yard thus decorated as it seemed by the hand of Memory, and shining, if I may so say, in the light of love, I have been affected by sensations akin to those which have risen in my mind while I have been standing by the side of a smooth Sea, on a Summer's day. It is such a happiness to have, in an unkind World, one Enclosure where the voice of detraction is not heard; where the traces of evil inclinations are unknown; where contentment prevails, and there is no jarring

---

Extracts from 'Essays upon epitaphs', in *Prose Works of William Wordsworth*, ed. W.J.B. Owen and Jane Worthington Smyser, Oxford: Clarendon Press, 1971, pp. 63–7, 93.

tone in the peaceful Concert of amity and gratitude. I have been rouzed from this reverie by a consciousness, suddenly flashing upon me, of the anxieties, the perturbations, and, in many instances, the vices and rancorous dispositions, by which the hearts of those who lie under so smooth a surface and so fair an outside must have been agitated. The image of an unruffled Sea has still remained; but my fancy has penetrated into the depths of that Sea – with accompanying thoughts of Shipwreck, of the destruction of the Mariner's hopes, the bones of drowned Men heaped together, monsters of the deep, and all the hideous and confused sights which Clarence saw in his Dream [in Shakespeare's *Richard III*]!

Nevertheless, I have been able to return, (and who may not?) to a steady contemplation of the benign influence of such a favourable Register lying open to the eyes of all. Without being so far lulled as to imagine I saw in a Village Church-yard the eye or central point of a rural Arcadia, I have felt that with all the vague and general expressions of love, gratitude, and praise with which it is usually crowded, it is a far more faithful representation of homely life as existing among a Community in which circumstances have not been untoward, than any report which might be made by a rigorous observer deficient in that spirit of forbearance and those kindly prepossessions, without which human life can in no condition be profitably looked at or described. For we must remember that it is the nature of Vice to force itself upon notice, both in the act and by its consequences. Drunkenness, cruelty, brutal manners, sensuality, impiety, thoughtless prodigality, and idleness, are obstreperous while they are in the height and heyday of their enjoyment; and, when that is passed away, long and obtrusive is the train of misery which they draw after them. But, on the contrary, the virtues, especially those of humble life, are retired; and many of the highest must be sought for or they will be overlooked. Industry, oeconomy, temperance, and cleanliness, are indeed made obvious by flourishing fields, rosy complexions, and smiling countenances; but how few know anything of the trials to which Men in a lowly condition are subject, or of the steady and triumphant manner in which those trials are often sustained, but they themselves! The afflictions which Peasants and rural Artizans have to struggle with are for the most part secret; the tears which they wipe away, and the signs which they stifle, – this is all a labour of privacy. [. . .] The encomiastic language of rural Tomb-stones does not so far exceed reality as might lightly be supposed. Doubtless, an inattentive or ill-disposed Observer, who should apply to the surrounding Cottages the knowledge which he may possess of any rural neighbourhood, would upon the first impulse confidently report that there was little in their living Inhabitants which reflected the concord and the virtue there dwelt upon so fondly. [. . .] Besides, to slight the uniform language of these memorials as on that account not trustworthy would obviously be unjustifiable. Enter a Church-yard by the Sea-coast, and you will be almost sure to find the Tomb-stones crowded with metaphors taken from the Sea and a Sea-faring life. These are uniformly in the same strain; but surely we ought not thence to infer that the words are used of course without any heart-felt sense of their propriety. Would not the contrary conclusion be right? [. . .] We learn from the Statistical account of Scotland that, in some districts, a general transfer of Inhabitants has taken place; and that a great majority of those who live, and labour, and attend public worship in one part of the Country, are buried in another. Strong and inconquerable still continues to be the desire of all, that their bones should rest by the side of their forefathers, and very poor Persons provide that their bodies should be conveyed if necessary to a great distance to obtain that last satisfaction. Nor can I refrain from saying that this natural interchange by which the living Inhabitants of a Parish have small knowledge of the dead who are buried in their Church-yards is grievously to be lamented wheresoever it exists. For it cannot fail to preclude not merely much but the best part of the wholesome influence of that communion between living and dead which the conjunction in rural districts of the place of burial and place of worship tends so effectually to promote. [. . .]

An experienced and well-regulated mind will not, therefore, be insensible to this monotonous language of sorrow and affectionate admiration; but will find under that veil a substance of individual truth. Yet, upon all Men, and upon such a mind in particular, an Epitaph must strike with a gleam of pleasure, when the expression is of that kind which carries conviction to the heart at once that the Author was a sincere mourner, and that the Inhabitant of the Grave deserved to be so lamented. This may be done sometimes by a naked ejaculation; as in an instance which a friend of mine met with in a Church-yard in Germany; thus literally translated. 'Ah! they have laid in the Grave a brave Man – he was to me more than many!'

> Ach! sie haben
> Einen Braven
> Mann begraben –
> Mir war er mehr als viele.

An effect as pleasing is often produced by the recital of an affliction endured with fortitude, or of a privation submitted to with contentment; or by a grateful display of the temporal blessings with which Providence had favoured the Deceased, and the happy course of life through which he had passed. And where these individualities are untouched upon it may still happen that the estate of man in his helplessness, in his dependence upon his Maker or some other inherent of his nature shall be movingly and profitably expressed. Every Reader will be able to supply from his own observation instances of all these kinds, and it will be more pleasing for him to refer to his memory than to have the page crowded with unnecessary Quotations. [. . .]

In an obscure corner of a Country Church-yard I once espied, half-overgrown with Hemlock and Nettles, a very small Stone laid upon the ground, bearing nothing more than the name of the Deceased with the date of birth and death, importing that it was an Infant which had been born one day and died the following. I know not how far the Reader may be in sympathy with me, but more awful thoughts of rights conferred, of hopes awakened, of remembrances stealing away or vanishing were imparted to my mind by that Inscription there before my eyes than by any other that it has ever been my lot to meet with upon a Tomb-stone.

63

For Rose Albert
(26 June 1895–19 May 1988)

Ellen Jaffe Bitz

Go, lovely Rose!

(Edmund Waller)

Bloom of my childhood
Grandmother
Today everything bursts into flower
Green, pink, white
while you wilt softly
in hospital nursery
glass and tubes around you.

Rose, bloom of my childhood
Dressing up in your clothes,
your high-heeled shoes
(on my last visit, I
peeked in your drawer
like a curious child,
found nests of gloves
white and black, neatly folded
waiting for occasions . . .
a lady is never without
decorum.)

We came to your 90th birthday party
You came to my 43rd,
a surprise planned by my son
You wore a paper hat
over your newly-done hair,
elegant – as always.

I remember
        your rose-painted nails
        and nestling in your feathery bed
                when I slept over

You gave me
      cantaloupe and ice-cream
      balloons and kisses
You were never old to me
        (even now
           even now)
And I am not really grown-up,
it is all an act
still dressing up in your clothes,
putting on plays.

Rose, bloom of my childhood
Your light goes out
Your scent
      will remain
in our hearts

64

How to live with ghosts

Ellen Jaffe Bitz

Navajos leave a hogan where someone has died
inside, before there was time
to go out to cleansing air, before
there was time
to say goodbye, letting loose
the spirit, *chindi*, to wander the earth
not poison the house and its survivors
with deadly ghost-sickness

they block up the entrance-way, facing sunrise
stop up the chimney
chop a hole in the side of the house
to let the *chindi* escape and warn the living
here is a house where someone has died
inside

even the best hogans, near plenty of grass,
water, high in the mountains,
are abandoned this way
in the breath of death

we do not leave our houses so easily
rooted down like trees with our possessions,
wood, silver, electric,
our phone lines, mailing addresses, lifelines
to the world
and the deaths need not be complete, just slowly
inside, where it matters . . .
the *chindi* is always following us, here in the
        bathroom,
or there on the ceiling, with scars of rotten fruit,
slivers of broken glass behind the door, never quite
in reach of the broom,
back in the bedroom, with its unmade secrets

our houses store up memories, helter-skelter,
oranges and coal, like needles of last year's Christmas
tree, forever underfoot . . .
perhaps we should just leave, while the wounds are
    fresh
seal up the door to the heart, chop out a ghost-hole
and start again

in a new location, uncontaminated
sweet.

65

December

Douglas Dunn

'No, don't stop writing your grievous poetry.
It will do you good, this work of your grief.
Keep writing until there is nothing left.
It will take time, and the years will go by.'
Ours was a gentle generation, pacific,
In love with music, art and restaurants,
And he with she, strolling among the canvases,
And she with him, at concerts, coats on their laps.
Almost all of us were shy when we were young.
No friend of ours had ever been to war.
So many telephone numbers, remembered addresses;
So many things to remember.
The red sun hangs in a black tree, a moist
Exploded zero, bleeding into the trees
Praying from the earth upward, a psalm
In wood and light, in sky, earth and water.
These bars of birdsong come from another world;
They ring in the air like little doorbells.
They go by quickly, our best florescent selves
As good as summer and in love with being.
Reality, I remember you as her soft kiss
At morning. You were her presence beside me.
The red sun drips its molten dusk. Wet fires
Embrace the barren orchards, these gardens in
A city of cold slumbers. I am trapped in it.
It is December. The town is part of my mourning
And I, too, am part of whatever it grieves for.
Whose tears are these, pooled on this cellophane?

From *Elegies*, London: Faber & Faber, 1985, p. 53.

Index